Existential Psychology East-West will appeal to anyone with an interest in understanding themselves and the nature and nurture of the human condition. Reading EPEW is like encountering a great river. It courses through the existential terrain and draws from many tributaries. It is both mysterious and inviting, beckoning the reader: ride the currents, plumb the depths, drink from the water.

Kevin Keenan, PhD
Faculty, Michigan School of Professional Psychology

Existential psychology is more relevant to the contemporary world than ever before. This dynamic and provocative anthology not only presents an authoritative history and descriptions of the topic, but includes chapters by Chinese psychologists who have found ways in which existentialism both resonates and contrasts with Asian wisdom traditions. This is a cutting edge book that needs not only to be read, but to be applied to the human condition, both East and West.

Stanley Krippner, PhD
Professor of Psychology, Saybrook Graduate School
Co-Editor, *The Psychological Impact of War Trauma on Civilians*

Face-to-face interaction in China led to virtual collaboration in writing this book. With the perspectives of scholars in both the USA and China represented, a true dialogic relationship is evident in this collection. Differences and difficulties in cultural understandings of existentialism are addressed forthrightly which deepens the reflection process that is a hallmark of existential psychology. *Existential Psychology East-West* also serves as a bridge to Chinese/Asian traditions as they are articulated from an existential perspective. What a terrific model for cross-cultural collaboration and dialogue!

David Lukoff, PhD
Core Faculty, Institute of Transpersonal Psychology

It is high time that an edition like this should appear. Toward the end of his life, Martin Heidegger noted parallels between his own thought and that of Eastern religious thinkers. Following in the tradition of Heidegger's pupil and friend, existential analyst Medard Boss, Hoffman, Yang, Kaklauskas and Chan have initiated an impressive dialogue between Eastern and Western thinkers on existential issues in psychology. Bravo!

Betty Cannon, PhD
Author of *Sartre and Psychoanalysis*

In this collection of 20 chapters entitled *Existential Psychology East-West*, the authors have brightly limned the commonalities and differences in Eastern and Western mentalities and their respective approaches into the "vasty deep" of human joy and anxiety, pleasure and suffering, enduring human values and personal ephemerality, and the emic and personological peculiarities of individuals in the various cultures that are clustered in these two hemispheres. The indigenous existentialism they each, separately, have in common provides a bridge for readers to understand each other in both universes of discourse. The Human in its sociality and individuality is treated without sentimentality and with scholarship. This book is not an ideational blender. Free of bromides and clichés, *Existential Psychology East-West* respects the distinctness and beauty of stand-alone paradigms for, and cultural visions of, the Human. This book makes a significant contribution to its domain of interest.

Frank Dumont, EdD
Full Professor (retired), McGill University, Montreal, Quebec

Existential Psychology East-West

Edited by
Louis Hoffman,
Mark Yang,
Francis J. Kaklauskas,
& Albert Chan

University of the Rockies Press
555 E. Pikes Peak Avenue, #108
Colorado Springs, Colorado 80903

First Published in 2009, University of the Rockies Press.

ISBN-10:	0-9764638-6-5
ISBN-13:	978-0-9764638-6-3

University of the Rockies Press
555 E. Pikes Peak Avenue, #108
Colorado Springs, CO 80903

Cover Design by Laura Ross, 2009

This book is dedicated in memory of

Rollo May
&
James F. T. Bugental

Table of Contents

Translation Note

Many challenges arise when editing a book which includes chapters from various languages and academic cultures. The current volume includes chapters written in English by authors from the United States; Chinese authors writing in English, which is not their native tongue; and chapters written in Chinese that were translated into English. The editors have attempted to balance the spirit of the APA writing style with cultural and academic differences across cultures. Both cultures have a rigorous academic tradition; however, there are significant differences in academic writing styles. For instance, APA style places a stronger emphasis on page numbers than is necessary in the Chinese academic culture. As these quotes have been translated in to English by the author or translator, and most English readers would not have access or be able to track down the quotes, we did not find it necessary to include page numbers in all the translated passages. We have, however, been ardent in giving due credit for ideas, which is consistent across both academic traditions. In addition to learning a great deal about existential thought in two cultures, we have also learned a great deal about the differences in the academic cultures. These, too, have been valuable lessons emerging from the cultural interchange.

We have also worked hard to honor the personal and cultural style in the translations. This has necessitated a good deal of communication between the original writers, the editors, and the translators. As should be evident, there are also cultural differences in communication style. The editors believe this is an important aspect of cross-cultural dialogue. Due to this, we did not try to make the translated chapters sound like traditional academic English. Instead, we have honored the original voice of the author as much as possible. It is our hope, and belief, that this adds to the cultural interchange evident in this book.

Acknowledgements

Compiling a book with contributors writing in different languages and located in different countries is an enormous challenge. There are many people who have played a pivotal role in the idea of this book, its development, and the final product. This truly was a collaborative process that entailed the help and support of many people.

First, the editors would like to thank the many talented contributors to this book. We were pleased with the excitement of the authors and amazed that everyone who we extended an invitation to write a chapter accepted our offer. This speaks to the timeliness and importance of this project. The contributors to this volume include many prominent scholars in the United States and China, as well as a number of rising stars in the profession. We are deeply humbled by their contributions to *Existential Psychology East-West*.

The idea for this book emerged from a trip to China in 2008 to conduct trainings in existential psychology in Hong Kong and mainland China. Many individuals who participated in this trip deserve our thanks including J. Christy Dyer, Michael M. Dow, Elizabeth Saxon, Yang Yuchuan, Simon Chow, and Reverend David Yip. We also owe a special gratitude to the University of the Rockies, who provided support for the 2008 trainings in China and for this book. The University of the Rockies Foundation also provided financial support for the training in China; our deepest gratitude goes to the foundation, especially the Steve Caruthers and former board member Emory Cowan. When in China, a number of organizations provided support in various forms. The Hong Kong Institute of Christian Counseling provided space and funding for the trip; we are deeply thankful for their generosity and hospitality. Lutheran Theological Seminary and Alliant University, Hong Kong Campus hosted talks and discussions on existential psychology. In Beijing, the China Youth University of Political Science was gracious in providing us with space and providing meals.

Al Dueck and Buxin Han also deserve special acknowledgement for organizing a series of psychology of religion conferences in mainland China, where the editors of this book met and began formulating plans for bringing dialogues on existential psychology to China. It was at these conferences where the editors also met several of the contributors to this volume. Drs. Dueck and Buxin also provided a model for holding an international conference in a culturally sensitive manner. Wang Xuefu has been an invaluable contributor to this volume in many ways, through helping make connections, providing feedback and insight, editorial support, assistance with translation, and contributing to this volume. We would also like to acknowledge a number of people who provided editorial support on particular chapters or portions of the book, including Kate Calhoon, Ed Mendelowitz, Kirk Schneider, Katie McGuire, Cheryl Deloia, John Chavis, Glen Moriarty, and Cathy Calvert. We owe special gratitude to Angela Nazworth, who was the copy editor for the book and worked with us on a tight timeline.

Last, we want to thank the family and friends of all those who contributed to this volume for their support, encouragement, and generosity in sharing their loved ones with us.

Louis Hoffman would like to thank his co-editors: Mark, Francis, and Albert. It has been a terrific honor to work with the three of you. I would like to give a special thanks to Kirk Schneider, the leading scholar and advocate of existential psychology in the United States, whose support and encouragement has been extremely meaningful to me. Ed Mendelowitz and Stephen A. Diamond, who I look to as two of the most talented writers in psychology, deserve deep gratitude for your encouragement of my writing and contributions to existential thought. I am also deeply grateful for the encouragement of Ilene Serlin and David Elkins. I would like to acknowledge H. Newton Malony and Winston Gooden, who helped introduce me to existential psychology during my graduate school days. Several friends and family members who provided early encouragement and feedback will always deserve credit on any writing I do throughout my career; without them, I may have never found my voice or the courage to write: Robert Murney, Brittany Bowser, and John Hoffman. I would also like to acknowledge my good friend and colleague Glen Moriarty whose collaboration and friendship has been a wonderful blessing and influence, and Sandra K. Knight, whose collaborations, friendship, and encouragement has been an incredible blessing in my life. I am appreciative of two great friends, Clarence Leung and Jonathon Choi, who first introduced me to Chinese culture over dim sums. These conversations opened my eyes to the excitement of diversity and forever changed my life.

I would like to thank Emory Cowan, a wonderful mentor and friend, who modeled existential applications in many areas of life. Several people at the University of the Rockies also deserve acknowledgement for their support and encouragement of my writing: Jim Ungvarsky, Susan Cooper, Lorri White, Sharon Trivette, and Jean Jones. However, I would also like to thank the entire faculty and administration at the University of the Rockies; I am so blessed to work with such wonderful people! I am deeply indebted to Al Dueck and Buxin Han, who first invited me to China. There are many students who throughout the years helped me become a better professor and I wish to thank all those who taught me while I was in the role of teaching them; good learning is always mutual! In particular, I would like to thank J. Christy Dyer, Michael M. Dow, and Elizabeth Saxon, who participated in my first trip to China focusing on trainings in existential psychology. I am deeply thankful to my friend and colleague, Mark Yang, who first invited me to present in Hong Kong and China on existential psychology. I am deeply thankful for our friendship as well as the opportunities to work together, hopefully for many years to come. My odd, but genuinely appreciative acknowledgement goes to Panera Bread in Colorado Springs, where the atmosphere, good coffee, and wireless internet seemed to provide the perfect environment for the writing and editing of this book. Last, and most importantly, I am thankful to my family. I need to thank my mother-in-law, Helen Rolle Rahming, a fellow writer, whose presence and help staying with us the last few months allowed me the time to finish this book; without this help we would not have finished by our deadline. My parents, Clarence and Lynn, have supported me in my education and career, but also in becoming a person of compassion. You deserve credit for any and every success in my life. My brother, John, and sister-in-law, Joy, have been wonderful supports as friends and colleagues as well as family members. My wife, Heatherlyn, and sons, Lakoda and Lucaya: You are my motivation in life and my greatest blessing; all these years of writing and I can still never find words enough to voice my love and appreciation of you.

Mark Yang would like to thank his co-editors Louis, Francis, and Albert. It has been a great learning experience to work with the three of you. A most special and warm gratitude is offered to Louis Hoffman who has become a friend, colleague, and even mentor of mine even though you are younger in age. Your wisdom, grace, and humility have become models for me. Your sharing about your own faith journey encourages me to face my own existential isolation and know that the All-Mighty can be found in unexpected places that may sometimes require that I let go of my "old wineskins." I would also like to thank Wang Xuefu who, through the work of this project and other teaching collaborations, has introduced and given me deeper insights into what Lu Xun and you have to say about the Chinese psyche. The knowledge I have gained from you helps me to have a better understanding of myself and my life here in Asia. I look forward to future projects and continuing in my process of learning with the two of you. I would also like to thank Winston Gooden, the dean at the Graduate School of Psychology at Fuller Seminary. Winston, you modeled and introduced to me the field of existential psychology. You helped me to explore my own ethnic identity and your belief in me sustained me through graduate school and beyond. You made my Fuller experience worthwhile. Finally, I would like to thank Irvin Yalom who has become my written mentor. I channel your writing and your wisdom on a daily basis. If it were not for your writing, I would not have known that I was an existential psychologist who is also interested in group and grief work; all because of you. Even though I have not met you yet, I feel like you have already made a significant part of yourself known to me. You are my teacher and mentor!

Francis Kaklauskas would like to thank Louis Hoffman for his continual encouragement and mentorship, as well as the wonderful opportunities and experiences of sharing our professional lives and families together. I would also like to thank my other co-editors, Mark and Albert, whose open hearts and gracious spirits made me quickly feel as if we were brothers. I would like to thank my sister, Kathy Graber, for countless generosities of time, spirit, and scholarship, as she was responsible for me considering Leibniz's monads and Schopenhauer's will to life instead of paying attention in high school. Finally, I can not thank my wife, Elizabeth, and my son, Levi, enough for their gift of love.

Albert Chan: I never thought of myself as someone who was going to write a chapter on myths of Chinese culture and especially writing a chapter on existential psychology, although in my undergraduate years, I had written some poems and did some editorial work for a university magazine and for a church. I am grateful to Dr. Louis Hoffman who initiated my involvement in this writing project. I am also indebt to his faith and trust in my writing, even though I feared that I would most likely fail badly with my inexperience in writing. I am particularly grateful for Dr. Francis Kaklauskas' editorial work on my chapter. I am thankful for his friendship and passion to make this chapter both truthful and readable. To my friend and mentor Dr. Frank Dumont, I am thankful for your kind companionship in reading my chapter before I had courage to submit it to the other editors. Dr. Mark Yang, I thank you for your comradeship in Hong Kong. Without this I would not have started this chapter in my life. With my editorial friends, I would like to show my gratitude; because of you and our meeting in Beijing, 2008, I come to appreciate existential psychology which reminds me of my early years of studies in philosophy, theology, and literature, a long overdue revisit.

I thank my daughters Hannah and Erin who keep up my interest in writing, as they share their writings with me and their faith in me. In many ways the chapter I contributed is for you. I am inspired by my students in Hong Kong and Macau for their trust in my teaching and special thanks to Christina Leung's curiosity which assists me not only in my teaching but also in challenging me in my writing in existential psychology. I thank Mark Lam who introduced me to learn Chinese natural philosophy. I thank my mother and my late father who gave me all their blessings in my life. My mentors/professors Drs. Claude Guldner and Andy Hum encouraged me in different stages of my life. My friends Janice Maloney and Lorena Perna who have been accompanying me in my professional development and keep me as your friends, I have not thanked you sufficiently. Father, Dr. Vincente Sanchez, we have discussed so many issues on individual and collective culture and life in general; we are set sailing into an exciting journey. Lastly, I thank Lillian Ko, who accompanied me in my life journey till now, words will not express my appreciation, love, and gratitude.

Poetic Preface

Tom Greening

PING

Let us now our praises sing
of a humble duck named Ping.
Dynasties may come and go,
governments put on their show,
emperors orate and strut—
All seek fame and power, but
a hundred years from now you'll see
who goes down in history.

Floating with the Yangtze's flow,
he knows as only ducks can know
when to fly and when to dive,
how to keep his hope alive,
and so of wisdom he is king,
even though he's only Ping.

This poem was inspired by the Chinese children's book, Ping, *which was read to me in 1935.*

Forward

Donadrian L. Rice

Every once and awhile we are treated with a text that adds a completely new dimension to our understanding of the world around us and the people who inhabit that world. While there are a plethora of disciplines that attempt to assist us in our understandings, psychology has emerged as the sine qua non among the disciplines that attempt to teach us about ourselves. Of the many theoretical approaches to psychology, Existential psychology has offered us the ability to illuminate and highlight the salient characteristics of human existence in ways that go beyond what psychology "as usual" has been able to achieve. While I readily admit to my bias, I am persuaded by the many volumes of literature published over the last six decades devoted exclusively to this important mission of apprehending the significant features of human existence.

The introduction of Existential psychology to the United States in the 1950s was literally a breath of fresh air to those psychologists who found the dominate theories of behaviorism and psychoanalysis lacking in their abilities to address the important questions about life posed by their clients in the consulting room. Leaders in this field such as Rollo May provided a template and direction in this emerging field that has allowed others to advance further the theory and practice of Existential psychology. The present volume, *Existential Psychology East-West* is firmly grounded in the foundations of European Existentialism while at the same time advancing into what many might consider to be terra incognita.

Prior to the writings of notable figures such as Alan Watts, little was known in the west of the psychological concepts found in Eastern philosophies and religions. While some of the concepts were new and quite different from Western understandings of psychology, there were other instances of considerable overlap. However, the traditional approaches to psychology did not have a means to explore and integrate the nuances of this rich and complex tradition. To be sure, Existential psychology, along with its methodological companion phenomenology, was the only theoretical position in psychology that remotely approached topics and questions found in Eastern psychologies such as "who am I," " what is experience," and the nature of "consciousness and Being." I am aware, of course, of the contributions made by Humanistic and

Transpersonal approaches to psychology and their efforts to integrate Eastern concepts; however, I consider Existential psychology as a foundation for these approaches.

While the similarities found in Existential psychology and Eastern philosophies and religions have always been there; until now, no concerted effort has been made to explore in depth this relationship in a text that is both scholarly and practical. Hoffman and his colleagues have taken on the herculean task of elucidating the subject matter of two complex areas and providing the reader, whether for scholarly purposes or practical application, with a comprehensible volume that clearly advances our understanding of the subtle fabric that connects these two traditions. Scholars will find that this volume reveals new insights that are worthy of exploration apart from the theme of this text. Therapists will be delighted with the care taken to introduce the practical applications that will certainly increase their knowledge, comprehension, and effectiveness as Existential psychotherapists.

Lastly, I would emphasize that this volume could not have come at a more significant time in our history. As a long time member of the "existential choir," I have always believed that our clients are best served by an existential approach to therapy. I have also recognized, and explored several Eastern disciplines in scholarly and practical ways. From these experiences, I have come to appreciate the reality of how Existential psychology and the Eastern disciplines both contribute to quality "cross-cultural" understanding. Moreover, I have come to value the importance of both of these traditions as possibly the only ways to address the angst experienced by so many in our increasingly multifaceted world. As we move even faster into a global society, only philosophies, systems, and concepts that speak to the essence of experience of all of humanity will help facilitate the better understanding among cultures that we desire while helping us navigate the inevitable travails of life. It is my contention that this volume is a gigantic step in that direction.

Introduction

Louis Hoffman
Mark Yang
Francis J. Kaklauskas
Albert Chan

During a trip to China in 2008, three of us visited the Great Wall. One of the only human structures visible from space, it was a remarkable sight to behold. As we approached the Great Wall, we could not help being awestruck. The beauty, the power, and the emotion in the millions of carved bricks as far as the eye can see resonated across the ground, across time, and through our beings.

There was not enough time for a proper visit. One could walk the Great Wall for days, even months, and never reach the end; or the end of pondering the emotions it stimulates. Begrudgingly, we eventually realized we could no longer suspend returning to our lives and commitments in Beijing. When leaving, we came across a decorative stone with this inscription:

> Once intended to ward off enemy attacks. Today it brings together the peoples of the world. The Great Wall, may it continue to act as a symbol of friendship for future generations.

Re-envisioning. What has kept people apart can now bring them together. What arguably is the most monumental human structure ever built is also one of the great symbols of division. But a paramount truth about symbols is that their meaning can be recreated and re-envisioned over time. While on the wall, we felt an amazing sense of unity with people we met from all over the world. Each displayed a friendliness and openness that we had rarely experienced. There is something magical, something transcendent about the wall.

Existential philosophy began in Europe in the 1800s and sometimes has been unfairly characterized as a dark philosophy. It emerged during a time when individualism reigned in Western thought and, in many ways, it took on this individualism. But, again, some of the portrayals of existentialism as individualist are unfair and may be due to a misunderstanding of basic existential ideas. Even Sartre, debatably the most individualistic and pessimistic of the existentialists, valued the importance of human compassion and human relationships in his writing and his life. Existentialism promulgates the relational imperative. In many ways, relationships provide the container against the void in which the individual can feel, act, and exist.

Regardless, existentialism is not guilt-free; it must take responsibility for its mistakes. If it is going to reach its ideals, existential philosophy and psychology must extend beyond the limits of Western thought. This, in part, is the story of this book. Culture has served to be a barrier, much like the Great Wall, for the extension of existential thought. Although the indigenous similarities between Eastern thought and existentialism are striking, it seems that culture, politics, and language precluded existential thought from moving beyond its Western origins. Nothing, however, could be more unexistential than such rigid and narrow applications of existential thought! Existential thought, and of particular interest in this book, existential psychology, must transcend the cultural and temporal limitations of its origins.

The four editors of this book, along with J. Christy Dyer, Michael M. Dow, and Elizabeth Saxon, had the opportunity to begin discussions of existential psychology in the East. In earlier eras, where international communication and travel were more difficult and rare, it was easier for schools of thought to become stuck in a singular cultural context. Now, in postmodern times, this same stuckness is the death of any theory sophisticated enough to gain prominence. Theory, especially psychological theory, must be culturally adaptable and must remain fluid enough to acclimate to the times and the contexts in which they exist. Although existential thought has not always followed this guideline, it has been implicit in its anti-dogmatic and contextual understanding of human existence.

Existential Psychology East-West seeks to re-envision existential thought beyond its original limited cultural context while remaining true to the core values of existentialism. Few experiences can transform a person's understanding of the world more than cross-cultural exchanges. This is evident in the classroom. No amount of within group differences can account for the same richness that is available in cross-cultural dialogues. Different cultures experience the world in such variant ways that it is often hard for us to leave our own culture behind long enough to truly understand the perspective of others. Similarly, we believe that there can be no better teacher about existential psychology's weakness and the direction that it needs to go than cross-cultural dialogue.

As is evident in the chapters in this book, there are some challenges. At times, it seems that existential psychology may have to soften on core principles in order to be culturally respectful and culturally relevant. It is our belief, however, that the core elements of existential psychology are culturally adaptable. We do not believe that there is a need to sacrifice any core principles of existential thought to be applied cross-culturally, but many may need some re-envisioning. It is our hope that this book is the beginning of a dialogue that will grow and develop for many years to come.

In the first part of this book, Louis Hoffman provides an overview of the practice of existential psychology and psychotherapy. The focus of this chapter, and this book, is primarily on the existential psychology strands emerging from Rollo May and James F. T. Bugental. This chapter introduces existential psychology's theory and practice, and sets the philosophical and historical foundation for the later chapters. In chapter two, a case illustration by Louis Hoffman and Nathaniel Granger helps to put a face to what existential psychotherapy looks like in practice.

In part 2, the focus shifts to the theoretical development of existential psychology in a cross-cultural context. The first chapter by J. Christy Dyer and colleagues sets the stage for issues examined later in the book. This chapter uses the information gathered during the 2008 trip to China to identify the major challenges of applying existential psychology in the East as well as the opportunities that can be built upon in moving toward understanding and integration. As the stage is set, these issues then are addressed by a number of leading Eastern and Western scholars. A primary theme in these chapters is the religious influences. Religion often reflects the indigenous values and the indigenous psychology of a culture. The existential and religious dialogues illuminate many of the challenges and opportunities of this dialogue in a rich manner. Other chapters address the interface of Jungian and existential psychology, global authenticity, mindfulness and existential psychology, and the similarities between several Chinese theories, such as Lu Xun, and existential thought.

The final section of this book draws on the ideas Rollo May (1991) initiated in his book *The Cry for Myth*. In the first chapter, Hoffman examines how myths reflect the universality of the existential givens and the need for cultural specific answers to the givens. In the following chapters, various authors build upon Eastern and Western myths to illuminate the various existential givens, while at the same time illustrating the culture-specific answers which emerge.

In closing, we hope this is the beginning of a long and rich dialogue. We hope readers will join us in this journey of exploration and bring along their openness, curiosity, and critical reflections. Existential truths are rarely easily attained. They are sought after, revised, and re-envisioned over time. This is only the beginning.

References

May, R. (1991). *The cry for myth*. New York: Delta.

Part 1

Overview of Existential Theory & Practice

1

Introduction to Existential Psychology
in a Cross-Cultural Context:
An East-West Dialogue[1]

Louis Hoffman

...the purpose of [existential] psychotherapy is to set
people free.

~ Rollo May, 1981, p. 19

*Viewed from an existential standpoint, questions of choice,
freedom and responsibility cannot be isolated or contained
within some separate being (such as 'self' or 'other')....*
Viewed in this way, no choice can be mine or yours alone,
no experienced impact of choice can be separated in terms
of 'my responsibility' versus 'your responsibility', no sense
of personal freedom can truly avoid its interpersonal
dimensions.

~ Ernesto Spinelli, 2001, p. 16

Existential thought is rooted in *the study of what it means to exist*.
With such a vague basic definition, it is no wonder that much confusion
exists about existential thought and existential psychology. This dry
philosophic definition cannot capture the rich unfolding nature of the
therapeutic encounter that is central to existential psychotherapy. When
applied to therapy, existential refers to a type of psychotherapy embedded
in a rich process of self-discovery.

Still, it is common for existentialists to hear questions such as "isn't
everything really existential?" Or, on the other end of the continuum, some

---

[1] Writing an introduction to existential psychology and psychotherapy today must be
engaged with a certain degree of humility due to the many great introductions which
already exist. In particular, the reader is encouraged to also consider Mendelowitz and
Schneider (2007), Schneider (2008a), May (1958a, 1958b), and Yalom (1980).

individuals will claim that existentialism is really Sartian philosophy (i.e., philosophy based upon the works of John Paul Sartre). These common misconceptions of existential thought, making it overly inclusive or overly restrictive, create a great amount of confusion about what could be considered existentialism.

The study of existence is only the starting point of existential thought. As with any school of thought, it must evolve beyond its starting point if it is to retain utility and meaning. If the study of human existence in any form is to be considered existential, then all psychology and most art could be considered existential. Therefore, such oversimplifications are rejected as naïve and problematic.

Similarly, relegating existential thought to being based upon the work of one thinker is rather *anti-existential*, as will become evident. Sartre deserves credit for popularizing the term existential; however, most existential scholars trace the origins of existential thought to Soren Kierkegaard and Friedrich Nietzsche. Rollo May goes back even further to identify Blaise Pascal as the original existentialist. Regardless, few existentialists would identify Sartre as the primary exemplifier of existential thought; a mistake is more likely to be made by those outside existentialism.

Before moving on to define the existential movement, let me make one last important distinction. Many existentialists do not label themselves as such and have voiced deep concern about such labels as being overly constrictive. Therefore, many of the early figures I will discuss never referred to themselves as existentialists, and many contemporary existentialists do so with some reticence. While empathizing with their concern and recognizing the need of protecting existentialism from succumbing to overly restrictive and narrow definitions, the label serves an important purpose in bringing together writers, theorists, practitioners, and students who share the basic values of existential thought.

The purpose of this chapter is to provide the reader with an introduction and overview of existential psychology; a difficult task given the various approaches to existential psychology and psychotherapy. We begin with the assumption that there is no one essential idea or value upon which all existentialists agree. Instead, we understand existentialism as a collection of values that emerge from the beginning point of the study of human existence. In each of these, there is some disagreement. For example, although most existentialists will adhere to a belief in the unconscious, Spinelli (2004) does not and provides a reinterpretation of what is traditionally construed as the unconscious.

In this chapter and throughout the book, we will focus primarily on the existential phenomenological school that can be traced to Rollo May in the United States and Ludwig Binswanger in Europe. At points, we will make reference to other schools of existential psychology, such as Frankl's logotherapy or Boss's existential analysis.

A Brief History of Existentialism[2]

The early existential writings of Blaise Pascal, Friedrich Nietzsche, and Soren Kierkegaard were connected with romanticism and the anti-enlightenment movement in Europe. Embodied in both these trends, existential thought was concerned with the dominance of rationalism over and against other ways of knowing. It sought more holistic ways to pursue knowledge. In many ways, the origin of existentialism is a reaction to scientific modernism,[3] which explains the many similarities between existentialism and postmodernism.

A second dominant theme early existentialists demonstrated was a commitment to honesty about the entirety of the human condition, or *existence*. With the ascendancy of scientific modernism and method, which emphasized a study of parts over wholes, there emerged a way of studying and understanding human nature in discrete parts. There was also a move toward valuing reason and science over and against the arts and emotions. The existentialists sought to bring things back into balance. The central themes of existential thought emerged out of a foundation premised upon holistic methodology; and a resultant brutal honesty about the human condition emerged the central themes of existential thought.

Phenomenology, or the study of subjective experience, is a third central theme in existential thought. The existential method, although emphasizing subjectivity, seeks to bring objective realities (i.e., the existential givens) into dialogue with the subjective self. Even here, existentialists tend to be more concerned with the subjective experience of the objective realities than with the objective realities themselves.

These three themes provide a basis for existential thought. One would note, however, that these three themes are devoid of specific

---

[2] For an introduction to many of the existential thinkers identified in these sections, see Schneider and May (1995). Brief descriptions of this and other works are available in the Appendix.

[3] "Scientific" is used as an adjective for "modernism" here to distinguish it from modernist literary figures, such as Franz Kafka, Virginia Woolf, and Samuel Becket, who have been very influential on many existential writers.

content; rather, *they are values that inform existential methodology*. In other words, one would be hard-pressed to find an existential approach that does not seek a holistic understanding of what it means to be human, an appreciation for one's subjective experience, and the intent to be honest about the human condition. However, from this foundation, many perspectives emerge.

The Beginning of Existential Psychology.

Existential psychology began in Europe with the writings of Ludwig Binswanger. Unfortunately, Binswanger remains relatively unknown outside of Europe, even among existential psychologists. The primary introduction to Binswanger are the translations of his work included in the book *Existence* (May, Angel, & Ellenberger, 1958), often cited as the origins of existential psychology in the United States. This book also thrust Rollo May, the lead editor of the book, into role of the father of American existential psychology.

Beginning with May, the early family tree of existential psychology in the United States can be established. The most notable offshoot of May's existential approach is James F. T. Bugental's *existential-humanistic psychology*. Although Rollo May was also active in humanistic psychology and the founding of the Association for Humanistic Psychology, he eventually favored the label *existential* because of key differences with Carl Rogers, a leading representative of humanistic psychology (see May, 1982; Rogers, 1982). For Bugental, conversely, the existential approach was strengthened and balanced by humanistic psychology.

The most famous follower of Rollo May is Irvin Yalom. Yalom's (1980) *Existential Psychotherapy* served as the classic introductory text to existential psychology for many years and still is preferred by many. Yalom, a former client of May, provided the most commonly used organizational structure for existential psychology through what he called the four existential givens: death, freedom, isolation, and meaninglessness. This continues to be the most common classification of the existential givens. Yalom also popularized existential psychology through writing several novels (1993, 1997) and case study books (1989, 1999).

More recently, Kirk Schneider has moved into the role of the most prominent figure in existential psychology in the United States. In 1995, Schneider co-edited with Rollo May the book *The Psychology of Existence*, which served as the first introductory text book on existential therapy since Yalom's *Existential Psychotherapy*. More recently, Schneider (2008a) published *Existential-Integrative Psychotherapy: Guideposts to the Core of*

Practice, which has served as the most significant contribution to existential psychology in the United States since May's death. He is currently co-authoring the forthcoming book *Existential-Humanistic Therapy* (in press) with Orah Krug.

Existential Psychotherapy as a Depth Psychotherapy

Existential psychotherapy is generally considered a *depth psychotherapy*. Depth psychotherapy, however, suffers from many of the same definitional problems that plague existential psychology. Similar to what has been discussed about existential psychotherapy, depth psychotherapy often is assumed to be a set of approaches that takes seriously the idea of the unconscious and values its exploration. However, not all depth psychotherapies, and not all existential therapists, embrace the idea of the unconscious. When the concept of the unconscious is challenged by depth psychotherapists, there is generally another cognitive construction that replaces the unconscious, or at least the concept of unconscious is redefined in a new manner. For example, insight, which traditionally has been linked to the concept of the unconscious, remains important even when the unconscious is dismissed.

Bugental (1987) discussed the idea of "life-changing psychotherapy," which could be equated to depth psychotherapy. Bugental distinguished life-changing psychotherapy from forms of therapy that are solution-focused, skill based, or centered on coping. This form of therapy was assumed to be a longer-term therapy in most instances, often lasting 6 months or more, as compared to the 8-20 sessions that are generally assumed in most brief therapies today.

Although Bugental's distinction is helpful in the therapy realm, depth psychotherapy emerges from depth psychology, which does not benefit much from this distinction focused solely on application. It is possible to infer some values from the idea of the unconscious and life-changing psychotherapy to extend this distinction. The depth psychotherapies posit that there are multiple layers of consciousness and/or experience that are part of human existence. A complete understanding of the human being therefore needs to be holistic, looking beyond the surface layers. In other words, depth psychology embraces a complex and holistic understanding of human nature.

Although the non-depth psychologies may also claim to embrace a complex and even holistic understanding of what it means to be human, this is generally defined more narrowly. Additionally, these other psychologies tend to focus on significantly circumscribed aspects of being human as the central aspect of their psychology. For example, the various cognitive and behavioral therapies focus primarily on the aspects of being human bearing their name: cognitions and behaviors. Although many acknowledge human existence is more complex than this, they do not see the need for their psychologies or therapies to delve into these realms in any great detail.

Implications for Existential Therapy as a Depth Psychotherapy

The depth emphasis in existential psychotherapy is quite essential to the therapeutic practice. Although there have been a number of attempts at brief forms of existential psychotherapy (Bugental, 2008; Galvin, 2008; Strasser & Strasser, 1997), the authors of these approaches often acknowledge the limitations inherent in such attempts. This should not discourage people from attempting to modify existential therapy for short-term applications, but does distinguish the brief existential approaches from the more traditional longer-term therapies.

Existential psychotherapy is an *ontological* therapy. Stated differently, existential therapy maintains that many of the challenges that bring people to psychotherapy are inherent in the nature of being. To this end, Yalom (1989) states:

> I believe that the primal stuff of psychotherapy is always... existence pain--and not, as is often claimed, repressed instinctual strivings or imperfectly buried shards of tragic personal past... basic anxiety emerges from a person's endeavors, conscious and unconscious, to cope with the harsh facts of life, the "givens" of existence. (p. 4-5)

This quote distinguishes existential from other depth psychotherapies through freeing it from the "instinctual strivings" and "personal past," but does not denounce the importance of these. Instead, Yalom is pointing to something more primal, more basic in our suffering and pathology—something ontological. The only other depth psychotherapy that comes close to taking on the ontological aspects of suffering as seriously is Jungian psychotherapy.

The ontological nature of existential psychotherapy is the primary challenge when adapting it to a short-term approach. How can one deal with ontological suffering in 12 to 20 sessions? Lest this be interpreted as being too harsh on the short-term existential approaches, let me clarify. It is not that the short-term approaches to existential therapy are superficial or antithetical to the core of existential practice, but rather *they are a fundamentally different from existential psychotherapy*. They remain a depth psychotherapy in the sense that they are rooted in a complex, holistic understanding of what it means to be human; however, they are more limited in scope.

Strasser and Strasser (1997) do, however, point out that there are some advantages of these "time-limited" models, which is their preferred language to identifying it as a brief psychotherapy. The imposed time-frame helps to bring forth existential issues. When one knows therapy is to end, and this is maintained in the forefront of one's consciousness, this changes the therapy. When therapists hold a frame with sensitivities to the existential condition, they can skillfully bring these issues into the discussion.

Therefore, there are advantages to the time-limited approach that cannot be denied and, in certain situations, this may be a preferred method. Often, the therapist does not have the luxury to extend therapy over many months or even years due to client factors, economic conditions, time limitations, or other externally imposed realities. Therefore, it is a valid and important endeavor to seek out short-term adaptations.

The depth emphasis, however, suggests that time-limitations are not the ideal. The very nature of seeing the condition as having "depth" suggests there is more to explore and process. Again, this is not to discourage or discredit brief approaches to therapy – existential or otherwise – but we do intend to distinguish between them.

In a critically important article, David Elkins (2008) challenges the limitations of the various "short-term, linear approaches to psychotherapy" (p. 413). Elkins reviews the research, including important recent meta-analytic studies, discrediting claims of the superiority of short-term models. Furthermore, he elucidates how the research points to the likely superiority of longer term approaches over time. From a philosophical and pragmatic perspective, Elkins points to many other limitations in the short-term, linear approaches to which we will return at the end of this chapter.

Many psychotherapists believe that the future of psychotherapy is the brief modalities and that the depth approaches will need to adapt or they will fade away. I disagree. There will always be a place for the brief psychotherapies, as well as a place for longer-term approaches. It is important for the depth therapies to be able to adapt in time-limited scenarios; however, longer-term therapy also has its place and will remain a demand in the marketplace.

The challenge of long-term therapy is, in part, economic. However, it is also *cultural* if we use this word in the broadest sense. In the West, a primary challenge to longer-term therapy is what seems to be a decreasing valuing of mental health and self-awareness. As will be discussed in Chapter 4, in China, as well as many other countries where the idea of psychotherapy is relatively new, there are different challenges inherent in getting people to invest in a longer-term therapy. These will be addressed in various ways throughout the book; however, at this point, I would maintain that this *problem* is a problem of creativity. The need for long-term and short-term depth psychotherapy approaches is there, but creativity is needed help clients access and recognize the value of these approaches.

Existential-*Integrative* Psychotherapy

It was just asserted that a primary challenge for existential and other depth psychotherapies in contemporary times is one of creativity. In the United States and Europe, this innovation is already in place. The face of psychotherapy needs to be ever changing with the times, needs, and cultural contexts. Existential-*integrative* psychotherapy is particularly well suited for this (Nathan, 2008; Schneider, 2008b). Although outside of this section the use of "existential-integrative" will not be used much throughout book, the integrative often will often be implied.

Integrative psychotherapies navigate between two extremes in the manner in which therapists relate to the theoretical foundations of therapy. First, there is the danger of theoretical fundamentalism. Many clinicians rigidly adhere to a particular theoretical orientation and the accompanying frame or structure. This typically negatively impacts the effectiveness of therapy. Although being rooted in a particular approach to therapy is beneficial, rigid adherence limits creativity, innovation, and the utilization of good ideas from other approaches to psychotherapy.

At the other extreme is eclecticism. Within the eclectic approaches, the common idea is to *use what works*. There are many problems with this idea. First, you have to ask, "To what ends does the therapy work?" These ends are necessarily determined by a theoretical frame; however, there is no universal intended outcome for therapy. Even if all therapists agreed upon an end, such as symptom reduction and improved quality of life, it is not likely they could agree upon what this means.

Second, eclecticism assumes that one can easily shift one's theoretical orientation to fit the needs of the client. It is simply not realistic for therapists to be competent, let alone expert, in a number of varied orientations. Although some orientations and techniques are easy to learn, most depth psychotherapies, including existential, take years of training to establish competency. As we will discuss later, being grounded in an approach to therapy that one believes in is more predictive of successful outcomes in therapy than the particular techniques used (Elkins, 1008a; Wampold, 2001).

Integrative denotes an approach in which the clinician has a foundation in a particular style of psychotherapy and then integrates other approaches with this foundation. Although this sounds fairly straightforward, it can be more complicated than it initially seems. Many therapists integrate ideas that end up working against each other. An example may help illustrate this.

Existential therapists generally align with anxiety, or utilize anxiety in the process of therapy. Therefore, a certain optimal level of anxiety is preferable to facilitate the therapy process. This can be challenging for integrating certain cognitive-behavioral strategies when working with anxiety. If the anxiety is overly controlled, repressed, or alleviated, the therapist and client have lost one of their best guides in the therapy process. This does not mean that strategies to help modulate anxiety should always be avoided. Often it is necessary to help the client gain some competency in modulating their anxiety in order to enter into it and learn the lessons that await. Cognitive-behavioral strategies, therefore, are utilized very differently in an existential paradigm when compared to the orthodox cognitive-behavioral paradigm.[4]

In many ways, it is easier to integrate the other depth psychotherapies with the existential approach as they share many of the same values; however, there are advantages to moving beyond this. Many theories have made important contributions to the understanding of human nature and how to help people struggling with issues of existence. Existential therapists should remain open to drawing on these diverse sources while retaining a critical and thoughtful approach to integration.

---

[4] Schneider's (2008) *Existential-Integrative Psychotherapy: Guideposts to the Core of Practice*, provides a number of examples of how different therapists have integrated existential therapy with other modalities, including cognitive-behavioral.

Core Tenets of Existential Psychological Theory

Thus far we have established that existential psychology is a depth psychotherapy that provides a solid foundation for integration with other psychotherapy approaches. Now it is time to shift our focus to the core tenets of the theory before moving on to the practice of existential psychotherapy.

The Existential Givens

The existential givens maintain a core place in existential theory, something that will become self-evident throughout the rest of this book. In particular, in Section 3, we will discuss the existential givens in the context of culture. The existential givens reflect core or universal aspects of the human condition that each of us must deal with on some level. Death is the most evident of these themes. Few would claim that they will not have to face death, even if they believe they have attained some resolution to this reality.

Each of the givens is understood as having a problematic aspect. In other words, they are not easily resolved. However, for optimal psychological health and authentic living, it is imperative that individuals face these givens. The givens, however, often have a highly symbolic nature and therefore may not always be dealt with directly. Instead, they emerge symbolically. The existential lexicon and direct address of the givens of existence infrequently occurs in psychotherapy. However, the themes are always present.[5] The art of existential psychotherapy resides in large measures in learning to talk about these givens of existence in the language of the client instead of the intellectual language of existential theory.

Earlier, I claimed these existential givens are universal, which is likely to create concern to readers with postmodern proclivities. However, to proclaim the existential givens universal is not the claim of them as a *metanarrative*.[6] Indeed, I maintain that the existential givens are *not* a metanarrative. Rather, these are realities each of us must address. The

---

[5] On one occasion when teaching a course on existential and humanistic psychotherapy, I walked into the clinic to see the four givens written on a white board in a therapy room with notes about the givens underneath. This is not the recommended approach to dealing with the givens with clients; indeed, this approach is strongly discouraged.

[6] In postmodern theory, metanarratives are understood as grand or totalizing narratives often forced upon different people and cultures. These are generally assumed to be oppressive in nature, particularly as they generally represent value systems or worldviews that are imposed upon people.

answers to the existential givens are what could potentially form a metanarrative. For example, any religion comprehensive enough to sustain over time must deal with the existential givens and, in its claims, generally ought to provide definitive answers, or ultimate truths, about these givens. This is a metanarrative. The givens themselves are merely conditions that often spark people into creating these grand metanarratives.

As we will discuss in Section 3, the existential givens form universal challenges or questions, but they necessitate local or cultural answers. In other words, *the existential givens are universal questions or problems with culture-specific answers*. In this section, Yalom's (1980) categorization of the existential givens is utilized as the initial framework. This section will, however, make some adjustments to Yalom's basic language and extend the discussion of the givens beyond Yalom's contribution. Additionally, a fifth given relating to embodiment and human emotion is added.

Death, Finiteness, and Human Limitation. Death can be seen as the ultimate given because, in many ways, it contextualizes each of the other givens. Each given is intimately connected to death. For example, death focuses meaning. It is almost cliché today to ask the question of what one would do if one had only a small amount of time to live. Yet, this simple, common exercise may help bring into focus the aspects of one's life that has the most personal value. Death can even be seen as being necessary for meaning. Although over stated, there is nonetheless a grain of truth in this. Without death, without endings, meaning would not be the same.

The other side of the question posed above is "what would you do if you knew you would live forever?" When I have asked this question when teaching, the most common response from my students indicates that things would not seem as important or urgent. Often at least one honest student will say, "I would probably start to take my family for granted." Occasionally, students remark that they would finally be able to live. This illustrates that for some, the fear of death is so pervasive and intense that it causes them to develop a fear of life. As Yalom (1980) suggests, once we embrace life we implicitly also embrace the reality that we are going to die; it is emotionally easier to remain unaware.

Becker (1973), in his existential classic *The Denial of Death*, suggests that death denial is at the core of the human dilemma. In considering Freud's theories, Becker states that Freud was not so far off base; his basic structure was correct, but he was wrong in placing sex at the center. Instead, Becker states that our most basic repression today is not sex, but death. To truly live we must face the reality of death, and the reality that we are going to die. Becker also realizes that death can become overwhelming. If we were to constantly be aware of death and our fragility, we would be immobilized, unable to do anything! Indeed, the denial of death is, to some degree, necessary. We have, however, taken this too far. Although it may not be possible to fully resolve the issue of death, it is necessary to face it, balancing death awareness with appropriate death denial.

Death must also be understood as symbolic of all forms of human limitation. This is why some thinkers, such as Bugental (1987, 1999) and Tillich (1952), prefer to focus on finiteness. *Finiteness* is used to indicate the basic limitedness of human nature. Human nature is full of limitations: limits of freedom, the longevity of life, our influence upon others and our environment, and limits on knowledge and understanding. For Tillich (1952, 1957a), who was a theologian and philosopher first, the ultimate sin or idolatry was to claim to know more than we know. In the psychological realm, the parallel form of this is the defense of *reification*, or making real or known that which is abstract or ambiguous.

In returning to Becker (1973), he argued that the root or basis of evil was the denial of death. Although there is debate among Becker scholars as to whether he intended death to be interpreted only literally or if he intended it to be interpreted symbolically, there is great power in this idea if interpreted symbolically. The root of all evil is the denial of our finite nature, the denial of our limitation, or, returning to Tillich's theology, the denial that we are not gods ourselves. This point has been repeatedly illustrated by history; when individuals, groups, or countries lose sight of their own limitations, they often engage in great evil.

In existential thought, the motive of becoming comfortable with the unknowns has a moral implication. We must come to grips with the limitations inherent in our own nature to avoid doing harm to others. This is a difficult, but necessary, truth. To resolve the issues of human death and limitation, the therapist does not help the client overcome these issues, but helps her or him to face this reality. In the end, the best way to prepare for a good death is by living a good life. Yet, paradoxically, it is often the fear of a bad death that keeps people from engaging life.

Yalom (1980) purports that most therapists do not recognize or engage death issues when they surface, which is often largely due to the therapist not having faced his or her own death issues. This is a great tragedy and something that existential therapy can teach the broader psychological community. Although there are no clear answers to death and human limitation, we can walk with clients as they face these terrifying issues. In doing so, we help clients find their answers and their peace. In helping clients face death, the therapist helps the client to truly live. When the fear of death remains unconscious, or is too much in the forefront of consciousness, it can dominate our entire existence.

Freedom, Responsibility, and Destiny. Freedom cannot be properly understood without also considering responsibility; one necessitates the other. Indeed, it can be considered a fundamental form of "pathology" to attempt to have freedom without responsibility. This, then, is fundamental to psychotherapy. Yalom (1980) states, "For the patient who will not accept such responsibility... no real therapy is possible" (p. 218).

It is for this reason that many perceive freedom as a burden; a burden they try desperately to escape. True freedom is a terrible curse as well as a wonderful blessing. Through freedom, we become responsible for the good which flows from our life, but also for pain, suffering, and even tragedy that may also ensue. It is the nature of our imperfect human condition that freedom makes us guilty.[7] We are destined, or perhaps condemned, to be free, but also destined to be guilty. The person who tries to claim perfect purity can only do so in denouncing their freedom.

In the United States, freedom is talked about frequently, but it is often talked about poorly, at least from an existential perspective. Freedom becomes idealized and there seems to be a consequential fanciful belief that if we are free, we will be happy; that if we are free, we will do the "right" thing. But freedom is not so ideal. This is not to say that people should not treasure the freedoms that they have, or even that freedom is not something worth standing for; rather, it is to acknowledge that freedom is not a perfect state.

People in the United States also tend to confuse political freedom with a more existential, or personal, freedom. It seems ironic that many will fight so hard for political freedom only to give up all of their personal freedoms. They abandon personal freedom to conformity, groupthink, and the tyranny of normalcy. This is truly a tragedy.

Freedom also cannot be understood apart from destiny, which May (1981) used to balance freedom. But destiny is not mere determinism; instead, there is an element of responsibility, of meaning in destiny. May states:

---

[7] This topic of guilt may need more discussion; however, for the purposes here let me address two aspects of this guilt. First, existentialists will often discuss guilt in terms of an *existential guilt* resulting from not fully living one's life. However, guilt is also a necessary condition of human limitation; we have inherent limitations in our moral and ethical abilities. Furthermore, the existential emphasis on paradox will often maintain that all choices are less than perfect, therefore including some element of guilt.

> The radical shift from determinism to destiny occurs when the subject is self-conscious about what is happening to him or her. The presence of consciousness creates the *context* in which the human being's responses to his or her destiny occur. (p. 88)

Destiny, then, entails an acceptance of our determinism, to a degree, but also the ability to be aware and accept requisite responsibility in the face of it. Destiny is accepting that one's freedom is always bound or limited, while also accepting that one is responsible for how one faces one's lack of freedom and how one will act given these limitations. Frankl (1959/1984), in talking about the limited freedoms during his experience in the German concentration camps, similarly states, "...everything can be taken from man but one thing: the last of the human freedoms—to choose one's attitude in any given set of circumstances, to choose one's own way" (p. 86).

No matter how determined we are, we are still free. Tillich (1957b) maintains that freedom and destiny are intertwined: "But freedom is the possibility of a total and centered act of the personality, an act in which all the drives and influences which constitute the destiny of man are brought into the centered unity of a decision" (pp. 42-43). Therefore, destiny is part of every decision, but so is freedom. We are never completely free, but we also are never completely determined. It is this element of freedom with which we are most concerned in existential psychotherapy.

To a degree, existentialists believe that *we are as free as we become*. However, it must always be emphasized that how free we become is tremendously limited. Rank (1929/1978) noted that all those conditions that influence us have greater control over us when they remain outside of our conscious awareness. Through increasing our awareness of what influences us, we increase our freedom. Although we can never become completely free, we can become freer. Given the connection between freedom and responsibility, we could then maintain that the responsible life is one in which we pursue freedom and, with it, responsibility.

Relationship, Intimacy, and Encounter

Human beings are relational creatures; this is one of our most basic needs. Yet, our relational needs are destined to be at least partially unfulfilled. We can never fully overcome loneliness. We can never conquer basic existential isolation. As with all the existential givens, relationships run into inherent limitations in our ability to resolve them.

Bugental (1987, 1999) uses the phrasing of *a-part-of* and *a-part-from* to illustrate the paradoxical nature of relationships. This can be understood in two senses. First, we all have a desire to be a-part-of, or to be connected, and to be a-part-from, or to be separate. Second, most people's reality is such that they are both connected, yet distinct. But being a-part-of and a-part-from is not necessarily as distinct as it would seem.

O'Donohue (1998) maintains that solitude is an essential part of relationship. In order to be fully present and able to relate on a deep level with others, some solitude, or time apart, is necessary. The amount of time may vary from individual to individual, but the basic need remains. Solitude, for O'Donohue, has a reflective quality; it is not merely being alone. Solitude is a time focused on one's relationship with oneself, their *intrapersonal* relationship. A healthy *intra*personal relationship, or connection with oneself, allows one to genuinely and subjectively engage with others in *inter*personal relationships.

When in connection with others, emphasis is placed upon the way one is relating with the other person. It is not just being in relationship that is important, but *the way* one is in relationship. Many approaches to psychotherapy today, including many approaches to couples and group therapy, focus on communication skills, including efficient, effective communication. It is evident that being able to communicate effectively is important to a healthy relationship, but how tragic if this is all that is sought after! This may be a proper ideal for working relationships, but how dreadful and unfulfilled as the ideal for an intimate relationship.

Existential perspectives value relationships that are rooted in genuineness and authenticity; relationships that have depth. These relationships require a certain amount of risk and vulnerability. One aspect of these relationships is the encounter, a way of relating in which both people are impacted and changed through the connection that is made. Vulnerability, risk, and a bi-directional relationship signify a considerable difference from what is focused on in other therapeutic modalities. From an existential perspective, however, it seems unrealistic to help clients improve their relationships and ability to make deep connections if we are unwilling to go there with them in therapy. Relationships are necessary and, as the common therapy adage goes, *it is the relationship that heals*.

Meaning. Yalom (1980) begins his discussion of meaning pointing to paradox: We are innately meaning seeking creatures; yet, there is no ultimate meaning for us to attain. Other existentialists (Frankl, 1959/1984; Tillich, 1957a, 1957b) may disagree with Yalom's skepticism about the lack of evident meaning; however, there is general agreement that humans are never fully fulfilled in terms of meaning; we are always left lacking and yearning to some degree. Still, we are destined to search for meaning; to attain the greatest level of meaning we can attain. As Becker (1973) states, in a quote we will return to later in the chapter, "Man cannot endure his own littleness unless he can translate it into meaningfulness on the largest possible level" (p. 196).

Meaning is not a simple concept; many distinctions can be made between different types of meaning. A primary distinction Yalom (1980) makes is between attempts to *discover* meaning and attempts to *make* meaning. Those who believe that ultimate meaning exists out there often spend their life trying to *discover* it, or locate it with sufficient confidence. The most common of the meaning discoverers are the religious, who believe that meaning is found in religion. The religious also tend to be suspicious of the idea of created meaning. For them, the only true meaning is that which is discovered in religion. For the religious existentialists, though, this meaning can never be completely attained while in our finite, human form. Because of this, meaning must be connected to faith, or a belief in what cannot be fully known (Tillich, 1957a).

Conversely, individuals aligning with the meaning creators position generally believe that there is no inherent meaning in the world; the only meaning that exists is that which the individual creates. The most radical of these positions was held by John Paul Sartre, who stated, "All existing things are born for no reason, continue through weakness, and die by accident... It is meaningless that we are born; it is meaningless that we die" (as cited in Yalom, 1980, p. 428). But this position is more extreme and nihilistic than most taken by the existentialists. Yet, there still is, and always will be, a great deal in life that is meaningless; this we cannot escape.

The problem with meaning, whether created or discovered, is located in the question: "How do we know what is truly meaningful?" Meaning is something that gives a person a sense of purpose and coherence (Yalom, 1980). But this is not enough, for there are many ways a person could a have sense of purpose and meaning that, in actuality, are radically destructive and problematic. For example, terrorists often see their acts of killing and destruction as highly meaningful. Meaning must be held to a greater accountability and this can be found returning to Becker (1973):

> What is the ideal for mental health, then? A *lived, compelling illusion* that *does not lie about life, death, and reality*; one honest

> enough to *follow its own commandments*: I mean, not to kill, not to take the lives of others to justify itself. (p. 204, emphasis added)

This quote is perhaps the most compelling existential view of mental health and meaning. In breaking this down, it is possible to make a distinction between what is referred to as sustaining meaning versus false meaning or *pseudo-meaning*.

First, Becker (1973) states that meaning is an illusion. From Becker's writings, it was never clear where he stood on religion. At times he seemed skeptical, almost antagonistic, about religion, and at other times more optimistic. What is evident is that Becker struggled with the religious questions all his life. In *The Denial of Death*, Becker stated, "the best existential analysis of the human condition leads directly into the problems of God and faith" (p. 68). Religion, for Becker, whether true or not, was something that could not be escaped. Even if the essence of religion is true, Becker seemed to believe that it was still an illusion; religion was a matter of faith, not proof. This conception of illusion is essentially the same as May's (1991) conception of myth.[8]

Next, Becker (1973) states that meaning must be a *lived, compelling* illusion. By lived, it must be embodied; it must impact our life and daily living. If an illusion is not lived, it has no meaning or purpose. In stating that the illusion is compelling, Becker maintains that one must truly believe in the myth and it must provide a sense of coherence. In some instances, it is evident that people are adhering to illusions or belief systems as a protection or a defense, not out of genuine belief. As Nietzsche (1894/1990) states, "The most common lie is the lie one tells oneself" (p. 185). These illusions are not sustaining.

Becker (1973) then states that the sustaining illusion "does not lie about life, death, and reality" (p. 204). This brings us back to a basic existential premise: *Existential theory attempts to be honest about the human condition*. Last, Becker states that this illusion must "follow its own commandments" (p. 204). Again, it must be lived, and it must be lived honestly. Becker also points to a topic we will return to later: evil. Implicit in this quote is that when one lives by a meaning system that is not embodied, compelling, and honest, then one must engage in destructive acts, such as killing, to justify himself or herself. The person with sustaining meaning does not need to resort to such ends.

---

[8] See also chapter 13.

Pseudo-meaning now should be evident: It is not honest about the human condition; it is not lived; it is not compelling or truly believed; and one often must resort to extreme defenses to justify and protect it. Sustaining meaning, then, is not even necessarily true meaning, but it is a meaning that promotes healthy ends. As the postmodernists say, true meaning or ultimate meaning may not exist or may not exist in a form that we can access, but this does not render meaning meaningless (Hoffman & Kurzenberger, 2007). Rather, meaning remains a key criterion in psychological health even if the full comprehension of it is elusive.

Embodiment and the Nature of Emotion. This given was not addressed by Yalom, but was central to Bugental (1987, 1999). In one sense, *embodiment is the embodiment of the existential givens*, the acknowledgment of these as lived realities. But embodiment, as understood here, also goes beyond this; it refers to the experience of these givens in our bodies. The most primary form of this experience is emotional.

From the beginning of existential thought, the emotions were seen as something to be embraced. Kierkegaard (1843/1985) wrote the first ever book on anxiety, *Fear and Trembling*, in 1843. He saw anxiety, which is often considered the mother of all emotions, as something that was natural. Anxiety was not something to be feared, avoided, controlled, or repressed; it was something to be learned from. Later, May (1950/1970) wrote his doctoral dissertation on anxiety, later published as the book *The Meaning of Anxiety*.

May (1950/1970) drew on Kierkegaard's ideas to develop some central thoughts on an existential theory of emotions. Kierkegaard distinguished between what today is referred to as *neurotic anxiety* and *normal anxiety* (or existential anxiety). Neurotic anxiety is "a more constrictive and uncreative form of anxiety that results from an individual's *failure* to move ahead in situations of normal anxiety" (May, 1950/1970, p. 38). All anxiety has, at its roots, normal anxiety. What makes anxiety normal or neurotic is not its presence, but the way the individual relates to the anxiety.

Nietzsche (1889/1990) discussed similar ideas with his basic premise that we should not fight that which is natural. In today's psychological language, Nietzsche was, in part, saying we should not fight, deny, or repress our emotions, which broadens Kierkegaard's ideas to other emotions. Indeed, this normal and neurotic distinction could rightly be applied to all emotions. However, he is not saying that we should just go with or act upon any urge that we have. Instead, Nietzsche is arguing that all that is natural needs to find expression. As will be discussed in the next section, this is the role of the daimonic, creativity, and integration. Returning to Kierkegaard and May, what is often needed is a creative expression of this emotion. Still, learning from Becker, we could also say that what is needed is a creative expression of the emotion that does not lie about the basic reality of the emotion.

This, we recognize, is an existential position that lends itself to challenges cross-culturally. Some cultures, including many Eastern cultures as well as many Northern European cultures, tend to be restrictive with emotions. This is where the *creative* element is essential. Existentially, it is still maintained that emotions need to find expression and that denying, controlling, and repressing them does not serve psychological health or well-being. However, *how* they are expressed will differ across cultures. For example, Eastern and Northern European cultures may seek out more subtle forms of emotional expression than what is typical in most places in the United States, African/African American cultures, and Southern European cultures.

The Daimonic and the Nature of Being Human

According to May (1969) the daimonic is "any natural function which has the power to take over the whole person" (p. 65). The daimonic itself, however, is not good or evil:

> While the daimonic cannot be said to be evil in itself, it confronts us with the troublesome dilemma of whether it is to be used with awareness, a sense of responsibility and the significance of life, or blindly and rashly... When the daimonic is repressed, it tends to erupt in some form. (p. 129)

The daimonic, then, is an aspect of what it means to be human that confronts the nature of our being. Existential therapy is generally classified as a humanistic psychology, however, this is an essential divergence with most humanistic psychologies (Hoffman, Patz-Clarke, Looney, & Knight, 2007; Hoffman, Warner, Buck, & Fehl, 2007). While humanistic psychology focuses primarily on human potential, existential psychology responds stating that it is also imperative that we recognize the potential for evil and human limitation.

Much of the field of psychology seems to have fallen into one of two camps. First, mainstream psychology has taken on the medical model in which the darker aspects of human nature are relegated as pathology.

Conversely, many in humanistic psychology and positive psychology focus on human potential to the exclusion of human limitation. Popular culture reflects a third distinction that identifies many individuals or groups as being essentially morally corrupt or evil (See Bernstein, 2005; Hoffman, Patz-Clarke et al., 2007; Hoffman, Warner, et al., 2007).

According to Diamond (1996), the daimonic is essentially tied to what is labeled as evil in the world. In the definition of the daimonic discussed before, several themes can be highlighted. First, the daimonic is a natural tendency. It is not something foreign or external; it is part of our nature. Second, the daimonic is not inherently negative, only potentially so. For example, drawing upon Diamond's focus on anger, it is natural for a person to experience anger. However, when the capacity for anger is denied or repressed, it does not go away. As it is relegated to the latent, unconscious, and denied realms, its potential grows and it begins to develop the strength to "take over the whole person." However, this same daimonic capacity can also be used positively or creatively. The creative use of anger, for example, has been the source of many social justice movements and great works of art.

According to Diamond (1996), self-awareness, integrity, and creativity are keys to dealing with the daimonic:

> Integrity is unity of the personality; it implies being brutally honest with ourselves about our intentionality. Since intentionality is inextricably bound up with the daimonic, this is never an easy, nor always pleasant pursuit. But being willing to admit our daimonic tendencies - to know them consciously and to wisely oversee them - brings with it the invaluable blessing of freedom, vigor, inner strength, and self-acceptance. (p. 233)

The beginning of utilizing the daimonic is awareness. From here, the individual must learn to accept this as an aspect of the self and creatively integrate it into one's self understanding.

Before moving to the good life, it is important to address one more aspect of evil. Becker (1973, 1975) placed denial of death, which could be interpreted to include the denial of all human limitation, as the root of evil. This runs parallel to the conception of the daimonic. Again, we see the denial of an aspect of human nature as the essence of evil. It is only through self-awareness and self-honesty that we can contain evil in the world. As May (1982) stated, "I am not predicting doom. But I am stating that if we ignore evil, we will move closer to doom, and the growth and triumph of evil may well result" (p. 20). This could be broadened to state that if, as a collective, we continue to deny human limitation and other negative aspects of human nature, we will continue to see evil abound. Instead, through encouraging everyone to recognize one's own potential for evil, as well as one's potential for good, we can work to dramatically reduce the amount of evil promulgated in the world.

The Good Life

> The point of both May and Nietzsche, and one of the major tenets of existential psychology, is the idea that what most of psychology calls "negative emotions" are in fact integral parts of being a human being and possessing the potential of both good and evil. Tragedy is part and parcel of human life. The attempt to deny this, whether it be carried out by utopian therapists who label nearly all of existence "pathological," or by psychiatrists who wish to obliterate such moods with mind-altering drugs, runs the risk of repressing the daimonic or Dionysian. (Hoeller, 1999, p. 120)

Maybe the greatest distinction between existential psychology and most of the rest of the psychology is its view of "the good life." Throughout most of the field of psychotherapy, it has become so implicit that the good life is one that seeks pleasure and the avoidance of discomfort (i.e., basic hedonism) that it seems unnecessary to even discuss (see Slife, 2004). As Hoeller (1999) states, *this* is a tragedy.

Throughout this chapter and the book, variations of the existential good life will be discussed, so here we wish to simply make explicit some common themes. First, however, it should be noted that in removing pleasure and happiness from the unquestioned pinnacle of mental health, it is not intending to state there is anything wrong with happiness. Instead, as Frankl (1959/1984) was fond of illustrating, happiness is best understood as a "side effect" of a life well lived and the more we pursue it directly the more elusive it becomes. Similarly, there is nothing wrong with helping clients decrease uncomfortable or painful experiences; however, at times, suffering is normal and even healthy.

The existential perspective on the good life is not, and should not be, agreed upon by all existentialists; however, here are some central themes:

1) *The meaningful life*. Frankl (1959/1984) was the strongest advocate of this position; however, this is one perspective shared by all, or nearly all, existentialists.

2) *The free life*. As May stated, "the purpose of [existential] psychotherapy is to set people free" (p. 19) and a major purpose of life is to become free.

3) *The aware life*. Existentialists tend to believe that there is an inherent goodness in self-awareness and self-honesty. It also serves to help one become free.

4) *The ethical or moral life*. Existentialists are highly focused on what is right and wrong, good and evil, but also talking about Nietzsche's (1886/1966) idea of "beyond good and evil." According to Nietzsche, ethics is not rooted in an ethical system, but rather in character. Furthermore, ethics should not be about conformity, or allegiance to a belief system, but should be personal and subjective. This is not to suggest relativism, but, rather, suggests a need for a degree of personal responsibility in all ethical determinations.

5) *The life fully embraced, or the passionate life*. Existentialists tend to believe, as Nietzsche did, that we should embrace all aspects of life, the good and the difficult. Suffering should be faced directly, not avoided, and the varied emotions embraced. Passion is illustrated through one's character, living a life in which one embraces her or his emotions and personal convictions.

6) *Transcendence*. May (1958) illustrates that transcendence is a central value of the existentialists, but he also is cautious about misunderstanding this term. Existentialists are not talking about transcendence in an other-worldly sense, but rather in the potential to see oneself as continually emerging, and to see oneself beyond the immediate context. Transcendence refers to the ability to see things fluidly and symbolically (as part of a meaning system) and in the context of a broader meaning system.

7) *Intimate relationships and encounters*.   Existentialists value relationships and many are surprised when theorists, such as Yalom (1980), state that in the end, the good life is about love. But it is not just being in contact with others that is valued, but rather a particular *way of being* or *way of relating* that includes genuineness and a depth of encounter.

8) *The compassionate life*. Although a bit more hidden in the literature, this theme emerges through Adler's influence on May.

Adler (1929/1969) believed that a lack of social interest was a sign of pathology and an end of successful therapy would be the increase in social interest. This, again, is a significant shift from the business of psychology as usual. The more hedonistically based therapies can often promote a self-interest and selfishness that is quite the contrary to this end of therapy.[9]

It is imperative to point out that these are not values to impose upon clients. This is not what many clients are seeking from therapy, at least not at first. Even if clients like the idea of the above formulated goal of the good life, many begin therapy with more immediate goals of decreasing or managing intense suffering. Existential therapy often needs to be adapted or adjusted to help clients meet a mixture of short-term goals, which may focus on intense suffering and a compromised level of functioning, and the long-term goals that may be more consistent with this picture of the good life.

Core Tenets of Existential Psychotherapy

After this book [on therapy technique] is read, it should be given away, or put in a forgotten corner. The therapist should be a healer: a human being concerned with engaging other human beings, therapeutically, around areas and issues that cause them pain… The goal, in other words, is to transcend technique. Only a person who has mastered technique and then contrived to forget it can become an expert therapist. (Minuchin & Fishman, 1981, p. 1)

I mistrust all systematizers and avoid them. (Nietzsche, 1889/1990 p. 35)

Aspects of this section of the chapter are the least existential of the book. As will be discussed, the idea of techniques, and even structure, is often viewed as antithetical to existential therapy. In this section, I will attempt to "break down" and "categorize" processes that existential therapists often employ in the therapy. In some ways, this reductive

---

[9] As many therapists have experienced, it is a very common end of therapy for clients to become more socially active in causes important to them, more compassionate to their friends and family, more concerned about what is going on in the world, and sometimes even consider becoming a therapist themselves. As one client near the end of therapy stated, "It's amazing how much my therapy has benefited my friends."

methodology does not fit with the spirit or essence of existential therapy. However, there is also a value to it, particularly for the therapist struggling with how to envision this type of therapy.[10]

I have often heard comments such as, "That existential psychology stuff is interesting, I just don't know what to do with it in therapy." This has led some, such as Yalom, to maintain that existential psychotherapy cannot stand on its own. I disagree. To explain, first it is necessary to dismiss the misnomer of theoretical purity. One can read Freud and see shades of behaviorism, cognitive therapy, humanistic therapy, and many other approaches. All therapies are naturally integrative to a degree.

This should not, however, lead us to the equally naïve conclusion that all therapies are really the same, each merely incorporating a different vocabulary. Although a behaviorist could maintain that transference is nothing other than learned behavior, mere classical conditioning, this does not make these concepts the same. Changing transference through a corrective emotional experience, too, could be explained by unlearning old patterns and relearning new ones. But there are many nuances of difference. When one only has a limited grasp of these concepts, or a very concrete understanding of them, it is easy to say that both explanations are the same. However, the more that one understands these concepts the more evident it becomes that *behaviorist principles can only explain part of the transference reaction*.

Similarly, the common existential therapy processes can be broken down and isolated to talk about them; however, as soon as they are removed from the context and fluid process of therapy they are changed. From an existential perspective it is essential that even when specific "techniques" are incorporated, they are never used in the same way twice. The Minuchin quote at the beginning of this section illustrates this point. The reason he encouraged the reader to forget what he says is not because of its lack of utility, but because techniques that are *applied* are not as effective as techniques that *emerge*. This is the art of psychotherapy. As therapists, we are not technicians who apply techniques that "fix" the client; we are guides and fellow sojourners who walk with the client, at times illuminating insights, encouraging them to consider certain

---

[10] It is interesting to note that shortly after completing the initial draft of this chapter, I was reviewing May's chapters in the book *Existence*, which introduced European Existential Psychotherapy to the United States. May similarly struggled when getting to the portion of technique, but also for similar reasons decided that it was necessary to include this section in order to give a practical illustration of existential therapy.

alternatives, and challenging them, but primarily engaging or encountering them.

Too much structure and planning stifles psychotherapy, despite the good intentions. When a therapist begins to plan interventions and apply techniques, she or he begins to objectify the client; no longer encountering the client in the moment. This is not to say that clients do not, at times, benefit from the application of technique; it is evident that they do. Indeed, in regard to symptom reduction and other more objectively identified changes, the outcomes may be very similar when therapy focuses on techniques. However, important differences remain between the application of technique versus engagement.

One of the great errors in the mental health field is that we have too often blindly settled into a utilitarian ethic that the ends justify the means. We seem to think that if the client reaches the goals presented in the first session that therapy is a success; it matters not how we get there. There are some exceptions to this. Many therapists recognize that there is a difference between alleviating depression through medication and through psychotherapy. However, we have too often failed to consider the difference between achieving goals through means that objectify the client and means that rely upon encountering the client as a valuable, subjective person. The method, or means, conveys a message.

The implicit message given in therapy approaches rooted in techniques that objectify the client is that the person is more akin to a machine. If we provide the right resources–coping mechanisms, skills, and knowledge–they will function optimally. Second, there is an implicit reductionist mindset that what we need to do is "fix" a part of the client, not address the client as a whole being. In the machine metaphor, therapy is more nearly akin to replacing the radiator on a car than helping the car. But a human being is very different than a car! A third implicit message given is that efficiency is valued over depth or substance.

Although this model may sound distasteful to many who are drawn to reading this book, it could also be noted that this fits with much of the historic Western view of human beings. Furthermore, it is important to point out that this is what many clients want and expect from therapy. However, many clients also end therapy having achieved their goals, but still having a nagging feeling that something is amiss, something has been left undone.

Existential therapy prefers to work with the person as a whole and to deal with what it means to be human. It balances helping the person function better with the higher aspirations of humanity such as intimate connections, meaning, and compassion. Therefore, existential therapy is a holistic, relational therapy at its core; it is a therapy that believes that the process of therapy, or the journey, is an essential part of the outcome, or the ends. In other words, *the ends do not justify the means, the means are a part of the end.*

Process and Technique

Existential therapy, as noted, has a reputation for lacking technique, which has been part of the reason many have hesitated to identify with this approach. It is also a frustration for many who have attempted to teach the process of existential psychotherapy. Teachers of existential psychotherapy are fond of encouraging their students to "be in the moment," "let the client guide," and "follow the process." These ideas sound nice, even somewhat romantic; however, they also create a good deal of ambiguity and anxiety. These are acceptable ideals for therapy; however, many students may need more guidance in the fundamentals of this process in order to grow into the ideals. In this section, I will attempt to break down existential psychotherapy into some of these fundamentals, which may appear very technique-like even if only to illuminate their application.

Some of the resistance to techniques is due to linguistic issues. Existential therapy stands firm against mechanized, linear, reductionistic, and manualized approaches to therapy (see Elkins, 2008). Imposing a false structure on psychotherapy, although easing the therapist's anxiety, is not seen as beneficial to the overall therapy process. Therefore, existential therapy seeks a less structured, more fluid approach.

The language of technique is viewed with suspicion by existential therapists because it often typifies manualized and over-structured therapies. Instead of technique, existential therapists would prefer to talk about stances or processes occurring in therapy. However, this should not be seen as simply a linguistic distinction. By shifting from technique to stances or processes, the therapist moves into a different type of relationship with the client and a different form of therapy. The therapist is not so much applying something to the client (i.e., objectifying them), but rather trying to relate to her or him in a particular manner.

In the rest of this section, I will engage in some of what I just strongly critiqued: breaking down existential therapy processes and providing more structure to them. I will even introduce a few "techniques," of sorts. However, this is done in the spirit of moving beyond the techniques. Stated differently, the hope is that the reader will read this section and then forget it. Once forgotten, the therapist may find these emerging naturally from the flow of the therapy process.

Relationship and Presence

Existential psychotherapy is rooted in the therapy relationship. This is most succinctly stated in the adage Yalom (1980) frequently repeats: "it is the relationship that heals" (p. 401). Throughout his writing, Yalom (1980, 2002, Yalom & Elkin, 1990) frequently uses anecdotal evidence and informal research, as well as some references to more formal research, to illustrate that there is often a significant difference between what the therapist and the client think are the most important aspects of therapy. Therapists want to believe that it is their penetrating interpretations or artful use of technique that helps the client; however, clients generally point to empathy, compassion, and other aspects of the therapy relationship as being the most important ingredients.

Empathy and Genuineness. When talking about the therapy relationship, most therapists point to Carl Rogers (1951, 1980) as the central figure. It has become cliché to say that "Rogerian therapy is a nice foundation for all therapies." The second part of the sentence generally points to the limitations of this therapy approach. For many making this statement, one has to wonder if they have ever read Rogers! What is generally being referred to in Rogers work is his *therapeutic triad* of empathy, genuineness, and unconditional positive regard, which is often reduced to acting nice and caring about clients. Although I agree that there are limitations to Rogers's approach, I would also suggest that there are more significant limitations to how Rogers' work is often interpreted.

Empathy and genuineness have received a good deal of attention in the therapeutic literature, especially in the literature on empirically supported therapy relationships (see Norcross, 2002a, 2002b). Outcome literature, which will be discussed in more detail later, has consistently identified the quality of therapeutic relationships as the second most influential contributor to therapy success after client factors (Elkins, 2008; Lambert & Barley, 2002; Wampold, 2001). As an aspect of the therapy relationship, several therapist characteristics have been found to be important predictors of therapy success including empathy (Bohart, Elliott, Greenberg, & Watson, 2002), positive regard (Farber & Lane, 2002), and congruence (Klein, Kolden, Michels, & Chisholm-Stockard, 2002).

The establishment of the therapy relationship as central to psychotherapy remains ambiguous and the therapeutic triad remains largely misunderstood. Empathy, for example, is often very poorly used by therapists. When supervising therapists, it is often evident that they are *applying empathy as a technique* instead of *being empathetic*.[11] Empathy as a technique is rarely effective and often can damage the therapy relationship.

Similarly, many therapists misapply genuineness. A colleague, Mark Stocks (personal communication), is fond of saying, "You can't try to be genuine. As soon as you are *trying* you are no longer genuine." Genuineness and empathy are qualities of the therapist, not techniques. These are qualities that the therapist *allows to come forth*, not something they *try to do*. In other words, it is more of a letting go process in which the therapist lowers his or her own barrier in order to connect with the client on a deeper level.

Contemporary psychoanalytic thinker Martha Stark (1999), provides important guidance on the application of genuineness (or authenticity) and empathy. According to Stark, when engaging in empathy one decenters from her or his own subjective self in order to take on the experience of the client. Conversely, genuineness is rooted in the therapist's subjective experience:

> (1) I am suggesting that empathy involves a kind of selflessness on the therapist's part, which she is able to achieve when she steps aside (decenters) from her own experience of self.
> (2) I am suggesting that authenticity involves the therapist's use of self... which she is able to do when she remains very much present—centered—within her own experience of self. (Stark, 1999, p. 46)

Although many therapists confuse empathy and genuineness, Stark illustrates that these are very different therapeutic processes in that one is centered while the other requires a degree of de-centering. For therapists, it can be quite difficult to keep in touch with their own subjective (centered) experience of the client while also remaining in touch with their empathetic (de-centered) experience of the client. Furthermore, it often becomes difficult to distinguish between these two experiences. A

---

[11] In teaching and supervision, I will often ask the student/supervisee these questions: "Think of a time when someone was 'applying the technique' of empathy to you, or acting empathetic. How did it feel? What did you want to do in reaction to this?" Most students/supervisees will respond stating that they were angry and just wanted to get away from the person who was "acting empathetic." Yet many therapists continue to apply empathy as a technique instead of being empathetic.

common psychoanalytic illustration of a parallel process questions, "Whose unconscious is it?" The existential parallel could be, "Whose subjectivity is it?"

These relational illustrations demonstrate why it is very difficult to become an existential or depth psychotherapist. When journeying beyond technique-based therapies, many nuances of relationship emerge. Without good self-awareness and ability to identify and understand complex relational processes, the therapist can easily venture onto dangerous ground. This illustrates why the process of becoming a depth psychotherapist is generally longer and more focused on the person of the therapist.[12] It is this person that becomes the primary "tool" of therapy. Technique is replaced with the person of the therapist and genuine encounter.

Encounter. The word *encounter* is preferred by many existential therapists (May, 1983, 1999; Mendelowitz, 2008a). Encounter brings depth to the idea of relationship. It also suggests a mutual impact. In many traditional therapies, impact is thought to be primarily in one direction (upon the client, not the therapist) and, when it is not, it is countertransference that needs to be kept under control and hidden by the therapist. Conversely, in existential therapy, the impact is seen as something that is natural, something healthy.

In supervision, I have encountered students who apologetically reported that they felt like crying when the client shared a powerful story. Many are shocked when they hear my response, "So why didn't you?" Of course, crying with a client is not always therapeutic. It is important to determine if this emotional response has mostly to do with the therapist's issues (i.e., countertransference) or rather emerges out of empathy and the genuine impact of being present when hearing the client's story. Many times, shedding a tear with a client can be the most effective intervention in the moment.

Olthuis (2001) tells a beautiful story of crying with a client who responded by commenting that they did not know they were worth crying for! Clearly, this illustrates the power of encounter. Often, the greatest mistakes therapists make, especially neophyte therapists, is not what they do, but what they hold back. Unfortunately, by the time many therapists

---

[12] This also illustrates why it is important for therapists to have had their own depth therapy, whenever possible, and to undergo extensive supervision from a depth psychotherapist. Additionally, this points to the need of ongoing consultation across one's career. In fact, we would suggest that ongoing consultation is equally important to the continuing education required by most licensing boards.

graduate they are so scared of making an ethical blunder that they do not allow themselves to care for or encounter their clients!

Presence. In many ways, presence is the basis for the psychotherapy relationship. This should not be confused, however, with the idea of *being fully present*. Being fully present refers to a relational process in which a person is attending to the other while simultaneously "present" to their own subjective experiences and the experiences of the other person. Presence refers to the emotional feel or quality experienced with another person. Being fully present is often an aspect of presence, but not the full concept. Although presence is always subjectively experienced by the person we are in relationship with, it can also be understood to have a quality of presence that comes from us.

May (1988) discussed Paul Tillich as an illustration of the idea of presence. Tillich, after moving to the United States, drew large crowds to many of his lectures, even though his lectures were such that the listeners often could not understand them either because of his German accent, his struggles with English as a second language, or the abstractness of his ideas. There was a quality in his presence, how people tended to experience him, that drew people in. He also noted that it seemed almost impossible to have a shallow conversation with Tillich; he drew people to the depths of experience.

Presence bears similarity to Rogers' (1980) idea of "a way of being." Essentially, Rogers argued that the craft of therapy was largely about developing a way of being that was healing, or growth facilitating. Most of us have experienced people in our lives whom simply by being in their presence created the impulse to want to grow, heal, or be a better person. This is a type of presence.

There are limitations to presence, too. We all have aspects of presence that we do not like. For example, I recognize that many people, especially students, initially feel intimidated by me. This is not very therapeutic. I recognize that it comes, at least partially, from my introspective nature, my tendency to be drawn toward abstract ideas, and also my physical presence (6 foot, 1 inch tall, broad shouldered). Some of this I cannot change, and other aspects are connected with things I like about myself. Fortunately, most people, when sitting down with me one to one (therapy clients) do not experience this, and most students report this fades as they get to know me, often through the more one to one conversations. It is not always necessary to change our presence to become more therapeutic, but it is important to be aware of how people generally experience us (i.e., our presence).

Similarly, presence is always experienced subjectively and, therefore, is often distorted or skewed. In other words, transference often occurs. As Yalom (1980) suggests, *transference happens*. While traditional psychoanalytic individuals often purport that transference occurs most readily when the therapist is a "blank slate," or the client knows little about the therapist, knowledge of the therapist does not stop the transference process. As an illustration, I once worked with an individual who had a strong negative reaction to me. She had a prior boyfriend who was abusive to her. This man was about my height and stature and also had blond hair and blue eyes like I do. Once she was able to identify that her reaction to me was based upon her feelings toward her former boyfriend, the transference decreased. However, it would re-emerge at times throughout therapy even after establishing a solid, trusting therapeutic relationship. Her general experience of me was as warm and caring, but at times she would continue to experience me as threatening. Although we were careful to not just assume this was the old transference and always explored things that I could have done or other transferences that could have caused her to experience me as threatening in the moment, it often would return to the abusive boyfriend.

Therapists can learn to use presence therapeutically through being aware of their presence and, at times, by developing their presence. For example, therapists may be able to improve their presence by increasing their empathy, becoming more comfortable in the therapy setting, working on issues that impact their presence in supervision and/or their personal therapy, and developing an increased awareness of their presence.

Reflective Listening Beyond the Misconceptions

Reflective listening has been a cornerstone of client-centered therapy (Rogers, 1951, 1980) and is often used in existential psychotherapy. However, there is tremendous confusion about what reflective listening is. It often is thought that reflective listening is only reflecting the content the client just shared, and maybe also reflecting the emotion. These are two aspects of reflective listening, but the mirror of reflective listening is much larger than this. Reflective listening can include reflecting the moment, reflecting the process, and reflecting the person in context.

Reflecting the moment includes reflecting the content and emotions, but can also include the non-verbals. For example, Bugental would consistently reflect to clients their non-verbals, often asking them to repeat them. He would also use his intuition to reflect many subtle changes that were ambiguous. For example, it was not uncommon to hear Bugental make statements such as "something changed there." He did not always know what that was, but he recognized a shift. In reflecting the shift, he and the client together could begin to understand what the shift was.[13]

Reflecting the process broadens the reflections beyond the moment. Therapists may make reflections such as, "in the first several minutes of the session today, you have shifted between several different topics." This type of reflection can help the client identify the reason for such topic jumping. Sometimes there is an underlying theme of which the therapist, and often the client, is unaware of. Other times, this may be the client's defense to avoid going into any topic in detail. The therapist can also reflect shifts in emotion, changes in the way the client is relating to the therapist, and other therapy processes.

Reflecting the person in context draws from a broader reflective pool. May (1958b) indicated that the root of individuals' problems often reflected their own inability to see themselves in context. As the therapist gets to know the client, and becomes more aware of the broader context of her or his life situation, she or he can help the client build this context. This can serve several purposes. First, it can help the client become more empathetic with his or her life situation through understanding the various influences on one's current life and life experience. Second, it can highlight their potential. Through the broader reflections one identifies many influences on who one has become (i.e., their destiny, in May's terms), but also helps one understand one's potential for change (i.e., transcendence).

Each type of reflection serves to promote self-understanding, although each does so in different ways and to different degrees. Contrary to how reflective listening is often portrayed, it is a rather complex process that can be difficult for therapists to learn. Reflecting content in the moment is fairly easy for most therapists to master; however, it is more difficult to reflect the various layers of what is occurring in the moment. It requires the ability to attend to several lines of information at once. When reflecting the process and the person in context is added, there is a large amount of information that is being held by the therapist to reflect to the client. In order to master this broader aspect of reflective listening, therapists need to develop their *therapeutic attention* to keep many lines of information readily accessible. At this point, for some, reflective listening may have changed from being overly simplistic to a nearly

---

[13] These observations were made based upon trainings with Bugental in which he provided therapist demonstrations.

impossible skill. However, with experience and intentionality about developing these skills, most therapists can develop them.

Embracing Emotion and the Unknowns

We have already discussed in detail that existential therapists believe it is important to experience a broad array of emotions and learn to accept their limitations and the unknowns of life. The challenge becomes how the therapist helps the client to accomplish this. Typically, this is a slow process that occurs over time. Initially the therapist often guides clients into these realms in during therapy session; however, gradually clients expand these explorations into their life outside of the therapy context. In the next several paragraphs, I will attempt to break this down into specific processes and illustrations.

The starting point is inviting the client into these realms in therapy, beginning with helping the client identify her or his feelings in the moment and then *sit* or *be* with those feelings. Being with emotions is a complex act of consciousness that includes experiencing the emotions, observing one's bodily sensations, impulses, cognitions, and other aspects of one's phenomenological experience. For example, the therapist may invite the client, in session, to sit with her or his anxiety, sadness, or anger. Or the therapist may ask the client to sit with her or his "unknowing," which often leads into some emotions. Although this may seem overwhelming for the client to do on her or his own, the therapy setting and the therapist's presence provides some containment for the client. As one becomes more comfortable sitting with the emotion or the unknown, one will become able to reflect upon it.

Some clients may need additional resources to be able to do this. For example, some clients resist going into their emotions even in session because they fear, "If I begin crying I'll never stop," or "If I allow myself to experience my anger, I may hurt someone." In these instances, the therapist may help the client utilize some coping resources to manage emotions. However, this is different from how these are typically used in therapy. In many therapy approaches, the end goal is the teaching of resources is to enable the client to manage or control his or her emotions. In existential therapy, coping strategies are used to help clients go into their emotions more deeply and understand them.

At this point, a client enters a different phase of relating to her or his emotions and the unknown: one begins reflecting on them. The client has moved from avoiding emotions to trying to understand them. Typically, as clients are able to start bringing understanding and meaning to their emotions, they are better able to engage them.

Becker (1973) made the statement, "Man cannot endure his own littleness unless he can translate it into meaningfulness on the largest possible level" (p. 196). The feeling of littleness is often connected to one's finiteness, one's limitations, or one's inability to know. Other times, clients may feel very small in light of the enormity of their emotions. When they begin to connect their emotions and limitations to meaning, they are able to begin venturing into them.

The meaning and value of vulnerability can also facilitate the client moving into her or his emotions. As an illustration, clients often associate their intense negative emotions as merely suffering not connected to anything good, beneficial, or meaningful. When a client journeys into this emotion in session, it can be quite powerful in this moment to highlight another aspect of this experience. For example, the therapist may comment, "I feel particularly close to you right now." This often shocks the client, but if they are able to reflect upon it, they will often acknowledge that they, too, have a feeling of intimacy and connection with the therapist. This simple statement helps the client move to a paradoxical understanding of negative emotions: They can create pain and intimacy at the same time. In other words, suffering with another is typically not pure suffering; there is some good or positive in this experience.

Experiential Processes and "Techniques"

Schneider (1998) states:

> The experiential mode is diversely interpreted by existential therapists. For example, Yalom (1980) appears to stress the immediate and affective elements of his therapeutic contacts, but he refers little to kinesthetic components. Bugental (1987) stresses kinesthetic elements of his encounters but places lesser emphasis on interpersonal implications of those elements. Tillich (1952) and Friedman (1995) accent the interpersonal dimension of therapeutic experiencing but convey little about the kinesthetic aspect, and so on. (p. 105)

Despite the lack of agreement on how to understand or identify the experiential mode of psychotherapy, existential therapists consistently agree that it remains important, if not essential. In terms of the existential givens, the experiential mode is closely connected with the given of embodiment and emotions. This makes it a universal struggle, but not a universal way of answering this challenge. Without tapping into the experiential mode, therapy is not holistic, not complete. In my view, optimal experiential psychotherapy would include kinesthetic or embodied processes, attention to the immediate (e.g., here-and-now), and the interpersonal realms, although not necessarily at once.

The primary approach to engaging in the experiential aspects of therapy is through attending to them as they naturally arise in psychotherapy. For example, when the therapist notices changes in the client's nonverbal behaviors, she or he may make note of this by bringing it to the client's attention or asking the client to focus on sensations occurring in their body. When the therapist senses a change in the therapy relationship, she or he may comment on this change or ask the client about this. Existential therapists may also engage in specific techniques or processes to facilitate the client's immersion in the experiential realm. For many existential therapists, the "techniques" may be a last resort; however, others may utilize these more readily.

The Kinesthetic Mode. The kinesthetic mode has received increasing attention in the psychological literature over the past several years. The increased attention is largely due to the emergence of many approaches to integrating mindfulness into psychotherapy (Avstreih, 2008; Nimanheminda, 2008; Olson, Unger, Kaklauskas, & Swan, 2008).[14] However, existential and Gestalt therapies have long utilized the kinesthetic mode (Bugental, 1987, 1999; Zinker, 1977).

As the world gets busier and most people spend less time in inactivity, it seems people are growing less and less aware of their bodies. This can be true even with fairly strong somatic sensations. Many therapists are surprised how much information can be gathered through simply asking clients to pay attention to what they are experiencing in their body. Unfortunately, increasing kinesthetic awareness is often not as easy as merely asking a client to focus on their body.

Clients often need assistance gaining bodily awareness due to having been largely unaware of their bodily sensations through much of their life. This can be quite easily done with most clients through some mild relaxation and focusing. For example, a client can be instructed to do a *body scan*, which is simply having one pay attention to different parts of one's body. The client may be guided with some simple questions or comments such as, "Notice if your hands feel warm or cold." and "Pay

---

[14] See also chapter 11.

attention to how your legs feel on the chair and your feet on the floor."
These simple comments help a client begin to attend to more subtle bodily
sensations. Next, the client can be guided through a gradual relaxation
process through breathing exercises. After obtaining some relaxation, even
if minimal, ask the client if she or he can recognize a difference in how the
body feels.

Therapists can also help clients identify bodily sensations in the
moment. For example, therapists can make observations about what they
see in the client such as, "Are you aware of how you normally hold your
shoulders up?" "Were you aware you just made fists with your hands?"
"Wow, your whole body just seemed to sink when you said that." "That
was a big sigh." Although very simple, these observations can gradually
help a client increase their bodily awareness. Therapists do need to be
careful not to overuse this lest a client become self-conscious.

Increasingly, as a client becomes more aware of her or his body,
the therapist may inquire what the bodily sensations and gestures may
mean. Most clients, as they grow accustomed to this process, begin making
these observations on their own and spontaneously attributing meaning to
them.

Gendlin (1982, 1996) developed the concept of a *felt sense* as what
could be described as the most remote of the bodily sensations that could
be classified as kinesthetic. Although a felt sense is not necessarily
experienced at the level of a physical sensation, it is experienced in the
body. According to Gendlin, it is a form of awareness that lies somewhere
between the conscious and unconscious. Initially, it is usually experienced
as something ambiguous; however, as bodily awareness increases, clients
are able to improve their ability to identify it.

The felt sense is significantly more difficult to identify than the
stronger bodily sensations. Additionally, it may take clients longer to begin
identifying them. When working at this kinesthetic level, it is important to
take time to prepare clients, which, in part, is letting them know that it
may take some time to become efficient at identifying the felt sense.

One aspect of the kinesthetic mode is the emotional realm;
however, many assume the kinesthetic realm is only about emotions.
Emotions are largely socially constructed and people will use different
terms for varied emotional and body states. In other words, individuals will
label emotional states differently; there is not a universal agreement about
what bodily experience signifies any particular emotion. Still, at times,
various kinesthetic sensations may have meaning, yet not be associated
with emotions for the client. It may be an urge, or the result of a repressed

emotion, but not actually an emotion. At times, part of the job of the therapist is to bring language, including more nuanced labels, to different bodily states. Through applying language to emotional states, the client is able to develop an emotional language and ascribe meaning to the experience in a fuller manner.

Bringing awareness and meaning to the kinesthetic and emotional realms connect to the development of insight, which will be discussed shortly. One aspect of the kinesthetic level is, to use the classic psychoanalytic language, making the unconscious conscious. As a parallel, it also can be helping the client make the preverbal verbal or the subsymbolic symbolic. Finally, tying to another therapeutic realm we will address shortly, this allows the client to integrate these various levels of experience into one's self-understanding and meaning system.

The Immediate Mode. The immediate mode is often discussed as the *here-and-now*. It involves attending to what is occurring in the moment. Many people live their lives so stuck in the past or obsessed about the future that they never experience "the now." At times, the past or future focus serves as a defense against the present. Other times, there may be particular events from the past or fears of the future which create a feeling of stuckness.

Existential therapy sees *the present as inclusive of the past and the future as experienced in the present moment*. Within this context, existential therapy is always pointing toward the future, but not to the neglect of the present (May, 1999).[15] This can illustrate important differences from other approaches to therapy. Psychoanalytic therapy, with the exception of contemporary psychoanalysis, works on the past in the past. In other words, they focus on the past experience believing once it is resolved, then it will no longer have such an impact on the present. Conversely, the existential therapist is concerned more with how the past is impacting the person in the here-and-now. When the client is discussing the past, instead of inquiring about one's experience at the time of the past incident, the therapist is more prone to inquire about the client's current experience of the past.

Similarly, while many goal-directed therapies talk about the future, they focus largely on making plans and goals. Existential therapists, conversely, have greater concern with how the person's goals, dreams, fears, and worries impact the present moment. Again, this will lead to a

---

[15] Some variations occur pertaining to the role of the future. For some, such as May, the future overshadows the present more than presented in this section. For others, such as Yalom, the present is more central.

different process of inquiry and exploration as opposed to when the focus is in the future. Existential therapists do, at times, also deal with the past as past experience and the future in terms of goals for the future, but the main focus is on the here-and-now.

This illustrates that the past and the future can be talked about in the *there-and-then* or the *here-and-now*. For some issues, such as past trauma, the existential therapist may spend just as much time talking about the past event, but they will do so from a different stance; the stance of the here-and-now. Therefore, the essential element of the here-and-now is not about content, but about the stance the therapist takes in addressing the content. From this here-and-now stance, the person is always pointed toward the future, but in a holistic sense, not limited to just planning for future goals and events.

The Relational Mode. The relational mode emphasizes that healing and growth occur in an interpersonal context. Stolorow (2007), from an existentially informed psychoanalytic perspective, suggests that all experience occurs in an interpersonal context. He focuses on trauma to illustrate this point. According to Stolorow, trauma is more about the relational context in which the trauma occurs than the traumatic event. Most individuals can identify this readily in their own life. Sometimes very small traumas will leave a big impact because it occurred in an interpersonal context that did not allow the event to be processed; however, other "bigger" traumas may have relatively little impact because they occurred in a different interpersonal context.[16] As the creation of a problem arises out of an interpersonal context, so does the healing, growth, or adjustment. It is not just relationship, or mere contact with others, that promotes change; it is a particular type of relationship, which we have already discussed in detail.

Experiential Techniques. Many of the experiential processes in existential therapy have been derived from its close relative, Gestalt therapy. Some of these, such as "micro-focusing on the observed behavior and emotions of the patient at each moment" (Yontef, 1998), have already

---

[16] When teaching I often as students to identify one or two small events from their childhood that have had a long impact on them. I then ask them to identify a bigger trauma that has had little long term impact, and to examine the interpersonal contexts of the events. Most of the time, people will identify there was not opportunities to talk about, process, or make meaning of the small traumas with big impact, but the larger traumas with little impact were sufficiently processed. Parents often facilitate this without bad intentions. The small events, because they seem minor, are assumed to be something that needs little attention; however, with the larger trauma, parents often help the child process and make sense of these events more attentively and fully.

been discussed in the previous sections. Although existentialists may de-emphasize the technique aspect when promoting this type of awareness, it is a common process in existential therapy.

Forms of the empty chair technique are used across many therapy modalities. This approach can be used in many variations. Often, the client is encouraged to speak to someone in the empty chair with whom they have unresolved issues. However, it can also be used to encourage a client to talk to different aspects of oneself. One example of this technique commonly used is having clients talk to themselves when one was much younger.

Engle and Arkowitz (2008) developed a variation of the empty chair technique applying an existential perspective on resistance. Bugental (1987, 1999) viewed resistance in a more positive light than many traditional therapies. He advocated that resistance always serves a purpose that can be adaptive in certain contexts, but may not be adaptive in therapy or at the present point of the individual's life. Existential approaches also recognize that resistance, to a degree, is a given. Clients are generally in the paradoxical condition of moving toward change while also resisting it; moving toward relationship while also moving away from it. The two conflicting motives or directions create ambivalence, or what Engle and Arkowitz refer to as *resistant ambivalence*.

Engle and Arkowitz (2008) seek to bring the different aspects of resistance into dialogue with each other. For example, it is common for clients to experience fears of intimacy because of the increased possibility of being hurt; however, they also desire greater intimacy and connection with others. The empty chair technique can be used to facilitate a dialogue between the aspects of the self. The client may begin sitting in one chair, taking the perspective of resistance, and then switch to the other chair, taking the perspective of seeking connection. This can help create insight and well as mobilize the client to make a decision.

Another experiential technique relevant to resistance is what Schneider (2008b, 2008c) discusses as *vivifying and confronting resistance.* Essentially, this is helping the client become aware of her or his resistances through one of a variety of techniques or processes. Vivifying refers to intensifying the experience of the resistance in order to bring it to the client's awareness. Confronting, on the other hand, is not necessarily experiential; however, the way it is typically employed in existential therapy *is* typically experiential. One way it becomes experiential is through its emergence in the moment, while the resistance is occurring, and through addressing of its emotional aspects. In psychoanalytic therapy, for example, the confronting of resistance is often more through interpretation and cognitive means; in existential therapy the relational and emotional aspects are highlighted.

Another approach to getting clients into the experiential realm is through the incorporation of *stark statements*. Essentially, stark statements are short comments that jar the client into awareness. This bears some similarity to interpretation, but with the primary difference being that these are more ambiguous, making the clients connect the dots, and, therefore are intended to evoke emotions. They are not intended to anger or upset the client, but rather to jar something into her or his consideration thereby eliciting emotion. The intention of eliciting emotions is to facilitate an experiential processing of the content instead of merely a cognitive processing of it. Rarely does this approach work when the therapist uses it with the intention of angering or upsetting the client.

An example can help illustrate the difference. It is common for clients to feel protective of their spouse in therapy. Whenever the therapist says something mildly critical of the spouse, the client may respond discounting it, correcting it, justifying the spouse's behavior, or talking about the good aspects of the spouse. An interpretation would focus on explaining this to the client. For example, the therapist might state, "I notice any time I say something critical of your spouse you respond by defending [him or her]. It seems you are worried that if you acknowledge anything negative about your spouse, that then the security you feel in your relationship with your spouse is no longer there." This can be effective in increasing insight, but it is also more likely to push the client into deep reflection incorporating the affect dimensions.

Using the same example, stark statements may take a client in a different direction. For example, consider the following possibilities: "Wow, you really need to defend your spouse from me," "You are really angry at your wife," "You are really angry at me for being critical of your spouse," or "You really need to protect your spouse from your disappointment with them." Another aspect of the stark statement is that they feel somewhat out of context. The above statements may not be jarring if stated following the interpretation or as part of the interpretation above. However, when the client is engaged in defending her or his spouse and the therapist makes one of these statements, it becomes jarring because it seems out of context. The difference from an interpretation is that the stark statements are more likely to take the client into their emotional experience instead of thinking about what is occurring.

The therapist must always be aware that the use of stark statements can also create some anger at the therapist. As a general rule, they should not be used near the end of a session. There must be time to work through emotions or any breaches to the therapeutic alliance that may result. They also should not be used until the therapeutic alliance is strong enough that the therapist feels confident in being able to work through any breaches to the alliance that may occur. As with all experiential techniques, this should not be overly used, but can be quite effective at times.

Other experiential techniques that can help clients engage with the experiential realm include letter writing, use of the arts or creativity, role-playing, and visualization, among others. Schneider (2008b, 2008c) talks of many of these experiential techniques and processes as *invoking the actual*. They are used to highlight what is relevant in the moment. May (1979, 1981), however, warned against over-relying on what he referred to as "gimmicks." Experiential techniques should be used with caution and sparingly. They can deepen therapy, especially when a client is stuck, but they can also derail therapy. Ironically, appropriate use of experiential techniques can help a client connect with her or his subjectivity; however, over-reliance on them can objectify the client. Additionally, these techniques should always be used in the context of an ongoing therapy *relationship*. It is essential that the relationship remain primary and the technique secondary.

Normalizing and Paradoxical Intention

Existential therapists tend to normalize what others pathologize. They emphasize that many "symptoms" were at one time adaptive and, in many instances, have helped clients to survive difficult situations. They may also be natural to the given moment in which they occur. Furthermore, existential therapists tend to have a different view of human nature and the good life. As discussed, the good life is not the hedonistic idea of increasing pleasure while decreasing suffering; instead, the good life contains a variety of experiences. As discussed previously, "pathology" is understood as often arising from the resistance to normal or existential emotions. Therefore, consistent with Nietzsche's (1889/1990) premise, we should not fight what is natural, and a wide variety of emotions and experiences are accepted as normal. In a sense, "pathology" arises, to a degree, out of labeling something as pathological.

For example, when a client labels grieving as unhealthy, she or he resists doing it and may feel guilty for the grief. This is the root of a more complicated form of grief that is often much more painful than the original response to the loss. Therefore, an existential therapist would normalize the grief and help the client to engage it. In doing so, the client is able to work through the normal grieving process. This does not leave her or him without some feelings of sadness, but the negative feelings are no longer as distressing or overwhelming. As will be discussed in the integration and meaning section below, the client often will also come to experience the grief different, recognizing that the grief is part of the intimate connections, pleasant memories, and other positive aspects of the relationship before the loss.

Frankl (1946/1988, 1959/1984) coined the term *paradoxical intention* for a technique that often provides a normalizing effect. When using paradoxical intention, the therapist will *prescribe the symptom,* or encourage the client to intentionally increase what she or he is afraid of. This often serves to create a shift in the client in which she or he recognizes the irrationality of what she or he was afraid of , and also recognize that, to a degree, what he is afraid of is a normal reaction, even if experienced excessively at times.

Therapists may take a softer approach to this. For example, in working with clients with obsessive-compulsive disorder (OCD), I will often encourage the client to allow themselves to engage in the behavior. In one instance, a client was compulsively checking to see that all the doors were locked during a period of increased stress. At one point, she had been up much of the night checking the lock. The therapist explained to the client that this seemed to be a reaction to stress and she should allow herself to continue to do this. The next week the client returned reporting she never had to check the lock more than three times a day since the last session. The symptom never returned during the course of therapy. Examples this dramatic are rare, and there are many instances where this sort of suggestion would not be appropriate, such as compulsions that could have negative consequences if engaged in more frequently.

In similar situations, clients have shown periods of significant improvement in symptoms and deepened insight following encouragement to allow themselves to be depressed, spending time alone when that is what they feared, or sitting with their anxiety. One shift that often occurs with this technique is that the client is able to stop trying to cope with or control the problem, which often leads to gaining insight. When the energy is no longer being used in the resistance to the symptom, it is then freed for trying to understand it. As the root of the problem becomes identified, then therapy can focus on the base problem instead of the symptoms.

Insight and the Unconscious

A consistent feature of all depth psychotherapies is the belief that increased insight is beneficial. However, the nature of insight and why it is important is more open to variation. In some depth therapies, insight is seen as valuable primarily because it serves to alleviate the symptoms. At other times, it is valuable as an end to itself. Some existential thinkers understand insight as important, but the conception of the unconscious as unnecessary (Groth, 2001; Spinelli, 2004). However, as May (1958b) illustrates, it is not necessary for existential psychology to dismiss the unconscious. May and other existentialists share concerns about the defining of the unconscious as a separate realm of consciousness (dualism) and that the unconscious controls a person thus freeing them from conscious responsibility.

Existentialists who value the unconscious suggest that it is not a separate consciousness, but another realm of a broader conception of consciousness (May, 1958b). In other words, the unconscious and conscious are all part of the same spectrum of consciousness. Additionally, existentialists believe that the unconscious must be understood as part of an individual's subjective experience (May, 1958b; Mishalani, 2001). They are concerned with the tendency to view and interpret the unconscious objectively and separate from the experience of the person to whom the unconscious belongs. For example, a dream should not be interpreted objectively in terms of universal symbols; instead, it must be interpreted and understood in the context of being a part of the individual's subjective experience, even if triggered by an archetypal image.

From an existential perspective, insight helps to serve a primary goal of therapy: setting one free (May, 1981). As noted earlier, Rank (1929/1978), a forerunner of existential therapy, advocated that all those things that influences us (i.e., the unconscious, environment, relationships, instincts, etc.) have control over us to the degree that we are unaware of them. Through bringing these influences into awareness, we begin to have more control over them.

May (1981), however, provides an important balance to this idea. Freedom can only be understood in the context of destiny, or those things which limit our freedom. May emphasized the constraints on our freedom and influences on our behavior are great. Yet, even if our freedom is small in comparison to our destiny, it is still incredibly valuable. Elsewhere May (1979) conceptualized freedom as the "pause between stimulus and response" (p. 191).

The primary purpose of insight is to serve freedom, which often has positive impacts on mental health. But the goal of insight is to increase freedom or to enable living the good life, not happiness or the removal of painful emotions. However, insight may also have direct positive effects, including increased happiness. It has become popular to maintain that insight does not produce change. The existential response is that while insight may not always produce change, it is often necessary for it to occur. Insight, however, also does occasionally have a jarring effect that has a more immediate impact. Most people can identify a moment of insight, or a shift in awareness, where they were powerfully and emotionally impacted and, after that moment, could never be fully the same. Although this type of insight is rare and is not the reason for seeking insight in existential therapy, it is also something that most people experience at some point of their lives. These jarring insights are more common when one is engaged in psychotherapy or other forms of self-discovery.

Moving In and Out of the Depths of Psychotherapy

Bugental (1987) clarifies an important misconception about the depth realm of therapy. When supervising existential therapists in training, I noticed it is common for them to be apologetic about not keeping the client at the depth realm or emotional realm throughout the session, every session. Many therapists think that "depth therapy" means that the therapist always pursues and tries to stay at the emotional and depth realms. This is not only difficult, but also counterproductive and often leads to the client abandoning therapy.

Therapists should move in and out of the various depth realms, with depth representing emotional depth, depth of insight, and depth of ideas. Holding clients at the depth realm is often similar to holding their head under water—eventually they need to come up for air! The longer the client is in therapy, the longer she or he will be able to stay at these depth realms before coming up for air, still eventual ascent will be necessary.

A primary reason that existential therapy is an experiential therapy is because of the belief that healing, growth, and change should be holistic. It involves the biological, behavioral, cognitive, emotional, and interpersonal realms. It entails the surface realms and the depth realms. To remain only at the depths renders therapy just as incomplete as when it remains only at the surface.

Integration and Meaning.

The instillation of meaning is a primary component of all existential approaches to psychotherapy. The deepest forms of meaning can be experienced on the various realms of biological, behavioral, cognitive, emotional, and interpersonal; in other words, it is a holistic meaning.

The attainment of meaning does much for the individual, but also should be distinguished from false forms of meaning. Meaning provides the basis for transcendence, or the ability to see one's life in context and to recognize one's potentialities. Meaning helps us to go into suffering, difficult emotions, and the unknowns. For, as Nietzsche (1889/1990) stated, "If we possess our *why* of life we can put up with almost any *how*" (p. 33). Meaning also can bring joy and happiness to our lives, even, sometimes, in the midst of suffering.

Existentialists understand meaning largely in terms of symbols and myths (May, 1961, 1991), which are, in part, culturally derived and, in part, personally derived. According to May (1961), "*Symbols* are specific acts or figures, while *myths* develop and elaborate these symbols..." (p. 44). We always discover or create meaning in the context of a culture, but these do not determine personal meaning. Still, it would be a mistake to separate meaning, symbols, and myth from culture.

May (1958a; 1991) was concerned about the way that meaning is impacted by cultural transitions. Although he did not use the terminology of postmodernism until his final publication (Schneider & May, 1995), he seemed to be acutely attuned to the transition from modernism to postmodernism that was occurring. Part of this transition was the deconstruction of the modern myth, but there were not yet cogent postmodern myths to provide sustaining meaning. New meaning systems were, and are, needed.

For meaning to be sustaining, it must help the individual address the existential givens. As is discussed in chapter 12, sustaining myths address the universality of the existential givens in a culturally specific manner. Thus, in sustaining cultural myths, there is always universality, and also a distinctive culturally-specific element. Individuals may also have personal myths, which generally exist in dialogue with one's culture and cultural myths. The realms of personal and collective myths are the central focus of the third section of this book.

Suffice it to say at this point, the attainment of meaning is one of the most central aspects of human existence and necessary to address in existential therapy. Additionally, myths have an integrative function. They help us make sense of the varied aspects of our existence, weaving them into a meaning system, albeit inherently incomplete due to our finite and limited nature. Similarly, myths of self can serve the integrative function in how individuals understand oneself (Hoffman et al, in press). In other words, personal myths can assist us in bringing meaning to the daimonic, to personal suffering, and our future direction in life.

Creativity and the Arts in Therapy. A powerful way to address the element of meaning is through creativity and the arts. Many existential therapists will integrate writing, poetry, dance, drawing, and painting into the therapy process. This serves both a cathartic purpose as well as insight-oriented and integrative purposes when utilized well. For example, the unconscious often finds expression in poetry or drawings that may be used in therapy or when the client brings them to therapy. These can be utilized similar to dreams to facilitate insight into the unconscious.

The arts, in their integrative function, create meaning. For example, when a client turns painful emotions into a beautiful painting, one is able to directly and symbolically see some beauty in the pain. In other words, it serves a transcendent purpose through moving the painful experience into a broader context and allowing it to serve a different purpose.

Art can also facilitate encounter or be used in a progressive nature. For example, the therapist may draw with the client in the therapy sessions, which can facilitate encounter and a shared creation of meaning. The therapist may also provide alternative visions of what is being expressed in the creative venture. When the client draws a picture illustrating the threats in their current environment, the therapist may illustrate a safe space in the drawing which the client did not recognize, or suggest integrating this into the painting. Similarly, the therapist may have the client paint the same theme over the course of therapy in order to see how it changes. In this way, the art work documents the progress of therapy while bringing meaning to the change.[17]

Finally, arts can facilitate encounter in a different way. As the use of arts generally entails very deep and personal aspects of oneself, the sharing of art can facilitate a deep encounter between the therapist and client through vulnerability. The use of art can often take therapy in a direction that was not anticipated, unveiling deeper levels of meaning, vulnerability, interpersonal connection, and choice. They also promote healing through bringing meaning to aspects of experience that, previously, seemed meaningless.

---

[17] See Mendelowitz (2008a) for a beautiful example of this use of art in therapy.

Therapy Outcomes: Does Existential Therapy Work and Why

Little traditional outcome research has been conducted directly on existential psychotherapy and, at times, existential therapists, along with other depth psychotherapists, have been highly critical of the idea of outcome studies. Despite the limitations of outcome research, it is vital that all forms of psychotherapy engage in some self-critique and examination to demonstrate its respective effectiveness toward the intended goals or desired outcomes of psychotherapy. In this section, I will briefly discuss some of the philosophical problems that have contributed to existential therapists not conducting outcome studies along with an overview of the literature that provides support for the effectiveness of existential approaches.

Philosophical Limitations of Outcome Research [18]

The philosophical critiques of outcomes research from an existential perspective can be summarized as being epistemological, or relating to how we know what we know, and ontological, or related to the basic nature of being. Most outcome research is reductionistic, which deflates the ontology while utilizing an overly simplistic epistemology.

Epistemological Limitations. The epistemological limitations are fairly straightforward, but also tap into the deeper ontological problems. Most outcome studies focus on the reduction of symptoms, although a few may also look at increasing positive states. In trying to avoid the temptations of moving on to the ontological problems with this, there are many problematic assumptions with most outcome measures. First, they are rooted in the idea of generalizability, focusing on shared aspects of human existence and states. For example, most depression measures focus on common traits of depression without taking into account that there are many forms of depression and that all forms of depression are experienced subjectively by the individual. Therefore, a very sterile, depersonalized form of depression is what is measured.

Most outcome research is rooted in "objective," quantitative research. One of the oddities about such research is that most of us, when completing an "objective" questionnaire, are filled which questions and frustrations about the wording of many items. When a subjective individual reads these "objective" questions, they are interpreted differently as far as basic meaning, temporal elements, and intensity. For example, what is

---

[18] For more extensive and detailed critiques see Elkins (2007, 2008a, 2008b), Wampold (2001), Hubble, Duncan & Miller (1999), and Norcross (2002a, 2002b).

little distress for some may be interpreted as severe distress by others. Similarly, what is recent for some may seem more distant for others. Last, many with depression and other distressing emotional states experience distortions in time that often make it difficult to remember specific time frames.

Furthermore, outcome research assumes a hedonistic bias that may not be appropriate for all individuals. This, as is evident, has ontological implications as well. However, from the epistemological perspective, many individuals seek therapy not simply to decrease discomfort while increasing pleasant feelings (i.e., the *hedonistic bias*); they often want to learn how to cope with or find meaning in their suffering. Many clients, although not knowing the language, are looking not to rid themselves of suffering, but rather learning to "suffer well" or change their experience of their suffering. When presented with this concern, therapists often interpret this within the dominant paradigm as wanting to decrease suffering.

From an existential perspective, the initial phase of therapy can be conceptualized as helping the client identify what she or he wants from therapy. However, as Elkins (2008) illustrates, it is problematic to assume that the reason for being in therapy will remain the same; indeed, an important aspect of good therapy is being able to track the client's ever-changing outcome desires and recognizing the fluid, emergent nature of wants and desires. When the entire direction of therapy is based upon what comes up in the first session the very constraints of this relegate the therapy goals to assumptions and needs that the therapist projects upon the client. As Elkin states,

> If clinicians cannot divine a client's problems in one or two initial sessions, then any treatment plan based on information gained in those sessions is clinically naïve at best and dangerous at worst. Clinicians who assume, because of institutional demands or their own clinical naïveté that the presenting problem is always the real problem may spend the ensuing therapy sessions dealing with the pseudo-problems and never getting to the client's real problems. (p. 416)

This penetrating analysis by Elkins provides the basis for an essential difference in the assumptions about clients' ability to know or divine their needs and desires in therapy. In depth psychotherapies, such as existential, it is assumed that for most clients, therapy is a journey in which they understand their primary problems, needs, and desired outcomes over time. Clients usually do not or are unable to clearly construct or identify a complete, realistic picture of their desired outcomes of therapy in the initial meetings. This is not intended to question the intelligence, intentions, or potential of clients; instead, it is simply noting that most clients do not have the psychological background, life experiences, and frame of reference to be able to make such decisions. Indeed, many therapists, often because of their rigid allegiance to a particular approach to therapy, are not effective in assisting clients identify and make these discoveries and determinations.

Many clients base their initial treatment goals largely on their preconceived ideas about psychotherapy. Often these ideas are inaccurate, such as the depictions of the psychotherapeutic process found in mass media portrayals. In the United States, what clients expect to experience in psychotherapy is heavily influenced by popular figures such as Dr. Phil and the very skewed and inaccurate depictions of therapy presented in the movies and on television. Additionally, many clients begin therapy during times of desperation. Their initial therapy needs may be based largely upon symptom alleviation; however, many shorter-term approaches to therapy do not continue to watch for emergent concerns after the crisis with which one had last adequately dealt. Bunting and Hayes (2008), along with Wolfe (2008), have nicely elucidated how cognitive-behavior interventions can successfully treat initial presenting concerns while remaining open to transitioning into a more existentially rooted approaches. In doing so, a more holistic therapy experience is offered while avoiding the dangers identified by Elkins (2008).

This idea that client's presenting problems are fluid and emergent indicates a need for a paradigmatic shift in psychotherapy that has broad implications for psychotherapy training. Given these factors, regardless of whether an existential approach is being utilized or not, the initial phase of therapy should focus on establishing rapport and then helping clients identify what they want from therapy. This often may take anywhere from 3 to 12 or more sessions; the entire time often allotted to reach the outcome in therapy from many perspectives.

Last, existential therapy points toward the need for more qualitative and subjectively based approaches to outcome research. This is not to suggest that quantitative, "objective" approaches are bad or should be discontinued; to the contrary, these remain very important and, to a degree, it will be important for existential therapy to consider engaging more in this type of research in the future. However, *it must be recognized that there are always significant epistemological limitations in outcome research.* Quantitative research must be balanced with qualitative. Let us close this section with a couple of examples.

First, some clients dealing with chronic conditions, including chronic contextual conditions, may not have significant changes in some of their symptoms, including the intensity of their symptoms; however, they may experience a significant change in *the way they experience and utilize these symptoms.* For example, an individual who is subjected to chronic racism, sexism, or homophobia may continue to feel hurt and angry about their situation, but learn to experience it as less personally wounding, and utilize this hurt and anger to promote positive social change. For this individual, becoming too comfortable in their unjust situation would serve to enable an unjust system and decrease their motivation to be involved in advocating for social change. Although "successful therapy" in the traditional sense of reducing discomfort and symptoms may help an individual feel better at some levels of experience, the person may also experience a loss of meaning, and on deeper levels experience existential guilt for their passivity about the injustice.

Second, many people who have lost a person they love connect the sadness of the loss with the joyful memories of the good times. They may not desire to give up the pain of the loss because it would symbolize the fading of the good aspects of the relationship. Many of these clients experience a transition in the way they experience their suffering that often contains a degree of reduced "symptomology" while placing ongoing suffering in a meaningful context. In this new context, the suffering is transformed, or transcended, and the client is able to experience her or his suffering differently; one is able to experience one's suffering as part of the joy and meaning of the relationship. In many ways, existential therapy helps people embrace the complexity of their subjective experiences and, in doing so, experience their "symptoms" differently.

Ontological Limitations. In this last section, we have already begun to transition into the ontological problems with outcome research. The problems are evident just in the following questions: How does one measure existence or ontology? How do you evaluate the ontological levels of depression and anxiety? How does one differentiate between existential/normal anxiety and neurotic/"pathological" anxiety? In other words, there is a measurement problem. This is where the ontological meets the epistemological.

May (1958a) says that existential therapy in its essence is an ontological therapy. In other words, existential therapy is, at its roots, dealing with the issue of what it means to be human. As already noted, what many therapies label as pathology existential therapy conceptualizes as *existence pain*. In other words, existential therapy often seeks to normalize what other therapy approaches seek to pathologize. I have already discussed Nietzsche's (1889/1990) premise that we should not fight our basic nature. In many or most situations, it is fighting of what is natural that turns what is normal, or existential, into what is neurotic, or pathological. In other words, it is the avoidance, denial, or repression of normal anxiety, normal guilt, and normal suffering that turns these into their more destructive symptoms. In existential therapy, the transition to health is more about learning to accept, integrate, and utilize these symptoms than coping, reducing, or controlling them.

The challenge, then, is how does one measure this type of change? How does one measure the transition from symptoms as problematic to symptoms as integrated and accepted? Undoubtedly, this will vary between individuals. For example, individuals who have transitioned from constant denial and resistance to anxiety and its root causes to embracing them will likely experience some reduction in their overall subjective experience of anxiety. However, their perceptions of their anxiety may become more disparate. Because they experience their anxiety differently, some may rate the same levels of anxiety lower on objective measures than they rated the same levels of anxiety previously. Existential therapy, therefore, demands a paradigmatic shift in the way outcome therapy is conceived. This also demonstrates why different measures are necessary to evaluate different forms of therapy.

The greatest problem of outcome research is that it assumes everyone is seeking a similar personal ontology or a similar way of being. This is implicit in the idea of generalizability and singular, "objective" outcome measures. In this way, outcome research can be understood as an oppressive type of conformity which imposes a universal, socially sanctioned view of mental health. While this is problematic in the Western psychology paradigm in which it was developed, it is even more problematic when applied to cross-cultural and international psychology.

The religious and spiritual traditions also provide important contradictions regarding this approach to ontology. All of the major world religions advocate that suffering is an essential part of being human; it is an ontological reality. It becomes problematic if psychology imposes a different value system upon people than that which is natural (i.e., suffering). Natural human experience and emotions are then viewed as something unnatural and pathological. To be sure, there are forms of suffering which most religious and spiritual individuals would agree is pathological; however, Western psychology as a whole has not adequately addressed the issue of how to distinguish between normal suffering and pathological suffering. Furthermore, it has not considered individual differences in values pertaining to this distinction between the variations of suffering. As many psychotherapy clients also consider themselves religious and/or spiritual, this places clients in a world with two very different value systems being pushed upon them.

In my view, *any psychology that advocates for a singular way of being, or personal ontology, as being the only psychologically healthy way has an inherent value problem.* The field of psychology has not adequately engaged in the self-reflective process advocated for, in different ways and differing degrees, by most psychotherapies. If it did, maybe Western psychology would begin to recognize its internal inconsistencies. We may hope that cross-cultural and international psychology will bring this issue more to the forefront.

Support for Existential Therapy as an Evidence-Based Practice

Despite the strong critique of outcome literature provided, it is quite clear that even within the limitations of conventional outcome research there is significant evidence for the efficacy of existential therapy. Numerous extensive reviews of this literature are available, therefore this section is limited to highlighting the important findings and literature reviews more directly relevant to existential psychology.[19] Through a review of the literature, including the research, meta-analytic studies, and critical reviews of the research, there are four important conclusions relevant to existential therapy that can be made:

1) Psychotherapy tends to be effective regardless of the treatment modality (Bacher, 2008; Elkins, 2007, 2008a, 2008b; Wampold, 2001, 2005; Wampold, Mondin, Moody, Stich, Benson, & Ahn, 1997).

2) Common factors, generally identified primarily as client factors and relationship factors, account for the majority of psychotherapy effectiveness while specific ingredients account for little variance (Ahn & Wampold, 2001; Bacher, 2008; Cooper, 2008; Elkins, 2007,

---

[19] For a more extensive review of the literature, one is guided to Schneider (2008b), Elkins (2008a), Wampold (2001), Hubble, Duncan, and Miller (1999), and Norcross (2002b).

2008a, 2008b; Hubble, Duncan, & Miller, 1999; Messer, & Wampold, 2000; Wampold, 2001, 2005).

3) With increasing consistency it is being demonstrated that after client factors, the therapeutic relationship is the most important ingredient in successful psychotherapy (Farber & Lane, 2002; Fischer, 2008; Klein et al., 2002; Lambert & Barley, 2002; Norcross, 2002a, 2002b; Wampold, 2001, 2005; Wampold, Mondin, Moody, Stich, Benson, & Ahn, 1997).

4) Based upon the preceding evidence, existential therapy, particularly when rooted within the existential phenomenological or existential humanistic traditions of Rollo May and James F. T. Bugental, has strong empirical support (Elkins, 2008a; Nathan, 2008, Schneider 2008a, 2008b; Wampold, 2008) and provides an ideal foundation for integrative psychotherapy (Nathan, 2008; Schneider 2008a, 2008b, 2008c). Given this, *existential therapy, particularly when practiced in a manner consistent with the existential humanistic (Bugental), existential phenomenological (May), and existential-integrative (Schneider) traditions, should rightly be considered to be an evidence-based therapy.*

The first of these premises is very well established and hard to dispute as a valid interpretation of the literature, even by those who may disagree or come to a different conclusion. The fourth point, however, may be viewed as more controversial. There has not been as much direct research on existential psychotherapy; however, I believe there is still reason to consider it an evidence-based practice.

There is still significant confusion about the precise meaning "evidence-based practice." According to Wampold, Goodheart, and Levant (2007):

> *Evidence* is not an unambiguous term and is usually undefined, but the term exists in a context and has a particular meaning. Evidence is not data, nor is it truth. Evidence can be thought of as inferences that flow from data. (pp. 616-617)

It is clear, however, that evidence-based practice was conceived and then developed partially in response to the overly restrictive idea of the empirically supported treatments that had a strong inherent bias toward many short-term, linear, and manualized treatments (see American

Psychological Association [APA] Presidential Task Force on Evidence-Based Practice, 2006).

The APA Task Force on Evidence-Based Practice (2006) indicated that multiple types of research evidence were valid, including clinical observation (which includes case studies), qualitative research, systematic case studies, single-case experimental design, public health and ethnographic research, process-outcome studies, randomized controlled trials, and meta-analytic studies. They also advocated for the validity of clinical experience and expertise as a basis for evidence-based practice. This includes clinical experience and training; interpersonal expertise; the ability to utilize appropriate research; understanding of cultural, individual, and contextual differences; ongoing self-reflection; seeking additional resources when needed (e.g., consultation, supervision, supplementary or alternative services); and a cogent rationale for treatment approaches. Finally, the task force suggested that patient characteristics, culture, and preferences should be considered. Thus, for a therapy to be considered evidence-based, it should be able to demonstrate 1) research support (broadly defined), 2) evidence based upon clinical experience, expertise, and well-developed theory, and 3) consideration of individual differences and preferences. As will be demonstrated, existential therapy clearly meets these three criteria.

Research. Research support, when defined broadly as is suggested by the APA Presidential Task Force on Evidence-Based Practice, should come from multiple formats. The literature is replete with numerous published examples of case studies on existential therapy (Bugental, 1976, 1990; Curtin, 2008; Greening, 2008; Hoffman, 2007, 2008a; Hoffman, Margiotta, Granger, Moriarty, 2008; Mendelowtiz, 2008a; 2008b; Moats, 2008; Rice, 2008; Rubin, 2008; Serlin, 2008; Spinelli, 1997; Yalom, 1989; 1999, Yalom & Elkin, 1990).[20] A limitation of these studies, which should be addressed in the future, is that many of them are not systematic case studies, some were combined characters (i.e., several clients combined into a single narrative for illustrative purposes), and these have been primarily developed for therapy illustration purposes. However, the aforementioned studies are drawn from actual existential therapy cases that have had successful outcomes. Further, as is noted by Mendelowtiz (2008a; 2008b), success must be defined contextually and is not necessarily synonymous with "a cure." Rather, success, from an existential perspective, should be defined by the client and therapist in accordance

---

[20] See also Hoffman & Granger, current volume, and Yang, current volume.

with the client's values and desired outcome. With this caveat, existential therapy has research support for its efficacy in both the traditional understanding of symptom reduction and the existential perspective based upon the client's desired outcome and subjective experience. The following will focus primarily on the traditional understanding of successful outcome as symptom reduction.

Meta-analytic research provides support for existential psychotherapy through the common factors as well as existential psychotherapy as a relationally based psychotherapy (Elkins, 2007, 2008a, 2008b; Schneider, 2008b). Although this may not apply to all variations of existential psychotherapy, those based in the existential phenomenological tradition of Rollo May, the existential-humanistic tradition of James F. T. Bugental, and the existential-integrative approach of Kirk Schneider clearly fall within the category of relationally-based psychotherapy.

Although there has been limited traditional research on existential therapy, there is some strong support in a few studies. One of the most interesting research projects, the Soteria Project, is a long-term study on the treatment of schizophrenia and schizophreniform disorder in a setting utilizing minimal psychotropic medication and focusing on an existentially and relationally based treatment model (Bola & Mosher, 2003; Mosher, 2001). The results of research on this model provided support for this treatment model through a two-year follow up. This is particularly note-worthy given that it is widely believed that schizophrenia is largely untreatable except with medications.

Additionally, there is significant empirical and neurological support for emotion-focused therapy (Elliott, Greenberg, & Lietaer, 2004; Greenberg, 2008; Greenberg & Johnson, 1988; Greenberg & Watson, 2005), which bears close similarity to the existential approach to working with emotion in therapy. Both of these approaches emphasize the importance of experiencing emotion and not over-controlling it. As already noted, there is significant support for relationally based therapies (Farber & Lane, 2002; Fischer, 2008; Klein et al., 2002; Lambert & Barley, 2002; Norcross, 2002a, 2002b; Wampold, 2001, 2005; Wampold, Mondin, Moody, Stich, Benson, & Ahn, 1997). As existential therapy is relationally based, there is significant empirical support for this approach.

Schneider and Krug (in press), in their broad review of the research support, report that existential-humanistic therapy has support in elaborate and formalized qualitative research, case studies, and quantitative research. Although there are areas that need further development from a traditional research perspective, the existence of varied types of research supporting the existential approach is undeniably strong and consistent. It is also diverse in that support emerges from traditional research as well as research that fits better epistemologically with existential theory. Last, it is broad in that it has been shown to have research support in working with a broad range of disorders, including depression, anxiety, and the psychotic disorders, amongst others, and individuals from diverse cultural backgrounds.

Maybe the most important support for the research basis of existential therapy comes from the words of one of the leading researchers on the effectiveness of psychotherapy, Bruce Wampold (2008), in his review of Schneider's book *Existential-Integrative Psychotherapy*:

> I have argued that the principles of change in EI [Existential-Integrative Psychotherapy] are as scientific as those of any other psychological treatment (Wampold, 2007); I have no doubt that EI approaches would satisfy any criteria used to label other psychological treatments as scientific. (¶ 13)

Wampold's endorsement of the research basis of existential-integrative therapy addresses the most commonly cited weakness of this approach. It is particularly valuable given that Wampold is an outsider; he is not an existential therapist.

Terror Management Theory and other experimental existential psychology approaches have also provided a good deal of empirical support for existential theory. Drawn from the work of Ernest Becker, Terror Management Theory has received considerable empirical support. Along with its offshoots, it provides significant evidence of existential theory as a way for understanding the human condition and experience. However, as Terror Management Theory is not a therapeutic theory, we will not go into detail about it here. Readers are directed to Greenberg, Koole, and Pyszczynski (2004), *The Handbook of Experimental Existential Psychology*, for more information on this theory.

Theory, Expertise, and Well Developed Theory. The support for existential therapy in regard to these criteria is clearly beyond question. The Task Force for the Development of Practice Recommendations for the Provision of Humanistic Psychosocial Services (1997, 2004) appointed by Division 32 (Society for Humanistic Psychology) of the American Psychological Association has developed very clear guidelines and strategies for the various humanistic psychotherapies, including existential. In reading through these guidelines, the existential influence is clear and the leading existential psychologist in the United States, Kirk Schneider, served on this task force. These recommendations have received approval by the Society for Humanistic Psychology and the American Psychological Association.

Kirk Schneider and Orah Krug (in press) have a forthcoming book, *Existential-Humanistic Therapy*, and an accompanying video being published by the American Psychological Association in addition to another recent video of Kirk Schneider published by the American Psychological Association. In addition to the current book, several important books have been published on the process of existential therapy including *Existential-Integrative Psychotherapy* by Schneider (2008), *The Art of Psychotherapy* (1987) and *Psychotherapy Isn't What You Think* (1999) by Bugental, *Existential Psychotherapy* by Yalom (1980), *The Psychology of Existence* by Schneider and May (1995) and *Ethics and Lao-Tzu* by Mendelowitz (2008), among others. Existential therapy also has had a strong and regular presence in the *Journal of Humanistic Psychology* and *The Humanistic Psychologist*.

An increasing number of training opportunities in the United States and beyond are available in existential psychotherapy. The International Institute for Humanistic Studies, the Existential-Humanistic Institute, and the Depth Psychotherapy Institute provide regular opportunities for training including conferences, retreat style training, and consultation groups. An increasing number of schools offer specialized training in existential therapy at the masters and doctorate level including Duquesne University, the University of the Rockies, the Michigan School of Professional Psychology, Saybrook University, and West Georgia University, among others.

Individual Differences and Preferences. In part, this criterion can be interpreted to indicate that clients are provided with the freedom to choose the type of therapy they desire and work toward goals that fit with their values. As discussed by Schneider (2008b, 2008c, 2008c) and Nathan (2008), existential-integrative therapy provides an ideal foundation to adapt psychotherapy to the needs of the client. The anti-dogmatic core of the existential-integrative approach facilitates adaptation to the unique needs of the client, including the ability to integrate other psycho-therapeutic approaches as needed. However, existential therapy is not for everyone and, as with any psychotherapy, therapists should work with clients to determine if this is an appropriate modality for what the client wants from therapy.

Recent trends in existential therapy have also sought to overcome previous weaknesses in addressing diversity issues (Hoffman, 2008c; Hoffman, Oumarou, Mejia, & Alcahé, 2008) and this issue continues to be addressed through many chapters in the current volume. Adaptations and illustrations have been developed for working with African American clients (Rice, 2008), Latino clients (Comas-Diaz, 2008), Chinese clients (Galvin, 2008), Native American clients (Alsup, 121), gay and lesbian clients (Monheit, 2008), female clients (Brown, 2008; Serlin, 2008), religious and spiritual diversity (Comas-Diaz, 2008; Hoffman 2007, 2008a, 2008b), elders (Bugental, 2008), and children (Curtin, 2008; Rubin, 2008). Furthermore, existential therapy demonstrates its adaptability to the needs of clients through the integration with other approaches such as feminist therapy (Brown, 2008), cognitive-behavioral approaches (Bunting & Hayes, 2008; Wolfe, 2008), and psychodynamic therapy (Dorman, 2008; Portnoy, 2008; Rubin, 2008; Stolorow, 2008).

Concluding Thoughts on the Evidence for Existential Psychotherapy's Effectiveness. A case has been built that there is clear and strong evidence about the effectiveness of existential psychotherapy demonstrated in the empirical and professional literature. *It is advocated that existential therapy meets and exceeds the requirements to be considered an evidence-based practice* including external verification on the most controversial aspect of this appraisal: research. The publication of the current volume further solidifies existential therapy's status. As Wampold (2008) stated, what this means for existential approaches is still unclear, particularly in regard to greater acceptance in the mainstream psychological community. Furthermore, as the application of existential therapy in Eastern cultures is a primary concern of this volume, it will be necessary to extend this evidence through research and critical reviews of existential therapy and its cultural adaptations in various Eastern cultures.

Conclusion

One repays a teacher badly if one always remains nothing but a pupil. (Nietzsche, 1892/1966, p. 78)

Despite the length of this chapter, it is only touching the richness of the existential psychotherapy literature. As indicated at the beginning, the reader is also reminded that this is one perspective on existential therapy that focuses primarily on the traditions emerging from Rollo May and James F. T. Bugental. Nothing is more antithetical to the idea of existential thought than to presume that any one approach is best or to turn the existential approach into a rigid system to be followed. Indeed, in some ways it is anti-existential to refer oneself as an existentialist!

Therefore, the ongoing mission of existential thought should be to continuously develop and expand existential thought. Existential therapists should fight ardently to assure that existential thought never becomes stagnant. At the same time, existential thought advocates strongly against accepting any revision without critical thought. This is the dual mission of the rest of this book. The editors and contributors to this book seek to help existential theory and psychotherapy continue to evolve through the intercultural dialog. At the same time, it is hoped that the entirely of this book is subjected to critical consideration. My hope is that in this chapter and this book we have not repaid Rollo May and James F. T. Bugental badly; that we have extended, broadened, and adapted their ideas taking them into some new places. We invite the reader to do the same.

References

Adler, A. (1969). *The science of living*. New York: Anchor. (Originally published in 1929)

Ahn, H. & Wampold, B. E. (2001). Where oh where are the specific ingredients? A meta-analysis of component studies in counseling and psychotherapy. *Journal of Counseling Psychology, 48,* 251-257.

Alsup, R. (2008). Existentialism of personalism: A Native American perspective. In K. J. Schneider (Ed.), *Existential-integrative psychotherapy: Guideposts to the core of practice* (pp. 121-127). New York: Routledge.

American Psychological Association Presidential Task Force on Evidence-Based Practice. (2006). *Evidence-based practice in psychology. American Psychologist, 61,* 271-285.

Avstreih, Z. (2008). The body in psychotherapy: Dancing with the paradox. In F. Kaklauskas, S. Nimanheminda, L. Hoffman, & M. Jack, (Eds.) *Brilliant Sanity: Buddhist Approaches to Psychotherapy* (pp. 213-221). Colorado Springs, CO: University of the Rockies Press.

Bacher, A. (2008). Shaking the foundations. In D. N. Elkins (Chair), *A shaking of the foundations.* Symposium conducted at the Existential Humanistic Institutes Second Annual Conference, San Francisco, CA.

Bernstein, R. J. (2005). *The abuse of evil: The corruption of politics and religion since 9/11*. Malden, MA: Polity Press.

Becker, E. (1973). *The denial of death.* New York: Free Press.

Becker, E. (1975). *Escape from evil.* New York: Free Press.

Bohart, A. C., Elliott, R., Greenberg, L. S., & Watson, J. C. (2002). Empathy. In J. C. Norcross (Ed.), *Psychotherapy relationships that work: Therapist* contributions and responsiveness to patients. (pp. 89-108). New York: Oxford University Press.

Bola, J. R. & Mosher, L. R. (2003). Treatment of acute psychosis without neuroleptics: Two-year outcomes from the Soteria project. The *Journal of Nervous and Mental Disease, 191,* 219-229.

Brown, L. S. (2008). Feminist therapy as a meaning-making practice: Where there is no power, where is the meaning? In K. J. Schneider (Ed.), *Existential-integrative psychotherapy: Guideposts to the core of practice* (pp. 130-140). New York: Routledge.

Bugental, E. K. (2008). Swimming together in a sea of loss: A group process for elders In K. J. Schneider (Ed.), *Existential-integrative psychotherapy: Guideposts to the core of practice* (pp. 333-342). New York: Routledge.

Bugental, J. F. T. (1976). *The search for existential identity.* San Francisco: Jossey-Bass.

Bugental, J. F. T. (1987). *The art of the psychotherapist.* New York: Norton.

Bugental, J. F. T. (1990). *Intimate journeys: Stories from life-changing therapy* (Rev. ed.). San Francisco: Jossey-Bass

Bugental, J. F. T. (1999). *Psychotherapy isn't what you think: Bringing the psychotherapeutic engagement into the living moment.* Phoenix, AZ: Zeig, Tucker & Co.

Bugental, J. F. T. (2007). Preliminary sketches for a short-term existential-humanistic therapy. In K. Schneider (Ed.), *Existential-integrative psychotherapy: Guideposts to the core of practice* (pp. 165-168). New York: Routledge.

Bunting, K. & Hayes, S. C. (Ed.), Language and meaning: Acceptance and commitment therapy and the EI model. In K. J. Schneider (Ed.), *Existential-integrative psychotherapy: Guideposts to the core of practice* (pp. 217-234). New York: Routledge.

Comas-Diaz, L. (2008). Latino psychospirituality. In K. J. Schneider (Ed.), *Existential-integrative psychotherapy: Guideposts to the core of practice* (pp. 100-109). New York: Routledge.

Cooper, S. L. (2008). Review of *The Heart and Soul of Change: What Works in Therapy.* In D. N. Elkins (Chair), *A shaking of the foundations.* Symposium conducted at the Existential Humanistic Institutes Second Annual Conference, San Francisco, CA.

Curtin, S. (2008). The inner sense of the child: The case of Joey. In K. J. Schneider (Ed.), *Existential-integrative psychotherapy: Guideposts to the core of practice* (pp. 321-331). New York: Routledge.

Diamond, S. A. (1996). *Anger, madness, and the daimonic: The psychological genesis of violence, evil, and creativity.* New York: State University of New York Press.

Dorman, D. (2008). Dante's cure: Schizophrenia and the two-person journey. In K. J. Schneider (Ed.), *Existential-integrative psychotherapy: Guideposts to the core of practice* (pp. 236-245). New York: Routledge.

Elkins, D. N. (2007). Empirically supported treatments: The deconstruction of a myth. *Journal of Humanistic Psychology, 47,* 474-500.

Elkins, D. N. (2008a). Short-term, linear approaches to psychotherapy: What we now know. *Journal of Humanistic Psychology, 48,* 413-431.

Elkins, D. N. (2008b). A shaking of the foundations: Research findings on what actually helps the suffering client. In D. N. Elkins (Chair), *A shaking of the foundations.* Symposium conducted at the Existential Humanistic Institutes Second Annual Conference, San Francisco, CA.

Elliott, R., Greenberg, L., & Lietaer, G. (2004). Research on experiential psychotherapy. In M. Lambert (Ed.), Bergin & Garfield's handbook of psychotherapy & behavior change (pp. 493–539). New York: Wiley.

Engle, D. & Arkowit, H. (2008). Viewing resistance as ambivalence: Integrative strategies for working with resistant ambivalence. *Journal of Humanistic Psychology, 48,* 389-412.

Farber, B. A. & Lane, J. S. (2002). Positive regard. In J. C. Norcross (Ed.), *Psychotherapy relationships that work: Therapist contributions and responsiveness to patients.* (pp. 175-194). New York: Oxford University Press.

Fischer, D. (2008). A summary of John Norcross, Psychotherapy Relationships that Work: Tailoring the Relationship to the Individual Patient. In D. N. Elkins (Chair), *A shaking of the foundations.* Symposium conducted at the Existential Humanistic Institutes Second Annual Conference, San Francisco, CA.

Frankl, V. E. (1984). *Man's search for meaning: An introduction to logotherapy* (3rd ed.). New York: Simon & Schuster. (Original work published in 1959)

Frankl, V. E. (1988). *The will to meaning: Foundations and applications of logotherapy.* New York: Meridian. (Original work published in 1946-1947).

Galvin, J. (2007). Brief encounters with Chinese clients: The case of Peter. In K. Schneider (Ed.), *Existential-integrative psychotherapy: Guideposts to the core of practice* (pp. 168-175). New York: Routledge.

Gendlin, E. T. (1982). *Focusing.* New York: Bantam.

Gendlin, E. T. (1996). *Focusing-oriented psychotherapy: A manual of the experiential method.* New York: Guilford Press.

Greenberg, J. Koole, S. L. & Pyszczynski, T. (Eds.). (2004). *Handbook of experimental existential psychology.* New York: Guilford.

Greenberg, L. S. (2008). Emotion and cognition in therapy: The transforming power of affect. *Canadian Psychology, 49,* 49-59.

Greenberg, L. S. & Johnson, S. (1988). *Emotionally focused therapy for couples.* New York: Guilford Press.

Greenberg, L. S. & Watson, J. (2005). *Emotion-focused therapy of depression.* Washington, DC: American Psychological Association Press.

Greening, T. (2008). Reflections on the depressed and dying: The case of carol. In K. J. Schneider (Ed.), *Existential-integrative psychotherapy: Guideposts to the core of practice* (pp. 342-345). New York: Routledge.

Groth, M. (2001). Existential psychotherapy today. *Review of Existential Psychology and Psychiatry, 25,* 7-27.

Hoeller, K. (1999). The tragedy of psychology: Rollo May's Daimonic and Friedrich Nietzsche's Dionysian. *Review of Existential Psychology and Psychiatry, 14,* 111-125.

Hoffman, L. (2007). Existential perspectives on God image theory and practice. In G. Moriarty & L. Hoffman, *The God image handbook for spiritual counseling and psychotherapy: Theory, research, and practice* (pp. 105-137). Haworth Press.

Hoffman, L. (2008a). An existential-integrative approach to working with religious and spiritual clients. In K. J. Schneider (Ed.), *Existential-integrative psychotherapy: Guideposts to the core of practice* (pp. 187-201). New York: Routledge.

Hoffman, L. (2008b). An existential framework for Buddhism, World Religions, and Psychotherapy: Culture and Diversity Considerations. In F. Kaklauskas, S. Nimanheminda, L. Hoffman, & M. Jack, (Eds.) *Brilliant Sanity: Buddhist Approaches to Psychotherapy* (pp. 19-38). Colorado Springs, CO: University of the Rockies Press.

Hoffman, L. (2008c, November). *Applying existential therapy in a culturally sensitive manner.* Paper presented at the Second Annual Existential Humanistic Institute Conference, San Francisco, CA.

Hoffman, L. & Kurzenberger, M. (2008). The miraculous in mental illness (Premodern, modern, and postmodern interpretations of the miraculous and mental illness from religious and psychological perspectives). In J. H. Ellens (Ed.), *Miracles: God, science, and psychology in the paranormal* (Vol. 3, pp. 65-93). Westport, CT: Praeger Books.

Hoffman, L., Margiotta, D., Granger, N., Jr., & Moriarty, G. (2008, August). *Experiential processes in working with spiritual issues in therapy: An existential approach.* Paper presented at the Second Annual Humanistic Psychotherapies Conference, Boston, MA.

Hoffman, L., Oumarou, S., Mejia, M., & Alcahé, A. (2008, August). *Exploring diversity issues in existential-integrative therapy: Embracing difficult dialogues.* Presented at the Humanistic Psychotherapies Conference, Boston, MA.

Hoffman, L., Patz-Clark, D., Looney, D., & Knight, S. K. (2007, August). *Historical perspectives and contemporary needs in the psychology of evil: Psychological and interdisciplinary perspectives.* Presented at the 115th Annual Convention of the American Psychological Association Annual Convention, San Francisco, CA.

Hoffman, L., Warner, H. J., Buck, C., & Fehl, S. (2007, August). *Existential-integrative perspectives on the psychology of evil: Clinical implications.* Presented at the 1st Annual Conference of the Division of Humanistic Psychology, San Francisco.

Hubble, M. A., Duncan, B. L., & Miller, S. D. (1999). *The heart and soul of change: What works in therapy.* Washington, DC: American Psychological Association.

Kierkegaard, S. (1985). *Fear and trembling* (A. Hannay, Trans.). New York: Penguin Classics. (Originally published in 1843)

Klein, M. H., Kolden, G. G., Michels, J. L., & Chisholm-Stockard, S. (2002). Congruence. In J. C. Norcross (Ed.), *Psychotherapy relationships that work: Therapist contributions and responsiveness to patients.* (pp. 195-215). New York: Oxford University Press.

Lambert, M. J. & Barley, D. E. (2002) Research on the therapeutic relationship and psychotherapy outcome. In J. C. Norcross (Ed.), *Psychotherapy relationships that work: Therapist contributions and responsiveness to patients.* (pp. 17-32). New York: Oxford University Press.

May, R. (1970). *The meaning of anxiety.* New York: Norton. (Originally published in 1950)

May, R. (1958a). The origins and significance of the existential movement in psychology. In R. May, E. Angel, & H. F. Ellenberger (Eds.), *Existence* (pp. 3-36). Northvale, NJ: Jason Aronson.

May, R. (1958b). Contributions of existential psychotherapy. In R. May, E. Angel, & H. F. Ellenberger (Eds.), *Existence* (pp. 37-91). Northvale, NJ: Jason Aronson.

May, R. (1961). The meaning of the Oedipus myth. *Review of Existential Psychology and Psychiatry, 1,* 44-52.

May, R. (1969). *Love and will.* New York: Delta.

May, R. (1979). *Psychology and the human dilemma.* New York: Norton & Company.

May, R. (1981). *Freedom and destiny.* New York: W. W. Norton & Company.

May, R. (1982). The problem of evil: An open letter to Carl Rogers. *Journal of Humanistic Psychology, 22,* 10-21.

May, R. (1983). *The discovery of being.* New York: Norton & Company.

May, R. (1988). *Paulus: Tillich as spiritual teacher* (Rev. ed). Dallas, TX: Saybrook.

May, R. (1991). *The cry for myth.* New York: Delta.

May, R. (1999). Existential psychotherapy. *Review of Existential Psychology and Psychotherapy, 14,* 3-9.

May, R., Angel, E., & Ellenberger, H. F. (Eds.). (1958). *Existence.* Northvale, NJ: Jason Aronson, Inc.

Mendelowitz, E. (2008a). *Ethics and Lao Tzu: Intimations of character.* Colorado Springs, CO: University of the Rockies Press.

Mendelowitz, E. (2008b). Meditations on dissociation: Kristina and the enigmatic self. In K. J. Schneider (Ed.), *Existential-integrative psychotherapy: Guideposts to the core of practice* (pp. 245-266). New York: Routledge.

Mendelowitz, E. & Schneider, K. J. (2007). Existential psychotherapy. In R. J. Corsini & D. Wedding (Eds.), *Current psychotherapies* (8th ed.; pp. 295-327). Brooks-Cole.

Messer, S. B. & Wampold, B. E. (2000). Let's face the facts: Common factors are more potent than specific therapy ingredients. *Clinical Psychology: Theory, Research, Practice, 9,* 21-25.

Minuchin, S. & Fishman, H. C. (1981). *Family therapy techniques.* Cambridge, MA: Harvard University Press.

Mishalani, J. (2001). On making conscious: An existential interpretation. *Review of Existential Psychology and Psychiatry, 26,* 27-38.

Moats, M. (2008). *An existential-humanistic case study using cinematherapy as a catalyst for growth.* Paper presented at the Second Annual Humanistic Psychotherapies Conference, Boston, MA.

Monheit, J. (2008). A lesbian and gay perspective: The case of Marcia. In K. J. Schneider (Ed.), *Existential-integrative psychotherapy: Guideposts to the core of practice* (pp. 140-146). New York: Routledge.

Mosher, L. R. (2001). Treating madness without hospitals: Soteria and its successors. In K. J. Schneider, J. F. Pierson, & J. F. T. Bugental, & (Eds.), *Handbook of humanistic psychology* (pp. 389-410). Thousand Oaks, CA: Sage.

Nathan, P. (2008, November). *Contextual factors as a point of integration for diverse psychotherapies.* Paper presented at the Second Annual Existential Humanistic Institute Conference, San Francisco, CA.

Nietzsche, F. (1966). *Beyond good and evil: Prelude to a philosophy of the future* (W. Kaufmann, Trans.). New York: Vintage. (Original work published in 1886)

Nietzsche, F. (1966). *Thus spoke Zarathustra: A book for all and none* (W. Kauffman, Trans.). New York: Penguin. (Original work published in 1892)

Nietzsche, F. (1990). Twilight of the idols. In R. J. Hollingdale (Ed. & Trans.), *Twilight of the idols and the anti-christ* (pp. 31-122). New York: Penguin Classics. (Original work published in 1889).

Nietzsche, F. (1990) The anti-christ. In R. J. Hollingdale (Ed. & Trans.), *Twilight of the idols and the anti-christ* (pp. 125-199). New York: Penguin Classics. (Original work published in 1894)

Nimanheminda, S. (2008). Group as a mindfulness practice. In F. Kaklauskas, S. Nimanheminda, L. Hoffman, & M. Jack, (Eds.) *Brilliant Sanity: Buddhist Approaches to Psychotherapy* (pp. 161-174). Colorado Springs, CO: University of the Rockies Press.

Norcross, J. C. (Ed.). (2002a). *Psychotherapy relationships that work: Therapist contributions and responsiveness to patients.* New York: Oxford University Press.

Norcross, J. C. (2002b). Empirically supported relationships. In J. C. Norcross (Ed.), *Psychotherapy relationships that work: Therapist contributions and responsiveness to patients.* (pp. 3-16). New York: Oxford University Press.

O'Donohue, J. (1998). *Anam cara: A Celtic book of Wisdom.* New York: Harper Collins.

Olson, E. A., Unger, H., Kaklauskas, F. J., & Swan, L. (2008). In F. Kaklauskas, S. Nimanheminda, L. Hoffman, & M. Jack, (Eds.) *Brilliant Sanity: Buddhist Approaches to Psychotherapy* (pp. 309-334). Colorado Springs, CO: University of the Rockies Press.

Olthuis, J. H. (2001). *The beautiful risk: A new psychology of loving and being loved.* Grand Rapids, MI: Zondervan.

Portnoy, D. (2008). Relatedness: Where existential and psychoanalytic approaches converge. In K. J. Schneider (Ed.), *Existential-integrative psychotherapy: Guideposts to the core of practice* (pp. 268-281). New York: Routledge.

Rank, O. (1978). *Truth and reality* (J. Taft, Trans.). New York: Norton & Company. (Originally published in 1929)

Rice, D. L. (2008). An African American perspective: The case of Darrin. In K. J. Schneider (Ed.), *Existential-integrative psychotherapy: Guideposts to the core of practice* (pp. 110-121). New York: Routledge.

Rogers, C. R. (1951). *Client-centered therapy.* New York: Houghton Mifflin.

Rogers, C. R. (1980). *A way of being.* New York: Houghton Mifflin.

Rogers, C. R. (1982). Notes on Rollo May. *Journal of Humanistic Psychology, 22,* 8-9.

Rubin, S. A. (2008, August). A return to depth. In K. J. Schneider (Chair), *Psychology, science, and the sea: A return to depth.* Symposium conducted at the 116th Annual Convention of the American Psychological Association Annual Convention, Boston, MA.

Sartre, J. P. (1956). *Being and nothing* (H. E. Barnes, Trans.). New York: Washington Square Press. (Originally published in 1943)

Schneider, K. J. (1998). Existential processes. In L. S. Greenberg, J. C. Watson, & G. Lietaer (Eds.), *Handbook of experiential psychotherapy* (pp. 103-120). New York: Guilford Press.

Schneider, K. J. (Ed.). (2008a). *Existential-integrative psychotherapy: Guideposts to the core of practice.* New York: Routledge.

Schneider, K. J. (2008b). From segregation to integration. In K. J. Schneider (Ed.), *Existential-integrative psychotherapy: Guideposts to the core of practice* (pp. 15-22). New York: Routledge.

Schneider, K. J. (2008c). The theory of the existential-integrative (EI) approach. In K. J. Schneider (Ed.), *Existential-integrative psychotherapy: Guideposts to the core of practice* (pp. 35-48). New York: Routledge.

Schneider, K. J. (2008d). Therapeutic implications of the theory. In K. J. Schneider (Ed.), *Existential-integrative psychotherapy: Guideposts to the core of practice* (pp. 49-87)). New York: Routledge.

Schneider, K. J. & May, R. (1995). *The psychology of existence: An integrative, clinical perspective.* New York: McGraw-Hill.

Schneider, K. J. & Krug, O. T. (in press). *Existential-humanistic therapy.* Washington, DC: American Psychological Association.

Serlin, I. (2008). Women and the midlife crisis: The Anne Sexton complex. In K. J. Schneider (Ed.), *Existential-integrative psychotherapy: Guideposts to the core of practice* (pp. 146-163). New York: Routledge.

Slife, B. D. (2004). Theoretical challenges to therapy practice and research: The constraint of naturalism. In M. J. Lambert (Ed.), *Bergin and Garfield's handbook of psychotherapy and behavior change* (5th ed.; pp. 44-83). New York: Wiley.

Spinelli, E. (1997). *Tales of un-knowing: Eight stories of existential therapy.* Washington Square, NY: New York University Press.

Spinelli, E. (2004). *The mirror and the hammer.* Thousand Oaks, CA: Sage.

Stark, M. (1999). *Modes of therapeutic action: Enhancement of knowledge, provision of experience, and engagement in relationship.* Northvale, NJ: Jason Aronson.

Stolorow, R. D. (2007). *Trauma and human existence: Autobiographical, psychoanalytic, and philosophical reflections.* New York: The Analytic Press.

Stolorow, R. D. (2008). Autobiographical and theoretical reflections on the "ontological unconscious." In K. J. Schneider (Ed.), *Existential-integrative psychotherapy: Guideposts to the core of practice* (pp. 281-290). New York: Routledge.

Strasser, F. & Strasser, A. (1997). *Existential time-limited therapy: The wheel of existence.* New York: Wiley & Sons.

Task Force for the Development of Practice Recommendations for the Provision of Humanistic Psychosocial Services (1997). Guidelines for the provision of humanistic psychosocial services. *The Humanistic Psychologist, 25,* 65-107.

Task Force for the Development of Practice Recommendations for the Provision of Humanistic Psychosocial Services (2004). Recommended principles and practices for the provision of humanistic psychosocial services. Alternative to mandated practice and treatment guidelines. *The Humanistic Psychologist, 32,* 3-75).

Tillich, P. (1952). *The courage to be.* New Haven, CT: Yale University Press.

Tillich, P. (1957a). *The dynamics of faith.* New York: Harper & Row.

Tillich, P. (1957b). *Systematic theology* (Vol. 2). Chicago: University of Chicago Press.

Wampold, B. E. (2001). *The great psychotherapy debate: Models, methods, findings.* Mahwah, NJ: Erlbaum.

Wampold, B. E. (2005). Do therapies designated as ESTs for specific disorders produce outcomes superior to non-EST therapies? Not a scintilla of evidence to support ESTs as more effective than other treatments. In J. C. Norcross, L. E. Beutler, & R. F. Levant (Eds.), *Evidence-based practices in mental health: Debate and dialogue on the fundamental questions.* (pp. 299-308). Washington, DC: American Psychological Association.

Wampold, B. E. (2008, February 4). Existential-integrative psychotherapy: Coming of Age [Review of the book Existential-integrative psychotherapy: Guideposts to the core of practice]. *PsycCRITIQUES-Contemporary Psychology: APA Review of Books, 53 (No. 6)* Retrieved November 21, 2008, from the PsycCRITIQUES database.

Wampold, B. E., Goodheart, C. D., & Levant, R. F. (2007). Clarification and elaboration on evidence-based practice in psychology. *American Psychologist, 62,* 616-618.

Wampold, B. E., Mondin, G. W., Moody, M., Stich, F., Benson, K. & Ahn, H. (1997). A meta-analysis of outcome studies comparing bona fide psychotherapies: Empirically, "All must have prizes." *Psychological Bulletin, 122,* 203-214.

Wolfe, B. E. (2008). Existential issues in anxiety disorders and their treatment. In K. J. Schneider (Ed.), *Existential-integrative psychotherapy: Guideposts to the core of practice* (pp. 204-216). New York: Routledge.

Yalom, I. D. (1980). *Existential psychotherapy.* New York: Basic Books.

Yalom, I. D. (1989). *Love's executioner.* New York: HarperPerennial.

Yalom, I. D. (1993). *When Nietzsche wept: A novel of obsession.* New York: Perennial.

Yalom, I. D. (1997). *Lying on the couch: A novel.* New York: Perennial.

Yalom, I. D. (1999). *Momma and the meaning of life.* New York: Perennial.

Yalom, I. D. (2002). *The gift of therapy.* New York: HarperCollins.

Yalom, I. D. & Elkin, G. (1990). *Every day gets a little closer: A twice-told therapy.* New York: Basic Books.

Yontef, G. (1998). Dialogic Gestalt therapy. In L. S. Greenberg, J. C. Watson, & G. Lietaer (Eds.), *Handbook of experiential psychotherapy* (pp. 82-102). New York: Guilford Press.

Zinker, J. (1977). *Creative processes in gestalt therapy.* New York: Random House.

2

An Existential Psychotherapy Case Illustration

Louis Hoffman
Nathaniel Granger

This chapter provides an overview of existential therapy with the intent of illustrating the theoretical concepts, therapeutic processes, and clinical techniques discussed in Chapter 1. In order to accomplish this, the following is a fictionalized client drawn from several real clients and real therapeutic experiences of both authors. Any references to identifying information have been altered. To avoid confusion, we will refer to the therapist in the first person singular.

Anastasia[1]

History

Presenting Problem. Anastasia arrived for her first therapy session meticulously plain. It was soon evident that there was no mistake in her presentation. Anastasia could easily fit in where ever she went, but more importantly she could just as easily fade into the background. Yet, when she desired, Anastasia could also stand out and make her presence known. These days, this did not happen so often; she preferred to remain hidden.

In the first session Anastasia reported that she was coming to therapy to work through issues of grief. One year ago, Sarah, her 2-year old daughter, died following an allergic reaction when at a babysitter's house. At the time, Anastasia was engaged to her daughter's father, Tim, who left Sarah with the babysitter while he put in a few extra hours of work over the weekend. He had neglected to tell the babysitter about the allergy. Anastasia was grieving the loss of her daughter, Sarah, but also grieving because she believed that at 34-years old she may not have another opportunity to have children.

---

[1] Anastasia means resurrection, or one who will be reborn.

Family History. Anastasia was the oldest of 3 children born to her parents who remained unhappily married. Her father was Chinese American and her mother was Caucasian. Anastasia's father worked many hours and was rarely home. Anastasia perceived him as being dominated and controlled by her mother, who was a very powerful figure in her life. Her mother did not work regularly, but kept very busy through involvement in the community. Anastasia's mother was also highly critical of her, as well as everyone else in her life. This led to Anastasia both fearing and admiring her mother.

As the oldest child, Anastasia was expected to fill the mother role while her mother stayed busy in her many activities. There were high expectations that came with this role. She was to keep her young brother and sister in line, but never loose her temper. Because of the role in which she was placed, Anastasia was never close with her siblings who often aligned against her. In general, Anastasia's family tended to avoid emotion, although her mother was, at times, prone to fits of rage. When this occurred, as Anastasia learned, it was not acceptable to respond in like. Instead, she learned to passively take in her mother's anger.

As an adult, Anastasia became closer to her father, who often provided financial support and verbal encouragement, although little emotional support. She avoided talking to her mother and her talks with her father were often kept secret. Anastasia longed for a closer relationship with her parents, even though she was too scared to seek it out. She had vowed that someday she would have a better relationship with her own children.

Personal History. Describing her college years, Anastasia stated, "I rebelled against my parents in any way I could think of that would make them mad." She reported wanting to "punish them" for what they could not provide for her. She had a number of tumultuous relationships, romantic and otherwise, that often involved her initially idealizing the other person to some degree. She would quickly attach to the person, but when the emotions became too intense, she became scared and distanced herself.

One rebellion Anastasia reported was joining a small, extremist political group that also had some unusual religious ideas. She stayed involved with this group through college and several years after graduating, gradually becoming less involved while retaining the belief system. She joined not for the specifics of the group's beliefs, but for a mixture of the support the group offered and the reaction of her parents.

Through her 20s, Anastasia was in several long term relationships, but never married. She described these as "safe and lifeless." She also occasionally struggled with alcohol through this period of her life, often drinking more heavily toward the end of the relationships. Two of her boyfriends ended the relationship because of her increasing struggles with alcohol.

After a couple years of sobriety and no significant dating relationships, Anastasia became very depressed shortly after her 30th birthday. She began to drink more heavily and focused on "finding a husband, any husband." She met Tim, who, like many of her boyfriends, was stable but not very exciting. Anastasia described Tim as a "workaholic who tolerated my drinking and occasionally partied with me." When Anastasia become pregnant, Tim immediately proposed and she accepted; however, Tim wanted to "secure his finances" before they got married. After the birth of Sarah, they remained engaged but did not live together because Tim's family strongly opposed living together outside of marriage due to their religious beliefs. This was one of the few times Tim stood up to Anastasia.

Anastasia and Tim's relationship began having problems before the death of their daughter. Tim, on the nights that he joined Anastasia drinking, became increasingly concerned about her flirting with other men and experimenting with methamphetamines. She reported she was doing this in order to try to make Tim jealous and get him to commit to a wedding date, even though she knew rationally this was not the best approach. Tim did, however, become more motivated to get their finances in order to get married and began spending more time at work. Sarah, meantime, was spending more time with various babysitters. Anastasia often complained that Tim did not thoroughly check out the babysitters before hiring them, but she was not willing to stop drinking and stay home with her.

The night of Sarah's death, Anastasia was drunk and high. When she arrived at the hospital, she was checked into a detox unit after becoming unruly at the hospital. Both Tim and Anastasia were devastated. As she sobered up, the guilt set in. Usually very controlled and void of emotions, she frequently went into rages against Tim blaming him for Sarah's death. Although they tried to work through the problems, they ended their relationship a little more a month after Sarah's death.

In the year since ending her relationship with Tim, Anastasia had several short relationships with "increasingly poor choices." She continued to sporadically use methamphetamines "when the alcohol wasn't working." About 3 months before beginning therapy, Anastasia reported that she "went to church out of desperation." She reported a "conversion experience" that changed her life. She stopped drinking and was happy for the first time since Sarah's death. This lasted 3 months before, "I had a lapse in faith and was tempted into a relapse." Two times, she went out drinking, used methamphetamines, and "went home with a complete stranger." After the second of these, she decided to resume therapy. She tried therapy a couple of times before her religious conversion, but reported she "never connected" and that her therapists "just wanted to tell me that it would get better with time and then tell me what to do."

Therapy

Early Phase. The first session, Anastasia reported that she sought out a therapist with a specialty in grief work, knowing that, "I know I need to work on grief, but I'm pretty messed up in general." She also reported a pattern of increasingly unhealthy relationships with men and substance use as primary concerns. Her presentation was very flat emotionally, even though she was quite open in disclosing a detached description of her life beginning with the period shortly before her daughter's death. After giving this overview she flatly stated, "I need therapy to work this time." Her words suggested a sense of urgency, but she displayed no hint of emotion.

The first several sessions focused on building a therapeutic relationship and clarifying Anastasia's motivation for coming to therapy. Although Anastasia appeared to have good insight into her reasons for coming to therapy, often additional issues surfaced that she had a difficult time perceiving. Anastasia was able to recognize quickly that she had problematic relationship patterns that went beyond her romantic relationships, and she was open to the possibility that her desired outcome of therapy may change over time. I also encouraged Anastasia to begin identifying and expressing her emotions, something she was quite resistant to doing.

It often will take between 6 to 20 sessions to solidify a therapeutic alliance and even after this the relationship continues to deepen, often allowing new, more difficult issues to rise to the surface. This shift from the early to middle phase of therapy is signified by a deepening of trust, often related to interactions in these first sessions. With Anastasia, several events helped the transition into the second phase of therapy.

First, as noted, Anastasia was very resistant to experience her emotions. As this was explored in therapy, she made comments such as, "I'm afraid if I start crying I'll never stop." As it was evident that Anastasia would not be willing to go into her emotions until she had some confidence in her ability to modulate them, I began helping her to develop some coping skills.[2] I began with some relaxation techniques that we used in session. As part of this, I included a focus on developing body awareness [kinesthetic mode]. Anastasia quickly began identifying body states or sensations present when she was attempting to control and repress her emotions. For example, she noticed that she kept a lot tension in her jaw and the back of her neck. I also observed some non-verbal behaviors during these times. For example, when trying to hold in emotions, she would often clench her jaw and push her thumb against her fingers. At first, Anastasia became somewhat self-conscious about these physical expressions; however, her recognition of my empathetic response helped to soften her discomfort into curiosity and awareness.

I also used many reflections, but avoided content reflections most of the time. Anastasia already focused her attention to the content and the cognitive levels as a defense against emotions. Therefore, while providing some content reflections, I focused more on reflecting the underlying subtle emotions. It was evident that Anastasia often was not aware of an emotion when it arose in her, but she would begin to notice her feelings more when I asked about them. At times, she was surprised I noticed emotions she thought she had hidden from me. Again, this would, cause Anastasia to become self-conscious and back away or hide. When this occurred, I would reflect this process, too.[3]

These process reflections were very important. Anastasia often felt overwhelmed by the streams of awareness being brought to her attention. The switch to discussing the process allowed for a break from the more intense focusing on her emotions and kinesthetic levels. However, more importantly, it also allowed for opportunities to normalize her experience

---

[2] In comparison to many solution focused approaches, an existential approach will emphasize the danger in using coping skills to over-control one's emotions. Therefore, with Anastasia, it was discussed with her that there were approaches to therapy that just focused on coping skills, but that this was not my approach [informed consent]. Additionally, I explained that the coping skills, instead of controlling her emotions, could be used to help her gradually begin experiencing her emotions without becoming overwhelmed.

[3] The reader may notice a couple of processes here. First, the type of reflection used was heavily influenced by various client factors. Second, multiple forms of reflection were utilized. An over-reliance on any one type of reflection can also become stagnant and may even feel patronizing to the client. Different reflective patterns encourage the client to become aware of different aspects of her or his experience, broadening their overall awareness.

and make sure she was in control.[4] The process reflections, at least in this context, were more cognitive and allowed Anastasia to step back from the intensity of the emotions and return to the safe space of thinking. During these times, I would also comment that her avoidance of emotion had served her well as a defense [aligning with the resistance]. Additionally, I encouraged her to use this as needed [similar to paradoxical intention], especially in her life outside of therapy. Gradually, Anastasia began to *experience* that she was able to have some control over her emotions through retreat to the cognitive levels of processing. I experientially helped Anastasia gain some confidence over her emotions, and only rarely would I draw on psychoeducation or the teaching of coping skills in our sessions. In part, these process comments were used to begin to help her form a relationship with her emotional life. This was essential as we moved into more difficult emotional issues. Nonetheless, she was gaining confidence in her ability to experience and manage her emotions.

Another process, which involved a shift in the content focus, helped deepen the therapy relationship and transition into a working phase of therapy. Anastasia, despite regularly stating she wanted to work on grief issues, regularly avoided this topic. An interesting parallel process seemed to emerge. In life, Anastasia would often use promiscuous sex, which she was engaging in with regularity again during the first months of therapy, to distract her from her emotions. In therapy, she would often switch to the topic of sex when the emotions became too intense, which often occurred when discussing Sarah's death. This led to the following exchange:

> **A**: I was thinking of Tim again last night. He really was good in bed and I miss that. I almost called him up, but didn't want to revisit that relationship. So instead I went to the bar and found some random guy to go home with.[5]
> **T**: You've been doing that a lot lately.

---

[4] This also reflects the process of moving in and out of depth. Anastasia was not used to being aware of her emotions and non-verbal communication styles. She so quickly became overwhelmed with emotional reflections that it was appropriate to move back to some cognitive discussions so she could "come up for air." Also, my attunement of when she needed a break was an important part of this pacing and conveyed respect for her process.

[5] The dialogues included are generally abbreviated, which sometimes may give the appearance of appearing "too easy." Although there are limitations in presenting the dialogue in this matter, it provides demonstrations of general themes and examples of therapeutic responses that hopefully are helpful to the reader.

A: Yeah, I know, it's not good. But, hey, I'm single and I just really like men.

T: You've always "liked men," but you haven't always gone out looking to hook up with random men.

A: I'm okay with it. I enjoy it and, as I said, I just really like men and I like sex.

T: It's not sex or men, you like the distraction that sex provides [stark statement].[6]

A: (noticeably reacting, upset). What? (pause, I do not respond) What do you mean?

T: It's not about the men, not about the sex. It's about you.

A: Yeah, *I* want sex.

T: It's more than that.

A: Well, sure, it's better than the pain, but I enjoy the sex, too.

T: I know. But I've noticed a pattern. Since you've begun here, when you are having a difficult week, and often after a difficult session, you go out looking for sex. In therapy, when we are talking about Sarah, you often shift to talking about your sexual relationships [reflection the person in context]. I'm not saying you don't enjoy men and sex, I am just saying sex comes up as a topic or something you seek out when you are in pain.[7]

Anastasia was upset by this conversation, but some progress had been made. She gained some awareness through this exchanged, and she allowed herself to show some small degree of anger. However, when I asked about her feelings she still denied that she was upset. A follow up to this occurred in the next session that seemed to symbolize the transition into deeper therapeutic work.

T: I wanted to start off with something today. Last week it really seemed like you were mad at me.

A: No, I was a bit frustrated, but not mad.

---

[6] Notice here that this statement was somewhat jarring. It didn't flow naturally in the conversation. Similar to an interpretation, it brought something uncomfortable quickly to her attention, but it did so without explanation. This pushed Anastasia to connect the meaning, but also quickly brought up emotions.

[7] This is a *big mirror reflection* in that it reflects several pieces of information and places them in context. This is largely the same process as an interpretation; however, it is left a bit less clear than most interpretations. There are intentionally some gaps that Anastasia will still need to connect for herself. Stated differently, some unknowns were intentionally left in place.

T: You looked mad. I'm a little unclear about the difference between being mad and being frustrated in your experience.

A: (long pause). I guess it is that I wasn't very upset, it wasn't a big deal.

T: It doesn't feel very safe to be angry at me.

A: What do you mean? I wasn't angry. (slightly irritated)

T: Okay, but would it be safe to be angry at me?

A: I guess.... I just really don't get angry.

T: Everyone gets angry. You just don't allow yourself to express it.

A: I guess, maybe.

T: Now that makes me angry. You're just blowing me off.

A: (surprised). I didn't mean to make you angry. I just meant I'm not sure. I'm not comfortable with anger... I did have something I wanted to bring up today.

T: Just wait, I think this is important.

A: I just don't want to talk about anger. You said I was in charge of what we talk about.

T: You are, and if you really want to move on, we will. But I imagine this would still be on your mind, on both of our minds. I don't think either of us will really be able to focus on something else if this is sitting there unresolved.

A: Alright (with a look of disgust).

T: See, there, you seem angry again.

A; Yeah, maybe, because you're trying to piss me off.

T: No, I'm not. I just think it is necessary for us to be completely honest with each other.

A: I never lied to you, what are you talking about?

T: I never said you lied. I just think you weren't telling me everything, maybe not telling yourself everything. It seemed you were not acknowledging your anger.

A: It doesn't feel safe. This is supposed to be a safe place.

T: It is. But how can it truly be safe if you cannot be angry at me?

A: (pause, Anastasia appeared to be considering this). I guess that makes sense. It's just that I was never allowed to get angry before. It was not okay in my family. If you got angry, then you were really going to get it.

T: And you're afraid I'm going to let you have it, too.

A: Or you'll get rid of me.

T: (leaning in) I'm not getting rid of you. In fact, I feel quite close to you right now.

> **A**: (long pause) I do feel close to you right now, too. I'm not sure what that means.
>
> **T**: Maybe it means, in part, that this is something you needed to talk about in here. You can't get too close to someone when you're hiding something that needs to be talked about.

This was a key moment in therapy. Anastasia was able to recognize the paradox in that moment: in the midst of very uncomfortable feelings of anger and sadness, she also felt connected, which felt good.[8] Through this exchange, Anastasia began to believe that I was not going anywhere. Even if both of us were mad, the relationship would go on.

A second aspect of this is important to note, too. I had role modeled my anger and expression of anger to Anastasia. It was not a dramatic expression of anger, but rather expressed directly and calmly. Some clients need to be able to raise their voice and express their anger more dramatically. For Anastasia, part of her resistance to anger was associating it with the more dramatic outbursts her mother occasionally had. As she learned that she could experience and express her emotions subtly, without the dramatic expressions of it, it began to feel safer. From an existential perspective, it is important to be able to experience and express emotion, but it is not dictated how that should be done.[9]

Middle Phase. As we transitioned into the next phase of therapy, Anastasia seemed to feel comfortable addressing a broader array of issues. Despite this, she still avoided talking about Sarah. Instead, she focused mostly on her relationship with men. It became apparent that Anastasia saw most men as weak and she felt like she could control them with sex or manipulation. A pattern seemed to emerge, even in her short relationships, that she would use her sexuality to attract men and control them while in relationship with them, but then would get bored with the relationship.

---

[8] In our experience, examples such as this are very common, although they may not always be centered on the emotion of anger. Sadness, for example, is equally as common. The essence of this experience therapeutically is twofold. First, the client recognizes that the intense emotions will not drive off the therapist. Second, this helps *change the experience of the emotion*. The emotion is the same, but it is not experienced as painful. Through these encounters, clients also learn that it is okay to go into their emotions and explore their meaning.

[9] There are also important cultural variations in emotional expression. As will be discussed in Chapter 3, many Eastern cultures tend to be leery of intense emotional expression. With Anastasia, once she learned that the emotional expression did not need to be the dramatic style of her associations, it became much easier for her to acknowledge, experience, and express emotion.

When seeking out a relationship and then in the relationship until she became bored, she dressed up to draw attention to herself. Once she became bored, she started to try to look plain again. During this time, the following interchange occurred.

> **T:** Anastasia, I've noticed you've been dressing quite differently for therapy lately.
> **A:** How so? (It was evident that she knew and was playing coy.)
> **T:** Well, you've been dressed up more and wearing more make-up. I'm curious as to what that is about.
> **A:** I'm just feeling better so I'm dressing up.
> **T:** That's a little different from what you are saying in sessions, though. It doesn't sound like you're feeling better. It seems there is something different.
> **A:** Like what?
> **T:** Well, I'm feeling a bit uncomfortable with your dress at times. [here-and-now therapist self-disclosure]
> **A:** How? Like you are attracted to me?
> **T:** That's not what I am getting at. We've talked about your pattern with men that you dress up to get their attention and to get control over them. I can't help but wonder if that is what you're trying to do in here.[10]

Erotic transferences in therapy happen more often than most therapists realize or are willing to admit to themselves. In this situation, it did not appear as if there was an erotic transference; however, Anastasia was using her sexuality as a defense. This pattern emerged after several very emotionally difficult sessions. As Anastasia started to dress up for therapy, she also become more resistant. This pattern, again, is not uncommon when an erotic transference emerges as the client will then often try to present themselves in the best light.

My instinct was that this was a resistance pattern, not an erotic transference; however, I could not be certain. The above opened the conversation in a way that could allow the erotic transference to emerge, if that was the case, or could deal with using sexuality as a resistance pattern. Through the exploration that followed this discussion, it became

---

[10] This illustrates a couple of challenges for many therapists. First, therapist self-disclosure was utilized. It focused on the here-and-now, not personal details again. Second, therapists are often overly hesitant in addressing issues of sexuality in therapy. In this instance, it was necessary to address sexuality straight on.

clear that it was a resistance pattern. As we discussed this during the next several weeks, the client was able to become aware that she felt overwhelmed by the intensity of the previous sessions, so she began to act out a pattern from her life in the therapy relationship. In this next brief excerpt, we discussed the relationship implications for this:

> **T:** Anastasia, when you were "dressing up for therapy," my experience was that I felt much more disconnected from you.
> **A:** (surprised) Most guys seem to like that.
> **T:** I would guess so, but I am more curious about your experience in here.[11]
> **A:** I guess I was more disconnected, too.
> **T:** You guess? Come on, you know that doesn't cut it in here. Look inward, what was your experience like?[12]
> **A:** Alright, alright. (pause). I really was disconnected. But I also felt powerful.
> **T:** Powerful... like you could control me.
> **A:** Yeah, I guess.... I mean, yeah, that seems right. I do that a lot with men. It is safer to be with them when I'm in control.
> **T:** But there is something missing, too.
> **A:** The intimacy is gone. It's not really a relationship anymore.

Anastasia was starting to see that many of her relationships did not meet her relational needs; they were just a distraction.

Not long after this issue was addressed, Anastasia reported feeling that she needed to "get back to church and get back to God." During the next several weeks, she became more focused on talking about her church and religious issues. She discussed feeling guilty about her sexual promiscuity, but there never seemed to be any emotional connection when she talked about her guilt. Her nights out at the bar and looking for men decreased and then desisted. The desire to go out remained, but now

---

[11] Anastasia was getting much better at reflecting on the moment in therapy, but she often needed guidance or pointing back to this process, which I regularly provided. Over time, clients generally begin to make these reflections more naturally in response to the therapist's own reflection on the process.

[12] I established pretty early on in therapy that "I don't know" and "I guess" are not acceptable answers in most situations, which is something I commonly do in therapy. When Anastasia used this as an answer, I regularly made a comment such as the one in the dialogue in a bit of a teasing voice tone. This tone made the confrontation easier to take, but also pointed her to looking inward to find her answer. Eventually, she would catch herself when she said, "I don't know" or "I guess" and correct it on her own.

she was talking about urges to go out partying as "the devil tempting" her. She spent more and more time at church growing increasingly active.

The impression I developed was that Anastasia had a genuine religious commitment and faith, but that she was increasingly using religion as a psychological defense. It is often difficult to challenge particular religious *beliefs* of the client without challenging their *faith* or *spirituality*. At the same time, Anastasia was not getting the deeper meaning benefits of being religious, because it was being utilized in the role of a psychological defense. The challenge in working with this issue with Anastasia, as with many clients, is to help her retain the meaningful aspects of religion while encouraging her to gradually explore and recognize the destructive aspects of her beliefs. It was particularly challenging to do this while respecting Anastasia's beliefs, even though I had concerns about them. Still, I knew that as long as her beliefs were being used as a psychological defense, they lacked the genuineness to provide sustaining meaning. By working through the defense aspects of the religious or spiritual beliefs, Anastasia would gradually be able to have a more authentic faith or spirituality that is sustaining and meaningful.

I had been encouraging Anastasia to explore her religious beliefs and how it was impacting her with some limited success. I began encouraging Anastasia to look at the grief issues that she had initially said she wanted to work on in therapy. Whenever Sarah came up, she responded saying, "She's in a better place now. God has freed me of that concern." During this period Anastasia came in with the following dream:

> **A:** I was at the beach on a retreat with friends. Sarah was there. It was a beautiful spot on the beach with high cliffs behind us. It was just a small beach area with a single road leading to it. We were having a celebration, partying. Sarah was playing down by the water. I was distracted by the others and lost track of Sarah. Next thing I knew, Sarah was swimming and getting caught in the waves, pulled out to sea. As I tried to get down there, Sarah was caught in the undertow and pulled under. I knew she was going to drown and there was nothing I could do about it. Then things changed. It was night and there was a fire on the beach. I was still trying to get to Sarah. It was no longer my partying friends with me; now it was my church friends. They were holding me back, telling me Sarah was okay and to come and join the singing. But I knew Sarah was not okay. I was mad, furious. I wanted them to help me find Sarah, but no one would listen. Then Tim was there. I made him get in this

little air raft by himself and go out looking for Sarah. He was trying to navigate the boat among the rocks and being sucked out to sea. Then I woke up.

As she finished telling the dream, Anastasia was sobbing. She had never gone into emotion like this before, never allowed herself to just cry. After several minutes she said, "I don't know why I am crying so hard."

We began to process the dream. I encouraged Anastasia to think about what the dream could mean to her. She responded with the following:

> **A:** Some of it is obvious. I can't save Sarah. And I know I can't. But I don't understand the rest. Why did my friends change? Why wouldn't my church friends help me find Sarah?

The dream led into some powerful therapy work and it unveiled itself over the next several sessions. The dark, vastness of the sea seemed symbolic of the unconscious, the great unknown. This was something that Anastasia was terrified to face, something she did not want to know about herself, yet there was part of her that was being beckoned by the sea. She could not deny that. All along she had been seeking meaning from the depths, but terrified of where she needed to go to get there.

Anastasia, through the dream, recognized that her partying friends represented her own guilt hidden away in her unconscious. She began to acknowledge that she felt it was her fault that Sarah died, not Tim's. She said Tim was being responsible, working, while she was out partying. Although she was able to recognize that Tim also made mistakes, she was facing her guilt and how it connected to the grief. She also began recognizing that she felt that she had treated Tim unfairly: "I often sent him on dangerous and unfair missions. Sarah was my excuse for doing so. I'm not sure I ever wanted him to succeed, but he would diligently go out among the rocks for me." She, too, began to understand the sea as symbolizing her great needs and all her unfinished business with the pain of her past that drove her to the lifestyle she was living when Sarah died.

In many ways, the most difficult symbolism that Sarah faced in the dream was that of her church friends. Early on, she ardently maintained that her church friends were there to provide her comfort. She said that they were encouraging her to move on and be thankful for what God had given her, but she was resistant. I was suspicious of this interpretation, but did not want to force my own opinion upon her. In one session, she began looking at this differently:

> **A:** I keep coming back to the dream, to the church friends that were there with me. I can't get that part of the dream off my mind.
>
> **T:** And the rest of the dream, that is not as pressing anymore?
>
> **A:** No, I don't seem to think about that much anymore.
>
> **T:** Maybe there is something else in that part of the dream, something you haven't recognized yet.
>
> **A:** There must be; I can't let it go. I even had another dream last night. I was back at the beach. The church friends were there singing away and I was so mad at them. Finally, I grabbed one of their guitars and threw it on the fire.
>
> **T:** Wow, it sounds like you were pretty mad at them.
>
> **A:** I was furious, but I don't know why. They weren't doing anything wrong.
>
> **T:** I wonder if you can just sit with that image from the dream for a minute. Go ahead and close your eyes, focus in on the image…. Notice how you feel… Check in with the different parts of your body… (I continued with some imagery work, just having her bring the image to mind combined with some body scans).
>
> **A:** (Crying). I'm so mad at them.
>
> **T:** Something about them is making you mad. Yet, you are crying. [13]
>
> **A:** (pause, still crying). I am so alone.
>
> **T:** (pause) Even with your friends there, you still feel alone.
>
> **A:** They are not really there; they are not there for me. They are only there for me if I can feel good.
>
> **T:** They won't go with you into your suffering, your pain.
>
> **A:** No, that's a weakness to them. Christians aren't supposed to suffer. God, if another person tells me Sarah is in a better place I'm just going to punch them. I know she's in a better place, that's not the point.
>
> **T:** The point is that you miss her.

---

[13] Several things can be noticed here. First, the temptation here would be to ask a question, yet I did not want to do this. When the therapist asks a question, this often draws the client into thinking, into her head; I wanted Anastasia to stay with the emotion. Statements and comments are much more effective in keeping a client with her emotions. Second, I pointed out the incongruence, which made Anastasia confront why she said she was mad when she was crying.

A: I miss her! Dammit (sic), I miss her! No cliché is going to make that go away. I miss her! (crying)

T: You feel even more alone when they discount your feelings with their simple answers.

A: I can't stand it. I just want them to be there with me. I want someone to let me cry, let me be mad; to let me even be mad at God!

This encounter was a powerful experience for Anastasia. She was able to gain important insight, as well as do some powerful experiential work by exploring her emotions. The next couple of sessions were also very intense as she continued to process her emotions around Sarah's death and her anger at her church, to which she hadn't gone back.

The day of third session after this dialogue, Anasasia called a few minutes before the appointment to say that she was drunk and unable to drive herself to the appointment. She went to have lunch at a bar and had a couple of drinks that led to a couple of more drinks. She never went back to work. I made sure that she was not planning to drive home, as she was still at the bar, and confirmed the appointment for next week.

The next week Anastasia arrived a few minutes late for her appointment and appeared nervous:

T: You appear nervous today.

A: I'm worried about how you're going to react about me missing last week.

T: Let's start there. How do you imagine I reacted to the events of last week?

A: I'm guessing you were mad at me.

T: And how did you imagine I was going to respond today?

A: I don't know, maybe that you were going to let me have it, or you would be disappointed in me.

T: Anastasia, I was concerned about you last week. In particular, I wanted to make sure you had a way to get home safely, without attempting to drive yourself.

A: You weren't mad?

T: It doesn't seem you really believe me.

A: Well, no, I mean, you had a right to be mad at me.

T: I supposed I did, but have I ever not been honest with you about how I was feeling or what I was thinking before?

A: There's always a first for everything.

T: Fair enough, but does it seem like I am mad at you or disappointed with you? Or did it seem that way on the phone last week?

A: No, it didn't. You just seemed concerned.

T: I was. I was very concerned. And I was concerned that your getting drunk may be connected to the work we've been doing in here.

A: Really?

T: We've been doing some pretty intense work in here. Alcohol has been one of your escapes. I wonder if we were going to fast pushing too hard. [14]

A: Yeah, but that's my responsibility.

T: You going out drinking, that is your responsibility. Us going too fast in here, that's *our* responsibility. And I think that *our* pushing hard in here impacted your choices out there. It was still *your* choice; I don't mean to let you off the hook for that. But, many factors and forces influence our choices.

A: But I thought you said this is what we needed to be doing.

T: I do believe we've been on the right track of important things for you to work on. Maybe we need to just be more aware of the pace we are going at, and how you feel about being able to manage it at the time. [15]

As the discussion continued, we addressed many patterns. I commented to Anastasia that although she had improved tremendously in tolerating her emotions, she still tended engage in certain old patterns to help her escape difficult emotions. At this point, it had been 6 months since our conversation about using sex to avoid talking about Sarah's death. I made the following reflection to Anastasia:

T: Anastasia, a while ago we discussed that you had been using sex, either as a topic of discussion or engaging in it, to avoid dealing with the difficult emotions around Sarah's death. We worked

---

[14] This illustrates a couple of points. First, it again illustrates the need to move in and out of the depths. Second, it demonstrates Bugental's idea of aligning with the resistance. I am demonstrating to Anastasia, through the dialogue, that various defenses have been used to help her survive. However, it is also communicating to her that we all have our limits. These may change over time, but at this point we were pushing Anastasia beyond what she could handle.

[15] This dialogue shows the shared responsibility of therapy, while also not taking away Anastasia's own freedom of choice and accompanying responsibility.

through that and you were focusing more on your emotions again. After engaging in your emotions for a while, you turned to religion. We discussed that you had been using religion, at the encouragement of your friends, to avoid dealing with the difficult aspects of your emotions, particularly around Sarah's death. We also identified that there seemed to be a part of you that felt it was necessary to deal with Sarah's death. Following the dream, we went back into your emotions rather intensely again for several weeks. Then you called in drunk, numbing out your emotions. Each time, in these avoidant patterns, I also have felt that you were pushing me away; I didn't feel as connected to you.[16]

In the next session, we picked up with this theme using the empty-chair (or two-chair) technique. I asked Anastasia to identify the part of her that was resistant to going into her emotions, and to talking about Sarah. Then I had her imagine in the other chair was the part of her that recognized the need to deal with her emotions and Sarah's death. Anastasia spoke for about 5-minutes, expressing her feelings and fears. One theme that emerged was that she was afraid that if she fully grieved for Sarah then she would really be gone—from her life and her memories.

As Sarah moved to the other chair, speaking to the resistant part of herself, she expressed how unhappy she was with her life. For the first time, she acknowledged that she did not really know what she was living for [meaninglessness]. She was not expressing any thoughts of suicide or wanting to die, but rather speaking to the depths of her feelings of emptiness about Sarah's death. After stating this, she stopped and looked at me saying:

A: You're not going to have me locked up now, are you?

T: No, I don't see any reason, as of now, to have you locked up.

A: I didn't mean to say that. I kind of got lost in talking to myself there, but when I said it I all of a sudden realized what I had said. I thought you therapist types generally lock people up for statements like that, don't you?

---

[16] This looks very much like an interpretation again, but my intent is different. I want to focus on reflecting the patterns. I am trying to help Anastasia see the various ways she tries to escape her emotions through defense patterns. I am also highlighting how it impacts our relationship.

T: You therapist types?[17]

A: Sorry, but you know what I mean.

T: Yes, I know what you mean. Listen, I didn't hear you saying that you were going to kill yourself. I heard you saying you were in a lot of pain.

A: Yes, my life feels pretty empty right now. I miss Sarah and the meaning she brought to my life. I miss my church, even though I am still mad at them and don't want to go back. And I even miss Tim.

T: Those were sources of meaning in your life, things worth living for.

A: Yes, they were.[18]

This interaction was another critical point in therapy. First, I again earned Anastasia's trust. Previous therapists had quickly rushed to consider hospitalizing Anastasia when she made any statement that could have suggested the possibility of suicide. She stated that she has never really considered harming herself, but her previous therapists could never hear her when she stated she was not intending to harm herself.

Second, Anastasia was able to deepen her understanding of her resistance to dealing with Sarah. She had been in therapy for close to a year at this point. Anastasia had made significant progress over this time, including increasing her ability to tolerate and process emotions, decrease

---

[17] This shift in language is important, and I would return Anastasia to it later; however it was not the critical issue at this point. The shift to refer to me as "you therapist types" is an objectifying language, something that had not occurred in a while in our therapy relationship. We later returned to this to better understand its meaning. Anastasia was able to identify that when she thought of me in these terms, as another of the "therapy types," that she was not relating to me as a person, but based on her past experiences (i.e., transference). I continued to point this out when I observed it, often saying, "Am I one of those therapy-types now?" Over time, she became more aware of when this was occurring and would bring it up directly on her own.

[18] Notice I never focused on the suicide issue. If by the end of the session I did not have adequate assurance that Anastasia was not going to harm herself, I would have evaluated this at the end of the session. However, if I had evaluated for suicide at this moment, it would have breached her trust. Anastasia had already told me pretty bluntly that she was concerned that I would react by hospitalizing her. I wanted to make sure that if suicide became a concern in the future that she would feel safe to talk with me about it and know that I would not jump to conclusions. Instead, I was communicating trust to her and implicitly telling her that in the future I would work with her on these issues and not just immediately rush to hospitalizing her without considering other options. Furthermore, this showed that even though we had a very strong therapy alliance, she still had difficulty fully trusting me on certain issues.

her reliance on sex, alcohol, and drugs to numb out her emotions, and she did not experience depression as frequently or as profoundly. Additionally, she had worked to develop a solid therapy alliance and she had greater insight and awareness. However, two important issues were becoming increasingly evident as necessary to face at this point of therapy. First, she was still avoiding grieving for Sarah. Second, Anastasia was starting to recognize that she had been avoiding developing any sustaining meaning or new relationships of any depth. She had developed many surface relationships, but none that were really meaningful to her.

Anastasia and I used this opportunity to review what she had accomplished in therapy and refocus the future direction of therapy. It was important that Anastasia recognize the gains she had made, particularly to help give her confidence to address these next phases of therapy. I had Anastasia reflect on her own perception of her progress and then I followed by sharing with her how I felt she had grown and changed. We then set course for these next two issues.

Part of integrating and grieving the loss of a loved one is a returning to engagement in the world. Often this means deepening existing relationships or developing new, meaningful relationships. Anastasia had lost both Sarah and Tim, but not replaced these relationships with any new relationships. Because of this, I would, at times, encourage Anastasia to talk about Sarah in her relationships outside of therapy, too. She gradually began to focus on the grieving process. As she did this outside of therapy, she started to develop some new relationships with sustaining meaning. The grieving was difficult and painful for Anastasia. In some sessions, I had her bring pictures of Sarah. She told me about the picture sometimes, sharing stories about Sarah that she had not spoken of since her death. Sometimes we would place the picture in a chair and use the empty chair technique to facilitate the grieving. She apologized to Sarah several times for not being there more when she was alive, and also for not being there the night of her death. She told Sarah what she missed about her and, gradually, was also able to talk about and grieve the things she did not always like or appreciate about Sarah. It became a full grieving process. It is important to note, too, that in spending almost a year before focusing on the grieving, therapy was able to address the issues that prevented her from being able to grieve for Sarah earlier. These same patterns had made it difficult for Anastasia to work through many other difficult emotions, too.

Anastasia was beginning to develop more sustaining sources of meaning in her life through the grieving process; however, this was still an area of concern for me, and I brought this up with her. She would regularly mention religion as having been important to her at times in her life, but also that she no longer trusted religion much. She recognized that the political/religious group from her college days was about rebellion. She had also recognized problems with the Christian church that she later attended.

> **T:** You know, I am noticing that religion seems to be coming up more and more in sessions again.
> **A:** I know, that must mean I haven't worked through my anger at them yet, right?
> **T:** Now you know I'm not going to answer that for you.
> **A:** Yeah, but I guess that must be what it is.
> **T:** Well, let's look at it. Give it some real consideration, not one of the "I guess" answers.
> **A:** Okay (pause). It seems like I must be angry at them, but I really don't feel it. I mean, I've kind of just come to accept that it was their limitations.
> **T:** What I hear you talking about with religion are the people who failed you. Is that all there was to your involvement in religion?
> **A:** No, well, at least I didn't think so, but… well, maybe it was.
> **T:** Anastasia, you have to decide if a spiritual perspective is something you want to pursue or not. But I think you have been focusing a lot on the religious people who let you down, and not much on what the religion itself was all about.

During the next several weeks, Anastasia began to re-examine her religious beliefs and what religion was all about for her. She elected not to return to her own church, but started to explore different avenues of spirituality, including different world religions. Eventually, she returned to a Christian church that was much more open to different perspectives as compared with her previous church. She became very involved in the service aspects of the church that she found deeply meaningful. She also started to develop new meaningful relationships at this church and began dating again. It was at this time that we began talking about ending therapy.

Final Phase. As we began talking about ending therapy, the topic of Tim came up regularly. Anastasia reported that she recognized that Tim was not the best person for her to marry, but that she deeply loved him. The ending process of therapy often brings up unresolved grief from the past, and it was evident that this was what was occurring with Tim. Anastasia had focused so much on grieving for Sarah that she never realized she also needed to grieve the loss of Tim. After a couple of sessions she called Tim and asked to get together. Tim, too, had struggled greatly since their separation. They were able to have a good talk and say a proper goodbye.

After this diversion, we resumed working toward the ending of therapy. I emphasized to Anastasia the importance of having closure on our relationship, especially given how difficult it had been for her to work through so many endings of relationships before. I encouraged her to write a summary of therapy, including what she felt she accomplished and what areas she still struggled with in life. Anastasia returned the next session having written about the process of therapy and her accomplishments, but was resistant to acknowledging what she wanted to change or improve. In discussing this, Anastasia said that she did not want me to leave with the feeling that I had not completed the process with her. After assuring her that I knew none of us are ever a "finished product," she was able to consider the issues that still lingered. She recognized that she stills struggled being open in relationships and felt guilty anytime she experienced anger. She also still deeply missed Sarah at times, especially on birthdays and holidays. However, Anastasia's statement in the last session helped me to know that she was ready to end therapy:

> **A:** I guess I know now that life is never complete and, after all, what fun would it be if it was. I am okay with still hurting and know that is part of what it is about. I'll think of you when I suffer from now on—not in a bad way—but in recognition that you helped me learn how to suffer and that its not such a bad thing. But I'll also be sure to think of you and be thankful sometimes when things are going well, too…. I'll miss you.

I let the "I guess" go this one time.

Concluding Remarks

This case, as is hopefully evident, illustrates Anastasia's wrestling with the existential givens and her own existence pain, while also illustrating the psychotherapy process. A few concluding comments may help to frame this case. First, many people are often surprised by the conversational tone used by many existential therapists. Many therapies utilize a special and seemingly mysterious way of communicating with their clients. Others rely upon an excessively technical language. Many existential therapists use these specialized styles of communication and they were utilized at times with Anastasia. However, part of the art of existential psychotherapy is being able to be therapeutic in a way that is not so distant from the communication of every day life. Even reflections, when not overused, appear more conversational. The dialogues chosen also intentionally include various types of reflections along with here-and-now self-disclosure, stark statements, and experiential techniques. Last, the existential themes were evident in the dialogues, even though they were never discussed in the abstract language of Chapter 1.

Therapy, for Anastasia, extended for a little more than 2-years. It was not always as intense as it may appear in the discussion above. As with any long-term therapy process, there were lulls and times where little progress seemed to be occurring. Generally, these did not last long. When they lasted more than several sessions, we addressed the issue together and were generally able to get therapy back on track. On a couple of these occasions, Anastasia responded with statements such as, "This is what I need right now." It is difficult for therapist not to be critical of the client or themselves when therapy progress is slow, but it is important not to force our expectations on our client in these situations. After the dialogue in which we addressed the pace of therapy, which was several months into the therapy process, Anastasia become very good at setting the pace and telling me when she needed to slow down.

As therapy concluded, I discussed with Anastasia that she could call me in the future if the need arose. It is not uncommon for clients to set up occasional "check in sessions," especially in the first couple of years after therapy. Therapy is an important part of an individual's life and the therapy relationship is often reflected upon well after therapy has ended. It is only natural that clients would want to check in from time to time and it is unfortunate that some therapy approaches pathologize such tendencies. As the lead character in Carol Gilligan's (2008) book *Kyra* tells her therapist, there is something unnatural about the conclusion of successful therapy relationship entailing the therapist leaving and a permanent ending of the relationship. For Anastasia, it would important for me to "still be real," in her words, so she would call from time to time with an update for several years. She did not want me to be one aspect of a memory of something she did, but rather an important person who accompanied her on a difficult part of her journey. Anastasia also continued a regular practice of sending a yearly birthday update, letting me know how her life was progressing. For my part, I looked forward to her birthdays. Anastasia would often conclude these updates echoing the sentiment of the final session, "Life is not perfect, but I no longer expect it to be that way."

References

Gilligan, C. (2008). *Kyra*. New York: Random House.

Part 2

East and West Perspectives
on Existential Psychology

3

Existential Psychology Dialogues in China: Beginning the Conversation

Jennifer Christy Dyer
Francis Kaklauskas
Michael M. Dow
Elizabeth Saxon
Albert Chan
Mark Yang
Louis Hoffman

The primary purpose of this chapter is to set the stage for the rest of the book. Thus far, the book has provided an overview of the existential approach to psychology as developed in the United States.[1] In this chapter, we begin to engage the East-West dialogue through the identification of many of the challenges and opportunities inherent in this dialogue. We introduce many of these questions and challenges, but will not fully address them as they will become the premise of the next 17 chapters. The journey of this chapter, and this book, began when a group of United States graduate psychology students and their professor journeyed to China to engage with Chinese psychologists about the theory and practice of existential psychology. The trip inspired countless conversations and revelations regarding the similarities and differences between "East" and "West," that often overturned expectations. We left with a deeper appreciation for not only how existential psychology might be relevant to China, but for how a Chinese perspective offers fresh insights for existential psychology.

---

[1] As noted in chapter 1, existential psychology began in Europe and there continues to be an existential therapy approach in Europe that bears many similarities to the schools in the tradition of Rollo May and James F. T. Bugental. This book focuses mostly on United States traditions with the exception of chapter 4, which draws heavily from the existential approach of Boss.

Background

On the morning of April 18, 1989, thousands of college students in Beijing filed silently into Tiananmen Square. Many laid wreaths around the Monument to the People's Heroes in memory of Yaobang, Secretary General of the Chinese Communist Party, whose death three days earlier would ignite the Protest Movement in May and June (Lin, 1993). One group from Beijing University spread a banner across the ground on which the following characters were inscribed: "Zhong-Guo-Hun – the Soul of China."

Chinese intellectuals have had to face the agonizing fact that for almost three decades virtually every one of them has forfeited their birthright as autonomous individuals and sold it almost willingly and unconditionally to become a cog in the machine, a "servile tool of the Party" (Lin, 1994). The tragic end of the Protest Movement of 1989 served only to intensify and accelerate the soul-searching process. Wang Ruoshui, the standard bearer of Marxist humanism in post-Mao China, closed his famous article "In Defense of Humanism," by asserting the reemergence of humanity:

> A specter stalks the earth of China.
> "Who are you?"
> "I am Humanity" (as cited in Lin, 1994, p. 614).

During the past twenty years, China has emerged as an economic, political, and military global power. The Communist Party's reform policies of the 1980s marked the start of China's transformation from an impoverished, agriculturally based society into an industrial powerhouse with a booming economy growing at a staggering rate of 10 percent per year over the past decade (The US - China Business Council, 2008). Along with the country's foray into global economic markets came the development of many Western institutions, ideas, and practices, including psychotherapy (Chang, Tong, Qija, & Zeng, 2005). Currently, the practice of psychotherapy in China is heavily influenced by Western approaches; however, differences between the cultures have led to the development of new hybridized forms of psychology that take into account Chinese cultural beliefs, philosophies, and help-seeking practices.

Chinese natives often demonstrate a preference for short-term, problem-focused psychotherapy that emphasizes symptom removal over personal growth (Chang et al., 2005). Psychotherapists are viewed as expert healers who can provide speedy results. Not surprisingly, behavioral therapy was identified as the most common mode of treatment in mainland China in a 1992 survey (Qian & Chen, 1998). Insight-oriented approaches such as existential and humanistic psychotherapy, with their emphasis on inner emotional life, are not taking hold as quickly in most places (Chang et al., 2005). Traditional Chinese culture dictates strict emotive control because it is believed that excessive emotions, desire, and self-indulgence adversely affect the balance of yin and yang and may lead to physical illness (Veith, 1997).

Since the goals of most Western models of psychotherapy emphasize individuation, self-efficacy, and self-actualization–goals that may conflict with the Chinese view that the self must be in harmony with the collective–the question of whether Western psychological interventions are appropriate and effective with Chinese nationals is often queried (Hoffman, Stewart, Warren, & Meek, in press; Mosig, 2006). In fact, the underutilization of mainstream mental health services by Chinese living in the United States is often attributed to disparities between Western models of treatment and traditional Chinese beliefs (Chang et al., 2005). However, demand for counseling services in China is growing at an exponential rate, far outpacing the ability of the country's 13,000 trained mental health professionals to provide services (Chang et al.). As the need for mental health services expands, no single therapeutic approach is likely to adequately and appropriately meet the variety of demands.

While existential psychology is just starting to be introduced to the Chinese, existential philosophy is not new to China. The most spectacular intellectual event in the reconstruction of Chinese consciousness during the 1980s was a great debate among academics on culture (Lin, 1993). The discussion included the study of Chinese premodern traditional culture, and then spread to the comparative study of Chinese and Western cultures and the theories and methods of cultural analysis (Lin, 1994). A much more radical departure was the "Sartre fever," "Nietzsche fever," and "Freud fever" that appeared in the early eighties and served as an antidote to the disoriented spiritual life, and filled the moral vacuum after Mao. Nietzsche's "transevaluation of all values" seemed to have caught the imagination not only of the academic circles, but also of the thinking public, who, no longer content with understanding and changing the world, began to search for the meaning and value of these activities.

Tradition-based scholars, who are versed in Chinese philosophy or familiar with the Chinese cultural heritage, also recognize the exceedingly rich metaphysical thinking in Confucianism, Taoism, and Buddhism (Lin, 1994). The other strand is Western-based, drawing its inspiration from the existentialist trend on the one hand and Christianity on the other. The debate on culture breathed life into the Chinese soul with ideas and values derived from various cultures, ancient and modern, Eastern and Western.

The discussions of the feasibility of applying natural scientific methodology to the study of humanities constituted another intellectual event in the post-Mao era (Lin, 1993). Jin Guantao, the most influential initiator of the scientific trend, explained that in the past twenty years of his philosophical exploration, epistemology and methodology were only "the beginning of the reconstruction of the edifice of rational philosophy," the peak of which is "the value, the meaningfulness, the ultimate concern for human life" (Guantao, as quoted in Lin, p. 178). Through self-assertion, self-exploration, and self-fulfillment (the humanist quest of the new intellectual discourse), a new soul was nurtured by a new culture reemerging in China, that cannot be stopped by tanks and guns.

Chinese scholars and reformers of the Post-Mao era were influenced by Western thinkers from Kant and Hegel to Nietzsche and Heidegger (Lin, 1994). Psychology, after decades of being denounced as pseudoscience, suddenly became a serious subject of inquiry with theories of psychoanalysis, Abraham Maslow's humanistic psychology, and Piaget's developmental psychology drawing the greatest attention. Representative works of Freud, Jung, Adler, Fromm, and others were translated and often cited to support new innovations in interpreting Marx.

Depth psychology emerged as the interest of reformers encompassed intuition, inspiration, and creativity as they sought to explore a multilayered, multidimensional, and multifunctional process. Scholars explain inspiration as "the power of intuitive thinking," which is "formed and developed when the subject uses his personal experience, feeling, and conceptual knowledge, forms, and methods in an integrative, holistic way" (Lin, 1993, p. 176).

Ancient Chinese philosophers and writers have also sought answers to many of the same existential questions posed by Kierkegaard and Nietzsche. For instance, Lao Tzu, author of the famous Taoist treatise, the *Tao Te Ching* (Lao-Tzu, Trans, Mitchell, 1998), emphasized that evil is not a force to resist but rather a state of disharmony with the universal process. This freedom from moral categories is similar to the existential notion that there is no absolute evil. Rather, human beings encompass both good and evil. Lao Tzu also talked frequently of paradoxes and the paradoxical nature of being human; a theme quite prevalent in existential psychology.

Despite the cultural challenges, there is a natural convergence between existential psychology and traditional Chinese thought. In fact, when teaching existential psychology in the West, it is not uncommon to hear students make reference to how similar it sounds to Eastern thought. It may very well be that no Western psychotherapy theory has as much natural convergence with Eastern thought as existential psychology. However, there are areas of dissonance that come into view when attempting to apply existential ideas to Chinese culture, such as the differing values placed on emotional expression, the importance of individual insight versus familial or societal harmony, and the duration of psychotherapy needed to produce meaningful change.

Beginning the Dialogue

Five representatives from the Colorado School of Professional Psychology of the University of the Rockies embarked on a trip to China in March, 2008. The goal of the trip was to engage in culturally-sensitive dialogues with Chinese graduate students, professors, and psychotherapists regarding existential-integrative psychology. Louis Hoffman, Francis Kaklauskas, Christy Dyer, Michael M. Dow, and Elizabeth Saxon were joined in Hong Kong by Mark Yang and Albert Chan in communicating with the Chinese academic psychology community regarding existential-integrative psychology and how such a psychology might be applied in the Chinese context. The forum for these dialogues included a series of workshops and guest lectures at Chinese colleges and universities in Hong Kong and Beijing. Informal avenues, such as site seeing, multi-course meals, and late night card games also gave rise to passionate and informative discussions. The expectation was that the Chinese participants would examine models of existential-integrative psychotherapy within their own cultural context and understanding of psychology while determining for themselves how well the model fit with their clinical settings and clientèle.

Existential Dialogues in Hong Kong

The first East-West dialogue took place at the City College of Hong Kong between the University of the Rockies group and Yang's class of masters level psychology students. After introductions, Yang lectured briefly on the basics of existential-integrative psychology. Λ case study was presented by a Hong Kong student and then utilized by the group to illustrate examples of the existential approach and to launch discussions and an exchange of ideas between the two groups. The Hong Kong students described typical challenges they faced in counseling clients who, due to cultural influences, were resistant to sharing emotions, felt burdened to meet familial obligations, and to succeed financially. Although the Chinese psychology students were enthusiastic about the existential approach, they believed that getting their clients to buy into this form of therapy would be difficult as the clients expect the psychotherapist to act as the "expert" and provide a quick, inexpensive fix to their mental health and interpersonal problems. Generally speaking, the existential model of psychology does not embrace the "quick fix" approach.

Louis Hoffman and Mark Yang lectured on existential-integrative psychology at three additional workshops held at the Hong Kong Institute of Christian Counselors. Francis Kaklauskas, Michael M. Dow, Christy Dyer, and Elizabeth Saxon gave brief presentations on related topics including mindfulness-based approaches to psychotherapy, Buddhist psychology, and Rollo May's theories regarding myth. Hong Kong students volunteered to provide case demonstrations and role plays. Hong Kong psychotherapists had already considered many of the difficulties of this cross-cultural integration, from the applicability of James' functionalism to contemporary Chinese culture to whether Freud, Adler, Jung, or Klein had the most accurate and applicable theory of personality.

Through dialogue, it was evident to all engaged in the discussions that while Hong Kong appears to be very Westernized on the surface, traditional Chinese cultural beliefs run much deeper than the recent impact of Westernization. For generations, the Chinese have emphasized the importance of the collective identity, group and familial affiliation, filial piety, traditional gender and family roles, and not "losing face." An applicable psychotherapy needs to incorporate these cultural subtexts.

To a surprising extent, the case examples that Hong Kong students presented were similar to those Western psychologists are familiar with, characterized by client complaints of financial stress, depression, relationship problems, and anxiety about career decisions. There were some striking differences as well. Among the Chinese, mental health issues continue to carry enormous stigma and shame, and homosexuality remains a somewhat taboo topic. A pressure to conform to societal norms appeared to occupy a more central place among the concerns of the average person, including both clients and psychotherapists.

In presentations on mindfulness and existential psychotherapy, it was interesting that this concept and practice originating in the East was largely unknown to the Hong Kong audiences (with the exception of the students of Helen Ma, a professor at the University of Hong Kong whose research and practice integrates mindfulness and psychotherapy). Instructors at the Hong Kong Institute of Christian Counselors explained that for most Hong Kong Chinese, Buddhism is generally viewed as an outmoded superstition associated with the distant past. Christianity and non-religious oriented thinking are more associated with a modern perspective. Although it is difficult to draw sweeping conclusions from this brief encounter, it appeared that the people of Hong Kong see themselves as quite different from mainland China, and pride themselves on being more modern and Westernized. Yet, they also retain a distinctly Asian identity and value system.

Existential Dialogues in Beijing

The next stop for the University of the Rockies contingent was Beijing, where Louis Hoffman and Mark Yang lectured on existential psychology at a one-day workshop held at the China Youth Polytechnic Institute. Louis Hoffman also demonstrated a role play with a Chinese student based on an actual case involving a hotline client experiencing suicidal and homicidal ideation. Group discussions between the Chinese students and the Western visitors followed. Topics included Maslow's *Hierarchy of Needs*, Victor Frankl's book *Man's Search for Meaning*, and the differences between existential guilt and neurotic guilt.

During the Beijing training, some of the challenges that arose included issues with translating very abstract, Western conceptualizations of existential psychology into language familiar to the Chinese. Quite often the nuance of ideas was lost in translation and, as a result, questions such as the one regarding the difference between existential and neurotic guilt were repeated. Additionally, the practical matter of translating Hoffman's role play with the Chinese student was slow as it required two interpreters translating consecutively so that both the Chinese-speaking and English-speaking audiences could understand the exchanges. These and other challenges, as well as congruences and future opportunities, will be discussed in the following section.

Challenges and Future Opportunities

There are many obstacles to the realization of existential-integrative psychology as a widely-used model of psychotherapy in China. Differences between Western and Eastern views of the self, specifically the importance that the Chinese place on the collective identity and their emphasis on group and familial affiliation, appear to contradict existential themes of individual introspection and choice. The widespread use of behavioral models of psychotherapy in mainland China poses another challenge to introducing existential psychology as a viable mode of treatment. Problems with translation as well as a history of censorship create a formidable obstacle to those wishing to convey the tenets of existential-integrative psychology to Chinese-speaking audiences. Furthermore, cultural taboos against the open expression of emotion are also viewed by many as a problem in adopting a mode of psychotherapy that encourages emotional exploration and expression.

In addition to challenges and obstacles, there are also many opportunities and convergences. When the disparities between Eastern and Western views are investigated at a deeper level, congruence begins to emerge, and opportunities for Eastern and Western schools of thought to engage in constructive dialogue present themselves.

Western and Eastern Views of Self

Historically, existential psychology focuses on an individualistic view of the self that is conceived as engaging in various personal struggles: between freedom and responsibility, expansion versus constriction, and the maladaptive defenses developed to avoid confronting the anxiety of death (Schneider, 2008a; 2008b). The interdependent, family-based nature of the Chinese self, cultural norms against emotional exploration and self-absorption, as well as differing views on issues of authority and power, all appear, at least on the surface, to be incongruent with these basic tenants of existential psychology.

Chinese society was built upon Confucian values, acknowledging piety, obedience, and respect as the primary virtues while maintaining a vast web of communications and economic relations on the basis of a shared sense of what could and could not be done (Malloch, 2006). The Chinese parents' perception of attributes of the ideal child are closely related to traditional values in Chinese culture and include good academic outcome, positive attitude toward studying, fulfillment of responsibility in studying, and high education attainment (Shek & Chan, 1999). The Chinese term "tinghua" carries the connotation of children conforming unquestionably their parents' bidding. It corresponds precisely to what Kant termed "self-inflicted immaturity" or the "incapacity to use one's own understanding without the guidance of others," in his famous definition of the Enlightenment (as cited in Lin, 1994, p. 628).

The concept of familial piety emerged repeatedly in the dialogues with Chinese psychotherapists. The contemporary Chinese often appear conflicted between respecting their long cultural and family histories and adopting the individualistic orientation towards life imported from the West. Individual growth, if too far afield, is often viewed as a threat that will disturb the harmony of the collective whole. These forces clash powerfully, and no simple answer for this dialectic is readily available for any unique individual or for the culture at large.

Conversely, the incongruousness offers a window of opportunity to explore how Eastern thought might sharpen and improve Western existential psychological theories. Rather than encouraging the Chinese to change their views of the world and the self, perhaps Western existential psychologists could strive to integrate more Eastern conceptions to their theories by giving more credence to the inter-relatedness of human beings.[2] In many ways, this is already inherent in the existential understanding of the paradoxes of self, but it has received only limited attention in the psychological literature (see Hoffman et al, in press) and more often has been misrepresented in many portrayals of existential thought. This challenge is also addressed by Chan in Chapter 17.

Emotional Expression

Emotion, as we have noted, is another challenge for existential psychology in Eastern settings. Again, this may not be as hard to overcome as it may initially appear. Traditional Chinese poetry, for example, is often described as expressing emotions directly via visual imagery of the natural world (Sun, 1995). The speaker implies emotion powerfully through his or her selection of images and word choice and, one could argue, expresses it even more directly, but without using emotion words attributed to the self (Owen, 1980; Sun, 1995). One might consider that there are alternative, less individually centered forms of emotional expression that represent equally existentially honest confrontations with life than the Western style

---

[2] It should be noted, however, that much of existential thought, including existential psychology, has been inaccurately portrayed as being more individualistic than it is in reality. Beginning with Kierkegaard, and even in Sartre who is considered by some as the height of individualism in existential thought, existentialists gave much credence to the need for and influence of culture, community, and others. For example, Sartre maintained that without others, there could be no self understanding. This, however, is different than the more culturally rooted understanding of community and the collectivist perspectives evident in the East-West dialogue.

of more overt personal expression of "deep" emotion. Both Americans and Chinese alike benefit from examining the ways in which cultural influences have shaped their understanding of human behavior and thought processes.

Many potential answers to the challenges also emerged through the dialogues. For example, the most difficult problem that seemed to repeatedly emerge was the avoidance of overt emotional expression in Chinese culture. Expression of emotion is considered risky as it threatens the peace of the collective. Over-emotionality is seen as the gateway to disharmony and conflict. Existential therapy, as a phenomenological and experiential therapy, values the experiencing and expressing of emotion. The example that emerged in one of the case discussions in Hong Kong was that the experiencing and expressing of emotion does not need to be "Hollywood emotion." A person can quietly and calmly experience deep levels of emotion and interact from this place without the more dramatic expressions of the emotional experience.[3] The lesson learned was that emotional expression is no less necessary in China, but may look quite different than it typically does in the United States.

Lost in Translation

Problems with translation offer another challenge to the development of existential psychology in China. Direct translations of Western texts into Chinese are limited by language, the translator's understanding of the topics, and are subject to cultural biases (Chang et al., 1998). The same limitations exist when English-speaking educators present complex, abstract concepts to Chinese-speaking audiences. Additionally, few existential psychological texts have actually been translated into Mandarin Chinese.

In Hong Kong, the dialogues were fast paced and fruitful, as most of the individuals in the audience were able to discuss the topics in English and even help with the translation of some difficult concepts. Many psychological words do not have an equivalent Cantonese translation, and it was typical to have discussions in which most of the words were spoken in Cantonese with terms such as "countertransference" and "meta-analysis" spoken in English. Some students used German, French, and Japanese words from original texts in addition to explaining the differences between the Cantonese and Mandarin understanding of psychological

---

[3] In actuality, this is likely more true to many of the early existentialists in their approach to emotion. For example, Nietzsche was a fairly emotionally contained individual, but he nonetheless advocated that emotions should not be denied and needed to be experienced.

terms. This created an atmosphere that clearly illustrated how powerfully language impacts thought and culture.

In Beijing, our dialogues were slower as most communication had to be translated by multiple interpreters. As in Hong Kong, the audiences wanted their Western guests to provide examples of what psychotherapy looks like in North America. Role playing produced a fascinating slowing of the therapeutic process. A Chinese student speaking Mandarin presented a client. This communication was translated into English and then the English reply was translated back into Mandarin. Although one might imagine that such a process would become tedious, the opposite was true. During the translation process, all involved had additional time to digest the content and feeling of each statement. The cultural norms and niceties of communication were stripped away. This produced more direct communication that quickly moved to the heart of the matter.

Other challenges include the Chinese psychology programs' lack of funding to purchase Western text books. Censorship of reading materials imposed by the Communist government may also restrict the availability of certain psychology books, especially those deemed of an inflammatory nature, a threat to social harmony, or critical of the government.[4] As some Chinese psychologists explained, while Christianity is tolerated in a few state-sanctioned churches, publications that include explicitly Christian themes are often subject to state censorship because they are considered an implicit threat to the communist regime and, in particular, the social harmony it is trying to protect.

Social scientists have recently engaged in addressing numerous aspects of religious revival in China (Holyoak, 2007). Religion, in ways, represents the ongoing dialogue regarding state control of social organizations and the willingness of local authorities to delegate responsibility for social welfare if acceptable substitutes arise (Sing-Kiat Ting & Watson, 2007).Time will dictate whether existential thought will be deemed acceptable by censorship authorities in mainland China, but we hope that if existential thinkers demonstrate appropriate respect for cultural differences that it will not be deemed a threat to social harmony. With these particular challenges of language and translation come the

---

[4] This illustrates an important point for respecting cultural difference. In the West, it is typical to view censorship as being entirely negative. However, in this context, the positive motivation of censorship is evident (i.e., the maintenance of harmony). It is important that Westerners do not impose their negative bias regarding censorship upon Chinese culture. Instead, it is important that Westerners, when writing to audiences that includes individuals in China, respect these differences and try to approach relevant topics with appropriate sensitivity.

opportunities for Chinese scholars to adapt concepts of existentialism to their own vernacular, essentially creating their own vocabulary in which to express existential concepts.

The Prevalence of Brief Therapy

As mentioned previously, the pragmatic approach of behavioral therapy is much more common in mainland China than insight-oriented therapies. According to Chang et al. (1998), mental health services are frequently provided in mainland China via general outpatient hospital clinics. These services generally consist of 10 to 20 minute drop-in appointments during which the patient receives a brief assessment, direct advice, psychoeducation, supportive listening, and prescription medication if needed. An on-going, therapeutic relationship is not commonly developed and follow-up appointments are not scheduled. For example, because many Chinese people put considerable emphasis on academic achievement, therapists can design courses or programs that are educational in nature. Instructions using a cognitive-behavioral training approach within a psychosocial educational intervention may generate better outcomes within a traditional Chinese population than an emotion-focused intervention (Chan & Palley, 2005). As the need is great and resources are minimal, such adaptations are necessary and appropriate. Until these conditions change and there are more psychological resources available, it may be beneficial for Chinese psychologists to develop similar educational and consulting adaptations with existential sensitivities along with the more traditional existential therapy options.

It is common for people to comment on the similarity between Eastern thought and existential psychology. Both share an appreciation of suffering, paradox, and introspection. The semblance between writers such as Lao Tzu and many existential writers is also quite startling. They share a recognition that the deeper changes often occur slowly. However, many in China, despite the recognition of needing discipline and time for deeper change, see psychotherapy in a different context. It may be that existential psychotherapy, even in the therapeutic applications, needs to be re-envisioned, at times, to meet certain cultural needs that mandate a more time-limited focus. Longer-term approaches could be conceptualized as connected to a different type of change that is slower, deeper, and akin to change as discussed by the Taoist philosophers. As noted in Chapter 1, similar adaptations already exist.

Given the huge need for mental health services and the shortage of mental health professionals, it is only to be expected that market forces will create a demand for brief, pragmatic approaches that allow a larger volume of patients to be seen. However, this need not be seen as antithetical to the development of more open-ended approaches. In fact, the familiarity of brief therapy among mainland Chinese is a potential stepping stone to introduce more ongoing, intensive models of psychotherapy such as existential-integrative psychology.

While there are many psychological problems that can be addressed in a brief way, there are many others that only yield to a more in-depth approach. Additionally, as the population becomes more sophisticated in terms of what they want and expect out of psychotherapy, such approaches will likely become more in demand. As awareness of the need for mental health services in China increases, especially in the wake of the devastating 2008 Sichuan earthquake, the Chinese are likely to be more willing to explore alternatives to short-term psychological interventions.

The Importance of Choice

Many Westerners who interact with Asian cultures and specifically communist countries, such as China, mistakenly believe that the natives embrace a collective identity blindly, without thought or choice. In fact, there has been an ongoing debate in China regarding the nature of self and culture for the past four decades. The first signs of the "revival of human nature" or the "humanist quest" appeared in the late 1960's and became a national movement with the "discussions on the criteria of truth," the first major intellectual event since 1978 (Lin, 1993).

When the era of "reform and opening-up" began in 1978, it was the emergence of central concern of the discourse of China's modernization (Lin, 1993). Two concepts preoccupied the participants: self and culture. The urge for self-realization merged with the quest for cultural identity, foreshadowing a long process of the rebirth of China's soul. The discussions yielded a decisive step toward the rediscovery of individuals in contemporary China by triggering a "Thought Emancipation Movement" that spread the message of independent thinking across the entire country. Deprived of its Marxist rhetoric, the central issue of the debate was: Does the person exist apart from being a tool of the Party, class struggle, or the proletariat cause of communist (Lin, 1994)?

Similarly, possible resolutions to the collectivist challenge also emerged. It may be, too, that much of existential psychology has been over identified with individualism. Perhaps deep in the Chinese collective psyche there is a fear that self-awareness of emotion creates conflict with others and personal growth is too individualistic (see also Ch. 17). Existential philosophy and psychology, engaged at a deep level, emphasizes the limitation of individual striving and recognizes the power and importance of many levels of inter-relationship.

Nonetheless, there remains an individualist slant to much of the Western existentialist thinking. The Chinese participants, however, did not consider this as big of a challenge as the presenters anticipated. The lesson that emerged was that the Chinese recognized the value of individual choice, but valued the choice to prioritize the collective. Thus, choice and the recognition that one must own one's choices are shared by both cultures; the different cultures just value different decisions.

Future Directions

A number of the contributors to this book besides the authors of this chapter, including Myrtle Heery, Erik Craig, and Kirk Schneider, have made trips to Eastern countries that have created excitement about the future of this dialogue. Preparations are being made for future and regular trips to China and other Eastern countries by individuals from the University of the Rockies with hopes to continue the dialogue and exchange of ideas. Additionally, an Existential Psychology East-West Conference is set to begin in 2010 in Nanjing and then continue every other year in different locations in the East. The excitement about the possibilities of continuing the dialogue on existential psychology is rapidly growing.

Due to the devastation left in the wake of the 2008 earthquake in Sichuan Province, China recently has been facing a mental health crisis of unimaginable proportions. The official death toll stands at 69,107, with an estimated 10,000 school children among the victims (Wong, 2008). Grieving parents who have lost their only offspring due to China's one-child per family law have been particularly traumatized. Brief therapy focused on symptom alleviation is not likely to bring relief to the thousands who have lost close family members and friends, not to mention their homes and livelihoods. Existential issues also have been brought to the forefront of Chinese mental health needs through this tragedy, and no doubt will need continued exploration over time.

Since the Sichuan earthquake, there has been an increased awareness in China of the need to train psychotherapists in trauma work. Hoffman and Yang are currently arranging for an existential psychology workshop to take place in Chengdu. Additionally, Saxon and Dyer will be holding discussions with earthquake relief workers as well as psychiatrists from West China University Hospital on working with survivors experiencing traumatic brain injuries and posttraumatic stress disorder. The potential for joint research and cultural exchange will further contribute to greater understanding of future directions facing both countries in the mental health field for the 21st century.

References

Chang, D.F., Tong, J., Qija, S, & Zeng, Q. (2005). Letting a hundred flowers bloom: Counseling and psychotherapy in the People's Republic of China. *Journal of Mental Health Counseling, 27* (2), pp. 104-114

Chan, C. L., & Palley, H. A. (2005). The use of traditional Chinese culture and values in social work health care related interventions in Hong Kong. *Health and Social Work, 30* (1), 76-78.

Hoffman, L., Stewart, S., Warren, D., & Meek., L. (in press). Toward a sustainable myth of self: An existential response to the postmodern condition. *Journal of Humanistic Psychology.*

Holyoak, L. (2007). Obstacles to rural development in China: Local minorities, cadres, and ritual. *Urban Anthropology & Studies of Cultural Systems & World Economic Development, 36* (1-2), 73-88.

Lin, T. (1993). A search for China's soul. *Daedalus, 122* (2), 171-181.

Lin, T. (1994). Subjectivity: Marxism and "The Spiritual" in China since Mao. *Philosophy East & West, 44*(4), 613-638.

Malloch, T. R. (2006). *Spiritual enterprise*. New York: Encounter Books.

Mosig, Y. D. (2006). Conceptions of the self in Western and Eastern psychology. *Journal of Theoretical and Philosophical Psychology, 26*, 39-50.

Qian, M. & Chen, Z. (1998). Behavior therapy in the People's Republic of China. In T. P. S. Oei (Ed.), *Behavior therapy and cognitive behavior therapy in Asia* (pp. 33 – 46). Glebe, New South Wales: Edumedia.

Schneider, K. J. (2008a). The theory of the existential-integrative (EI) approach. In K. J. Schneider (Ed.), *Existential-integrative psychotherapy: Guideposts to the core of practice* (pp. 35-48). New York: Routledge.

Schneider, K. J. (2008b). Therapeutic implications of the theory. In K. J. Schneider (Ed.), *Existential-integrative psychotherapy: Guideposts to the core of practice* (pp. 49-87)). New York: Routledge.

Shek, D. T. L., & Chan, L. K. (1999). Hong Kong Chinese parents' perceptions of the ideal child. *Journal of Psychology, 133*(3), 291.

Sing-Kiat Ting, R. & Watson, T. (2007). Is suffering good? An explorative study on the religious persecution among Chinese pastors. *Journal of Psychology and Theology, 35* (3), 202-211.

Sun, C. C. (1995). *Pearls from the dragon's mouth: Evocation of scene and feeling in Chinese poetry*. Ann Arbor, MI: University of Michigan Press.

Veith, I. (1997). *Huang Ti nei ching su wen: The yellow emperor's classic of internal medicine*. Selangor Darul Ehsan, Malaysia: Pelanduck Publications.

The US - China Business Council. (2008, January 31). *Forecast 2008: China's economy*. Retrieved July 31, 2008, from: http://uschina.org/public/documents/2008/02/2008-china-economy.pdf

Wong, E. (2008, June 4). Chinese Stifle Grieving Parents' Protest of Shabby School Construction. *The New York Times*. Retrieved July 31, 2008, from: http://www.nytimes.com/2008/06/04/world/asia/04china.html?scp=2&sq=Chinese+Parents&st=nyt

4

Tao, Dasein, and Psyche:
Shared Grounds for Depth Psychotherapy[1]

Erik Craig

Tao, Dasein, and Psyche: Such strange and disparate terms from such distant and yet resonant times and traditions. From ancient far Eastern philosophy, the venerable Tao discloses the Way, the Way of Being itself, the Ground or Source of all that is, as well as the teaching that arises from this fundament. From modern and post-modern Western philosophy, the miraculous Dasein, reveals that being who seems, among all others, to be concerned with understanding being, including its own being, that kind of being we call human. Finally, from Greek mythology and, later, from that branch of Western scientific medicine called psychoanalysis, the sonorous Psyche announces the human being's soul, the life of the soul, that richly textured, sumptuously colored fabric of lived experience that imbues our very own existence with passion and meaning. While the Tao reminds us of all that is and of our humble participation in this wholeness, it is Dasein as which we dwell that opens us to this wholeness as inseparable oneness with it, and Psyche that endows this open dwelling with pathos, value, and wonder. And all this, ultimately, a mystery and unspeakable.

This chapter dialogues the thought and practice of three traditions of psychotherapy: Tao psychotherapy, daseinsanalysis, and psychoanalysis, the first being from the East and the latter two from the West.[2] My hope is

---

[1] The original version of this chapter was written as an invited address for The Society for Humanistic Psychology at the American Psychological Association's 2006 Annual Convention in New Orleans, LA. Due to space constraints, some of the extended footnotes of the chapter had to be removed. For the full version of this paper including the extended footnotes, please contact the author.

[2] Today Western psychoanalytic and existential psychotherapies and Eastern psychotherapies can each count among their practitioners many distinctive approaches. I will be dialoging only one specific approach from each of these broader traditions: from psychoanalysis, Freud's classical humanistic psychoanalysis; from existential therapy, Medard Boss's daseinsanalysis, the first systematic approach to existential depth psychotherapy; and from the East, Korean psychiatrist, Rhee Dongshick's Tao

to uncover some shared grounds for understanding human existence and human suffering as well as our care for them in depth oriented psychotherapy. Ultimately my question is this: What is it that makes depth psychotherapy even possible in the first place? My approach will be one of open, immediate inquiry, not authoritative, apodictic speech: I intend to ask, not tell.

I will begin with a brief explication of what I mean as an existential psychotherapist by the term depth psychotherapy, and then go on to identify and discuss epistemological concerns regarding otherness and ownness. Next, I will briefly explicate the three ontological domains of being--Tao, Dasein, and Psyche--with which Tao psychotherapy, daseinsanalytic psychotherapy, and psychoanalytic psychotherapy are respectively concerned. Finally, I will address foundational depth psychotherapeutic premises and promises held in common by practitioners of psychoanalytic, daseinsanalytic, and Tao psychotherapies.

What is Depth Psychotherapy?

Depth psychology (*Tiefenpsychologie*, German), is a term first used by Eugen Bleuler (1910) to designate, in everyday language, the approach to psychological treatment, called *Psychoanalyse* founded by Sigmund Freud. Contrary to the common erroneous belief that depth psychology refers to Jungian psychology exclusively, today, depth psychology is more widely and accurately used to refer to all those psychologies that developed out of Freud's psychoanalysis, including, but not limited to, classical psychoanalysis, analytical psychology, object relations, psychoanalytic ego psychology, psychoanalytic self psychology, interpersonal psychiatry, psychodynamic psychology, intersubjective psychoanalysis, relational psychoanalysis, existential analysis, and so forth. Certainly Eastern psychologies, with their grounding in ancient philosophical traditions, are also among today's most significant depth psychologies.

The foundational claim of all depth psychologies is that the totality of the human remains largely hidden to the eye and even to thought at all. In other words, depth psychologies all acknowledge the indisputable reality of ontological secrecy, not only in the human but in everything that is. Thus, depth psychology is simply the kind of psychology that takes seriously the unseen, the unthought, and, even, the unthinkable and

---

psychotherapy that seeks the essential unity of Western depth psychotherapies with Eastern philosophical traditions such as Confucianism, Buddhism, Tao, and Zen.

unspeakable. Most simply put, depth psychology is *"a psychology of the invisible, a psychology of the secret, a psychology of concealment as such"* (Craig, 2007, p. 317). Depth *psychotherapies*, therefore, all have at least two purposes in common: first, to coax gently out of the darkness those secrets that contain the key to understanding the individual's suffering, and, second, to liberate those possibilities for being that have been held hostage by that suffering.

Ironically, one could say that the essence of Western depth psychology and depth psychotherapy was actually disclosed in the East millennia before psychology as a field even existed at all. Recall this from the first chapter of the *Tao Te Ching*:

> Free from desire, you realize mystery.
> Caught in desire, you see only the manifestations.
>
> Yet mystery and manifestations
> Arise from the same source.
> This source is called darkness.
>
> Darkness within darkness.
> The gateway to all understanding.
> (S. Mitchell, Trans. 1988, Ch. 1)

How is it with Otherness?

When engaging in a discourse within and between such radically different, culturally grounded, philosophical and healing traditions as those found in Eastern and Western psychologies, one can hardly avoid asking, "How can we aspire to understand the so-called other, or otherness as such?" In this case, for example, having grown up in a poor, little New England village, through and through an ordinary Westerner, and a 20th century one at that, how can I hope to understand something that arose millennia ago, from the opposite side of the earth, within a culture and ethos, a people and time, so palpably other than my own? What can I say of what I am not? How can we meet and understand one another within the complexity of unity and diversity, the predicament, within our common humanity, of our otherness? How can we bridge these remote cultures of the East and West which have given rise to such distinctive languages for being? How can we rise to the challenges inherent in comparative philosophy and practice? Ultimately, how can we realize and put to good account our own possibilities for human empathy.

It is this same question of whether we can truly grasp otherness that one evening nearly 80 years ago led to an impasse in a discussion with Martin Heidegger. According to Petzet (1993) and Pöggeler (1987), Heidegger joined some colleagues for discussion after a 1930 lecture in Bremen, Germany. When the conversation floundered on the problem of human empathy, Heidegger asked the host for a copy of Martin Buber's translations of the *Parables of Chuang-tzu* and, that delivered, proceeded to read the following allegory:

> Chuang Tzu and Hui Tzu
> Were crossing Hao river
> By the dam.
>
> Chuang said:
> "See how free
> The fishes leap and dart:
> That is their happiness."
>
> Hui replied:
> "Since you are not a fish
> How do you know
> What makes fishes happy?"
>
> Chuang said:
> "Since you are not I
> How can you possibly know
> That I do not know
> What makes fishes happy?"
>
> Hui argued:
> If I, not being you,
> Cannot know what you know
> It follows that you
> Not being a fish
> Cannot know what they know.
>
> Chuang said:
> Wait a minute!

Let us get back
To the original question.
What you asked me was
How do you know
What makes fishes happy?'
From the terms of your question
You evidently know I know
What makes fishes happy.

I know the joy of fishes
In the river
Through my own joy, as I go walking
Along the same river.
[Merton, Trans., 2004, pp. 109-110]

With this allegory Heidegger hoped to free up the discussion of how it is human beings can grasp the otherness of others. The philosopher's primary gesture, as I understand it, was to suggest the possibility that we know otherness by being fully in our ownness, that when we mindfully participate in the immediacy of our own individual human existence we also participate in our common humanity and, with this, in the event of Being itself. The key to the riddle is in the line "as I go walking along the same river." Only as you and I "walk along the river," that is, allow ourselves to be in the world freely and openly as we are, can we at all know what it is like for another to walk and to be as well. For Heidegger, to empathize with another meant, first of all, to be on our own way in the world. As the Zen saying goes, "The wondrous Tao consists in carrying water and chopping wood." Mindfully engaging in the immediate projects of our everyday lives, whether carrying water, chopping wood, cleaning the house, or driving to work, we experience the Tao and, through this, begin to know what it is like for others to do so as well. As Mitchell put it in his rendering of chapter 70 of the *Tao Te Ching* (trans.,1988): "If you want to know me, look inside your heart." Such advice comes close to the recommendation in our field that those who practice psychotherapy and psychoanalysis begin with themselves?

Naturally, we should not let Chuang Tzu's fishes allegory lull us into smugly thinking that, within our common humanity, human difference and diversity are insignificant. There were still differences between Chuang Tzu and Hui Tzu, as there are between you and me, between those of us from the East and those of us from the West. Certainly, human love relations give ample testimony that empathy is no easy achievement even among those who are closest to us. However, Heidegger's use of Chuang Tzu's allegory serves to remind us that the beginning of human empathy and human understanding is to be genuinely on our own way, or, as Le Guin (1997) put it, to "be the riverbed of the world" (p.38).

How is it with Ownness?

The problem of otherness always presumes the problem of ownness. How we are as ourselves inevitably shapes how we are with others. Our own origins and circumstances, whether Eastern or Western, unavoidably structure and color our understanding of each others' traditions, indeed, of each other as individuals. Whenever we seek to understand something, in this case Eastern and Western depth psychotherapy, we always bring our own fore knowledge, our own predispositions, our own pre-understanding to the table of our inquiry. For existential investigators, it is important to recognize and declare our pre-understanding or orientation in advance.

Explicating My Predisposition

It is with some apprehension that I write this chapter in the first place. Not only do I fear of my own possibilities for misappropriation, especially in the form of what I call Western academic colonialism, but also I am well aware of the even more fundamental circumstance that "The Tao that can be told is not the eternal Tao" (S. Mitchell, Trans., 1988, Ch. 1).

With respect to the first concern, Western misappropriation, it is important to at least declare my hermeneutic stance or *démarche*[3] as

---

[3] A phenomenological hermeneutic researcher understands that all knowledge or understanding is perspectival; one always has a predisposition to phenomena that unavoidably shapes one's understanding of them. Phenomenological researchers acknowledge and declare, at least to the extent possible or feasible, the nature and epistemological significance of their predisposition or foreknowledge. Naturally, the way researchers handle their predispositions depends largely on their own epistemological beliefs. Some phenomenologists believe that they can suspend or bracket out their presuppositions or, in the language of depth psychology, transferences, and thus achieve a pure, descriptive, and even transcendental understanding of a given phenomenon. Other phenomenologists, believe that one can never escape the influence of one's personal, cultural, and linguistic perspectives, sometimes called one's throwness. Such existential or hermeneutic phenomenologists are content with a fundamentally historical, contextualized, or relational understanding of phenomena; do not aspire to absolute, objective interpretations; and, therefore, necessarily live with more uncertainty than the more pure, descriptive, or transcendental phenomenologists, who find refuge in the certainty of

being guided, on the one hand, by the philosophically grounded hermeneutic phenomenology of Martin Heidegger's *Daseinsanalytik* and, on the other hand, by the everyday demands of an existential or daseinsanalytic psychotherapeutic practice. In the present situation, I justify the use of a daseinsanalytic approach on three grounds.

First, daseinsanalysis strives, above all and to the extent possible, not to impose predetermined concepts and theories on what is encountered but, rather, to proceed phenomenologically, that is, to allow *what* is to show itself precisely as that which it is and is on its way to being. In other words, a daseinsanalyst is forewarned by Hamlet's caution that there are more things in heaven and earth than are dreamt of in our philosophy. One of Freud's (1892-94/1966) favorite stories of Charcot also comes to mind: when Freud commented that one of the French physician's observations contradicted prevailing theory, Charcot rebuked him with the words, "La théorie c'est bon; mais ça n'empêche pas d'exister" (Theory is good; but it doesn't prevent things from existing, p. 139). Daseinsanalysis takes such openness to what is very seriously and it is just this commitment to radical openness in scientific, philosophic, and therapeutic inquiry that allows me to dare to employ a daseinsanalytic *démarche* in approaching or allowing myself to be approached by the Tao.

Another ground upon which I justify using a daseinsanalytic perspective is that we now know that the founder of *Daseinsanalytik*, Martin Heidegger, had studied Taoist texts and, in spite of his secrecy about them, these studies unquestionably influenced his own thinking. As Graham Parkes (1996) noted, Heidegger's contact with East Asian thought precedes even the writing of his magnum opus, *Being and Time* (1927/1962). Given that Heidegger's own thought was so significantly influenced by ancient wisdoms of the East, we ought not be surprised to find the profound thematic affinities that immediately strike us when reading his texts along with the *Tao Te Ching*.

---

objective, ahistorical, absolute meaning and truth. Daseinsanalysts, especially those who follow the spirit of the early Heidegger (1927/1962) of *Being and Time*, seek to be especially cognizant of their foreknowledge or predispositional relationship with phenomena, not with the vain aspiration of overcoming this predisposition but, rather, like the modern psychoanalysts use of transference and countertransference, with the hope of employing it in the service of minimizing concealment and maximizing disclosure of the phenomenon in question. In keeping with this spirit of Heideggerian, existential, or hermeneutic phenomenology, therefore, here I use the French word *démarche*, meaning "step" or "gait," to designate what more pure phenomenologists might call set, stance, or lens. The reason I prefer the word *démarche* is that it captures the sense of motion and "being on a path" of thinking that the other more commonly used English words do not.

The final ground upon which I to justify using a daseinsanalytic perspective is my intent: namely, to listen for and dialogue basic affinities between the thinking of the East and the West, without prioritizing either or establishing any apodictic, metaphysical equations. My "reading" here is purely heuristic, serving to discover what it is that the East and West share in order to enrich and open up our experience and understanding not only of our being human but also our being psychotherapists.

Explaining My Use of Language

Many students of Eastern thought have pointed out that Western thinkers are almost unnaturally attached to theory and verbal explanation, using it to establish their difference from others and authority over things and, thereby, unwittingly confining themselves to a self made "conceptual prison" (Barrett,1956, p. xvi). Western daseinsanalysts like myself also use concepts. So the question arises, "How might we understand language and our use of concepts such that they do not diminish but rather open up and liberate the phenomena with which we are concerned?" In other words, how might we use language lovingly?

In his little book entitled *Basic Concepts* (*Grundbegriffe*), Heidegger (1981/1993) distinguished basic or "ground concepts" (Grundbegriffe) that bring the world before us from "mere concepts," that "are nothing concrete and lead nowhere" (p. 2). Heidegger saw such basic concepts (*Grundbegriffe*) as a way to "con-ceive," to grasp, to hold that which "grounds everything and gives ground to everything." For Heidegger generally, an authentic language of experience is a way of giving Being a home, a way "to take into care beings as a whole" (p.3). With such care in mind, Heidegger (1947/1977b) once called language the "house of Being" and wrote that "In its home man dwells. Those who create with words are the guardians of this home" (p. 193). If I understand him correctly, the philosopher was not suggesting that language itself was the real, the Tao, but, rather, that language is our way of hosting or shepherding the real. Heidegger might say that it is with language that Dasein "lets beings be the beings they are" (Heidegger, 1943/1977c p. 127f). Thus, for Heidegger, language is our way of disclosing being, of allowing being to be and to show itself, like providing a chair, a bed, or a room for a guest whom we have invited into our home. Is it not often the case that when the guest leaves our home, the thought of the chair, bed, or room still holds the one who was so hosted? So it is with our words: they are not the beings themselves but they hold and host the beings, bringing them before us in the fullness of their being.

Here is an analogy from everyday life. I recall Medard Boss's obvious pleasure in showing me, on the ground floor of his home in Zollikon, Switzerland, the white arm chair where Heidegger would sit to read, meditate, or lecture. Boss always thought of that chair as the "Heidegger chair" and it held the famous philosopher and friend, whether he was in it or not. It seemed to me that whenever Boss spoke of the chair or sat in it, he was with Heidegger, or, rather, Heidegger became present with him. I would suggest that, in a similar way, our words hold, host, serve, or care for Being.

Nevertheless, just as Boss would never mistake or be willing to exchange that arm chair for the actual presence of his friend Heidegger, nor would we mistake or be willing to exchange our concepts of beings for the beings themselves, our concept of Tao for Tao itself. Lying infinitely beyond the concept of Being is Being itself. Here, the first lines of the *Tao Te Ching*:

> The tao that can be told
> Is not the eternal Tao,
> The name that can be named
> Is not the eternal Name.
> (S. Mitchell, Trans., 1988, Chapt. 1)

Those familiar with Eastern thought might be reminded here of the famous distinction between the finger pointing at the moon and the moon itself. This distinction is not intended to disparage fingers, names, or concepts. As limited as they may be, without fingers or words, with what could we host or care for the world? As Rhee Dongshick (2002), the founder of Tao psychotherapy, has suggested in the face of this conundrum, when you have really caught the experience, let go of the words, for only, "Then," as he puts it, "you become friendly with the Tao" (p. 94). Rhee's view concurs with Heidegger's: Although concepts first show us the way to beings, they are not the beings themselves which lie, beyond all pointing and holding, in the breath and heartbeat of lived experience. As Heidegger (1977b/1947) put it: "If man is to find his way again into the nearness of Being he must first learn to exist in the nameless" (p. 199).

With this preliminary disclosure of my own hermeneutic *démarche* at least begun, I can move on to the problems at hand. What are Tao, Dasein, and Psyche and what do they have to do with depth psychotherapy?

Tao, Dasein, and Psyche:
Ontological Grounds for Psychotherapy[4]

Each of the three particular approaches to depth psychology, namely, psychoanalysis, daseinsanalysis, and Tao psychotherapy are grounded in a concern for a particular ontological domain of being. I will touch briefly on each these ontological realms, beginning with the most familiar and delimited, the Psyche of psychoanalysis; moving from there to the least well known, the Dasein of daseinsanalysis; and ending with the oldest and most all encompassing, the Tao of Eastern Philosophy.

Psychoanalysis: The Realm of Psyche
    Even as a young man Freud was hungry for a vocation, a calling, an object of devotion worthy of his intense intellectual fervor. A few years after opening his private practice, he wrote friend and confidant, Wilhelm Fliess, that "a man like me cannot live without a hobby horse, without a consuming passion, without...a tyrant. I have found one. In its service I know no limits. It is psychology, which has always been my distant beckoning goal" (Masson, 1985). Thus it happened that Sigmund Freud, the founder of depth psychology, gave his existence to understanding what he

---

[4] Here we need to distinguish between two aspects of being, the ontic or ontical on the one hand and the ontologic or ontological on the other. The *ontic or ontical refers to the particular beings in the course of our everyday, mundane lives.* Ontic refers to the specific, individual beings that appear to us as we go about living our lives, to the particular beings that show themselves in our ordinary, prosaic existence. *The ontologic or ontological refers, not just to particular beings, but to their "being-ness," to what makes them the very kind of being they are, for example, the treeness of trees, the cowness of cows, the seaness of seas or the humanness of humans.* Ontologically speaking, our human beingness is that way of being in world in every moment of our lives that we have in common with all other human beings in every moment of their lives. The ontologic or ontological refers to what actually makes human beings human beings and not any other kind of being and, thus, to what necessarily obtains in every moment of every human being's life (See Craig, 2008,a). Generally speaking, ontology refers to the philosophical discipline whose task is the study of being. Historically, the aim of ontology is to understand the kind of being (beingness) any particular being is. Phenomenological ontology begins with the everyday appearance of a *particular being* (ontic) in order to understanding its *beingness*, the fundamental structure or essence of *what makes the particular being the kind of being it is*: not just this particular tree, but tree*ness*;, not just this particular human being, but human*ness*; etc. The task of disclosing the ontological characteristics of human beings, beings Martin Heidegger called Dasein, was the whole purpose of his magnum opus, *Being and Time* (1927/1962). This section addresses three different kinds of being (Tao, Dasein, and Psyche) that are not only central to each of the three representative approaches to psychotherapy but also to the existence of psychotherapy as such.

called "the life of the soul" (*Seelenleben*), describing his science of psychoanalysis as *Wissenschaft vom Seelenleben*, a science of the life of the soul (Freud, 1933/1940, p. 4). For Freud, the human psyche or soul (*Seele*) was an ambiguous and indefinable reality, but also that which we hold most dear in our lives. Indeed, the master recommended psychoanalysis, not for its healing potential but, rather for "the truths it contains (*Wahrheitsgehalts*)... about that which comes most near to human beings, namely, their very own essence (*Wesen*)" (Freud, 1933/1940, translation mine, p. 169). There can be no doubt that what he intended to designate by this essence was nothing other than the human "soul" (*Seele*) or "life of the soul" (*Seelenleben*). Freud did not understand the soul as any substantive or transcendental entity but as a kind of historical, cultural, experiential essence, the very heart of an individual's existence as lived. That such a reality eludes precise definition is obvious. In fact, among the many dictionaries of psychoanalysis one will rarely, if ever, find the words psyche, soul, or life of the soul listed among its entries. The limits of language in such ontological domains have been known by philosophers and thinkers from every age and culture. One only has to recall the first lines of the *Tao Te Ching*, cited above: "The tao that can be told is not the eternal Tao" (S. Mitchell, Trans., 1988, Chapt. 1). Not surprisingly, Freud seems also to have felt that to define the soul is to miss it entirely, that, like the Tao, the soul that can be told is not the true soul. But what is this human quiddity, the soul or psyche? Although it has been suggested that what we mean by soul, existentially speaking, is "an individual's *very own situated gathering of lived experience*" (Craig, 2008b, p. 257), even this language fails to capture the flesh and blood essence of our experience whenever we call upon the soul. Could it be that, as a devoted disciple of the unseen and mysterious, Freud was passionately obsessed with the life of the soul not in spite of but, rather, because of the impossibility of ever actually capturing its essence with words?

A thought: *Where Being and mystery lie, there language cannot go.*

Daseinsanalysis: The Realm of Dasein

Just as Freud grounded his entire work and life in the realm of being we call psyche, or soul, existential analysts ground the whole of their scientific and clinical endeavor in human existence as a whole, that is, in that realm of being the philosopher Martin Heidegger designated with the everyday German term *Dasein*. For Heidegger, Dasein meant the existing human both individually and collectively. Dasein refers not just to our human personality or our inner or subjective psychic life, what Freud called

Seelenleben, but rather to our whole existence. Dasein means, literally, a there (*da*)–being (*sein*), a being-there, underscoring our human existence as a realm of world openness, an ever unfolding opening up right here, right now. For Heidegger and his psychological protégés, Ludwig Binswanger and Medard Boss, the respective founders of the approach to existential psychology and psychotherapy called daseinsanalysis, we do not exist "in-there," inside our epidermis, but rather "out-there" in the world. Dasein, that is you and I, exist as being-in-the-world (*In-der-Welt-sein*). With this understanding of human existence as Dasein, Heidegger also sought to overcome what Rollo May (1958) refers to as "the cleavage between subject and object that has bedeviled Western thought and science since shortly after the renaissance" (p.11). Unfettered by such dualism, we no longer find ourselves existing as self contained intra-subjective entities, in any way separate from our world and merely interacting with it but, rather, as encountering our world as a unity, as our very self (See Buber, 1910/1957, p. 37). For example, right now, as I am writing and you are reading, we constitute one another's very existing, we exist inextricably as being-with-one-another, indeed, *as-one-another-being-with-one-another*. For Heidegger, Boss, and Binswanger, to be Dasein is to be a whole realm of world openness, of world open-ing (See Craig, 2008c). Here, Western daseinsanalysis and Eastern Taoist thought are impressively consonant; both perspectives understand that we exist together with one another and with world as a singular unity, as one, or, even better, as *one-ing*. In daseinsanalysis it is understood that we exist in, with, and for one another as a whole realm of relational possibilities. In Taoist thought, as the philosopher and allegorist Chuang Tzu put it, "The universe and I come into being together; and I and everything therein, are ONE" (Giles, 1926, p. 23, capitals original).

Another thought: *Where self lies, there also other: One.*

Eastern Thought: The Realm of the Tao

Just as Freud grounded his work in the intra-subjective realm of being we call psyche, or soul, and existential analysts grounded their endeavors in human existence as a whole, that realm of being human we call Dasein, much of Eastern philosophy is grounded in an even wider domain, that all encompassing realm called the Tao. Tracing the Tao to as early as the fifth or sixth Centuries B.C.E., today the term is generally understood to refer both to the Way of Being and to the virtue of being in accord with this Way of Being. The word Tao means literally means *the Way* and refers to the Way of all that is, the entire spatial-temporal horizon of all the beings that ever have been, that are now, and that will ever be. Therefore, the Tao refers to that which precedes and gives birth to beings as a whole. The realm of the Tao is the realm of the All, taken both as a whole and with respect to each and every particular being that comprises this Whole. Further, the Way is not some static condition but, rather, an immediately present, ever unfolding destining of Being itself. Thus, the entire cosmos, the entire universe of Being has its very own Way, its very own *Waying*, its very own coming-into-presence even right here and now. But more, each individual being manifests an individual Tao or Taoing. Thus, you and I each have our very own Tao, our very own Waying, our very own inimitable coming-into-presence, which has been and is now unfolding. So the Tao refers not just to the comprehensive Way of all Being, but to the distinctive Way of each and every particular being, including each and every one of us here and now as well as each and every one of those whom we serve in our practice of psychotherapy.

The Tao is often thought of as akin to certain Western understandings of Nature as primordial Being. For example, Ellen Chen (1989) speaks of the Tao as "an image (hsiang) of the unnamable Urgrund...the dark hidden Urgrund, the mother of all" (p.63). As this ground of all being, the Tao is the way of Nature itself, which Hölderlin (1952) describes as "older than the ages and above the gods of East and West" (p. 162, translation mine). As Le Guin (1997) puts it the Tao "was born before the gods" (p. 7) and signifies the immanently, unfurling destining of all that is. It is ineffable, mysterious, miraculous, unitive; both human and not human, particular and universal, concrete and unsubstantial, meaningful and meaningless, visible and invisible, real and unreal, something and yet nothing at all. In this ontological sense then, the Tao refers, in part, to what Heidegger called Beingness-as-such (*Seyn*) as well as his understanding of "world" in both the ontic and ontological senses that he designated as "the totality of entities" (*Das All des Seienden*).

Still another thought: *Wherever anything is, wherever you are, there also Tao.*

Tao, Dasein, and Psyche:
Ineluctable Grounds for Depth Psychotherapy

Now, you may be wondering what any of this has to do with the question, "What is it that makes such a process as psychotherapy possible in the first place?" Clearly, if any one of these three domains of being, Tao, Dasein, or Psyche did not exist, there would be no such thing as psychotherapy in the first place. That anything is at all, especially what we call the Tao or Beingness as such, is required for psychotherapy to be. Without Dasein, the kind of being we call human being, the one who has the capacity to be open to being, to perceive and understand being, without this Dasein, psychotherapy could not be. And finally, without psyche or Seele, without soul, that is, without individual and collective experience; without sentience or awareness; without memory, language, culture, and history psychotherapy would not only be unnecessary but nonsense and impossible. The Tao has given birth to the human, the human has given birth to the psyche; all three are necessary preconditions for the psychotherapy to even exist at all. So, ontologically speaking, Tao, Dasein, and Psyche all make any kind of psychotherapy possible in the first place. Remember, none of this has to be at all. It could just as well *not* be. Tao, Dasein, and Psyche are not the kinds of beings to be taken for granted.

As you may have already suspected from the above, whereas Freud's psychoanalysis provides the theoretical and technical foundation for almost all depth psychotherapies today, daseinsanalysis and Eastern thought bring to depth psychology a philosophical, ethical, and ontological foundation for that theory and practice. One's understanding Tao, Dasein, and Psyche is both necessary and essential for the theory and practice of depth psychotherapy, even if one's understanding remains prereflective or even largely unexplicated. In what follows I will show how such a synthesis of certain basic premises and promises of depth psychotherapy from Eastern, existential, and psychoanalytic thought and practice can strengthen and enrich our understanding and conduct of the art and science of depth psychotherapy.

The Shared Premises of Depth Psychotherapy

In the following section, I will briefly discuss four foundational premises for the theory and practice of depth psychotherapy shared by psychoanalysis, Tao psychotherapy, and daseinsanalysis.

The Problem of Suffering
Lying at the very heart of all three traditions of thought and practice is the recognition of the inevitable and unavoidable reality of human suffering. Although as a physician Freud was specifically concerned with the severest forms of what he called "neurotic misery," he also recognized that to be human at all was most assuredly to suffer. His conviction about the ubiquity of human suffering, first implied in his early

remark that the hope of psychoanalysis was in "transforming…hysterical misery into ordinary unhappiness" (Breuer & Freud,1893-1895/1955, p.305), was spelled out quite explicitly in his later works, particularly in his companion works, *Future of an Illusion* (1961b/1927) and *Civilization and its Discontents* (1961a/1930), where he described human suffering as "fatefully inevitable" and threatening from three directions: our bodies "which, are doomed to decay and dissolution," "the external world which, may rage against us with overwhelming and merciless forces of destruction" and, finally, our relations to other human beings, a suffering he acknowledged was "perhaps more painful to us than any other" (Freud,1961/1930, p. 77). Although Freud apparently read very little if any Eastern writings, he was as convinced of the ubiquity of human suffering as the Buddha, whose very first of Four Noble Truths was the "Truth of Suffering" (*Duhkha*, Sanskrit). Indeed for the Buddhist suffering is one of the three basic characteristics (*Trilakshana*) of existence. This understanding of suffering may also be found the great Taoist allegorist, Chuang Tzu as seen in this passage:

> Once we happen into the form of this body, we cannot forget it. And so it is that we wait out the end. Grappling and tangling with things, we rush headlong toward the end, and there's no stopping it. It's sad isn't it? We slave our lives away and never get anywhere, work ourselves ragged and never find our way home. How could it be anything but sorrow? People talk about never dying, but what good is that? This form we have soon becomes others and the mind vanishes with it. How could it be called anything but great sorrow? (Hinton, 1998, p.20)

As you can imagine, existential writers and philosophers from Dostoevsky to Hemingway and from Kierkegaard to Camus would find little to argue here. Just hear some of their titles: *Notes from the Underground*, *The Idiot*, *Crime and Punishment*, *Sickness unto Death*, *Fear and Trembling*, *The Concept of Dread*, *The Stranger*, *The Plague*, *No Exit*, *A Happy Death*, and *For Whom the Bell Tolls*. Perhaps, among these thinkers, none were more terse than Ibsen (1867/1963) when he wrote, "Life is a terrible price to pay for birth" (p. 155). Whether our suffering is neurotic, as in the case of psychoanalysis, existential, as in the case of daseinsanalysis, or mental, as in the case of Taoism and Eastern philosophy, what is inescapable for all three forms of depth psychology is the brute living reality of human suffering itself.

The Possibility of Virtue

Another basic premise shared by our three representative depth psychotherapies is the possibility of some kind of human virtue. As I mentioned earlier, the second fundamental meaning of the Tao denotes the teaching and practicing of the Tao, that is, being in accord with the Tao. This second signification of Tao is found in the little Chinese word, Te, as in *Tao Te Ching.* Usually understood as virtue, Te refers specifically to the way we do or do not find our very own reconciliation with what is and is becoming, with the Tao. Daseinsanalysis and psychoanalysis are also concerned with the possibility *the well lived life*, with virtue, broadly defined. In all three streams of thought, such virtue is not about how things are but, rather, how *we* are with how things are. Naturally, this virtue may appear in different linguistic costumes. For the Taoist, virtue is accordance with the Tao, with what is; for the daseinsanalyst, virtue is openness and authenticity; for the psychoanalyst virtue is worthwhile, minimally conflicted love and work and the capacity to live both realistically and well with the disappointments and sacrifices required in exchange for the reasonable protections and comforts provided by civilized existence. Fully recognizing their many specific differences, one can still say that all three traditions extol the virtuous life as one that is in harmony with the real, the true. Although I do not recall James Bugental, one of the founders of humanistic psychology, ever mentioning the Tao as such, he quite aptly articulated this second meaning of Tao, that is Te, the teaching and practicing of Tao, when he described the challenge of authenticity as follows: "A person is authentic in the degree to which his being in the world is in accord with the givenness of his own nature and of the world" (Bugental, 1965, pp. 31-32).

Now one rather inconvenient difficulty is that regardless of how desirable it may be, virtue is not a way of being that can be achieved without considerable personal effort and sacrifice. All that is given to us is existence and, with this, suffering. Virtue, however it is defined, is merely a possibility, and a possibility that comes, for all its benefits, at considerable expense including sacrifices in time and money; forsaken personal gratifications; the shouldering of inevitable sorrows and disappointments; the bearing of responsibility for one's own feelings, behaviors and attitudes; and a ready concern for others that at least matches our concern for ourselves. All this, not to mention the unfortunate circumstance that virtue is not always a particularly welcome attribute, can make the pursuit of virtue plainly unappealing. Indeed, in our own lifetime, we have all known extraordinary human beings who have paid for their virtue with their lives.[5]

The Primacy of Lived-experience

A third area of confluence is in the basic way to overcome human suffering or achieve virtue. All three traditions agree that one can neither overcome suffering nor achieve virtue vicariously or even intellectually but must engage these hopes through immersion in immediate, personal experience. Whether the path leads, as Freud put it, to "ordinary unhappiness," or all the way to clarity of mind (Shūnyatā), enlightenment and the highest form of transcendent consciousness (*Nirvana*), there is no other way except going on one's own way. Thus, another basic premise shared by these approaches to psychological life is that one must actually live them through to ever understand and appropriate their possibilities. As Chuang Tzu put it, "traveling the Way makes it Way" (1998, p. 23). One's destining is forged and found, ultimately, not in words or theories or trainings, but in living it through. As Heidegger (1927/1962) put it, speaking of the fundamental question of ontology, "One must seek a way...and this is the way one must go. Whether this is the only way or even the right one at all, can be decided only *after one has gone along it*" (p. 487, emphasis Heidegger's). The German poet, Friedrich von Schiller (1805/1972) wrote, speaking of the fate of the oppressive Swiss governor Gessler, "He has no choice but through this sunken way to come to Kussnacht...there is no other road" (p. 109) and, later, "all who travel make their destined way to their own tasks" (p.111). For psychoanalysis, too, there is no escaping the onerous trials of personal experience, namely in the form of a personal analysis. Although Freud's standard for analysts of "psychoanalytic purification" (1912/1958, p. 116) was more exacting than his standard for patients, namely, the transformation of "hysterical misery into ordinary unhappiness" (Breuer & Freud, 1893-1895/1955, p.305), the path through painful and uncanny personal experience was still unavoidable.

Psychoanalysis, daseinsanalysis, and Tao psychotherapy all agree that psychic liberation can only be achieved by passing conscientiously through the fires of one's own lived experience. The word conscientious is the critical one here because, although we must all live through our life in

---

[5] As the reader may well have guessed, I am thinking here of such individuals as Mohatma Ghandi, John and Robert Kennedy, and Martin Luther King Jr., all of whom represented certain kinds of virtuous lives that were perceived as threatening to others. That said, I am not attempting to idealize these men as they, like all of us, were far from virtuous in every aspect of their lives, however the term is defined.

one way or another, to do so conscientiously, that is, mindfully, with a heightened sense of awareness and personal responsibility, this is another thing entirely. Given the ubiquity of suffering, who would want to have to endure this suffering conscientiously? If our human existence is inevitably one of profound sorrow and suffering, who would not wish for an escape, a way around, a way out? Given the demands of a virtuous existence, the effort and sacrifices it requires, regardless of the means that are chosen, who would not at least consider the possibility of giving up virtue for the fantasy of a pleasurable, uncomplicated, mindless existence?

The Penchant for Flight

Thus, a fourth premise shared by all three representative approaches to depth psychology is that human beings have an understandable penchant to avoid that which is painful, unpleasant, or in some way threatening to their sense of themselves or their functioning status quo, even if this comes at the price of one's own authentic existence. For Freud, this elusiveness took the form of repression and a host of other tactical psychological defenses. Underlying all of these defenses was the human tendency to cling to familiar forms of suffering, rather that open up to what is new and true. As Freud (1905/1953c) put it "the patient clings to his disease and even fights against his own recovery" (p. 261). For Daseinsanalysts, the individual flees "in the face of itself," in the face of being-in-the-world as such, by falling into absorption by what Heidegger called the They-self (*Man-Selbtsein*), the everyday herd-like concern with whatever practical matters lie at hand. For Eastern thinkers, this flight from reality is achieved, not only by absorption in everyday concerns or what might be called the familiar appeal of the status quo, but also by the stubborn attachments to desires and "false views" (see Rubin, 1996). For Rhee Dongshick, such "false views" often come in the form of what William Barrett (1956) called a "conceptual prison" (p. xvi), that is, abstract concepts that keep an individual away from his or her own living experience.

Regardless of how this flight from reality is construed, all three of these depth psychologies recognize the ubiquity of fleeing in the face of what is, whether that fleeing is in order to avoid the exacting rigors of the virtuous life, or the unforgiving vicissitudes of human suffering. As one patient exclaimed to me recently, "I don't want to be human!" Another patient, chuckling almost proudly to himself, recently began his session by announcing a fantasy that had occurred to him earlier in the day. His image was of staging a one-man protest in front of my office. As the image had it, he was waving a placard reading on one side, "I don't want to be enlightened" and on the other, "I just want what I want." His ridicule accepted; we went on to discuss his understandable ambivalence about the relatively moderate promises of psychotherapy in relation to its immoderate demands. Somewhere along the way, hoping to assure him that his doubts placed him good company, I mentioned the American author, Saul Bellow's remarks that although Socrates said, "The unexamined life is not worth living," and Aristotle countered, "The unlived life is not worth examining," sometimes, Saul Bellow rejoined, "The examined life makes you wish you were dead." With this, the patient's proud, wry grin returned.

Considering these four shared premises as a whole naturally begs this question: If our suffering is so great, our virtue so demanding, our relation to the lived-experience of both so ambivalent, and our penchant for flight so ubiquitous, what could make depth psychotherapy at all possible in the first place? Who would want it? Certainly the possibility of some relief from acute suffering is one factor, but are there also certain characteristics of depth psychotherapy that contribute to its hospitality as a project?

The Promises of Psychotherapy

Following the medical customs of his day, when Freud first began his practice as a physician, he combined lengthy home visits with hypnosis, massage, and hydrotherapy with the hope of alleviating the various enigmatic sufferings to which his patients were prone. However, he soon realized the complication of such fashionable remedies, especially with respect to their untoward influence on his relationships with the individuals he promised to help. Gradually, with some quirky, but impeccable feedback, especially from gifted female patients, along with the impressive yields of his own self analysis, Freud developed psychoanalysis, the first systematic approach to modern depth psychotherapy. Although, psychoanalysis has since grown into a whole chorus depth psychological healing voices, they concur on a few basic therapeutic promises. Underlying depth psychotherapy's potential appeal and efficacy are three essential features: its framework, its attitude, and its mode.

The Framework of Depth Psychotherapy: A Sanctuary for Being

To my mind, with all their present day cultural and historical limitations, Freud's papers on technique (Freud, 1904/1953a, 1905/1953c,

1912/1958a, 1915/1958b, 1913/1958c, 1912/1958d, 1914/1958e) are still among the most sound, well-written treatises on the fundamentals of depth psychotherapeutic practice. These technical works include, among other things, time tested recommendations for establishing a sturdy, trustworthy framework within which the vicissitudes of analytic or psychotherapeutic relating may safely and freely proceed. Although in some ways contrived and artificial, the framework offers a reliable set of constants, a clearly defined environmental capacity for evoking, containing, and sustaining the radical, revolutionary, and often dangerous experiment conducted by the therapeutic partners involved. Agreements with respect to time, space, compensation, and the roles, rules, and responsibilities governing the behavior and attitude of each of the participants all contribute to building a structure or framework for the conduct of depth psychotherapy.

The term framework was first used by Marion Milner (1952) to describe the therapeutic pact, comparing it to the frame of a painting which sequesters its reality, preserving it from intrusion, and establishing for it a living refuge. Winnicott (1957) first referred to this same therapeutic structure as the setting, by which he meant "the summation of all the details of management" (p. 297). Winnicott went on to call this unique setting "the facilitating environment" and "the holding environment" (Winnicott, 1958, 1965, 1986, 1989) likening the later to the infants "being held by a mother." He emphasized that "the mother holds a situation" (pp. 262-263, italics Winnicott's) allowing both mother and child to "*live an experience together*" (1975, p. 152, italics Winnicott's). This therapeutic setting or framework has also been called a "therapeutic cocoon," an "analytic sphere" (Viderman, 1974), a "safe place" (Havens, 1989), and a "sanctuary" (Craig, 2000). However, whatever it is called, it is clear that this framework requires two fundamental features: first, *a sound but appropriately flexible perimeter* that contains, protects, and accommodates its contents, and, second, *an open, free area, a pregnant emptiness* where what is contained and accommodated may can appear and develop according to its own nature.

That being requires emptiness has long been known. In the *Tao Te Ching* we read that "being and non-being create each other" (S. Mitchell, trans., 1988, Ch. 2) and that the Tao itself is "like an eternal void: filled with infinite possibilities" (Ch. 3). In daseinsanalysis, it is the encounter with emptiness that brings us face to face with Being as such, with the very circumstance that we are at all. Although Heidegger (1929/1977) was speaking philosophically, not psychologically, his ontological assertions, are remarkably apt for the ontic everyday situation of depth psychotherapy: "For human existence the nothing makes possible the openness of beings as such" (p. 106). In the same paper he added, "human existence can relate to beings only if it holds itself out into the nothing" (p.111) and "From the nothing all beings as being come to be" (p. 110). Concurring with these psychoanalytic and daseinsanalytic perspectives are these from the East, presented here in side by side translations of the same passage from the *Tao Te Ching* on the pregnancy of the nothing, the empty:

We throw Clay	Hollowed out,
to shape a pot,	clay makes a pot.
but the utility of the clay pot	Where the pots not
is a function of the nothingness inside it.	is where it's useful.
We bore out doors and windows	Cut doors and windows
To make a dwelling,	to make a room
But the utility of the dwelling	Where the room isn't
Is a function of the nothingness inside it.	There's room for you
(Ames & Hall, 2003, p. 91)	(Le Guin, 1997, p. 14)

When read phenomenologically Freud's recommendations for therapeutic practice constitute a psychical pact, a "working alliance" (Greenson, 1965) that establishes in the midst of everyday life a concrete opportunity or opening up to and for the patient's being and becoming. Freud's depth psychotherapeutic framework is nothing less than a human refuge for the real. As Masud Khan (1974), the defrocked but still sage British psychoanalyst, put it, the essential yield of the framework or "holding" for patients is nothing less than their very own "experience of *being*" (p. 204, emphasis Khan's).

All three of our representative approaches to psychotherapy construe it as a deliberately structured situation that allows human beings to take their own being seriously, that wrests from the harried world of everyday existence an asylum within that the patient's own reality can show itself from itself in the very way in which it shows itself from itself.[6] One could fairly say that depth psychotherapy intentionally recreates in the ontic realm of everyday life, the ontological characteristic of Being Heidegger (1927/1962) called the Open or Clearing (*Lichtung*) and the Taoists call emptiness or nothing. Ontologically speaking "the Opening

---

[6] Heidegger's (1927/1962) famous exposition of the essence of phenomenology was "to let that which shows itself from itself be seen from itself in the very way in which it shows itself from itself" (p. 58).

means the beginning of Being, the unfurling of Being, the sheltering of Being, and the freeing of Being" (Craig, 2008c). Ontically speaking, the opening of psychotherapy evokes the beginning of the patient's being, the unfurling of the patient's being, the sheltering of the patient's being, and the freeing of the patient's being. In other words, again essentially speaking, psychotherapy is a kind of asylum or sanctuary (Craig, 2000) for the being and the becoming of the patient, a time, space, and human relationship the singular purpose of which is to open the way for human individuals to appear precisely as they are and are on their way to being.

The Attitude of Depth Psychotherapy: Letting Being Be

From this perspective, a major challenge is to keep therapeutic ambition from getting in the way of what is arising at the moment, to provide an open forum, imbued with the safety and freedom for the individual to be whoever or whatever he or she is at the moment. Indeed, this is the very foundation for Western psychoanalysis and all real depth psychotherapy. But, again, if suffering is so great, virtue so demanding, and the penchant for flight so ubiquitous, what could possibly entice individuals, even in the safest and coziest of sanctuaries, to undergo such an ordeal as depth psychotherapy in the first place?

Psychoanalytic letting be. Freud well understood that any intensive depth psychotherapy worth its salt was carried out in the grip of ambivalence, a wish to escape suffering that is at once sufficient reason for entering psychotherapy and for avoiding it. The person does not exist who is not profoundly reluctant about genuine, thorough, ongoing self knowledge. As noted earlier, the examined life does not cheery advocates make. Having seen for himself the value of self understanding, Freud was eager to discover a way to maximize self disclosure and minimize resistance.

Freud became convinced that if patients could follow one simple behavior, called *Einfall*, it would lead to the revelation of everything required for a cure.[7] Einfall or free association, involved letting whatever appeared in one's stream of consciousness do so without interference and

---

[7] Freud discusses his "Basic Rule," *Einfall"* translated free association a number of times throughout his collected works (see for example, 1900/1953b, pp. 100-106; 1904/1953, pp. 250-252; 1913/1958c, pp. 134-136; 1915-1916/1961, pp. 114 -115; 1916-1917/1963, pp. 287-289; 1923/1925, pp. 237-238; 1926/159, pp. 187-188;1940/1964, p. 140). However his first detailed discussion, found in chapter two of *The Interpretation of Dreams* (1900/1953, pp. 100-106) remains the most informative.

then reporting these "associations" directly. Thus Freud would say something like, "Let's not bother ourselves here with our customary habits of social discourse and decorum. Just lie down, relax, and simply say, without exception, whatever passes through your mind. Oh, and, by the way, don't be concerned with me: I'll get out of your way and just listen to whatever you have to say, without any of the kinds of personal feelings and judgments you've come to expect from others." With such reassurances setting the stage for the patient's practice of free association, Freud hoped to create as relaxed and open minded a situation as possible, essentially one in which the individuals could completely indulge themselves in the observation of their own experience, however irrational, ridiculous, or inappropriate it might appear. Here was a situation free of judgment, ridicule, interference, or retaliation. The entire design of which was to provide an opportunity to share one's deepest secrets, one's most private memories and longings with another human being, assured of that other's genuine interest, empathy, and care. All this in the interest of the patient's own self discovery, understanding, and acceptance.

Fine idea. The catch was no one could do it. Thus, Freud began taking great pains to help patients overcome their reticence to proceed as advised. For example, he would encourage patients to let go "as you would in a conversation in which you were rambling on quite disconnectedly and at random" (Freud, 1904/1953a, p. 251). Or he might advise, "So say whatever comes to your mind. Act as though, for instance, you were a traveler sitting next to the window of a railway carriage and describing to someone inside the carriage the changing views which you see outside" (Freud, 1913/1958c, p. 135). Still no one could do it.

So, in addition to these more persuasive methods, Freud also tried an educative approach to his technique for "the widening of consciousness" (Freud, 1904/1953a, p. 250). For instance, in *The Interpretation of Dreams* (1900/1953b) Freud distinguished between the everyday attitude of self reflection and psychoanalytic attitude of self observation with the former being influenced by the critical faculty and the later requiring its suspension. For such self observation, he wrote one needs only to "increase… the attention paid to [one's] own psychical perceptions" and to eliminate "the criticism by which [one] normally sifts through thoughts that occur to [one]" (1900/1953b, p. 101, brackets mine). "Suspend disbelief!" and "Accept what shows itself!" were the gentle battle cries of the couch.

Thus, well over a century ago Freud was claiming that to be helped by depth psychotherapy, you must practice a sophisticated form of mindfulness, a form of self-observation requiring that one be calmly interested in one's own unfettered stream of consciousness and accept the psychic reality of whatever occurs. However, Freud not only recommended this strikingly enlightened manner of being as the Fundamental Rule for patients, but also recommended essentially the same manner of being for the therapist. For instance, in his case study of Little Hans (1909/1955a) he describes his own therapeutic *démarche* as follows: "We... suspend our judgment and give our impartial attention to everything that there is to observe" (p. 23). Freud's name for this "fundamental rule for analysts," was *Gleichschwebende Aufmerksamkeit* (1912/1958c, p. 111), translated roughly as a "similar evenly hovering attentiveness."[8] So therapists, too, were advised to let themselves go, to be as open and free as possible in receiving whatever occurs in the moment. Again, as this is not a common everyday attitude, Freud offered a number of supportive instructions. For instance, he discouraged analysts from deliberately concentrating on anything in particular, instructing them, instead, to give "equal notice to everything" and to "simply listen, and not bother about... keeping anything in mind" (1912/ 1958c, p. 112). For Freud this rule of "evenly hovering attention" for the therapist was, he wrote, "intended to create for the doctor a counterpart to the 'fundamental rule of psycho-analysis' which is laid down for the patient."

> Just a patient must relate everything that his self-observation can detect, and keep back all the logical and affective objections that seek him to make a selection from among them, so the doctor must put himself in a position to make use of everything he is told...without substituting a censorship of his own...To put it in a formula: he must turn his own unconscious like a receptive organ towards the transmitting organ of the patient. (1912/ 1958c, p. 115)

Now, in order to achieve this kind of a radically open, objective mind, Freud also added that the therapist "must himself fulfill one psychological condition to a high degree. He may not tolerate any

---

[8] The German-English translations run somewhat as follows: Gleich = like or similar; schwebender = suspended, hovering, floating; Aufmerksamkeit = attentiveness or consideration. Although Strachey's English translation is "evenly-suspended attention," other common translations in psychoanalytic literature include "evenly hovering attention" or "free-floating attention," the latter attempting to emphasize the similarity with "free association" (*Einfall*).

resistances in himself" (1912/1958c, p. 115). For Freud, it was not sufficient for the therapist to be "an approximately normal person" but that he should undergo "psychoanalytic purification" and thus become fully cognizant of "those complexes of his own that would be apt to interfere with his grasp of what the patient tells him" (1912/1958c, p. 116). Other psychoanalytic practices shaping the therapeutic interaction are neutrality and abstinence. Whereas being neutral means the therapist makes every effort to avoid leaping into the patient's experience to take sides, offer opinions, or prize one idea, thought, feeling, or form of communication over any other; Being abstinent means not seizing the therapeutic situation to gratify either the patient's or the therapist's wishes but, rather, making every effort to allow what comes with those wishes to show itself in order that it can be more deeply understood. Given these basic Western depth psychotherapeutic attitudes, one could fairly say that the psychoanalyst's stance is not so different from what in the East is called "the empty mind" (*Shūnyatā*). Indeed, with this talk of the "widening of consciousness" (1904/1953a, p. 250), of radical openness and permissiveness toward what is, of neutrality and abstinence, Freud is not only sounding like an existentialist but also like a Zen Buddhist master worthy of his own robes![9]

Taoist letting be. Freud's recommendations regarding the two fundamental rules of depth psychotherapy were essentially an invitation for the patient and therapist alike to let what is be, to allow whatever is beginning to show itself to come into its own being.[10] But how does such thinking actually stand with the Tao? Remember, Tao is the Way, the immediate and ever unfolding path of all that is, Being's becoming. Ancient is this Way, older than memory, older than recorded history, older than the oldest thing of which we know.[11] According to the Tao, not only does all that is have a certain energy or impulse to be but also everything that is

---

[9] I do not want to suggest that free association and evenly hovering attention are the precise equivalents of meditative mindfulness. Nor do I claim that Freud had the same kind of wisdom one finds in the masters of the East. My point is mainly that the existence of such striking similarities deserves our attention and understanding.

[10] Years later, the British analyst Wilfred Bion (1967/1970) pithily summarized the primary requirement of evenly hovering attention as the "disciplined denial of memory and desire" (p. 41).

[11] The concept of the Tao is in this context akin to certain Western understandings of Nature as primordial Being. For example, Ellen Chen (1989) speaks of the Tao as "an image (hsiang) of the unnamable Urgrund," "the dark hidden Urgrund, the mother of all" (p.63). As this ground of all being, the Tao is the way of Nature itself, which Hölderlin (1952) describes as "older than the ages and above the gods of East and West" (p. 162, translation mine). As Le Guin (1997) puts it the Tao "was born before the gods" (p. 7).

has a certain essential Way of being. In other words, every being has its own Way of being that is tirelessly unfurling itself in time. It is this very Way that the psychoanalysts and depth psychotherapists are pledged to attune themselves to, to let be, and to serve. In Taoist thought there is a name for this "being in accord with being." It is called *wu wei* and has been the East's preeminent spiritual practice for millennia.

Exactly what is *wu wei*? The Chinese *wu* means "without" in the sense of "free of" or, more literally, "empty of" and *wei* means "to do," "to act," "to make," or "to work." Taken together, the term *wu wei* means to be "free of acting or doing," "empty of working or producing." Alan Watts (2000) prefers to think of *wu wei* as "not forcing" and John C. H. Wu (1989) has translated the term as "Non-Ado" (p.7) as in not making a fuss about. Thus, *wu wei* means "not tampering with," "grabbing," or "grasping after" (see J.C.H. Wu, 1989, p. 59). A basic distinction in the practice of *wu wei* is between "doing" and "being," with *wu wei* emphasizing the possibility of simply being what one is and letting other beings be what they are, rather than striving "to make" oneself or others or things into something else, some wished for something else, or some desired something else. Wu's translation of *wu wei* as not tampering or meddling with being means not interfering with the natural order of things, the Tao. For example, we find such aphorisms in the *Tao Te Ching* as "Practice non-doing and everything will fall in place" (S. Mitchell, 1988, Chapt. 3) and "When the beautiful strives to be beautiful it is repulsive... when the good strives to be good, it is no good... this is why sages abide in the business of non-action" (Ivanhoe, 2002, p. 2). We also find these words: "The Way does nothing, yet nothing is left undone" (Ivanhoe, 2002, p. 37).

Recalling the essential attitude required of free association, evenly hovering attention, neutrality, and abstinence, you find something very close to that non-interfering, non-manipulating presence that in the East is called simply, *wu wei*.

Daseinsanalytic letting be. Although Martin Heidegger's task was ontological and not at all concerned with the practice of psychotherapy, he spoke of the possibility of "letting being be." For example, in *Being and Time* (1927/1962), Heidegger described the task of phenomenology itself as "*to let (lassen)* that which shows itself be seen from itself in the very way in which it shows itself from itself" (p. 58, emphasis mine).[12] Later, in

---

[12] The German word here, lassen, which means to leave something in a certain state, that is, to let it be as it is, becomes what might be called a "way-word" or "play-word" for Heidegger's thought over the next several decades. In this paragraph I only briefly mention

"On the Essence of Truth" (1943/1977c), he writes that "the essence of truth is freedom," (p. 125) and then defines freedom as *"letting beings be"* (*Seinlassen vom Seindem*, p. 127, emphasis mine), or, from another translation of the same work (Heidegger, 1943/1949a), as letting "whatever is at the moment be what it is" (*Lässt das jeweilige siende das Seinde sein, das es ist*, p. 333). Finally, in 1949, Heidegger uses the term *Gelassenheit* which means "the-gathering-of-letting-be-ness"[13] and which he interprets as a *"releasement toward things"* (1959/1966, p. 54, emphasis Heidegger's). For Heidegger, such a releasement-toward-Being involved something quite like the practice of *wu wei,* in that it required a willing renunciation of willing (p. 59), a "letting-oneself-into-nearness" with beings or, in Eastern thought, a coming close to the Tao.

As Medard Boss (1958/1963, 1979/1971) tirelessly pointed out, of particular concern for the practice of psychotherapy is Heidegger's (1927/1962, pp. 157-159) distinction between the two different ways in which we care for human beings, namely, intervening care (*einspringende Fürsorge*) and anticipatory care (*vorauspringende Fürsorge*). Intervening care is that kind of care by which we "leap into" patients' lives to take responsibility for them when we determine that they are incapable of doing so for themselves. Such intervening care can take the form of anything from giving advice, to recommending medication, interventions for addiction, or hospitalization. On the other hand, anticipatory care is, as Boss points out, very close to the kind of care that Freud had designated for psychoanalytic or depth psychotherapy. When practicing anticipatory care, the therapist does everything possible to respect the patient's own integrity and capability and, instead of leaping in with recommendations and strategies, leaps "ahead," "out of the way" of the patient just in order to create an opening for a patient's existence, with all its limitations and possibilities, first, to show itself as it is and, second, to develop in accordance with its own circumstances and freedom. As a psychotherapeutic manner of being, anticipatory care aspires *to let* patients be in and as their truth, to let them be precisely who they are and who they are on their way to being. Thus, anticipatory care invokes an opening up and coming close to what is, a "releasement" to the very

---

a very few of the many different ways Heidegger follows the possible meanings and implications of the verb throughout his philosophical journey.

[13] See Heidegger's *Essay Concerning Technology* (1954/1977) for his translation of *Ge* in various German compound words as "gathering." For instance, *Gebirg* is a gathering of mountains, a mountain range. Thus, Ge-lassen-heit is, literally, the "gathering of- letting be - ness."

existing of the individual as such. Boss, drawing on Heidegger, often spoke of Dasein's ontological vocation as "a shepherd of being." For Boss (1988), it was this ontological understanding of the relation of Dasein to Being that gave us the philosophical ground for what it is that makes such an endeavor as psychotherapy even possible in the first place.

Perikles Kastrinidis (1990), a Swiss psychiatrist and Daseinsanalyst, has tried to clarify what shepherding or *Gelassenheit* (the-gathering-of-letting-be-ness) might mean in the context of human relationships. Although his main concern was everyday love relationships, his thoughts regarding "the development of serenity" or "the development of letting-be-ness" (Gelassenwerden) is evocative for psychotherapeutic relationships as well. Kastrinidis describes three constituents of *Gelassenwerden*: *zulassen*, *loslassen*, and *sich einlassen*. I will consider each of these with respect to the conduct of psychotherapy.

Following Heidegger, for Kastrinidis (1990) *zulassen* means "to let near," that is, to allow whatever it is that begins to show itself to continue to approach us, to come near to us, whether it be perceptions, dreams, fantasies, thoughts, feelings, or whatever. Such letting near refers not only to so called "mental things," but also to actual persons. For example, in psychotherapy, this means that patient and therapist alike allow each other to get close to one another, to come into each other's existence, to provide a home for the other in one's very own existence. The next constituent of *Gelassenwerden* is *loslassen*, which means "to let go." In psychotherapy this means, at least in part, letting go of old wishes, expectations, concepts, or prejudices. Whereas *zulassen* permits old, historically shaped ways of loving and being (i.e., transferential phenomena) to show themselves in the first place, *loslassen* allows patient and therapist alike to let go of those same old, rigid, or conflicted ways of being. For example, patients must let go of their idea of the therapist as the new, perfect, or omniscient parent, partner, or friend. Likewise, therapists must let go of their fantasies for the patient's life and allow each patient to follow his or her own-most way in life. On this, Freud (1919/1955a) was eloquent:

> We refused most emphatically to turn a patient who puts himself into our hands in search of help into our private property, to decide his fate for him, to force our own ideals upon him, and with the pride of a creator to form him in our image and see that it is good....*The patient should be educated to liberate and fulfill his*

own nature, not to resemble ourselves. (p. 164-165, emphasis mine)

Naturally, one of the most poignant implications of *loslassen* is that at some point both patient and therapist must let go of the other, once and for all, without clinging or resentment, bitterness or guilt, thus releasing each to live their own-most future. Such letting go is a central way of being in the East. Rhee Dongshick (1995), frequently paraphrases Lao Tzu's words: "the Tao is gained by daily loss. Loss upon loss until it comes to wu-wei" (p. 165). Kastrinidis's understanding of *Loslassen*, is thus very much in keeping with the wisdom of the Tao: to let things be means, in part, to let things go. The third constituent of *Gellassenwerden* is *sich einlassen*, which means "to let oneself near," that is, to let oneself get close to what shows itself. In psychotherapy, this suggests that therapist and patient alike dare *to let themselves* come close to whatever it is that shows itself, to have the courage to let oneself come close to whatever appears.

The above reflections reveal a remarkable consonance among these three approaches to depth psychotherapy with respect to the basic attitude of "letting be" that makes the depth psychotherapy possible at all.

The Mode of Depth Psychotherapy: Human Relationship

However crucial the framework of sanctuary and the attitude of letting be may be, these still do not touch the single most essential feature that makes depth psychotherapy possible at all and that one single most important factor is a human relationship. No one entering depth psychotherapy would want to bear its demands if it were not for the possibility of a genuine human relationship with a genuine, trustworthy companion.

Freud understood the importance of this indispensable aspect of psychotherapy even in his earliest years as a physician, when he wrote to his fiancée that he had come to realize that one cures patients more with one's own personality than with any kind of technique. In his earliest writing on psychoanalytic psychotherapy he spoke of the importance of the "personal relation" between the therapist and the patient. He called it *"a sine qua non* to a solution of the problem" (Breuer & Freud, 1893-1895/1955, p. 266). In addition to the time and effort expended on behalf of the patient, for Freud, the therapist was also expected to bring such human qualities as patience, respect, sympathy, and friendliness (pp. 282-283). Thus, very early on, Freud readily acknowledged the irreplaceable value of "the special solicitude inherent in the treatment" (p. 302), and the "affective factor" of "the personal influence" of the therapist that one "can seldom do without" (p. 283). Although Freud soon began to intellectually reify this human relation with a reductionistic and deterministic conceptualization of the therapeutic relationship as mere transference, he also wrote that "one has no right to dispute the 'genuine' nature of the love that makes its appearance in the course of analytic treatment" (Freud, 1915/1959, p. 388). Further, in more private contexts he acknowledged the importance of personal human emotions, especially love, in the therapeutic situation. For instance, in a December 6, 1906 letter to Jung, Freud wrote of psychoanalysis, "Essentially, one might say, the cure is effected by love" (in McGuire, 1974, p. 12-13). Although at the time Freud was speaking of the curative affect of the patient's love for the therapist, he also understood that therapists found themselves loving the person with whom they shared so many intimate hours. In a 1913 letter to Binswanger, Freud addressed the problem of what a therapist should "give to the patient," especially with respect to love. Although cautioning that a therapist should beware of "giving" out of their own countertransference needs, he also said that "to give someone too little because one loves him too much is unfair to the patient and a technical error" (In Fichtner, 2003, p. 112).

Subsequent to Freud's death, in the absence of such a powerful adjudicator of psychoanalytic thought and practice, depth psychotherapy as a whole became increasingly flexible and relational. For example, fifteen years after her father's death, Anna Freud (1954) expressed the importance of personal human relatedness in therapeutic situation even more forcefully. She wrote that,

> so far as the patient has a healthy part of his personality, his real relationship to the analyst is never wholly submerged….With due respect for the necessary strictest handling and interpretation of the transference, I feel still that we should leave room somewhere for the realization that analyst and patient are also two real people, of equal adult status, in a real personal relationship to each other. (pp. 618-619)

Today, at least in America, many psychoanalysts openly acknowledge the importance of the real human relationship that develops in intensive depth psychotherapy and even write about the significance of both the patient's love for the therapist and the analyst's love for the patient in the process of healing.

Daseinsanalysts from Ludwig Binswanger (1963) to Medard Boss (1957/1963, 1971/1979) to Paul Stern (1972) all emphasize the realness of the relationship that emerges in the context of depth psychological exploration. None would deny that of all the factors contributing to the patient's long term development and well-being, the genuine relationship stands without equal. The founder of daseinsanalytic psychotherapy, Medard Boss (1971/1979), said so explicitly: success in psychotherapy, he wrote, "depend[s] primarily on the physician's ability to allow this being-together to ripen in a way that [is] fruitful to the patient" (p. 259, brackets mine).

Tao psychotherapists also emphasize the importance of the human relationship in depth psychotherapy. For Rhee Dongshick (1995, 2002a) the therapist's genuine empathy and compassion are crucial for the patient's sense of well being while undergoing depth psychotherapy. Empathy comes from the Greek words *em* and *pathos*. The word pathos means suffering and is also akin to sorrow or mourning. The word *em* means with. So to be empathic is to be with the suffering, sorrow, or mourning of the other. Compassion comes from the combination of the Latin *pati*, which means suffering, and com, which means with. Thus, like empathy, compassion is to suffer with. However, compassion, even etymologically, has a hint of adding something else that was not quite present with empathy, namely, not only *feeling with* but also *feeling for.* Whereas empathy brings the therapist into a profound relationship with the patient in his or her moment of suffering; compassion adds to this a sense of concern *for* that suffering, a sorrow *for* that suffering, a desire for the other to be somehow relieved of that suffering when the time is right. This understanding of compassion of adding to empathy's *feeling with*, the hint of also *feeling for,* is certainly in keeping with the Buddhist notion of compassion (*Karunā*) which speaks of the heart being moved on behalf of a person who is suffering. Thus for Rhee, psychotherapy is essentially a cure brought about by a genuine human relationship.

How could it be otherwise? Depth psychotherapy is no vision quest. For all its potential benefits, it is a journey that can be full of terror, suffering, and uncertainty. In depth psychotherapy, the icons and illusions upon which individuals have relied for so long can disintegrate before their very eyes and soon lie crumbled in the sand like the great stone visage of Shelley's Ozymandias. As if this were not enough, individuals often find old friends and relatives haunting one's dreams, not as the saints or saviors once imagined, but as ghosts, ghouls, or goblins, prostitutes or gangsters, intent on seduction, oppression, or simply the taste of our own blood. To make matters even more unpalatable, individuals often discover equally mangy aspects of themselves lurking in dark, long overlooked corners of desire. Why would anyone undertake a journey of such unflinching truthfulness alone?

Relationship – rich, full, honest, empathic, gentle being together – is surely, of all the above factors, the most consequential promise of depth psychotherapy. Insight, structure, technique, and knowledge, though utterly necessary, all pale in significance to the power of human being-with-one-another as the indispensable factor making depth psychotherapy possible at all.

Summary

I have tried to touch on just a few very foundational matters regarding the nature and practice of psychotherapy, especially those matters on which there are important confluences between three specific approaches to depth psychotherapy: classical psychoanalysis, daseinsanalysis, and Tao psychotherapy. I began with a brief explication of the term depth psychotherapy and then went on to identify and discuss certain epistemological concerns grounded in the problems of otherness and ownness, concerns particularly relevant to understanding traditions arising from contexts so unlike one's own. Throughout the remainder of the paper I attempted to address the question "What is it that makes depth psychotherapy even possible in the first place?" Beginning with the implications of the ontological domains of Tao, Dasein, and Psyche, I went on to disclose and discuss four basic premises of depth psychotherapy: the problem of suffering, the possibility of virtue, the primacy of lived – experience, and the penchant for flight. I then concluded with a consideration of three promises of depth psychotherapy, namely, its framework as a sanctuary for being, its attitude of letting be, and its mode of genuine human relationship. Naturally, this is just a beginning exploration of such themes and correspondences and I hope this chapter will stimulate further reflection and investigation on the part of other psychotherapists regarding the essentially human or being-centered essence of depth psychotherapy.

As members of our own modern technological, results driven culture, not to mention our now compulsively evidence based profession, we have become increasingly pressured to focus on doing at the expense of being and, with this, increasingly forgetful of the very foundations of human existence and of our practice of psychotherapy. Psychoanalysis, daseinsanalysis, and Tao psychotherapy, though in varying ways and to varying degrees, all point to the importance of being, the importance of being open to being, the importance of being in accord with being. As Medard Boss (1988) once reminded us, "as human beings we are never alone in this calling to respond to Being. We are always together with other human beings...and therefore never isolated in this humble but dignified vocation" (p. 61). Hopefully, with this encouraging attitude, we can learn ways to more effectively resist the dehumanizing aspects of our profession and work together to develop forms of psychotherapy that honor what is deepest and truest in our gentle profession.

References

Ames, R. T. & Hall, D.L. (2003). *A philosophical translation of the Dao De Jing: Making this life significant.* New York: Ballentine Books.

Atwood, G. E. & Stolorow, R. D. (1984). *Structures of subjectivity: Explorations in psychoanalytic phenomenology.* Hillsdale, NJ: The Analytic Press.

Barrett, W. (1956). Introduction: Zen for the West. In W. Barrett (Ed.), *Zen Buddhism: Selected writings of D. T. Suzuki.*, (pp. vii-xx). New York: Doubleday Anchor Books.

Binswanger, L. (1963). *Being-in-the-world* (J. Needleman, Ed. & Trans.). New York: Basic Books. (Original works published 1930- 1957)

Bion, W.R. (1967). Notes on memory and desire. *Psychoanalytic Forum, 2,* 271-280.

Bion, W. R. (1970). *Attention and interpretation: A scientific approach to insight in psycho-analysis and groups.* New York: Basic Books.

Bleuler, E. (1910). Die Psychanalyse Freuds: Verteidigung und kritische Bemerkungen. Jahrbuch fur Psychoanalytische und Psychopathologische Forschungen, II Band (II Hälfte), 623-730.

Boss, M. (1963). *Psychoanalysis and daseinsanalysis* (L.B. Lefebre, Trans.) New York: Basic Books. (Original work published 1957)

Boss, M. (1979). *Existential foundations of medicine and psychology* (S. Conway & A. Cleaves, Trans.). New York: Aronson. (Original work published 1971)

Boss, M. (1988). Recent considerations in daseinsanalysis. *The Humanistic Psychologist, 16* (1), 58-74.

Breuer, J. & Freud, S. (1955). Studies on Hysteria. In J. Strachey (Ed. and Trans.). *The standard edition of the complete psychological works of Sigmund Freud* (Volume 2). London: Hogarth Press. (Original works published 1893-1895)

Buber, M. (1957) *Pointing the way.* New York: Harper & Brothers. (Original work published 1910)

Bugental, J. F. T. (1965). *The search for authenticity.* New York: Holt, Rinehart, and Winston, Inc.

Chen, E. M. (Trans.). (1989). The *Tao Te Ching: A new translation with commentary*. St. Paul, MN: Paragon House. (Original work attributed to Lao Tzu)

Craig, E. (1988a). An encounter with Medard Boss. *The Humanistic Psychologist, 16,* 24-55.

Craig, E. (Ed.). (1988b). Psychotherapy for freedom: The daseinsanalytic way in psychology and psychoanalysis. *The Humanistic Psychologist, 16.*

Craig, E. (2000). Sanctuary and presence: An existential view of the therapist's contribution. *The Humanistic Psychologist, 28* (1-3), 267-274.

Craig, E. (2007). Hermeneutic inquiry in depth psychology: A practical and philosophical reflection. *The Humanistic Psychologist, 35,* 307-321.

Craig, E. (2008a). A brief overview of existential depth psychotherapy. *The Humanistic Psychologist, 36,* 211-226.

Craig, E. (2008b). The human and the hidden: Existential wonderings about depth, soul, and the unconscious. *The Humanistic Psychologist, 36,* 227-282.

Craig, E. (2008c). The opening of being and Dasein. K. Hoeller (Ed.), *Review of Existential Psychology and Psychiatry (Special Issue: The Heidegger-Boss Relationship , 27,* 61-82.

Feng, G-F. & English, J. (Trans.). (1972). *Tao Te Ching*. New York: Random House. (Original work attributed to Lao Tzu)

Fichtner, G. (Ed.) (2003). *The Sigmund Freud-Ludwig Binswanger Correspondence, 1908-1938* (A.J. Pomerans, Trans.). London: Open Gate Press.

Freud, A. (1954). The widening scope of indications for psychoanalysis. *Journal of the American Psychoanalytic Association, 2,* 607-620.

Freud, S. (1953a). Freud's psycho-analytic procedure. In J. Strachey (Ed. & Trans.), *The standard edition of the complete psychological works of Sigmund Freud* (Volume 7; pp. 247-254). London: Hogarth Press. (Original work published1904)

Freud, S. (1953b). The interpretation of dreams. In J. Strachey (Ed. & Trans.), *The standard edition of the complete psychological works of Sigmund Freud* (Volumes 4 & 5, pp. 1-627). London: Hogarth Press. (Original work published 1900)

Freud, S. (1953c). On psychotherapy. In J. Strachey (Ed. & Trans.). *The standard edition of the complete psychological works of Sigmund Freud* (Volume 7, pp. 255-268). London: Hogarth Press. (Original work published1905)

Freud, S. (1955). Lines of advance in psychoanalytic therapy. In J. Strachey (Ed. & Trans.), *The standard edition of the complete psychological works of Sigmund Freud* (Volume 17, pp. 157-168). London: Hogarth Press. (Original work published 1919)

Freud, S. (1957). On the history of the psycho-analytic movement. In J. Strachey (Ed. & Trans.), *The standard edition of the complete psychological works of Sigmund Freud* (Volume 14, pp. 1-66). London: Hogarth Press. (Original work published 1914)

Freud, S. (1958a). The dynamics of transference. In J. Strachey (Ed. & Trans.). *The standard edition of the complete psychological works of Sigmund Freud* (Vol. 12, pp. 97-108). London: Hogarth Press. (Original work published 1912)

Freud, S. (1958b). Observations on transference-love (Further recommendations on the technique of psychoanalysis III). In J. Strachey (Ed. & Trans.). *The standard edition of the complete psychological works of Sigmund Freud* (Vol. 12, pp. 157-171). London: Hogarth Press. (Original work published 1915)

Freud, S. (1958c). On beginning the treatment: (Further recommendations on the technique of psychoanalysis I). In J. Strachey (Ed. & Trans.). *The standard edition of the complete psychological works of Sigmund Freud* (Vol. 12, pp. 121-144). London: Hogarth Press. (Original work published 1913)

Freud, S. (1958d). Recommendations to physicians practicing psycho-analysis. In J. Strachey (Ed. & Trans.), *The standard edition of the complete psychological works of Sigmund Freud* (Vol. 12, pp. 109-120). London: Hogarth Press. (Original work published 1912)

Freud, S. (1958e). Remembering, repeating and working through (Further recommendations on the technique of psychoanalysis II). In J. Strachey (Ed. & Trans.), *The standard edition of the complete psychological works of Sigmund Freud* (Vol. 12, pp. 145-156). London: Hogarth Press. (Original work published 1914)

Freud, S. (1959). Further recommendations on the technique of psycho-analysis: Observations on transference-love. In J. Riviere (Trans.), *Sigmund Freud collected papers* (Vol. 2, 377-391). New York: Basic Books. (Original work published 1915).

Freud, S. (1961a). Civilization and its discontents. In J. Strachey (Ed. & Trans.). *The standard edition of the complete psychological works of Sigmund Freud* (Vol. 21, pp. 57-145). London: Hogarth Press. (Original work published 1930)

Freud, S. (1961b). The future of an illusion. In J. Strachey (Ed. & Trans.). *The standard edition of the complete psychological works of Sigmund Freud* (Vol. 21, pp. 1-56). London: Hogarth Press. (Original work published 1927)

Freud, S. (1961c). Introductory lectures on psychoanalysis. In J. Strachey (Ed. & Trans.), *The standard edition of the complete psychological works of Sigmund Freud* (Vol. 15&16). London: Hogarth Press. (Original work published 1916-1917)

Freud, S. (1964). New introductory lectures on psycho-analysis. In J. Strachey (Ed. & Trans.). *The standard edition of the complete psychological works of Sigmund Freud* (Vol. 18, pp. 1-182). London: Hogarth Press. (Original work published 1933)

Freud, S. (1966). Preface and footnotes to the translation of Charcot's Tuesday Lectures. In J. Strachey (Ed. & Trans.). *The standard edition of the complete psychological works of Sigmund Freud* (Vol. 1, pp. 129-143). London: Hogarth Press. (Original work published 1892-1894)

Greenson, R. (1967). *The technique and practice of psychoanalysis* (Vol.1). New York: International Universities Press.

Hartmann, E. (1991). *Boundaries of the mind: A new psychology of personality.* New York: Basic Books.

Havens, L. (1989). *A safe place: Laying the groundwork of psychotherapy.* Cambridge, MA: Harvard University Press.

Heidegger, M. (1949a). On the essence of truth (R. F. C. Hull & A. Crick, Trans.) In W. Brock (Ed.), *Existence and being* (pp. 317-351). London: Vision Press, L.T.D. (Original work published 1943)

Heidegger, M. (1949b). What is metaphysics? (R. F. C. Hull & A. Crick, Trans.) In W. Brock (Ed.), Existence and being (pp. 353-392). London: Vision Press, L.T.D. (Original work published 1929)

Heidegger, M. (1962). *Being and time* (J. McQuarrie & E. Robinson, Trans.). New York: Harper and Row. (Original work published in 1927)

Heidegger, M. (1963). Preface (Letter to Father W. J. Richardson). In W.J. Richardson (Ed.), *Heidegger: Through phenomenology to thought* (pp. viii-xxiii). The Hague: Martinus Nijhoff.

Heidegger, M. (1966). *Discourse on thinking* (J. M. Anderson & E. H. Freund, Trans.). New York: Harper & Row. (Original work published 1959)

Heidegger, M. (1971). *On the way to language* (P. D. Hertz, Trans.). New York: Harper & Row. (Original work published 1959)

Heidegger, M. (1977a). *Basic writings* (D.F. Krell, Ed.). New York: Harper and Row. (Original works published from 1927-1976)

Heidegger, M. (1977b). Letter on humanism (J. Sallis, Trans.). In D. F. Krell (Ed.), *Basic writings* (pp. 189-242). (Original work published 1947)

Heidegger, M. (1977c). On the essence of truth (J. Sallis, Trans.). In D. F. Krell (Ed.), *Basic writings* (pp. 113-141). (Original work published 1943)

Heidegger, M. (1977d). *The question concerning technology and other essays* (W. Lovitt, Trans.) New York: Harper & Row, Publishers. (Original work published 1954)

Heidegger, M. (1977e). *What is metaphysics?* (D. F. Krell, Trans.). In D. F. Krell (Ed.), Basic writings (pp. 91-112). New York: Harper & Row. (Original work published 1929)

Heidegger, M. (1993). *Basic concepts* (G. E. Aylesworth, Trans.). Bloomington, IN: Indiana University Press. (Original work published 1981)

Heidegger, M. (1999). *Contributions to philosophy (from enowning)* (Parvis, E. & Maly, K., Trans.). Bloomington, Indiana: Indiana University Press.(Original work published in 1989)

Hinton, D. (Trans.). (1998). *Chuang Tzu: The inner chapters*. New York: Counterpoint.

Hölderlin, F. (1952). *Hölderlin poems* (M. Hamburger, Trans.). New York: Pantheon Books.

Ibsen, H. (1963). *Peer Gynt* (M. Meyer, Trans.). New York: Anchor Books. (Original work published 1867)

Ivanhoe, P. J. (Trans.). (2002). *The Daodejing of Laozi.* New York: Seven Bridges Press.

Kastrinidis, P. (1990). *Wenn Liebe krank macht (When love creates illness).* Zurich: Kreuz Verlag.

Kastrinidis, P. (2004, March). *Between human illusion and inhuman reality: A daseinsanalytic contribution to the understanding of masochism.* Paper presented at a symposium on daseinsanalysis, the 22nd Annual Symposium of the Simon Silverman Phenomenology Center of Duquesne University, Pittsburgh, PA.

Khan, M. M. R. (1974). *The privacy of the self: Papers on psychoanalytic theory and technique.* New York: International Universities Press.

Lau, D. C. (Trans.). (1963). *Tao Te Ching.* London: Penguin Books. (Original Work attributed to Lao Tzu)

Le Guin, U. K. (Trans.). (1997). *Tao Te Ching: A book about the way and the power of the way.* Boston: Shambala Publications, Inc. (Original work attributed to Lao Tzu)

Masson, J.M. (Ed. & Trans.). (1985). *The complete letters of Sigmund Freud and Wilhelm Fliess: 1887-1904.* Cambridge, MA: Harvard University Press.

May, R. (1958). Contributions of existential psychotherapy. In R. May, E. Angel, & H.F. Ellenberger (Eds.) *Existence: A new dimension in psychiatry and psychology* (pp. 37-91). New York: Basic Books.

Merton, T. (2004). The way of Chuang Tzu. Boston, MA: Shambala.

McGuire, W. (Ed.). (1974). *The Freud/Jung letters: The correspondence between Sigmund Freud and C. G. Jung* (R. Manhein & R. F. C. Hull, Trans.). Princeton, NJ: Princeton University Press.

Milner, M. (1952). Aspects of symbolism in the comprehension of the non-self. *International Journal of Psycho-Analysis, 33*, 181-195.

Mitchell, S. (Trans.). (1988). Tao Te Ching: A New English Version. New York: Harper Collins. (Original work attributed to Lao Tzu)

Mitchell, S. A. (1988). Relational concepts in psychoanalysis: An integration. Cambridge: Harvard University Press.

Parkes, G. (1996). Translator's preface. In R. May, Heidegger's hidden sources: East Asian influences on his work, pp. vii – xiii. London: Routledge.

Petzet, O. (1993). *Encounters and dialogues with Martin Heidegger, 1929-1976* P. Emad & K. Maly, Trans.). Chicago: University of Chicago Press.

Pöggeler, O. (1987). West-East Dialogue: Heidegger and Lao-tzu. In G. Parkes (Ed.), *Heidegger and Asian thought* (pp. 47-78). Honolulu: University of Hawaii Press.

Rhee, D. (1995). *The Tao and Western psychotherapy.* In Psychotherapy East and West: Integration of psychotherapies (Revised edition of the proceedings of the 16th International Congress of Psychotherapy), pp. 162-168. Seoul, Korea: Korean Academy of Psychotherapists.

Rhee, D. (2002a). *The Tao and empathy: East Asian interpretation*. In World Congress Proceedings, pp. 75-87. Seoul, Korea: Korean Academy of Psychotherapists.

Rhee, D. (2002b). The Tao, psychoanalysis and existential thought. In World Congress Proceedings, pp. 89-95. Seoul, Korea: Korean Academy of Psychotherapists. (Original work published 1990)

Rubin, J. B. (1996). *Psychotherapy and Buddhism: Toward and integration.* New York: Plenum Press.

Sartre, J. P. (1956). *Being and nothingness: An essay on phenomenological psychology* (H. E. Barnes, Trans.) New York: Philosophical Library. (Original work published 1943)

Stern, P.J. (1972). *In praise of madness: Realness therapy – the self reclaimed.* New York: W.W. Norton & Company.

Stolorow , R. D. & Atwood, G. E. (1992). *Contexts of being: The intersubjective foundation of psychological life.* Hillsdale, NJ: The Analytic Press.

Suzuki, D. T., Fromm, E. & De Martino, R. (Eds.). (1960). *Zen Buddhism & psychoanalysis.* New York: Grove Press.

Tzu, C. (2004). *The way of Chuang Tzu* (T. Merton, Trans.). Boston: Shambala Publications, Inc. (Original work by Chuang Tzu)

Viderman, S. (1974). Interpretation in the analytic space. *International Review of Psycho-analysis, 1,* 467-480.

Von Schiller, F. (1972). *Wilhelm Tell* (W. F. Mainland, Trans.). Chicago: University of Chicago Press. (Original work published 1805)

Watts, A. (1960). *Psychotherapy East and West.* New York: Pantheon Books.

Watts, A. (2000). *What is Tao?* Novato CA: New World Library.

Winnicott, D.W. (1957). Mother and child: A primer of first relationships. New York: Basic Books.

Winnicott, D. W. (1958). T*hrough pediatrics to psycho-analysis.* New York: Basic Books.

Winnicott, D. W. (1965). *The maturational processes and the facilitating environment: Studies in the theory of emotional development.* New York: International Universities Press.

Winnicott, D. W. (1986). *Holding and interpretation: Fragment of an analysis*. New York: Grove Press.

Winnicott, D. W. (1989). *Psycho-analytic explorations.* Cambridge, MA: Harvard University Press.

Wu, J. C. H. (Trans.). (1989). *Tao Te Ching*. Boston: Shambala. (Original work attributed to Lao Tzu)

5

Spiritual Warrior in Search of Meaning:
An Existential View of Lu Xun
Through His Life Incidents and Analogies

Xuefu Wang

With the emergence of Modern Chinese Literature and the upsurge of the New Cultural Movement in China, Lu Xun emerged as the most brilliant writer and acute observer of the Chinese psyche during the early 20th century. He directed his critical gaze at what he considered the cultural backwardness and the psychological cowardice of the Chinese people throughout history up to the time when he was writing. His penetrating perception and exposure of the shadowy realm of the Chinese Psyche is evident throughout his novels and essays.

Grandfather's Case

Lu Xun was born to a scholar/official family in Shaoxin, in Southeastern China. When he was 13 years old, his grandfather, a retired government official (of Qing Dynasty), was convicted of fraud and spent a number of years in jail. This led to the family's decline. Lu Xun's (1981a) early years were deeply affected by this sudden change, as he commented, "He who plummets from the heights may gain perspective to discern human snobbishness to the core" (p. 415).

Father's Illness and Death

Another incident that profoundly influenced Lu Xun was his father's chronic disease and eventual death. From the age of 14 to 16, Lu Xun was a frequent visitor to the pawnshops and drugstores in Shaoxin. He used to pawn his family belongings and "take the money given to me with contempt" (Lu Xun, 1922/2000). He went to all possible places to purchase unusual drugs and supplements prescribed by quack doctors of Chinese medicine. This included items such as aloe roots dug up in the winter, sugar-cane exposed to frost for three years, original mating pairs of crickets, and an essentially non-existent fecund ardisia plant that is usually characterized by its barrenness.[1] However, his father's illness went from bad to worse until he died at age 37. This experience engraved in Lu Xun's (1922/2000) mind with a skeptical view toward Chinese medicine: "I gradually came to the conclusion that those physicians were charlatans, either unintended or deliberate" (p. 5). Such skepticism deeply affected his later examination of the long feudal history of China.

Seeking a New Path

From his childhood to the age of 18, Lu Xun studied classical Chinese at the Three Flavor Study (三味书屋), which led to official examinations. After the death of his father, Lu Xun's family financial situation worsened. He decided to leave his hometown to study Western knowledge and technology, because it was a more affordable program. As Lu Xun recalled, "Anyone who studied 'foreign subjects' was a social outcast regarded as someone who could find no way out and was forced to sell his soul to foreign devils" (Lu Xun, 1922/2000, p. 5). To the contrary, Lu Xun's acting out of his own convictions "struck out on news paths, opening himself to novel places, while searching for a new breed of people with different characteristics – a new personality" (Lu Xun, 1981a, p. 415).

Lu Xun went to Nanjing to study physics, arithmetic, geography, history, drawing, and physical training at the Jiangnan Naval Academy (江南水师学堂). He also gained some knowledge regarding physiology. It was during this period that Lu Xun opened his mind and began to assimilate the influence of foreign cultures. By this time, many books on science, philosophy, and literature of the West were translated into Chinese. Lu Xun read Western literature through Lin Shu's translation of foreign novels (林译小说). He also recalled how he was engrossed in reading the works of famous figures in science and philosophy of the West, such as Huxley, Socrates, Plato, Tolstoy, and Nietzsche. After years of traditional education of classical Chinese, Lu Xun's worldview was, for the first time, broadened by the new thoughts from the West.

---

[1] The essence of all these quack remedies is that they are rare to the point of absurdity. The idea was, the more absurd, the more healing power was ascribed to these charlatans.

Slides at Sendai Medical College

Lu Xun's thinking on national salvation originated from the most profound recesses of his soul. In 1902, Lu Xun went to Sendai Medical College in Japan to study Western medicine. His intention was to save his fellow countrymen who, like his father, suffered from inadequate treatment. He continued to read widely in philosophy and literature while studying medicine. At the same time, he began to ponder the Chinese character: "What is the ideal human character? What is most lacking in the Chinese character? What is the root cause of the problem?" (Shouchang Xu, 1999, pp. 226, 443, 487). An incident occurring during this period of study at Sendai Medical College prompted Lu Xun to give up medicine for literature. In the preface to *Call to Arms*, Lu Xun (1922/2000) recalls, "If the lecture ended early, the instructor might show slides of natural scenery or news to fill up the time. Since this was during the Russo-Japanese War, there were many war slides." One day, during a class interval, Lu Xun saw his fellow Chinese compatriots on the slides. One of them was bound in the middle and the rest were standing around him. They were all strong and capable but appeared completely apathetic. According to the commentary, Lu Xun (1922/2000) stated:

> the one with his hands bound was a spy accused of working for the Russians, who was to be beheaded by the Japanese military as a warning to others, while the Chinese people beside him had come to enjoy the spectacle. (p. 7)

The disparity between his people's physical sturdiness and spiritual apathy caused Lu Xun much sadness. He became convinced that medical science was not as important as he originally assumed. Thus, Lu Xun decided to give up the study of medicine in order to pursue literature because he believed that literature had the ability to transform the mind, spirit, and character of the Chinese people.

The Boundless Desert and Huge Poisonous Snake

Lu Xun's enthusiasm was initially channeled into starting a magazine named *New Life* (新生). He put his all into this endeavor but, due to lack of support, the enterprise eventually failed. Lu Xun then dedicated his time and energy to the translation of foreign literature. In collaboration with his brother Zhou Zhuoren, he published two volumes. He sold only 21 copies of Volume 1 and 20 copies of Volume 2. Lu Xun returned to China in 1909, but the political situation caused him more disappointment. He became lonely and sighed,

> If a man's proposals were met with approval, this should encourage him to advance; if they were met with opposition, they should make him fight back; but the real tragedy was for him to lift up his voice among the living and be met with no response, neither approval nor opposition, just as if he were stranded in a boundless desert completely at a loss. That was when I became conscious of loneliness. (Lu Xun, 1922/2000, p. 8-11)

Lu Xun (1992/2000) continues, "And this sense of loneliness grew from day to day, entwining itself about my soul like a huge poisonous snake." Here, the huge poisonous snake and related themes, such as, poison, inner darkness, ghost, etc., were analogies symbolizing hopelessness or meaninglessness.

Lu Xun's greatness lies in the fact that he was able to respond to the tragedy of his times. He confronted the contradictions of his ego, undertaking an extremely painful self-critique in the form of vigilant self-observation and profound and trenchant self-analysis. In his self analysis, Lu Xun was conscious of inner darkness, which he sometimes referred to as ghosts dwelling in the recess of his mind. However, in his writings, Lu Xun conscientiously kept such darkness to himself lest he poison his young readers. His wife likened him to a cow eating grass but producing milk (rather than a snake eating grass while producing poison). Ultimately, upon consuming the "grass" of various other thinkers, Lu Xun realized that he could not avoid assimilating some poisonous ingredients such as the nihilism of the ancient Chinese philosopher, Zhuang Zi, or and the pessimism of Schopenhauer and various Buddhist teachers. Paradoxically, Lu Xun also admired the higher realm of wisdom to be found in these same poisonous ingredients.

Lu Xun was often in conflict. He frequently battled between his strong desire for meaning and his skeptical attitude toward life, which resulted in his occasional retreats into nothingness and despair. Yet, in the depth of his heart he maintained a fire that refused to be extinguished. And that fire was easily rekindled whenever new possibilities of life were presented.

Lu Xun was not a superficial optimist who chose to live by ignoring the negative aspects of life. On the contrary, he endeavored to seek meaning through staring directly at reality in the face (直面). His suspicious, discerning eye uncovered all kinds of duplicity in the feudal society, exposing its rotten roots. He sometimes fluctuated between hope and despair, but his despair could never keep him from seeking hope.

The Iron House

Lu Xun's loneliness stemmed from his experience of calling out but receiving no response. He reflected that he was not the type of hero who could rally multitudes with one call. Lu Xun's disappointment with his fellow countrymen led him to sink into a disheartened silence for nearly 10 years (1909-1918). During that time he lived a fairly secluded life at the Shaoxin Hostel in Beijing. Instead of standing out as a hero, he withdrew to the hordes of commoners. In order to deaden his senses to reality, he retreated to the past by copying ancient tablet inscriptions. This was the period that Lu Xun was entangled and poisoned by the serpent of helplessness from within his heart. He assumed that he could do nothing except allow his life to slip quietly away.

This changed with a visit from his friend, Qian Xuantong, who questioned Lu Xun's work on copying the inscriptions:

"What's the use of copying these?"
"There isn't any use," was Lu Xun's reply.
"What's the point, then, of copying them?"
"There isn't any point," again answered Lu Xun ("No use" and "No point" indicate *No meaning*).

After appreciating Lu Xun's current state, Qian Xuantong began to persuade him to write something for *New Youth*, a leading magazine of the New Cultural Movement. It was a light of hope brought into the darkness of Lu Xun's life that would ignite something for meaning.

Being fully aware of his mission as a writer, Lu Xun expressed his thoughts through an image of an iron house, showing an attitude of hesitation:

Imagine an iron house having not a single window and virtually indestructible, with all its inmates asleep and about to die of suffocation. Dying in their sleep, they won't feel the pain of death. Now if you raise a shout, and awaken a few of the light sleepers, making these unfortunate few suffer the agony of irrevocable death, do you really think you are doing them a good turn?

But if a few wake up, you can't say that there is no hope of destroying the iron house. (Lu Xun, 1922/2000, p. 12-15)

Symbolically, "the iron house" was the China in which people had long fallen asleep. Lu Xun was the man standing in front of "the iron house." Hesitating for some time, he finally determined to shout and bang on the outside of the house. Lu Xun had reason to hesitate. Even though the people inside might die if they were not awakened, their death would be peaceful. However, if they awoke and found no way out, they would die a painful death. Lu Xun also had reason to take action by calling them to awake. There was hope, however slight, that if awakened, they would be able to break "the iron house" and free themselves.

An examination of Lu Xun's past experience of his father's illness would also reveal a similar desire to bring about salvation and the related hesitation before uttering the shout. Interestingly, in the Chinese culture, filial duty would have the eldest son of the family repeatedly calling out to the father upon his deathbed. Lu Xun, being the eldest son, called numerous times for his father to "wake up," intending to hold him back from dying. However, Lu Xun's father was so annoyed that he asked Lu Xun to stop calling. This might explain some of the unconscious motivation behind Xun's reluctance for calling out. Nevertheless, over and over again, we hear Lu Xun's calls outside the gate of the "iron house" of China. Lu Xun never stopped calling for the rest of his life.

A Madman's Diary

A Madman's Diary (狂人日记) (1918) was Lu Xun's first short story published in *New Youth*. It is considered to be one of the first and most influential modern works written in vernacular Chinese, marking the beginning of modern Chinese literature. *A Madman's Diary* is Lu Xun's first "shout" (呐喊) in front of "the iron house," attempting to reveal the oppression of feudal values imposed upon the Chinese people. The imagery of cannibalism is applied to describe and symbolize the ways in which feudalistic Confucian values were eating away at the individual.

The main character of the story, a madman, suffers from paranoid delusions. However, this is not merely a medical case of schizophrenia; it has deeper implications. Symbolically, the madman is the one who sees through the hypocritical veil of the tyrannical tradition. He made an extensive study of Chinese history as outlined in the Four Books and Five Classics (四书五经), all of which were filled with statements of virtue and morality. But in a sleepless night he read them over and over again and saw the words "Eat People!" written between the lines of the texts. He therefore realized that the whole history of China is but a cannibalistic history. Seeing the people in his village as potential cannibals, he is gripped by the fear that everyone, including his brother, his venerable doctor, and his neighbors are plotting to eat him. The narrator (the author of the diary in the story) allegorically integrates two roles: one is a mental patient who sees a perverse, confused world through his delusional mental lens; the other is an acute thinker who discerns the covered-up truths of a feudal society that is the callousness of "cannibalism" under the gloss of virtue and morality. At last the madman, with the help of his brother and the doctor, is "restored to health" and went on to fill a vacant official position. This, again, is symbolic of a "warrior of the spiritual realm" (精神界之战士), or the loner in the crowd who, after a strenuous fight with feudal traditions, became compromised by the power of darkness, often represented by the ignorant masses or "subjects of the tyrant" (暴君的臣民), as termed by Lu Xun.

In *Subjects of the Tyrant* (1919), Lu Xun reveals, in extreme form, the indignation of the tyranny subjects:

> A tyrant's subject will, in the main, be much more violent and vicious than the tyrant. The tyrant's tyranny frequently cannot satisfy the wishes of the subjects under his rule. Instead of China, let us take an example from overseas. When the prosecutor wanted to release Jesus, the crowd demanded that he be crucified. The tyrant's subjects have a simple wish, that tyranny takes its toll on someone else. This they watch happily. Cruelty is their pleasure, the suffering of others their enjoyment and comfort. These subjects' own talents lie in their lucky escape, to safety, from which they again choose the sacrifice of others, satiating their thirst for blood, but no one understands. The one who is tortured to death is groaning in pain, saying 'aiya,' while others around him are enjoying his painful groans by showing much happiness. (Lu Xun, 1981a, p. 366)

This is what prompts Jesus, while dying on the cross, to say, "Father, forgive them, for they know not what they do."

Persecution of the hero by the subjects of the tyrant is a common theme in Lu Xun's literary creation. The persecution often takes the form of framing the madman. This is not uncommon in reality. Lu Xun's teacher, Zhang Taiyan, a radical thinker of modern China, was called "Zhang Fengzi" (Madman Zhang) . In some of Lu Xun's novels, there are characters who are revolutionaries and anti-tradition activists. These include Xia Yu in *Medicine* (1919, in Lu Xun 1981a), who is despised as 'mad' by the people in the teahouse; and the fool in the *Lamp that Was Kept Alight* (1925, in Lu Xun, 1981b), who claims to burn down the temple, extinguishing the lamp, symbolizing the spiritual oppression of the feudal tradition. Also in *Revenge II* (1924, in Lu Xun 1981b), Lu Xun wrote a new version of the crucifixion of Jesus, one that is contrary to the Biblical account in which Jesus pleads for the forgiveness of the persecuting crowds. In this new account, Jesus, tortured and mocked (as a madman who claimed himself a King) by the evil crowd, shouted forth accusations, curses, and threats of revenge upon the crowd and their posterity. However, in *A Madman's Diary* (1918), Lu Xun, through the lips of the madman, raised perhaps the most significant question regarding the cannibalistic history of China. As accounted in the novel, when the madman brought up cannibalism (symbolizing the cruelty of feudalism) from cover-up of feudal hypocrisy, his brother's (representing feudal moralist) facial expression grew ghastly pale as he said "That's the way it's always been…" "Does that make it right?" was the reply of the madman.(Lu Xun, 1922/2000, p. 41). This question directly points at the passivity of the Chinese national character.

The Dark House

The goal of Lu Xun's literary creation is based on the premise that to establish a nation, one must first establish its people. And, in order to establish the people, one must first enlighten them. In regards to enlightenment, Lu Xun chose to expose the rotten roots of the Chinese national character, such as servility, passivity, compromising attitude, and fear of change.

The dark house is another metaphor Lu Xun (1981a) created to expose the deep-rooted concessionary attitude in the Chinese psyche:

The disposition of the Chinese is an irredeemable compromise, ready to take a middle course with everything. Supposed that you are in a house that is too dark. If you suggest opening up a window, all others will not allow such a change. Yet if you make a strong enough proposition of removing the roof so as to let the light in, all the rest will then approach to make the concession by agreeing to your former suggestion of opening a window. So without a strong enough proposition people will not bother to budge even a moderate step for reform. (pp. 13-14)

So Lu Xun's observation is that in order to achieve any kind of significant change with such a conforming/concessionary/compromising society, one needs to simply rise above one's peers. If one's proposition is of sufficient strength, perhaps the masses will grant a small percentage of what was originally requested.

In Lu Xun's critical analysis, the compromising character is the result of self-yielding constriction under the deprivation of feudal tyranny. With limited space to live, people have to constrict themselves, almost without limits, in order to gain a margin for survival in this abnormal social environment. By way of unending concessions, they sink to the level of slavery, readily paying any price for security. From this perspective, Lu Xun divides the history of China, despite its many dynasties, into but two ages—one that people can live securely as slaves and the other where people cannot even gain themselves a secure life of slavery. This degradation of living status under the endless of feudal oppression has left a deep-rooted sense of insecurity in Chinese psyche and passivity in Chinese character. People become terrified of any change that might affect their minimum security. That is why in China, even present times, any kind of reform will be met with strong opposition.

Lu Xun's analogies of the iron house, the madman, and the dark house are reminiscent of Nels F. S. Fere's (1953) old barn parable. The parable described an old barn that was wide with no windows and a low ceiling. The lighting within the barn was dim as the lamps of the Law were smoky and easily extinguished. The people were busy keeping these lamps lit. The people sighed, waiting for a new and brighter light to appear. But century after century would pass while people went to their graves disappointed. Then one day a prophet with a bright countenance arrived telling the people of the bright sunshine outside. All they needed to do was to step outside and see for themselves. The prophet said, "I come from the Light. I know the Light. I am the Light. Trust me. Follow me into the Light" (p. 12). Many heard and marveled. But there was much fear. The prophet kept imploring the people to leave the dark barn and step into the Light but they became angry and hated him.

Similar to Lu Xun's allegories, this parable indicates that people living in the old barn have become habitually accustomed to the darkness. They may harbor a secret desire for light, but are also possessed by a stronger fear of the light. They are afraid of stepping out. They even deny the existence of the light outside. Finally, as the parable of the old barn points out, they eventually kill the prophet of Light.

So, contrary to Lu Xun's admonition regarding "zhi-mian" (直面), literally translated to mean "direct facing," people tend to employ innumerable defense mechanisms to escape the realities of life. They do not know who they are or what they are doing. Their behavior is motivated by an unconscious sense of insecurity. They avoid calls for change because they are afraid of activating a sensor that would bring trouble. In order to maintain security, they keep everything in order by adhering to status quo. Anyone who proposes change will be regarded as a potential threat and trouble-maker. If they cannot coax him to conform, they will plot to get rid of him.

In May 2008, Mark Yang and I led a workshop on existential psychology at Zhi-Mian Institute for Psychotherapy in Nanjing. Yang introduced the following story found in the opening of the chapter on meaninglessness in Irvin Yalom's (1980) book *Existential Psychotherapy*:

> Imagine a happy group of morons who are engaged in work. They are carrying bricks in an open field. As soon as they have stacked all the bricks at one end of the field, they proceed to transport them to the opposite end. This continues without stop and everyday of every year they are busy doing the same thing. One day one of the morons stops long enough to ask himself what he is doing. He wonders what purpose there is in carrying the bricks. And from that instant on he is not quite as content with his occupation as he had been before.
>
> I am that moron who wonders why he is carrying the bricks. (p. 419)

As Yalom informed us, this was a suicide note left behind by a despairing soul who killed himself because he saw no meaning in life.

How would Lu Xun understand this story? I imagined that Lu Xun would suggest that this moron has discerned the meaninglessness of traditional society and decided to depart and seek meaning from elsewhere. The moron may have even tried to raise similar questions to the other morons. In the beginning, the other morons do not respond. But gradually pressure is applied to the one questioning moron to conform. If the questioning moron continues his line of inquiry, the other morons may even plot to get rid of him. Perhaps it is this pressure that drives the questioning moron to end his life. This has been the case repeated many times in Chinese history.

The Wounded Wolf

Qu Qiubai (1953), one of Lu Xun's friends, likened Lu Xun to the legendary figure of Remus from Roman mythology. According to this myth, Numitor was the king of Alba Longa but was dethroned by his brother Amulius ('Romulus and Reomus,' 2008). Out of fear that Numitor's daughter, Rhea Silvia, would produce children who would one day overthrow him as king, Amulius forced Rhea to become a Vestal Virgin, a priestess sworn to abstinence. But Mars, god of war, was smitten by her and secretly, while she slept, bore her two sons. The twins were of remarkable size and beauty, and named Romulus and Remus. Amulius was enraged and ordered that Rhea be buried alive and the twins thrown into the Tiber River. The servant could not bear to carry out the order, but instead placed the twins in a basket and laid the basket on the banks of the Tiber River. The river, in flood season, rose and gently carried the basket downstream. Romulus and Remus were kept safe by the river god Tiberinus, who brought them up onto the Palatine Hill. There they were nursed by a wolf. Later, Romulus became the founder of Rome while Remus was killed over a dispute about which one of the two brothers had the support of the local deities to rule the new city and give it his name.

Similarly, Lu Xun was born into a official-scholar gentry but was symbolically nursed by the milk of wild animals, the revolutionary figures of both China and abroad. Under their tutelage, he grew up to be a rebellious son of the feudal patriarchal clan society. Instead of paying allegiance to the gentry class of the feudal society, he became a revolutionary leading thinker who spread forth his thoughts to many commoners. Lu Xun suffered numerous injuries in his battle against the "old stronghold" of feudalism, but he concealed his wounds and kept on fighting. He likened himself to a wounded wolf, limping deep into the woods. Sad and lonely, he lay down to lick his wounds and later emerged from the woods again, only to fight. From his own feudal gentry he is viewed as a rebellious wolf. But in the eyes of the Chinese people he represents a fighting spirit for the transformation of China. He fought continuously until the time of his death in 1936, and was eulogized as "the soul of the nation." (民族魂)

While studying abroad, Lu Xun began laying the foundation of his axiom: In order to establish a nation, one must first establish her people (立国必先立人). He searched all over China and abroad for a spiritual model that could become an antidote to the weakened Chinese personality. He exclaimed, "If we search all over China today, where will we find such a warrior spirit? Will anyone speak out in sincerity; anyone to call our people to goodness, beauty, strength and vigor? Where are the compassionate voices to save our people from desolation?" (Lu Xun, 1981a, p. 100). Then he found the rebellious "Mara Poets" in foreign, alien lands. "Mara" means the devil or Satan, representing the European Romantic thinkers who are the positive (originally perceived as negative) forces that moved society forward, but nicknamed by the ignorant society as "Mara poets." Lu Xun began to admire figures such as, Nietzsche, Schopenhauer, Kierkegaard, Shelley, Byron, to name only a few. Lu Xun's early writings, including, *On the Power of the Mara Poetry* (1907, in Lu Xun, 1981a), *On Extremities of Cultures* (1907, in Lu Xun, 1981a), etc., can be understood as a chronology of Western heroes of the spiritual/moral/intellectual[2] realm. It was Lu Xun's fervent hope that visionaries such as these would emerge in China and "speak with powerful voices, breaking bonds of loneliness, bringing new life to his compatriots, and helping to advance China's prominence in the eyes of the world."

At his birthday gathering, Lu Xun was presented with a couplet of praise from his friend Liu Bannong (刘半农). The couplet, loosely translated to mean "Teachings of Tolstoy and Nietzsche, Writing Style of Wei and Jin Dynasty" (托尼学说，魏晋文章), recognized Lu Xun's integration of the teaching of Tolstoy and Nietzsche with the literary heritage from ancient China. This accomplishment is especially enlightening given that the divergent teachings of Tolstoy and Nietzsche, not to mention the culture divergence between Russia, Europe, and China. Lu Xun, especially during his youth, advocated Tolstoy's humanitarian values derived from Christianity. As perceived by Cao Juren (2006), one of the Lu Xun's biographers, Lu Xun's protestations against war and advocacy for international communication and exchange are influenced by Tolstoy's writings. At the same time, he admired Nietzsche's individualism and the writing style of *Thus Spoke Zarathustra* 1892/1954). We find traces of Nietzsche's philosophy and writing style in Lu Xun's *Wild Grass*

---

[2] The Chinese word is difficult to translate here. It encompasses both the spiritual/moral and the intellectual realm. In the East, Lu Xun is understood more as a "spiritual" warrior. In the West, Lu Xun can be better appreciated as an "intellectual" warrior or giant akin to that of Nietzsche.

(1927/1981b), a collection of prose, especially pieces like *Preface to Wild Grass*, *The Passer-By*, *Such A Fighter*, etc. This collection of prose or short essays, possibly the most existential literary work by Lu Xun, touched on the topics of hope and despair, darkness and light, meaning and sense of void or nothingness, choice, fighting with hypocrites, and living and dying. In fact, Lu Xun, for a period of time, was regarded as "China's Nietzsche." The two figures shared many similarities. Both Nietzsche and Lu Xun launched vigorous, wholesale attacks on their respective cultural traditions. Nietzsche (1892/1954) declared "God is dead," which shocked the entire Western Christian world. Lu Xun (1981b), on the other side of the world, exposed unrelentingly how "Confucian morality was eating its people." Ironically, however, both figures were more deeply connected to the essence of their own cultures than most of their fellow countrymen. Upon deeper examination, we find Nietzsche's spiritual attachment to Jesus echoing Lu Xun's personal similarities with Confucius. Both figures were critical of the degenerated parts of their own culture. Both sought to enlighten and inspire people to transcend from lower realms of awareness and to seek freedom from their bondage to the culture and environment. In his treatment of the national character, Lu Xun, exactly like Nietzsche, enumerated all the drawbacks in order to draw attention to a cure. In one of Lu Xun's (1981a) letter to Qian Xuantong, we find this passage:

> Jesus said if you see a cart about to overturn, put out a hand to hold it up. Nietzsche said if you see a cart about to overturn, give it a push. I naturally agree with Jesus, but I also think that if a person is not willing to receive your support, then there's no reason to force it on him. Do what they say and be done with it. If later the cart hasn't overturned, all well and good. If it does overturn in the end, then go and give practical help in raising it. My elder brother, it takes less energy to raise a cart than to support it from falling; and in the latter case, the results are less evident. To raise the cart after it falls is much more beneficial than to give a supporting hand when it's on the verge of falling. (p. 36)

In this passage we find evidence of Lu Xun's preference to integrate both the teachings of Jesus and Nietzsche. Lu Xun was practical and unrelenting while holding up and raising the great and difficult task of reforming the national character. But other times, similar to Nietzsche, he would be deliberately provocative in his words and behaviors so as to "give a push," but harbor a private intention "to raise the cart." Lu Xun was deeply concerned about his country and his people and was persistent and sincere in raising his concerns. But often times he kept his fervent compassion behind an austere exterior. Lu Xun desperately sought to awaken the deep slumbering spirit of his people across the vast land of China. Yet, with profound sorrow, Lu Xun portrayed group after group of apathetic and cruel souls in his fiction, displaying an attitude of "Grief Over Their Misfortune" and "Indignant Toward Their Servility" (哀其不幸，怒其不争).[3]

The Lock Gate of Darkness

In *A Madman's Diary* (1918), Lu Xun depicts a world of callousness in which people eat people. However, Lu Xun's peers remarked to him that this novel was too dark. To which Lu Xun finally added the phrase "save the children" to the novel as the ending sentence, upon whom he placed the hope of the Chinese society, because, as he stated, "Perhaps there are still children who haven't eaten men?" (p. 53).

In his satirical essays, as well as in his life, Lu Xun was relentless in pointing his critical pen, or more exactly, the top of his writing brush at many of his enemies. But he always showed leniency toward the young, even if they offended him. He likened himself to a cow, ready to serve the young. He pinned his hope for change in China upon the young. In one of his early articles, *How Should We Be Fathers Today?* Lu Xun (1981) employed the metaphor of "the gate of darkness" by writing "We, as fathers, should 'shoulder' the sinking gate of darkness and guide our children out to a vast land full of brightness, to live happy lives as normal, upright human beings." This metaphor originated from a parable of a dungeon in the evil underworld. Every day a giant monster captured children from the human world and locked them in the dungeon. A hero ventured into the underworld to attempt to save the children. The dungeon is in complete darkness and the locked gate is heavy and impregnable. The gate is only lifted briefly everyday when the monster leaves the dungeon to snatch more children. This becomes the only chance for the hero to enter and rescue the children. The hero took the initiative one day and guided the children out while the gate was open. However, while the gate was dropping, the hero saw that some of the children have yet to escape. Thus, he propped up the sinking gate with his shoulder in

---

[3] A term most often used in association with Lu Xun's attitude toward Chinese, but its resource cannot be found.

order for the rest of the children to escape. This resulted in the hero's death in the end as he was crushed by the gate of darkness.

This is Lu Xun: a hero who chose to fight and even "sink with the darkness." In his contemporary periods of gloom, Lu Xun explored his own path and sometimes found nowhere to turn. Instead of crying and turning back at the end of the road, as the case with Ruan Ji (阮籍), one of his favorite ancient poets, Lu Xun chose to remain and ponder his fate, before eventually resuming his exploration. Throughout his life, Lu Xun never stopped exploring lonely paths in his quest to discover and create new meaning. His quest is not just for himself, but for China as a nation, and even for all humanity.

The parable of "shouldering the lock gate of the dungeon" expresses the full sense of existential psychology in terms of choosing suffering for meaning. This reminds me of Victor Frankl, who was thrown into the concentration camp by monstrous forces of evil. There he had to face the reality that his life was devoid of everything except for cold, hunger, and all kinds of brutal torture and humiliation. In his famous book *Man's Search for Meaning*, Frankl (1963) questioned his existence when everything was deprived. What does it mean for me to exist when living in such a state? What is there still left for me to live for? These were questions that launched his school of logotherapy. "The main tenets of logotherapy were justified by the acid test of the concentration camp" (as cited in Hall, 1968, p. 63). Frankl had to find answer for himself, for his inmates who despaired, and for all of us who cannot escape the suffering in our lives. Frankl witnessed that the basic motivation in humanity is the "will to meaning", rather than "will to pleasure" (as Freud assumed) or "will to power" (as Adler assumed). It is this "will to meaning" that motivates human beings to seek meaning in their life and to fulfill it in various ways. According to Frankl, there are three ways to make life meaningful: love, work, and suffering.

Similar to Frankl's experience, from the existential point of view, we find that Lu Xun's life is essentially also a process of the "will to meaning." First, he obtained the highest value of creativity through his literary work that turned out to be a spiritual contribution to his nation. Second, he practiced genuine love for his fellow countrymen, through which he gained what Frankl (1963) termed "the value of experience." Finally, through the experience of his personal suffering and the suffering of the Chinese people, Lu Xun realized "the value of attitude" by "shouldering the gate of darkness" so people may pursue a better, more meaningful life. His pain found its meaning. We can always hear his sincere voice calling his people of "the iron house" to wake up and seek meaning in a seemingly meaningless environment.

Lu Xun's (1981c) existential attitude is fully revealed in his term of "zhi mian," which means "directly facing" reality. He champions the "zhi mian warrior," as one who "dares to face life as it is, no matter how gloomy it might be" (真的猛士，敢于直面惨淡的人生; p. 271). Lu Xun lived out Nietzsche's axioms "He who has a *why* to live for can bear with almost any *how*" (as cited in Frankl, 1963, p. 12) and "That which does not kill me, makes me stronger" (as cited in Frankl, 1963, p. 103). These remarks found meaning with Frankl as well. Both Lu Xun and Frankl, in my opinion, are meaning-making heroes. They fully agree with Nietzsche in believing that, for human beings, ultimately, there is no other choice except the choice of living as heroes.

References

Ferre, N. F. S. (1953). *The sun and the umbrella*. New York: Harper & Brothers.

Frankl, V. E. (1963). *Man's search for meaning: An introduction to logotherapy*. New York: Washington Square Press.

Hall, M. (1968, Feb.). Conversation with V. E. Frankl. *Psychology Today, 1,* 56-63.

Juren, C. (2006). *Critical biography of Lu Xun*. Shanghai, China: Fudan University Press.

Lu Xun (1981a). *Complete works of Lu Xun* (Vol. 1). Beijing, China: People's Literature Publishing House.

Lu Xun (1982b). *Complete works of Lu Xun* (Vol. 2). Beijing, China: People's Literature Publishing House.

Lu Xun (1982c). *Complete works of Lu Xun* (Vol. 3). Beijing, China: People's Literature Publishing House.

Lu Xun (2000). *Call to arms* (Y. Xianyi & G. Yang, Trans.). Beijing, China: Foreign Languages Press. (Original work published in 1922)

Nietzsche, F. (1954). *Thus Spoke Zarathustra: A book for none and all* (W. Kaufmann, Trans.). New York: Penguin. (Original work published 1892)

Qiubai, Q. (1953). *Preface*. In *Seclected essays of Lu Xun. Collected works of Qu Qiubai* (Vol. 2). Beijing, China: People's Literature Publishing House.

Romulus and Reomus (2008, October). In *Wikipedia, the free encyclopedia*. Retrieved from http://en.wikipedia.org/wiki/ Romulus_and_remus

Shouchang, X. (1999). *Impressions on Lu Xun, my deceased friend,* The reminiscenes of Lu Xun. Beijing, China: Beijing Publishing House.

Yalom, I. D. (1980). *Existential psychotherapy*. New York: Basic Books.

6

Existentialism, Taoism, and Buddhism: Two Views

Kirk J. Schneider
Benjamin Tong

In this chapter, we focus on two contemplative styles—the existential style, which emphasizes the *mystery* of being; and the Taoist-Buddhist style, which accentuates the *harmony* of being. We then go on to consider how these respective emphases play out in a variety of life-contexts--individuality, development, society, and nature.

When tackling a subject of this magnitude, it is necessary to be explicitly frank about our objectives. While this chapter addresses several key issues in the debate/dialogue about the relation among existentialism, Taoism, and Buddhism it is but a very brief musing on a time-honored inquiry. For this reason, we have confined ourselves to general descriptions about the respective worldviews, rather than finely calibrated formulations. For those readers desiring an elaboration on these descriptions, see Aronson (2004); Barnes (1967); Barrett (1958); Batchelor (1990); Bradford (2008); Epstein (1995); Friedman (1991); Galvin (2008); Hoffman, Stewart, Warren, & Meek (in press); Jordan (1985); Mendelowitz (2008); Rubin (1996); Schneider (1999, 2002, 2004); Tong (1992, 1999, 2003, 2009); Walsh (2002); Watts (1961); and Welwood (2000).

In the passages to follow, we present two views on existential, Taoist, and Buddhist forms of contemplation (In Dr. Tong's section, Confucianism is also considered). From the outset, we wish to make clear that although these perspectives differ slightly in approach, they each share a common root—the elucidation of being. In this chapter, we hope to tease out the nuances of this common root and to dispel the stereotypes about the approaches that highlight either extreme differences or rigid similarities.

In the spirit of the many fruitful exchanges on this subject between the authors, we decided to divide this chapter into three basic parts. In the first part, we feature a reflection by Kirk Schneider, drawing on his background in existential-spiritual psychology. In the second portion, we present a commentary by Benjamin Tong, drawing on his background in Taoist studies and existential philosophy. In the final portion, the authors will discuss and summarize their views.

Agnosticism, Awe, and the Existential-Spiritual Lineage
Kirk Schneider

Below I consider "existential spirituality" or what I have more recently termed "awe-based awakening" (Schneider, 2004, in preparation), as a context for our Taoist-Buddhist dialogue. The basis for this examination is the existential-spiritual tradition, which, over and above the atheist existential heritage, embraces the humility and wonder, thrill and anxiety, or in short "awe" of life (Friedman, 1991; Schneider, 2004). By awe of life, I mean neither absolute godlessness nor certain theism, but the invigorating "space" between (Buber, 1970; Friedman, 1991; Heschel, 1951; Tillich, 1957). I am reminded here of a parable that I am fond of invoking when asked about the difference between atheistic and agnostic forms of existentialism: "Whereas the agnostic-existentialist stands before the cosmos and throws up his hands in amazement (a la Martin Buber and Abraham Heschel), the atheist-existentialist stands before the cosmos and just simply throws up!" (a la Jean Paul Sartre). To be sure, the dividing line between an atheist and agnostic existentialist is elusive. However, there is more than a grain of truth to the stereotypes of the atheist existentialist as a curmudgeonly loner in contrast to the agnostic existentialist as a "tragically optimistic" communalist (Frankl, 1984; Friedman, 1991).

At the same time, the agnostic and atheist existentialist lineages converge on several key points: the sense of puzzlement, or even absurdity concerning the ultimate questions of life, the stress on responsibility, or ability to respond to this problematic plight, and the accent on choice. On the other hand, the agnostic existentialist tends not to share the atheist's cynicism. Questions of the divine nature of being are held in abeyance for the agnostic existentialist, and the enigmatic qualities of life, while anxiety provoking, are also viewed as occasions for fascination, even revelry. Among the agnostic and theologically oriented existentialists pertinent to this chapter are Blaise Pascal, Soren Kierkegaard, William James, Emanual Levinas, Paul Tillich, Martin Buber, Gabriel Marcel, Abraham Heschel, Ernest Becker, Rollo May, and even, at points, Friedrich Nietzsche, Martin Heidegger and Albert Camus.

In the foregoing, I will draw mainly from the agnostic-theistic existential heritage in my comparison/contrast with Taoist-Buddhist traditions. Again, these comparisons are introductory, but may spark deeper considerations.

Mystery and Harmony in Dialogue

The core basis of agnostic existentialism is mystery. We know not from whence we came nor whither we are going. Or as Gabriel Marcel (1967) put it in effect: life is not a problem to be solved but a mystery to be contemplated. At the same time, agnostic existentialists tend to view mystery as more than simply "unverifiable data," as the tough-minded scientist might look at it, but as the wellspring of a profound paradox. Taking their cue from Rudolf Otto's (1923) classic study of the origins of religiosity, these existentialists define the mystery of being in terms of two entwined yet separable dimensions: The dimension of mysterium tremendum or dread, and the dimension of fascination or wonder. Add these together and you have an "awe-based" philosophy of life (Heschel, 1951; Schneider, 1993, 2004; Tillich, 1952, 1957).

While Taoism and Buddhism also affirm life's mystery (see Tong, this chapter), they take different approaches to that mystery. Buddhism for example, tends to view mystery or the unknown as "matter of fact" qualities of life. Life, for Buddhism is *impermanence* and impermanence is ultimately uncontainable. However, the Buddhist attitude toward impermanence is one of equanimity or harmonious accommodation. There is much less of the angst or daunting quality associated with the uncontained, as is common in the existential position; there is also less of the impassioned and fascinating element. From the Buddhist point of view, there is no need to be either daunted or enthralled by mystery, but simply to accept it.

Acceptance or "*suchness*" from the Taoist and Buddhist points of view are key sensibilities toward life. They lead to the ability to "relax" into and trust life rather than contend with it. Although existentialists also foster trust and acceptance of life "as is" they also seem more susceptible to being affected (or moved) by the "as is," or to experience it in some kind of tension. As previously intimated, whereas Taoists and Buddhists stress the correspondence of all things; existentialists emphasize the dialogical tension of being separate-yet-related (Tillich, 1957). What this means practically is that there is a comparatively greater emphasis in existentialism on struggle, passion, and poignancy in the face of the unknown. There is also a commensurately greater stress on the tragic dimension of life within the existential purview. From this standpoint, tragedy is viewed as an integral part of living *well*—richly, fully—not just living. Or to put it another way, suffering is more than merely an inevitable part of life, as stressed by Buddhism, but it is at the same time *key* to a life fully lived. This is a life marked by depth, intensity, and the impetus for reform.

Below I address this perspective in the light of a variety of life-contexts, beginning with individuality. Momentarily, Dr. Tong will address the same life-contexts.

Individuality. Existentialists view individuality as a dialogical *process* rather than as a discrete or static category (Bugental, 1987). As noted earlier, individuals are viewed by existentialists as neither separate, self-isolated monads, nor open, unbounded deities, but as "fluid yet centered," separate-but-related mortals (Becker, 1973; Schneider, 2004; Tillich, 1957). For existentialists, there is no absolute dividing line between self and not self, being and nonbeing, or even primitive ("prepersonal") and enlightened ("transpersonal"). But there is no necessary all-encompassing connection among these polarities either. To this degree, existentialists are skeptical of all attempts to bifurcate the human being, including, at points, the Buddhistic notion of nirvana, which implies a kind of absolute purity of consciousness juxtaposed to attached and suffering consciousness (Schneider, 1987; Smith, 1986). On the other hand, this does not mean that existentialists, as I have defined them, believe in a discrete, bounded self. To the contrary, the parameters of self are ambiguous for existentialists, and the potential for expansion indefinite. However, "indefinite" is not the same as "all-pervading" or "pure" and it is ever subject to challenge. To this extent, the deconstruction of the self is both encouraged and yet questioned at appropriate points in existential circles, just as the mysterium tremendum of creation is both marveled at and yet gasped before. The question as to where these junctures reside and who or what is best to address them is an ongoing, whole-bodied challenge.

For existentialists, a key component of this challenge is presence. The more we can be present to ourselves, the more we can open to and be responsive about the world; and this responsiveness (vs. reactivity) increases our latitude for *choice* (Buber, 1970; Heidegger, 1962; May, 1981).

Growth and development. As Dr. Tong notes in the section below, growth and development are integral to both existentialist and Taoist-Buddhist belief systems. Here again the question is one of approach. Whereas existentialists place a comparative stress on *active* transformation (e.g., grappling, encountering, clarifying, doing), Taoist-Buddhists place an emphasis on pliant, "being" oriented forms of maturation. Among these are experiences of beauty in simplicity (e.g., Japanese flower arrangement), humility (e.g., deference to others), and basic life acceptance.

Passion. The question of passion for existentialists is more subtly the question of *engagement.* Where is the line between engagement and fixation, effort and attachment to outcome? Is there a place for savoring (temporary) attachments, immersing in them with one's whole bodily being? And to what extent? On the other hand, when does savoring, lingering become fixating and therefore devitalizing? At what point do therapy clients, for example, need to "let go" of their internal battles, and at what point should they dwell in them, steep in their complexities? At what point do I give up wrestling with this essay and simply allow it to "write itself?" Will it write itself—gratifyingly--if I don't tussle with it, stay up nights over it? Correlatively, what is the place for sentiment, intensity, and depth? How much can I revel in my son's romp through the ocean waves, or the graceful slope of my wife's neck before they become obsessions? I always appreciated the Taoist notion of "effortless effort," or what I call "effortful nonattachment." This is the notion of full and deep engagement of a given inclination, but without the fixation on outcome. This notion strikes me as deeply existential, but also ideal. Maybe the best we can do is approach it, investigate it, and marvel at the perplexities.

Relationship to Society and Nature. As with most things, existentialists have an ambivalent relationship to society and nature. They are both potentially freeing and entrapping. Although I do not subscribe to the Sartrean notion that "hell is other people," I also do not buy into "group think." The dialogical imperative of existentialism intimates that our relations to the social milieu can be either deeply fulfilling or imprisoning, depending on how we interact with it and negotiate its demands. Tillich (1967) describes the approach of "listening love" to address the moral dilemmas of our society. Listening love "is a listening to and looking at the concrete situation in all its concreteness, which includes the deepest motives of the other…" (p.109). He goes on: "The more seriously one has considered all the factors in a moral decision"--the individual as well as social, past influences as well as long term possibilities—"the more one can be certain that there is a power of acceptance in the depth of life," and in our own lives, I might add, for the decision we risk (p. 111). Listening love, in other words, gives us a "whole-bodied," experiential way to engage with others and the world. It fosters neither robotic attachment nor nihilistic detachment, but a comprehensive and practical response. Buddhism says something similar about finding the middle way, and Taoism about attention to what we are not, in addition to what we are.

True Knowledge. For existentialism, as with Taoism and Buddhism, there is no absolute when it comes to either society or nature, the best we can do is be maximally present, and appreciate the poignancy of our predicament; we are neither worms nor angels, but we can thrive nonetheless.

.

Taoism and Existentialism/Existential Psychology: Brief Comparative Notes
Benjamin Tong

In juxtaposing Taoism with existentialism and existential psychology, a starting point needs to be the acknowledgment that Taoism is an inseparable part of a syncretic "whole" of longstanding in East Asian cultures – namely, Buddhism, Taoism, and Confucianism. While there are clear distinctions between all three, the differences between these "wisdom traditions" have frequently been viewed as largely matters of emphasis. A brief consideration of their commonalities will provide an appropriate backdrop against which to contrast Taoism with existentialism and existential psychology.

For one thing, this "whole" has the singular, common focus of *transformation.* The "point" of human existence to the Buddhists is the achievement of "nirvana." In everyday language, nirvana simply refers to "The Great Escape": That is to say, transcending the earthly realm of perpetual suffering and never having to return except by choice. This "psychospiritual" evolution involves virtually countless lifetimes of difficult karmic work and uncertain struggle.

With its more earth-bound, relational preoccupations, Confucianism envisions the mature individual – indeed, the mature civilization as well – as one in which only a single type of conflict is permitted. In concrete, everyday terms, this simply (and movingly) refers to "Who's going to pick up the check?" at a restaurant. The transformed human being is poised to be kinder than the next person. The popular bumper sticker imperative to "Commit Acts of Random Kindness" resonates to this interpersonal imperative. Akin to this state, another hallmark of the mature or properly transformed individual is the ability to know what questions one should worry about in life.

For Taoist people, the central aim in a world essentially without "meaning" is the achievement of "wu wei." In the contemporary language of Star Wars movies, this is a state in which the individual is "at one with the (Universal Life) Force." Also referred to as the Spirit of Nature, wu wei is characterized by both yin and yang forces being in balance. Put another way, action or being-ness in the moment, is an integral fusion of maximum involvement as well as maximum abandon. Focused, concerted effort is tempered with non-attachment to outcome.

An illustrative example from Nature: A wolverine and her cubs are cornered by a hungry bear and have very little hope of surviving. Either as a result of instinctual knowing or observational learning, she "knows" that their only chance is for her to lunge up in the air at the bear's exposed throat the moment the huge animal charges in for the kill. She does just that: She jumps straight at the huge animal's throat, fully aware that contact with even a casual swipe by the bear's paw would break every bone in her tiny body. She knows she might die while attacking but is not attached to the outcome. All that matters is getting her sharp teeth into the bear's exposed throat. In the existential moment, in the here-and-now, there is maximum involvement (yang) and maximum abandon (yin).

> Two other themes are equally pervasive in these three traditions: *mystery* and *harmony*. The "ways of the Force" are as much of a mystery to those in the Judeo-Christian tradition as they are to adherents of the syncretic wisdom tradition of Buddhism, Taoism, and Confucianism. It is a mystery, for example, as to why the almighty, omnipotent God or the Force would allow for the possibility of evil people mastering and abusing the Power of the Universe. As millions have come to know, it is a phenomenon of awesome dimensions--both fascinating and terrifying. (Conniff, 1994)

I am reminded of the story about the night the God of Jewish internees in a Nazi death camp was put on trial for failing his people. Following the verdict of "guilty as charged," and right before a sentence was to be pronounced, someone in the "court room" shouted, "Wait, it is eight o'clock, we must stop! It is time for evening prayer."

In his famous novel, *Walden Two*, B. F. Skinner (1948) envisioned the ideal society to be a harmonious one in which conflict of any sort does not exist. With a nod in the direction of ego psychology, we might say that this would be the ego's "sphere of conflict-free-ness" writ large. By way of contrast, *harmony* in the tripartite Eastern traditions is understood to emerge not from the *elimination* of conflicts but, rather, from the *management* of conflictual tensions. The classical Chinese metaphor for life is war. The achievement of, or the return to, the state of "wu wei" enables one to engage in the management of perpetual conflict or war in this arena of perpetual suffering -- without going mad.

Let us now turn to a few thumbnail comparisons between Taoism and existentialism and existential psychology. In particular, we will consider seven themes: the nature of being, non-being, individuality, growth and development, passion, one's relationship to society and Nature, and the essence of true knowledge.

The Nature of Being. Both traditions appeal to a reality underlying or standing behind subjectivity and objectivity. They differ, however, with respect to the means for achieving rapport with that *Tao* or *Ground of all being* (see Tillich, 1952). Martin Buber (1970) and Erich Fromm (1956) would emphasize the role of relationships: In authentic relationships that "work," the experience of the Other – the "Thou" – paves the way for the Tao. In feeling both united and separate at the same time, there is an experiential approximation of being that is *one with all that is*. Taoists, like Zen practitioners, have stressed the role of such disciplines as meditation, archery, healing and the martial arts in achieving increasingly close rapport with the Universal Life Force (Liu, 1979).

Non-being. Existentialists like Tillich speak of the perpetual "threat of non-being" as an experience that Westerners (with the possible exception of R. D. Laing) anticipate with dread (rf. also Cushman, 1990). Taoists, and other Eastern esoterics, refer to non-being as an experience to be actively pursued. Non-being, in fact, is the essential source and origin of all being (all things that exist). Zen practitioners sometimes use the synonym, *no-mindedness*, while at least one contemporary Taoist scholar, Chang Chung Yuan (1975), speaks of *no-identity as true identity*.

Individuality. Existentialism and existential psychology are concerned that the individual "stand out" separate from other beings. This is Nietzsche's "separate peace" that must somehow be won over and over again. Taoists are preoccupied with the same thing but they also stress – paradoxically, with Sartre – the importance of achieving a deep and thorough identification with all of Creation. Bad faith, to Sartre (1957), is failure to acknowledge that "in choosing myself, I choose [for] man" (p. 18].

Growth and Development. Both traditions insist a human comes into a fullness of self by immersing him or her self into the arena of worldly life. Both place a high premium on assuming total responsibility for oneself and one's actions, all the while living in a spirit of risk, adventure and freedom. For Sartre (1956), the choice of life "projects" is critical, as one is shaped entirely as a result of commitment to choices. Frankl (1984) would say that the discovery of one's very own special "meaning," through creative endeavor, is *the* project. Taoists stress the attitude of "non-attachment" in living out that meaning.

Passion. Existentialists frequently seek to acquaint mortals with their capacity for passion, particularly in a contemporary world wherein so many are *dead but not buried* as a result of lack of passion. Theater plays like "Equus" imply that the attachments in the lives of many Westerners lack passion – i.e., because they are lifeless, inauthentic, and alienated.

Taoists, on the other hand, seek to liberate themselves from *enslavement* to passion of any sort. All living beings are born, they live for awhile, and then they die. Other than for a few basic givens, we homosapiens really do not understand much else. In the interim between entry and exit in this earthly dimension, those human beings who would be serious about living "naturally" should endeavor to exist in much the same manner as plants and animals: simple, discrete, and without baggage. "Health" or "wellness" resides in not getting hung up on the necessary meaning or outcome of any event or behavior. Alan Watts (1994) reminds us of this path of "suchness" and simplicity in a marvelous story of old:

> Once a upon a time there was a Chinese farmer whose horse ran away, and all the neighbors came around to commiserate that evening. "So sorry to hear your horse ran away. This is most unfortunate." The farmer said, "Maybe." The next day the horse came back bringing seven wild horses with it, and everybody came back in the evening and said "Oh, isn't that lucky. What a great turn of events. You now have eight horses!" And he said "Maybe." The next day his son tried to break one of these horses and ride it but he was thrown, and broke his leg, and they all said, "Oh dear, that's too bad," and he said, "Maybe." The following day the conscription offices came around to conscript people into the army and they rejected his son because he had a broken leg. Again all the people came around and said, "Isn't that great!" And he said, "Maybe." (p.157).

Relationship to Society and Nature. "The most difficult thing in life is to see it as it really is" (Personal Communication, late professor at the California School of Professional Psychology, Murray Bilmes, 1974). According to existentialism and existential psychology, humankind must face this essential condition of "thrownness" (Heiddeger's "dasein"), and own up to what it actually is -- complete with its brutal contradictions, radical contingency, and dehumanization. This is an uncompromising honesty that necessarily involves the response of despair. One comes to feel empty, homeless, adrift and lost.

Taoists agree with the analysis. Paradoxically, they also contend that life is also not real: Our social and material "reality" is but an extremely minute part of a much larger and eternal Reality, without beginning or end. Earthly life is tantamount to Buddhism's "Wheel of Life and Death," to which an individual soul continually "returns" to work through karmic business until it is finished. In light of this perspective, the response need not be despair: It just isn't any big deal to come into human existence again and again. The feeling should be a kind of (cultivated) "no feeling." One should live as simply as possible, with a minimum of passionate attachments, and then die when the time comes.

True knowledge. Both traditions agree that we know what is really "true" only by being in its *grasp.* We do not "know" truth as much as we are _seized_ by it. (e.g. Kierkegaard's notion of "truth only as it produced in action"). Truth is always much more than logical judgments or that to which only the mind can attend. There are definite (finite) limits to ordinary human knowing.

Summary and Conclusion

In this chapter, we have examined several shared tenets of existentialism, Taoism, and Buddhism. Far from being exhaustive, this is a thumbnail overview. Among the themes highlighted are the shared inquiry into being, the shared concern with living—both individually and collectively--in the face of this condition, and the shared problem of truth. We have shown that although the respective worldviews converge on these points, they also exhibit nuances of difference. For example, while existentialists emphasize the mystery, and thereby (dynamic) tension of self-cosmic relations, Taoists and Buddhists stress the correspondence, and thereby (restorative) harmony of self-cosmic relations. Further, whereas existentialists stress the intensity, meaning, and passion of a life well lived, Taoists and Buddhists accent the acceptance, , and unfoldment of a life continually in flux.

In closing, it is our sincere hope that we have stimulated a fresh dialogue about existentialism, Taoism, and Buddhism. Undoubtedly, we have raised more questions than we have answered, but if these questions prove fruitful, if they inspire others to enlarge their horizons, then we will have more than fulfilled our task.

References

Aronson, H. B. 2004. *Buddhist practice on Western ground: Reconciling Eastern ideals and Western psychology.* Boston: Shambhala.

Barnes, H. (1967). *An existentialist ethics.* New York: Knopf.

Batchelor, S. (1990). *The faith to doubt: Glimpses of Buddhist uncertainty.* Berkeley, CA: Parallex Press.

Becker, E. (1973). *Denial of death.* New York: Free Press.

Bradford, G.K. (2007). The play of unconditioned presence in existential-integrative psychotherapy. *Journal of Transpersonal Psychology, 39,* 23-47.

Buber, M. (1970). *I and thou.* (W. Kaufmann, Tr.). New York: Scribner's.

Chang, Chung-Yuan (1975). *Tao: A new way of thinking.* New York: Harper and Row.

Bugental, J.F.T. (1987). *The art of the psychotherapist.* New York: Norton.

Conniff, R. (1994, March). Healthy terror (essay). *Atlantic Monthly.*

Cushman, P. (1990). Why the self is empty: Toward a historically situated psychology. *American Psychologist, 45(5),* 599-611.

Epstein, M. (1995). *Thoughts without a thinker: Psychotherapy from a Buddhist perspective.* New York: Basic Books.

Frankl, V. (1984). *Man's search for meaning.* (I. Lasch, Tr.). New York: Simon & Schuster.

Friedman, M. (1991). *The worlds of existentialism: A critical reader.* Atlantic Highlands, NJ: Humanities Press.

Fromm, E. (1956). *The art of loving.* New York: Harper & Row.

Galvin, J. (2008). Brief encounters with Chinese clients: The case of Peter. In K. Schneider (Ed.), *Existential-Integrative psychotherapy: Guideposts to the core of practice.* (pp. 168-175). New York: Routledge.

Heidegger, M. (1962). *Being and time.* (J. Macquarrie & E. Robinson, Trans.). New York: Harper & Row.

Heschel, A. (1951). *Man is not alone: A philosophy of religion.* New York: Farrar, Straus, and Giroux.

Hoffman, L., Stewart, S., Warren, D., & Meek, L. (in press). Toward a sustainable myth of self: An existential response to the postmodern condition. *Journal of Humanistic Psychology.*

Jordan, J.R. (1985). Paradox and polarity: The Tao of family therapy. *Family Process 24,* 165-174.

Liu, Da. (1979). *The Tao and Chinese culture.* New York: Schocken Books.

Marcel, G. (1967). *The philosophy of existentialism.* New York: Citadel.

Mendelowitz, E. (2008). *Ethics and Lao Tzu: Intimations of character.* Colorado Springs, CO: University of the Rockies Press.

Otto, R. (1923). *The idea of the holy.* London: Oxford University Press.

Rubin, J.B. (1996). *Psychotherapy and Buddhism: Toward an integration.* NY: Plenum Press.

Sartre, J.P. (1956). *Being and nothingness.* (H. Barnes, Trans.). New York: Philosophical Library.

Sartre, J.P. (1957). *Existentialism and human emotions.* New York: Philosophical Library.

Schneider, K.J. (1987). The deified self: A centaur response to Wilber and the transpersonal movement. *Journal of Humanistic Psychology, 27,* (196-216).

Schneider, K.J. (1999). *The paradoxical self: Toward an understanding of our contradictory nature.* Amherst, NY: Humanity Books.

Schneider, K.J. (2002). A reply to Roger Walsh. In K. Schneider, J. Bugental, & F. Pierson (Eds.), *The handbook of humanistic psychology: Leading edges in theory, research, and practice.* (pp., 621-624). Thousand Oaks, CA: Sage.

Schneider, K.J. (2004). *Rediscovery of awe: Splendor, mystery, and the fluid center of life.* St. Paul, MN: Paragon House.

Schneider, K.J. (2009). *Awakening to awe: Personal stories of profound transformation.* Lanham, MD: Jason Aronson.

Skinner, B.F. (1948). *Walden Two.* New York: Macmillan.

Smith, H. (1986). *The religions of man.* New York: Perennial Library.

Tillich, P. (1952). *The courage to be.* New Haven, CT: Yale University Press.

Tillich, P. (1957). *Dynamics of faith.* New York: Harper Torchbooks.

Tillich, P. (1967). *My search for absolutes.* New York: Simon & Schuster.

Tong, B. R (1992) The Tao of Chaos. *The Social Dynamicist, 3(4),* 9-10.

Tong, B. R (1999, Fall). Taoism: Concerned about wellness and then again not. *The Empty Vessel: A Journal of Contemporary Taoism 6(1),* 32-40.

Tong, B. R. (2003). Taoist mind-body resources for psychospiritual health and healing. In S. G. Mijares (Ed.), *Modern psychology and ancient wisdom: Psychological healing practices from the world's religious traditions.* Binghamton, NY: Haworth Press.

Tong, B. R. (in preparation). The Breath of the Tao and the Tao of Breathing. S. J. Mijares (Ed.), *The revelation of the breath: A tribute to Its wisdom, power and beauty* (working title).

Walsh, R. (2002). Authenticity, conventionality, and angst: Existential and transpersonal perspectives. In K. Schneider, J. Bugental, & F. Pierson (Eds.), *The handbook of humanistic psychology: Leading edges in theory, research, and practice.* (pp., 609-619). Thousand Oaks, CA: Sage.

Watts, A. (1961). *Psychotherapy East and West.* New York: Pantheon.

Watts, A. (1994). *Talking Zen: Written and spoken by Alan Watts* (M. Watts, Ed.). New York: Weatherhill.

Welwood, J. (2000). *Toward a psychology of awakening: Buddhism, psychotherapy, and the path of personal and spiritual transformation.* Boston: Shambhala.

7

Existential Themes in the Parables of Jesus

Mark Yang

This chapter explores the relationship between Christianity and existential psychology by presenting a few of Jesus' parables. Given that we will be presenting various myths from the East and the West in the following chapters, it is only appropriate that we understand Jesus' teachings through his parables. Parables, like myths are embodiments of great truths that challenge us to think and wrestle with symbolism and meaning. They represent truths, even if not literal truths. The first and main parable that I will present is the Parable of the Ten Virgins, which is found in the New Testament book of Matthew 25:1-13. It was a rather cryptic parable to me when I first read it. I was confused and could not believe that such a parable was told by Jesus and included in the Bible. However, my study of existential psychology helped to enlighten me to the wisdom in the moral of that parable. Similarly, existential themes helped me to have a deeper understanding of the parable that follows immediate after: The Parable of the Talents (Matthew 25: 14-30). Contrary to popular misconception, it is my passionate belief that existential psychology and philosophy share much more commonalities than differences with Christian teachings. My hope is that upon reading the existential themes presenting in this chapter and book, you too will come to a deeper understanding of the wisdom to be found in the parables told by Jesus.

Parable of the Ten Virgins

Then the kingdom of heaven will be like ten virgins who took their lamps and went to meet the bridegroom. Five of them were foolish, and five were wise. For when the foolish took their lamps, they took no oil with them, but the wise took flasks of oil with their lamps. As the bridegroom was delayed, they all became drowsy and slept. But at midnight there was a cry, 'Here is the bridegroom! Come out to meet him.' Then all those virgins rose and trimmed their lamps. And the foolish said to the wise, 'Give us some of your oil, for our lamps are going out.' But the wise answered, saying, 'Since there will not be enough for us and for you, go rather to the dealers and buy for yourselves.' And while they were going to buy, the bridegroom came, and those who were ready went in with him to the marriage feast, and the door was shut. Afterward the other virgins came also, saying, 'Lord, lord, open to us.' But he answered, 'Truly, I say to you, I do not know you.' Watch therefore, for you know neither the day nor the hour. (Matthew 25: 1-13, New International Version)

This is indeed one of the more cryptic parables told by Jesus. Usually the reader cannot understand why Jesus would tell a story in which the wise virgins will not share their oil with the foolish virgins. After all, isn't generosity and sharing some of the basic foundational teachings of Christianity and other religions? Furthermore, this parable is talking about the end times when the return of the bridegroom can be compared to the second coming of Jesus. The second coming refers to the time when Jesus will ireturn to take the believers back with him to heaven. So a lot is at stake here. We are talking about heaven, entering into the Kingdom of God! Thus, it is even more strange when this is compared to the Great Commission (Matthew 28:16-20, Mark 16:14-18, Luke 24:44-49, Acts 1:4-8, and John 20:19-23) in which the Christians are called to "make disciples of all nations . . ." Thus, one would think that Jesus would have rebuked the wise virgins for not sharing their oil instead of calling them wise. How can these "selfish" virgins be wise when they told the foolish virgins that "since there will not be enough for us and for you, go rather to the dealers and buy for yourselves" (vs. 9). Where is the wisdom in being selfish? However, upon the bridegroom's return, he took with him to the marriage feast (heaven) those wise virgins who were *ready* while the foolish virgins went to buy their own oil. The frightening thing is, when the foolish virgins returned and asked to be let into the marriage feast, Jesus said "Truly, I say to you, I do not know you. Watch therefore for you do not know neither the day nor hour" (vs. 12).

I am not sure of your reaction to this parable, but initially, mine was one of terror. But what helps to assuage this terror is an understanding of the existential themes throughout the parable. First of all, the key to understanding this parable hinges upon understanding the symbolism of the oil. The oil symbolizes *preparation*. The wise virgins were prepared and ready in anticipation of the bridegroom's return. They were alert (Mark 13:32-33). If the oil symbolizes preparation, the next question then is, "how do we become prepared?" In the language of the parable, "how or when do we buy the oil for ourselves?" I propose that being prepared and purchasing the oil for ourselves has everything to do with facing the four existential givens as proposed by Irvin Yalom (1980) in his classic textbook, *Existential Psychotherapy*: Death, Freedom, Isolation, and Meaninglessness. This chapter will endeavor to address the relationship between preparedness and these four all important existential givens.

Most Christians will immediately understand that this parable has to do with death and the end times. I believe that this understanding is not just intellectual, but also visceral as this is not a pleasant parable to read. My own reaction is to run away from this parable. Who would want to read about selfish people who refrain from sharing, only to be rewarded with eternal life; while the poor souls who were unprepared, perhaps simply lethargic, are punished by being kept out of the ultimate party and told by God, "I do not know you."? Most of the time, I prefer to avoid such unpleasantness, just as I prefer to deny the reality of death. Yet, Saint Augustine reminds us that "It is only in the face of death that a man's self is born" (as cited in Montaigne, 1965, p. 63). Seneca said likewise, "No man enjoys the true taste of life but he who is willing and ready to quit it" (as cited in Montaigne, 1965, p. 61). Cicero suggests that "to philosophize is to prepare for death" (as cited in Montaigne, 1965, p. 56). And finally, Irvin Yalom (2008) tells us "though the physicality of death destroys us, the idea of death saves us" (p. 7).

In regard to the first existential given, the importance of facing our own death or limits, it all begins with awareness or mindfulness. In the parable, both the wise and foolish virgins became drowsy and slept. The symbolism of drowsiness is powerful here. It is not just simply lethargy. Drowsiness can be understood as the lack of awareness, or the unwillingness to thinking more deeply - a certain kind of "forgetfulness of being" as proposed by Martin Heidegger (1962). In contrast, in this parable as in other parables, Jesus' followers are often warned to be watchful, to be alert. The majority of the time, these warnings occur in the context of Jesus' death and second coming: "Therefore keep watch, because you do not know on what day your Lord will come" (Matthew: 24:42).

> It's like a man going away: He leaves his house and puts his servants in charge, each with his assigned task, and tells the one at the door to keep watch. Therefore keep watch because you do not know when the owner of the house will come back—whether in

the evening, or at midnight, or when the rooster crows, or at dawn. If he comes suddenly, do not let him find you sleeping. (Mark 13:34-36)

Existentially, this alertness can be understood as mindfulness, what the Greeks referred to as the Ontological mode of existence where one remains not only mindful of the fragility of being (death), but mindful too of one's responsibility for one's own being. According to Heidegger (1962), this mindfulness entails being authentic, responsible for one's choices; where one embraces one's possibilities and limits; one faces absolute freedom and nothingness – and is anxious in the face of them (note, not the absence of anxiety). More on the theme of freedom and nothingness will follow later in the chapter.

To what are we to be aware of? First, the awareness begins with an attitude, the belief that life and death are simultaneous and interdependent. The fact that life and death are interdependent is well known. Most people know that in order to die well, one has to live well. In the words of Irvin Yalom (1980) "behind every fear of death is a life unlived" (p. 207) or "death anxiety is inversely proportional to life satisfaction" (p. 207). On the other hand, most people do not understand life and death to be simultaneous. Most people understand that death follows life; they are consecutive. Indeed, the pronouncement of death, also known as the Final Medical Act, is required to be performed by a physician. The barrier between life and death needs to be exact. Not so in the view of existential psychology. The act of baptism in Christianity symbolizes death followed by rebirth. Life and death were very much simultaneous in the life of Jesus as he warned constantly about his departure. The Triumphal Entry of Jesus (Matthew 21-22, Mark 11-12, Luke 19-20, John 12) also was very much about Jesus' awareness of his limited time on earth. Even the dual nature of Jesus being *both* human and divine is about the simultaneous existence of both mortality and immortality, life and death. The fact that Jesus' ministry and time on earth was very much limited added to the urgency and vitality of his ministry.

However, this awareness of the omnipresence of death is painful and anxiety producing. Indeed, one's confrontation with death is a terrible experience. It has been compared to *Staring at the Sun*, the title of Irvin Yalom's (2008) latest book on "Overcoming the Terror of Death" (e.g., the book's subtitle). One must not stare directly at the sun, this is utter foolishness. Instead, one confronts death obliquely, similar to how one is to experience the literal presence of God. Therefore, because the direct confrontation with death is so filled with anxiety, human beings have actively erected numerous defenses against this awareness. Such defenses are replete throughout the stories in the Bible. I have presented but two of these parables. The drowsiness on the part of the virgins, the beloved disciples of Jesus, and by extension to other followers, results not from passive laziness/lethargy or the lack of obedience, but from active denial. How else to explain Jesus' exasperation as he time and again warned the disciples of his imminent departure with statements such as "the Son of Man will suffer..." (Mark 8:31, Mark 9:12, Luke 9:22, Luke 24:7) and "the Son of Man comes at an unexpected hour..." (Matthew 24:44, Luke 12:40). One wonders how the disciples can be so thick-headed and ignorant. Yudhishtara understood this when he said "of all the world's wonders, which is the most wonderful? That no man, though he sees others dying all around him, believes that he himself will die" (as cited in Branfman, n.d.) Laziness has its limits and such ignorance can best be explained by an understanding of the active denial (versus passive laziness) that is required to avoid the unpleasant inevitable.

Instead of defending against death, existential psychology teaches that the best solution regarding the fear of death is to live life fully. In the words of Zorba the Greek, live life in such a way so as to "leave death nothing but a burned out castle" (as cited in Yalom, 2008, p. 50). Nietzsche implored us to "Consummate your life" And "Die at the right time" (as cited in Yalom, 2008, p. 50). Sartre (1981), in his autobiography, "I was going quietly to my end... certain that the last burst of my heart would be inscribed on the last page of my work and that death would be taking only a dead man" (p. 198). This is the principle behind the Parable of the Rich fool found in Luke 12:16–21, where Jesus warned about the foolishness of storing material things up when death comes calling. Instead, Jesus urges people to be rich towards God (v. 21) and store up our treasures in heaven (Matthew 6:19-21). This storing up of treasures in heaven is the essence behind the principle of rippling.

> Rippling is perhaps the singular idea that brings the most comfort in countering a person's death anxiety and distress at the transience of life. Rippling refers to the fact that each of us creates – often without our conscious intent or knowledge – concentric circles of influence that may affect others for years, even for generations. The idea that we can leave something behind of ourselves, even beyond our knowing, offers a potent answer to

those who claim that meaninglessness inevitably flows from one's finiteness and transiency. (Yalom, 2008, p. 83)

Rippling is also behind the idea of stewardship. In the parable immediately following the parable of the Ten Virgins, Jesus tells the Parable of the Talents (Matthew 25: 14-28). The moral of this parable is that we are all given talents according to our abilities. What is asked of individuals is that they put their talents to work so that the talents will multiply. The number and characteristic of the talents, and how we are to trade with them is individually defined. However, what is expected of Jesus' followers is that the talents will be used and this is where rippling applies. Christians are to steward their talents to allow the effects to multiply and ripple across generations. This is the work of the preparation that will assuage the fear of death and gain eternal life.

Parable of the Talents

Again, it will be like a man going on a journey, who called his servants and entrusted his property to them. To one he gave five talents of money, to another two talents, and to another one talent, each according to his ability. Then he went on his journey. The man who had received the five talents went at once and put his money to work and gained five more. So also, the one with the two talents gained two more. But the man who had received the one talent went off, dug a hole in the ground and hid his master's money. After a long time the master of those servants returned and settled accounts with them. The man who had received the five talents brought the other five. 'Master,' he said, 'you entrusted me with five talents. See, I have gained five more.' His master replied, 'Well done, good and faithful servant! You have been faithful with a few things; I will put you in charge of many things. Come and share your master's happiness!' The man with the two talents also came. 'Master,' he said, 'you entrusted me with two talents; see, I have gained two more.' His master replied, 'Well done, good and faithful servant! You have been faithful with a few things; I will put you in charge of many things. Come and share your master's happiness!' Then the man who had received the one talent came. 'Master,' he said, 'I knew that you are a hard man, harvesting where you have not sown and gathering where you have not scattered seed. So I was afraid and went out and hid your talent in the ground. See, here is what belongs to you.' His master replied, 'You wicked, lazy servant! So you knew that I harvest where I have not sown and gather where I have not scattered seed? Well then, you should have put my money on deposit with the bankers, so that when I returned I would have received it back with interest.' 'Take the talent from him and give it to the one who has the ten talents. For everyone who has will be given more, and he will have an abundance. Whoever does not have, even what he has will be taken from him. And throw that worthless servant outside, into the darkness, where there will be weeping and gnashing of teeth.' (Matthew 25: 14-30)

The Parable of the Talents also embodies the themes of freedom, responsibility, and destiny. In the parable, each of the servants was free and responsible to choose what to do with their talents. The same freedom applied to the wise and foolish virgins from the previous parable. The wise servants from the Parable of the Talents were cognizant of their responsibilities and chose to increase the value of their talents. The foolish servant, fearing the master, chose to run away from his responsibility and destiny, dug a hole in the ground, and hid his talent. As the result of his choice, even what he had was taken away from him and he was thrown into the darkness where there was gnashing of teeth (v. 30). Again a terrible story, full of terror! How then do we make sense of the fear of the foolish servant and such a strong reaction on the part of the master?

This is where an existential understanding of the concept of freedom can shed some light. Eric Fromm (1941) famous work *Escape from Freedom* informs us that we all are condemned to freedom. This is a very paradoxical understanding regarding the concept of freedom. Generally, freedom is something to be desired and people will lay their lives down for freedom, not to escape from it. Furthermore, condemnation is the antonym for freedom and yet Fromm states that we are condemned to freedom such that we want to escape from it. How do we understand this paradox?

According to Fromm, freedom is unavoidably tied to responsibility and destiny. Responsibility is equated with authorship. Jean-Paul Sartre

(1956) wrote that to be responsible is to be "the uncontested author of an event or a thing" (p. 633). To be aware of responsibility is to be aware of creating one's own self, destiny, life predicament, feelings, and, if such be the case, one's own suffering. Sartre, like Fromm, believes that human beings are *doomed* to freedom. Again, a paradox. One is entirely responsible for one's life, not only for one's actions but for one's failure to act. In the parables told by Jesus, the foolish servants failed to act, and the foolish virgins acted too late. Both were met with terrible consequences! Such responsibility is immense. Both to be responsible for oneself and one's world and to be aware of one's responsibility is a deeply frightening insight. Like the awareness of death, freedom is fraught with anxiety! James Truslow Adams observed that "Eternal anxiety is the lot of the free man" (see May, 1981, p. 185). Rollo May (1981) stated that "Freedom and anxiety are two sides of the same coin – there is never one without the other" (p. 190). And finally, Dostoevsky in his legend of the Grand Inquisitor in the *Brothers Karamazov* (1880/1990) said that "Man is tormented by no greater anxiety than to find someone quickly to whom he can hand over the gift of freedom with which the ill-fated creature is born" (p. 32).

Such anxiety is an unavoidable experience of freedom. Rollo May (1981) talks about the *anxious prophet* as one who experiences the anxiety that comes with his freedom to see into the future, to see beyond the usual limits in which other people see. May states,

> One way to distinguish between the authentic prophet or saint from the fanatic or charlatan is this: the authentic prophet feels anxiety about his role and the charlatan does not. Like the prophets in the Old Testament, the authentic ones do not want to be prophets; they do their best to decline the role. They would escape if they could because of the dizziness and dread such great freedom entails. Jonah even fled from Nineveh and had to be brought back by a whale to give his prophecies. (p. 193)

Indeed, we see Jesus struggling with his freedom, choice, responsibility, and destiny in the Garden of Gethsemane (Matthew 26: 36-45) when he prayed three times for the cup to be taken away from him. Jesus' prayer revealed his struggle with his destiny, "if it is possible, may this cup be taken from me" and with his freedom of choice, "Yet not as I will, but as you will" (v. 39). Even though Jesus' prayer was for the Father's will to be done, he still had to choose whether to obey God's will and the anxiety related that choice. The anxiety was distressing to the point to which Jesus uttered "my soul is overwhelmed with sorrow to the point of death" (v. 38).

Jesus' confrontation with freedom and destiny was evident throughout the entirety of his life, not only the end. Jesus' ministry began with the three temptations from the devil (Matthew 4:1-11) in which alternative choices were offered. In each case, Jesus made the *decision* to seek his own destiny, aligned with that of the Father, and follow the written word. Decisions are difficult because they require renunciation, relinquishment, exclusion, and limitation, all associated with death. For every yes, there must be a no, or a multitude of no's. The old priest in John Gardner's (1971) novel *Grendel* wisely told us that "Things fade; alternatives exclude.... The ultimate evil is that time is perpetual perishing and being involves elimination" (p. 115). As one therapist commented to an indecisive patient, "Decisions are very expensive, they cost you everything else." The temptations of Jesus make these points abundantly clear. The temptations were all about renunciation. Jesus talked about renunciation when he lovingly told a rich young man "to go and sell everything he had and give to the poor, and you will have treasure in heaven. Then come and follow me" (Mark 10:21). How difficult was/is this choice? Jesus later taught his disciples "that it is easier for the camel to go through the eye of the needle than for a rich man to enter the kingdom of God" (Mark 10:25). The decision was painful because it involved death.

As the quote above from the novel *Grendel* teaches us, death is associated with the painfulness of decisions. Things fading with time perpetually perishing is about death. The root of the word decide, *cidium*, means "slay," the "act of killing" as in homicide, suicide, pesticide. The rich young man knew of the wisdom of Jesus' words and went away sad (v. 22). The young man experienced the existential pain of renunciation, and knew that the decision involved death. Many think the rich young ruler was sad because the choice he was faced with involved the renunciation of his material wealth, but such an understanding does not go deep enough. The choice was also painful because it involves the death of his former life. Decisions are painful because they limit possibilities. Indeed Martin Heidegger (1962) defined death as the "impossibility of further possibility" (p. 93). The decisions that Jesus and the rich young man were faced with involved renunciation, death, and eternal life.

Furthermore, the difficulty of deciding is that decisions are continuous. Often, we think of monumental decisions. But decision making is often more of a gradual subtle process. Gaining awareness, therapists often help clients to appreciate that therapeutic change often does not consists of a single willful choice, but a gradual series of decisions each leading to the next. Although Jesus' ministry is bracketed by the monumental decisions above, we also read of Jesus making continuous choices to head toward Jerusalem and his destiny. Jesus choosing his destiny involved him explaining over and over again how the "Son of Man will be betrayed to the chief priests and teachers of the law. They will condemn him to death and will hand him over to the Gentiles, who will mock him and spit on him, flog him and kill him. Three days later he will rise" (Mark 10:33-34). In the words of Bronislaw Malinowsky (as cited in May, 1981), Jesus is making the choice to accept the *chains which suits him*:

> Metaphorically, freedom in its essence is the acceptance of the chains which suit you and for which you are suited, and of the harness in which you pull towards an end chosen and valued by yourself, and not imposed. It is not, and never can be, the absence of restrictions, obligations or law and of duty. (p. 83)

> Or in the poetic words of Lord Byron (as cited in May 1981, p. 204):

> My very chains and I grew friends,
> So much a long communion tends
> To make us what we are; - even I
> Regain'd my freedom with a sigh.

Jesus, in choosing his destiny, understands who he is, the Messiah, and the implications of him accepting his identity and his responsibilities. This is in contrast to the disciples who continually ignore Jesus' explanations and warnings about who he is and his destiny. How to explain such ignorance? One is tempted to view the disciples as simple fisherman who cannot grasp the reality of what Jesus was saying to them. Perhaps this is a passive kind of ignorance and lack of sophistication or intelligence. I do not think so. It makes more sense to understand the ignorance of the disciples as an active form of defense; a defense against Jesus' destiny and their own destinies, the defense against death. How else do you account for such repeated ignorance of Jesus' clear warnings. It is not that the disciples did not understand Jesus' warnings. At some level, they understood too well, and were struggling to accept their destinies as Jesus was marching toward his. Knowing in hindsight how most of the disciples were martyred, it is entirely understandable how one would repeatedly choose ignorance. Such existential courage is not easily found.

This constitutes Jesus' suffering. His beloved disciples were forever unaware of the reality of Jesus' destiny. We read of Jesus' exasperation as he beseeched the disciples over and over again, "How long will I be with you?" This is evidence of Jesus' loneliness; Jesus' suffering in the form of existential isolation. Although Jesus was surrounded by his disciples throughout the years of his ministry, we surmise that he was not suffering from interpersonal isolation or loneliness. In fact, Jesus often sought the sanctuary of solitude in order to pray and perhaps commune with himself. Indeed, Jesus was a model of balance between intrapersonal and interpersonal connectedness. He represented the ideal balance between being in relationship with others and maintaining time for solitude." As written above, Jesus began his ministry in isolation in the desert. Such solitude can be understood from the framework of Jesus nurturing his relationship with himself and with God, making sure that he is not intra-personally isolated. However, despite being interpersonally and intrapersonally connected, there is no escaping the suffering that Jesus is faced with in the form of Existential Isolation.

In addition to the constant disconnectedness between Jesus and his disciples in regard to Jesus' true destiny, perhaps the greatest instance of Jesus struggling with existential isolation was again his experience in the Garden of Gethsemane (Matthew 26:36-46). In the Garden, although Jesus had continually been headed toward Jerusalem and his death, he had to confront the fundamental decision once and for all whether to face up to his destiny. And again this decision was continuous for Jesus as he, both literally and symbolically, had to face up to this decision to take the bitter cup of suffering three times that early morning in Gethsemane. Such fundamental decisions confront each of us with existential isolation. Existential isolation refers to an unbridgeable gulf between oneself and any other being (Yalom, 1980). And death and dying is perhaps the most lonely of human experience. No one can die with one or for one. Martin Heidegger (1962) states that "though one can go to his death for another, such 'dying-for' can never signify that the other has had his death taken away in even the slightest degree. No one can take the other's death away from him" (p. 284).

Like death and freedom, a decision is a lonely act, and it is *our* act; no one can decide for us. No one can decide for Jesus. The decision was so painful that Jesus begged the Father on three occasions for "the cup to be taken away from him" (vs. 39, 42 & 44). Jesus also shared with Peter,

James, and John that "his soul is overwhelmed to the point of death." And in the midst of this pain, Jesus asked his most beloved disciples to "stay and keep watch with him" (vs. 38). Although Jesus took Peter, James, and John to be with him, he was fundamentally alone. No relationship can eliminate existential isolation. Each of us is alone in existence.

Yet, aloneness can be shared in such a way that love compensates for the pain of isolation. "A great relationship," says Martin Buber (1965), "breaches the barriers of a lofty solitude, subdues its strict law, and throws a bridge from self-being to self-being across the abyss of dread of the universe" (p. 175). But the disciples fell asleep at the Garden of Gethsemane and were not able to provide Jesus with the companionship he was seeking. Perhaps this is symbolic of that unbridgeable gap. Such was the depth of Jesus' isolation and sorrow. It is again interesting that the disciples, like the virgins in the parables, were also asleep. For it is difficult and painful to maintain awareness and alertness in the midst of such great suffering. Ah, for the relief and escape provided for by sleep to the depressed. Nevertheless, the courage to remain alert and aware is exactly what is required of companions, whether one be therapists or friend.

The episode in the Garden of Gethsemane is perhaps the penultimate event in Jesus' life and ministry. For Christians the world over, it cannot underestimate the importance of Jesus' decision for sacrifice and to follow the will of God unto death (with faith for resurrection). As written above, Jesus could not escape the fact that his decision at the Garden of Gethsemane was his alone. His ministry and his life necessitated that he face this all important decision and face it alone. It was the essence of his decision, for to "exist" means to stand-out. Often times, Jesus is characterized as fully integrated with the Father and the Holy Spirit in the Trinity. To the extent that this integration is not understood as three separate beings, such integration can be described as a form of fusion. However, it is my understanding that the meaning of Jesus being fully human (along with being fully divine, thus a mysterious paradox) meant that he had to depart and separate from the Father, taking on human likeness. Jesus' decision at the Garden of Gethsemane is perhaps the clearest illustration that there were two wills, Jesus' will and the Father's will. Jesus asked that "not as I will, but as you will" (Matthew 26: 39). So in many ways, Jesus' descent to be *with* us, meant that he had to separate, perhaps even individuate from the Father. This is the meaning of Jesus' existence—to stand out. The significance of Jesus' isolated decision, indeed the meaning of Jesus' redemption for the human race, required that he descend from heaven and make that isolated decision to pay the ultimate price. I do not think the decision, and the meaning and power of Jesus' decision to take on the sins of the world, would have had much significance if Jesus did not make a separate decision from the Father. For without struggle, suffering, thus faith, the decision and sacrifice would have been meaningless. In other words, if Jesus was fused with the Father so as to obviate the need to face this existential crisis, then the decision would have been meaningless; I argue that the meaning and redemptive power behind his decision and sacrifice would have been meaningless as well. In short, there are some who believe that the decision for Jesus to obey was "easy" because Jesus' will was so in-line (fused) with the Father. But I would view this as a form of fusion defense similar to the disciple's lack of understanding regarding the meaning of Jesus' decision to choose his destiny.

This theme of fusion-isolation, attachment-separation is a major existential developmental task. To relinquish a state of interpersonal fusion means to encounter existential isolation with all its anxiety and dread. But not to separate means not to grow up. The price for individuation is isolation. As Irvin Yalom (1980) teaches us:

> Existential isolation and interpersonal isolation are intricately interwoven. Emergence from interpersonal fusion thrusts the individual into existential isolation. A dissatisfying state of fusion–existence or too early or too tentative emergence leaves the individual unprepared to face the isolation inherent in autonomous existence. The fear of existential isolation is the driving force behind many interpersonal relationships and is, as we shall see, a major dynamic behind the phenomenon of transference. (p. 362)

James Bugental (1965) in his discussion of the problem of relatedness, plays on the word "apart" (p. 309). The human being's basic interpersonal task is to be at once *a-part-of* and *a-part-from*. Interpersonal and existential isolation are way stations for each other. One must first separate oneself from the other in order to encounter isolation; one must be alone to experience aloneness. But, it is the facing of aloneness that ultimately allows one to engage another deeply and meaningfully.

Bugental's discussion regarding a-part-of and a-part-from is an excellent understanding of Jesus being both fully human (a-part-of) and fully divine (a-part-from). In the end, Jesus is perhaps our greatest model of how to engage our developmental task of attachment-separation. He emerged from the unity of being in "perfect" relationship with the Father and individuated from the Father–acknowledged and resolutely confronted his isolation in human existence–and as the result was able to return to the unity with the Father while delivering salvation for the human race as the ultimate sacrifice of love.

Another way to understand Jesus' destiny was that his destiny was very much his purpose and meaning in life. Existential psychology places great emphasis upon the importance of one's meaning in life. Jung (1966) believed that meaninglessness was equivalent to illness. He wrote:

> Absence of meaning in life plays a crucial role in the etiology of neurosis. A neurosis must be understood ultimately as a suffering of a soul which has not discovered it's meaning... about 1/3 of my cases are not suffering from any clinical definable neurosis but from the senselessness and aimlessness of their lives. (p. 83)

Similarly, Victor Frankl (1959) stated that 20% of the neuroses he encounters in clinical practice derive from a lack of meaning. Frankl believed that the lack of meaning is the paramount existential stress. To him, existential neurosis is synonymous with a crisis in meaninglessness. Conversely, according to Frankl, there is nothing in the world that would so effectively help one to survive even the worse conditions as the knowledge that there is a meaning in one's life. There is much wisdom in the words of Nietzsche: "He who has a *why* to live for can bear almost any *how*" (as cited in Frankl, 1959) In Frankl's Nazi concentration camp experience, he could see that those who knew that there was a task waiting for them to fulfill were most apt to survive. Nicholas Hobbs (1962) agrees:

> Contemporary culture often produces a kind of neuroses different from that described by Freud. Contemporary neuroses are characterized not so much by repression and conversion... not by lack of insight but lack of a sense of purpose, of meaning in life. (p. 742–748)

Jesus' life was imbued with meaning. It is this meaning and purpose that helped him to endure the suffering that he encountered for much of his ministry. Nietzsche's words from above are illuminating because it was because Jesus' knew *why* he was in life that allowed him to know *how* to live his life and put up with the suffering he endured.

Meaning in life can be very simply categorized into two different categories: religious and secular. What I hope to show here is that although these are distinct categories, the similarities between them are far more important than their differences. Secular understandings of meaning in life, or more appropriately meaninglessness in life, are embodied by the nihilistic philosophies of Camus and Sartre. Camus (1955) used the world "absurd" to refer to the human being's basic position in the world–the predicament of a transcendent, meaning-seeking being who must live in a world that has no meaning. Camus referred to this as the absurd human condition. This is the essence of nihilism. Camus' solution for facing up to this absurdity is what he called "heroic nihilism." He heartened individuals to contemplate this basic absurdity and construct a new life meaning by cherishing our "nights of despair," by facing the very essence of meaninglessness and arriving at a position of "heroic nihilism." This would be Camus's understanding of Jesus' night of despair as Jesus fully faced up to his destiny and the meaning or possible meaninglessness of his life. It was only through this confrontation that Jesus was able to become fully who He wanted to or was meant to be. Thomas Hardy would agree as he said that "if a way to the Better there be, it exacts a full look at the Worst" (as cited in May, Angel & Ellenberger, 1958, p. 3). Similarly, a human being, Camus believed, can mature only by living with dignity in the face of absurdity. The world's indifference can be transcended by rebellion, a prideful rebellion against one's condition. So the values of heroic nihilism consists of courage, prideful rebellion, fraternal solidarity, love, and secular saintliness.

Sartre had a very similar understanding of the importance of being heroic in the face of this absurdity. Although Sartre's sense of freedom is uncompromisingly defined by meaninglessness, his solution, as embodied by the fictional characters in his book, is very similar to that of Camus. The characters in Sartre's books find meaning not by looking into "faith" in the religious sense, but by embracing commitment, action, and above all engagement. And this commitment and engagement is not characterized by self-fulfillment but service to others. Frankl (1959) agrees wholeheartedly when he described the "self-transcendence" of human existence He continues,

> I wish to stress that the true meaning of life is to be discovered in the world rather than within man or his own psyche, as though it were a closed system… It denotes the fact that being human always points, and is directed, to something, or someone, other than oneself – be it a meaning to fulfill or another human being to encounter. The more one forgets himself – by giving himself to a

cause to serve or another person to love – the more human he is and the more he actualizes himself. What is called self-actualization is not an attainable aim at all, for the simple reason that the more one would strive for it, the more he would miss it. In other words, self-actualization is possible only as a side-effect of self-transcendence" (p. 133).

Metaphorically, Frankl (1959) reminds us that a boomerang returns to the hunter who threw it only if it misses its target; in the same way human beings return to self-preoccupation only if they have missed the meaning that life has for them. Finally, in the words of Arthur Ashe (n.d.), the great American tennis champion, "From what we get, we can make a living; what we give, however, makes a life." What we get is destiny. What we give is freedom and responsibility.

In the end, what is important for both Camus and Sartre, is that human beings recognize that one must invent one's own meaning (rather than discover God's or nature's meaning). After that meaning is recognized, one then must commit oneself fully to fulfill that meaning. But however we classify that meaning, whether it is secular or religious, whether it arises out of meaninglessness or a dedication to a higher cause as in the case of Christianity, it is worthwhile to observe that there are very important common elements that consist of courage, commitment, engagement, fraternal solidarity, love, and secular/religious saintliness. Although the lack of understanding between Christians and existentialists would place the basic philosophies of Camus, Sartre, and Jesus at opposite ends of the spectrum, in the end both share some very important commonalities.

Camus and Sartre's call for individuals to be committed and engaged is embodied by the Parable of the Talents described earlier. The moral of the parable is engagement. The wrath of the master was reserved for the servant who buried his talent. The servant was labeled wicked and lazy for "burying" and refusing to trade with his talent. The servant refused to commit and engage. Instead of committing, he withdrew from the world. His fear was symbolized by his act of burial. It is interesting to note here that this servant's view of the master, perhaps his view of the world, was one characterized by harshness, unfairness and unpredictability (v. 24 & 26), similar to Camus's sense of absurdity. Yet, unlike the other two servants who traded and committed to action their given talents, this servant gave in to fear, and lacked the courage to engage and commit. Camus and Sartre would point out that this servant lacked courage, resoluteness, and even rebelliousness, and gave up in the face of absurdity. It is also interesting to point out that the "reward" for the other two servants were even greater talents, commitments, and actions, and the "sharing of the master's happiness" (v. 21 & 23). Perhaps this is illustrative of Frankl's (1959) wisdom in reminding us that meaning, success, love, and happiness *ensues*, they cannot be *pursued*. The servants in the parable were entrusted with their master's property. I imagine that they had to act upon some form of faith in order to make the decision to trade with their talents. It is also worth noting that both the two servants who traded with their talents were decisive and went at once to put their talents to work (v. 16-17). It can be said that they embraced their freedom, responsibility and destiny. But it was not certain that their reward and their happiness were sure to follow. For some reason, most likely out of faith, they chose to engage and trade; or perhaps it was simply out of the joy or meaning to be found in trading. Nevertheless, the meaning of their actions was to be found later. Meaning begets meaning; commitments and engagement begets more commitment resulting in happiness.

Another understanding of the lack of commitment from the "lazy" servant of the above parable is through the existential concept of authenticity. The parable begins with the master giving to each servant talents according to their individual abilities. To one servant he gave five talents and two talents to the other. Note that the master did not give equal numbers of talent to each servant. He gave according to ability and he was rewarded in the end according to ability. The master recognized individuality that has to do with authenticity. Existential philosophers and psychologists place great importance upon the concept of authenticity, being congruent and being true to oneself. Nietzsche challenged us to "become yourself" and to "consummate your life!" (as cited in Yalom, 1992). Similarly, Paul Tillich (1952), the Existential Theologian, wrote "man is asked to make of himself what he is supposed to become, to fulfill his destiny" (p. 52). Otto Rank (1945) also said "we feel ourselves guilty on account of the unused life, the unlived life in us" (as cited in Yalom, 1980, p. 278). Finally, the Hasidic rabbi, Susya, said this shortly before his death: "When I go to heaven they will not ask me, 'Why were you not Moses?' Instead they will ask 'Why were you not Susya?' Why did you not become what only you could become" (as cited in Friedman, 1965, p. xix)? Jesus had his destiny to fulfill. The different servants in the parable had their destinies to fulfill, and we all have our own destinies to fulfill. Frankl (1959) reminds us over and over,

Life's tasks form man's destiny, which is different and unique for each individual. No man and no destiny can be compared with any other man or any other destiny... When a man finds that it is his destiny to suffer, he will have to accept his suffering as his task; his single and unique task. He will have to acknowledge the fact that even in suffering he is unique and alone in the universe. No one can relieve him of his suffering or suffer in his place. His unique opportunity lies in the way in which he bears his burden. (p. 98–99)

Christians are called to be *like* Jesus, not to *be* Jesus.

Each of the two servants in the parable accepted their different talents and traded with them. The third servant was identified as being "lazy" and chose to bury his talent. A simple understanding of laziness has to do with physical laziness. But if he was so lazy, why did he even bother to dig a hole to hide his talent. His laziness had much more to do with fear, the fear of the master, and perhaps the fear of fulfilling his potential. The fourth cardinal sin in the Christian tradition is the sin of *accidie* which is defined as: sloth, torpor, acedia: apathy, boredom. As an aside, it is interesting to point out that boredom and apathy leads to lethargy and drowsiness which has been discussed above. A number of existential thinkers from Buber, Fromm, Allport, Rogers, Jung, Maslow, and Horney, have come to interpret accidie not in the simple terms of slothfulness but the sin of failing to live up to one's potential. Thus the sin of the servants and virgins were not sins of commission of having committed some criminal act, but the sins of omission, the regret of self-condemnation, of failing to act. Such regret is certainly thematically central to both the Parable of the Virgins followed by the Parable of the Talents.

Finally, the solution to "defeating" death in the Christian sense is to believe in Jesus and gain salvation. What does it mean to believe in Jesus and receive salvation? Both of these Parables above told by Jesus warns us that death is inevitable and that we must be prepared, which involves not burying but actively trading one's talent. Such preparation and trading in the existential sense involves Rippling. In the words of Irvin Yalom (2008):

Of all the ideas that have emerged from my years of practice to counter a person's death anxiety and distress at the transience of life, I have found the idea of ripping to be singularly powerful... Rippling does not necessarily mean leaving behind your image or your name... Attempts to preserve personal identity are always futile. Transiency is forever. Rippling as I use it, refers instead to leaving behind something from your life experience; some trait; some piece of wisdom, guidance, virtue, comfort that passes on to others, known or unknown (p. 83–84).

For existentialists, rippling is the solution that "defeats" death. Jesus' life is the ultimate example of rippling in Christianity. The effects and consequences of Jesus' death and sacrifice do not just ripple on at a nano level but powerfully across generations and generations of time. His legacy, what he left behind is the ultimate in self-transcendence and self-actualization according to the definitions above. It must have been his sense of purpose that helped him to cope with his suffering, his isolation, humiliation and the multiple rejections he faced. Again Nietzsche's words ring powerfully true here: He who has a "why" can bear with almost any "how." And as Christians, we are called to believe in Jesus, to follow him and to be like him. This means that each of us must "work out" our own salvations as Jesus worked out his own. As the parables of Jesus and the existential philosophers and theologians have reminded us over the ages, this has everything to do with how we deal with the unavoidable existential givens of life: Death, Freedom, Isolation, and Meaninglessness. We have been given our talents and the bridegroom will come for us all. How will we trade in preparation for his eventual arrival?

References

Ashe, A. (n.d.) *Quotes*. Retrieved December 7, 2008 from http://www. cmgww.com/sports/ashe/about/quotes1.htm

Branfman, F. (2008, Dec. 7). *The Salon Interview, Irvin Yalom: A Matter of Life and Death.* Retrieved December 7, 2008 from http://www.salon.com/weekly/yalom960805.html

Buber, M. (1965). *Between man and man.* New York: Macmillan.

Bugental, J. F. T. (1965). *The search for authenticity.* New York: Holt, Rinehart & Winston.

Camus, A. (1955). *The myth of Sisyphus and other essays.* New York: Alfred A. Knopf.

Dostoevsky, I. (1990). *Brothers Karamazov* (R. Peaver & L. Volokhonsky, Trans). New York: Farrar, Straus, and Giroux. (Original work published 1880)

Frankl, V. (1959). *Man's search for meaning.* New York: Pocket Books.

Friedman, M. (1965). Introduction. In M. Buber (author), *Between man and man.* New York: Macmillan.

Fromm, E. (1941). *Escape from freedom.* New York: Holt, Rinehart & Winston.

Gardner, J. (1971). *Grendel.* New York: Ballentine Books.

Heidegger, M. (1962). *Being and time*. New York: Harper & Row.

Hobbs, N. (1962). Principles of international psychotherapy. *American Psychologist, 17,* 742–748.

Jung, C.G. (1966). *Collected works: The practice of psychotherapy*, (Vol. XVI). New York: Patheon Bollingen Series.

Kazantzakis, N. (1952). *Zorba the Greek*. New York: Simon & Schuster. (Originally published in 1946).

May, R. (1958). The origins and significance of the existential movement in psychology. In R. May, E. Angel, & H. F. Ellenberger (Eds.), *Existence* (pp. 3-36). Northvale, NJ: Jason Aronson.

May, R. (1981). *Freedom and destiny*. New York: Norton & Company.

Montaigne, M. E. (1965). *The complete essays of Montaigne* (Ed. & Trans., D. Frame). Stanford, CA: Stanford University Press.

Rank, O. (1945). *Will therapy and truth and reality*. New York: Alfred A. Knopf.

Sartre, J. P. (1981). *The words*. New York: Vintage Books. (Originally published in 1964).

Tillich, P. (1952). *The courage to be*. New Haven, CT: Yale University Press.

Yalom, I. D. (1980). *Existential psychotherapy*. New York: Basic Books.

Yalom, I. D. (1992). *When Nietzsche wept*. New York: Basic Books.

Yalom, I.D. (2008). *Staring at the sun: Overcoming the terror of death*. San Francisco: Jossey-Bass.

8

The Heart of Jungian Analysis
and Existential Psychology[1]

Heyong Shen

My first formal class of Jungian psychology took place at the Institute of Transpersonal Psychology (ITP) in Palo Alto, California. Several important Jungians, such as June Singer and Thomas Kirsch were teachers there. I conducted a seminar on "Psychology of the Heart and the Heart of Psychology" at the ITP, and presented my work to integrate Analytical Psychology (i.e., Jungian) and Chinese Culture. The significance of Jungian psychology to me, my work, and the practice of Jungian analysis has been integrated with Chinese culture and further influenced by transpersonal and existential thought.

There are three important points in Jungian analysis: 1) the experience of the self; 2) active imagination; and 3) the individuation process. Each of these will be illustrated through stories about Jung.

After his separation with Freud, Jung went through a period of personal difficulty that proved highly formative on the development of his thought. He described this time in his autobiography *Memories, Dreams, Reflections*:

> After parting ways with Freud, a period of inner uncertainly began for me. It would be no exaggeration to call it a state of disorientation. I felt totally suspended in mid-air, for I had not yet found my own footing. (Jung, 1963, p.170)

Later, in the chapter "Confrontation with the Unconscious," it is important to keep in mind an old Chinese proverb that states, "the real learner learns from the heart, not from the master." In this chapter, Jung conveys how he stood his ground to face the unconscious by himself, which represents a

[1] The research was sponsored by the Foundation of China Ministry of Education for Humanities and Social Science Research (06 JJD 880021)

transition in Jung's thinking which emerged from working through these trials. He experienced many dreams and images later realizing, "dreams like this, and actual experiences of the unconscious, taught me that such contents are not dead, outmoded forms, but belong to our living being" (p. 173). He identified that below the threshold of consciousness, everything is seething with life. This is the most important point for Jungian psychology and represents a transition in the understanding of the unconscious in the depth psychologies.

In *Memories, Dreams, Reflections*, using the image of Philemon, Jung's inner Chinese Taoist teacher according to David Rosen (see Rosen, 1997), Jung made further exploration, "there are things in the psyche which I do not produce, but which prudence themselves and have their own life" (Jung, 1963, p. 183). Here we touch a key point of Jungian psychology, the autonomy of the psyche; the psyche produces things which have a life of their own. For Sigmund Freud, the heart of psychoanalysis is the Oedipus myth. For Jung, the Oedipus complex is very important, but most important is the fact that the psyche itself is producing myth.

This understanding is the key for the Jungian concept *Active Imagination*. Jung first formally expressed this idea in the book he wrote in conjunction with Richard Wilhelm: *The Secret of the Golden Flower* (Wilhelm & Jung, 1929/1931). He wrote commentary on the Chinese Taoist inner alchemy. Jung said in the book,

> What then did these people do in order to achieve the progress that freed them? As far as I could see they did nothing (*wu wei*), but let things happen, for, as Master Lu Tzu teaches in our text, the Light circulates according to its own law, if one does not give up one's accustomed calling. The art of letting things happen, action in non-action, letting go of oneself, as taught by Master Esckehart, became a key to me with which I was able to open the door to the 'Way'. The key is this: we must be able to let things happen in the psyche. (p. 90)

Allowing things to happen in the psyche is important for active imagination, as well as for healing, for personal growth, and for the individuation process.

For Jung, the goal of the individuation process is the synthesis of the self. As Daryl Sharp (1991) described in *Jung Lexicon: A Primer of Terms and Concepts*, the process of individuation leads to the realization of the self as a psychic reality greater than the ego. Thus, individuation is essentially different from the process of simply becoming conscious.

Jung expressed his early experiences encountered with Wilhelm through the cooperated work of *The Secret of the Golden Flower:*

> Some years later (in 1927) I obtained confirmation of my ideas about the center and the self by way of a dream. I represented its essence in a mandala which I called Window on Eternity. The picture is reproduced in The Secret of the Golden Flower. A year later I painted a second picture, like wise a mandala, with a golden castle in the center. When it was finished, I asked myself, Why is this so Chinese?
>
> It was a strange coincidence that shortly afterward I received a letter from Richard Wilhelm enclosing the manuscript of a Taoist-alchemical treatise entitled *The Secret of the Golden Flower*, with a request that I write a commentary on it. I devoured the manuscript at once, for the text gave me undreamed-of confirmation of my ideas about the mandala and the circumambulation of the center. That was the first event which broke through my isolation. I became aware of an affinity; I could establish ties with something and someone. (Jung, 1963, p. 197)

The experiences of the self, along with the way of Active Imagination, and the reality of the psyche, helped Jung journey through the process of his individuation. Jung presented such summery in the *Secret of the Golden Flower*.

> Its effect is astonishing in that it almost always brings about a solution of psychic complications, and thereby frees the inner personality from emotional and imaginary entanglements, creating thus a unity of being, which is universally felt as a release. (Wilhelm & Jung, 1975, p. 105)

Psychology of the Heart

There is a strong inner relationship between Jungian psychology and Chinese culture. Jung learned the Chinese language, studied *I Ching* and Daoist inner alchemy, and Chinese philosophy. I utilize the term Psychology of the Heart to present the system of Chinese cultural psychology that involves the integration of Jungian psychology and Chinese culture. To understand the Psychology of the Heart, we need to start with the following story from Jung.

In 1924, Jung traveled to America, where he visited the Taos Pueblos in New Mexico. He befriended the chief of the Taos Pueblo Indians, Mountain Lake. Jung asked Mountain Lake why he thought the European white people were all mad. Mountain Lake replied: "Because they say that they think with their heads." Jung said, "Why of course," and asked him in surprise, "What do you think with?" Mountain Lake said: "We think here" and pointed at his heart (Jung, 1963, p. 251). Jung, in *Memories, Dreams, Reflections*, said that he fell into a long meditation:

> this Indian had struck our vulnerable spot, unveiled a truth to which we are blind. I felt rising within me like a shapeless mist something unknown and yet deeply familiar. Something else that Mountain Lake said to me stuck in my mind. It seems to me so intimately connected with the peculiar atmosphere of our interview. (Jung, 1963, p. 248)

Jung believed that American Indians were native Chinese who had traveled to the America through the Bering Strait thousands of years ago.

Let us compare this to the Chinese way of thinking, which involves thinking with head and heart together. I call this the "thinking-heart."

This Chinese character has two parts: the upper part is the top of the head (the fontanel); and the lower section, like a support and container, is the heart. According to the dictionary, Shuo-Wen-Jie-Zi of the Han dynasty, the explanation of Si (i.e., thinking) is: "for thinking, following the heart and head, from the fontanel to the heart, consistent, non-stop connecting and communicating." What is most important in the image is that head and heart are combined together. This is the key point of Jung's transcendental function as well as the real meaning of the doctrine of thinking in Chinese tradition. Furthermore, in the Chinese character of Si, the relationship between the fontanel and the heart conveys the symbolic meaning of communication between the human heart and heaven. The image of fontanel in Chinese is described by the esoteric alchemist as "heaven top" (the head is usually compared to heaven in the symbolic system of *I-Ching*). So, in the image of the Si (the thinking-heart), the "ideal state" of "heaven and man" is combined together: *Tian-Ren-He-Yi*, the Unity of Heaven and Man.

The meaning of the heart in Chinese can be described in three dimensions. The first two dimensions are psychological and the third, metaphysical. First, the ancient Chinese believe that the heart is the root and nature of life, and at the same time, the heart is the changing of mind and spirit. Second, the heart represents thinking, emotion, will, love, and hate. The Chinese perceive the heart as the totality or synthesis of all psychological phenomena and processes. Third, the ancient Chinese used the heart to express the heaven mind, heaven heart, and the heart of Tao. The Heart of Tao is the most important image in the book of *I Ching*. As Confucius said in the *Great Commentary*: "the sage wash the heart with *I Ching*. In Chinese Confucian tradition, benevolence, righteousness, propriety, and knowledge (the four pillars of Confucianism), they are all rooted in the heart."

The heart is also the most important issue of Taoist tradition. Zhuang Zi once said, the highest essence of truth is used for examining the heart. Guan Yi Zi took the heart, matter, and the Tao as the three basic elements, but the three can become a unified one, and the most important thing is to use the heart to get the unified one. That is just what the Taoist Guan Zi expressed, cultivate your heart first, and then the Tao will come to you naturally.

The Chinese Chan Buddhism was called the Heart Sect. Hui Neng, the real founder of Chinese Chan Buddhism, once said to his teacher Hong Ren,

> Who would have thought, that the Essence of Heart is intrinsically pure! Who would have thought that the Essence of Heart is intrinsically free from becoming or annihilation! Who would have thought that the Essence of Heart is intrinsically self-sufficient! Who would have thought that the Essence of Heart is intrinsically free from change! Who would have thought that all things are the manifestation of the Essence of Heart.

This understanding and wisdom is the foundation for the Psychology of the Heart.

Existence, Expressive, and Embodiment

In both Jungian analysis, and the Psychology of the Heart, the purpose of psychotherapy consists of healing, the individuation process, wholeness, and pursuing the meaning of life. Feelings of meaninglessness lead to psychological diseases. These diseases can be overcome by creating one's own values and by finding the meaning of life.

For the Chinese, finding the meaning of the heart is to find the meaning of life. For example, while working in Sichuan recently after the 512 earthquake, the psychological support that was provided can be expressed in the two Chinese characters: Ci-Bei (grace, compassion, mercy), which I translate as "loving-grief"

Let us look at the following images of the two Chinese characters "Ci Bei":

They are both based on the heart, the lower part of the two characters is the image of the heart. The image of the first character, is nurturing the heart, and the second, is the lost heart. According to the psychology of grief and trauma, when we experience too much stress and trauma, disassociation and split occurs. The second character of Ci Bei (Bei) has an image of disassociation, the heart is lost, is not your heart anymore (fei, the upper part of Bei, in Chinese means lost and not), and the heart is flying away like a broken kite. When someone has lost his heart, grief and trauma take over. The image of the first character of Ci (grace and love) conveys the meaning of associating, and nurturing, and heart-growing. Healing occurs through associating the disassociated pieces of psyche, nurturing the heart, and understanding the meaning of life, through Ci-Bei (i.e., through love and grace).

We named our psychological aid work station at Sichuan area as the "Garden of the Heart and Soul." The main methods we are using is Jungian analysis, Jungian Sandplay, and the Psychology of the Heart. Dora Kalff (2004), who developed the Jungian sandplay, had learned Chinese when she was young. In her book *Sandplay: A Psychotherapeutic Approach to the Psyche*, she used Chinese philosophy as the most important foundation of sandplay therapy. She started with Zhou Dunyi`s I-Ching model and ended with Hexagram 29 of the I-Ching: "Only the heart can penetrate the difficulties and find the meaning of the situation." To me, the Jungian sandplay manifests the Chinese saying: "Receive from the heart, and respond with the hands." Combining active imagination and sandplay therapy, we can use the Chinese way of embodied imagination: through body-knowledge, embodiment process, to body-heart enlightenment.

The practice of both Psychology of the Heart, and Jungian analysis in China, involves healing and transformation. There is an old Chinese saying: "a sick heart (psychological disease) needs heart-medicine for treatment;" it needs creating peace in one's heart, as well as psychological education (i.e., enlightening the heart for the individuation process) and transformation. The most important principle for such a practice is from the I-Ching, especially from the 31st Hexagram: "Wholehearted influence" (touching by the heart and responding from the heart):

> Heaven and earth exert their influences, and ensure the transformation and production of all things. The sages influence the heart of men, and the result is harmony and peace all under the sky. If we look at (the method and issues) of those (wholehearted) influences, the true character of heaven and earth and of all things can be seen. (I-Ching, 31, The Great Commentaries).

So, Psychology of the Heart, combined with Jungian analysis, is the key point to understanding our work at the Sichuan earthquake area; it essentially involved heart-thinking and thinking-heart.

There are three important steps in our work for that involved a Jungian-style psychological intervention. First, we start with the association and building of the safe, contained, empathetic, free and protected relationship. Then, we utilize symbols, images, Jungian Sandplay, and expressive and embodied work to deal with grief and trauma issues. Finally, we have work to find the lost heart, to find the opportunity within the crises, to find the value of existence, to find the meaning of everyday life, and ultimately, to experience the meaning of transformation.

References

Jung, C. G. (1963). *Memories, dreams, reflections.* New York: Pantheon.

Kalff, D. M. (2004). *Sandplay: A psychotherapeutic approach to the psyche.* Cloverdale, CA: Temenos Press.

Rosen, D. (1997). *The Tao of Jung: The way of integrity.* New York: Penguin.

Sharp, D. (1991). *Jung lexicon: A primer of terms and concepts.* Toronto, Canada: Inner City Books.

Wilhelm, R. & Jung, C. G. (1931). *The secret of the golden flower: A Chinese book of life* (C. F. Baynes, Trans.). New York: Causeway Books. (Original work published in 1929)

9

Global Authenticity

Myrtle Heery

> I know what you want. You want a story that won't
> surprise you. That will confirm what you already know.
> That won't make you see higher or further or differently.
> You want a flat story. An immobile story. You want dry,
> yeastless factuality.
>
> ~ *Life of Pi*, Yann Martel

Dry factuality does not have the capacity to make meaning out of life, but surprise does. My global teaching experience has certainly been full of many dry facts and activities, such as gathering visas, organizing papers, purchasing airline tickets, and so on. These dry facts formed a container where surprises created in me what I have come to call *global authenticity*.

Over the past twelve years I have taught students of psychology and psychotherapists in Canada, China, England, Switzerland, Holland, Mexico, Russia, and the United States. I have introduced the basics and application of existential-humanistic psychotherapy in classes, seminars, and workshops. Some students had extensive knowledge of psychotherapy and others were beginners in psychotherapy. These years of global teaching have formed a colorful tapestry of rich and diverse stories from students, their clients, and me. The threads used to weave this tapestry are the givens of the human condition that are central to existential-humanistic psychotherapy.

Four Givens

Different theorists in the existential school (Yalom, 1980) and the existential-humanistic school (Bugental, 1965) expound on the givens of the human condition. I will review with you four givens that Bugental and I (2005) presented in a chapter titled *Listening to the Listener*, which focused on therapy with the therapist using the existential-humanistic model.

1. Embodiedness

Everyone has a body, a vehicle through which to experience life. This is the given of *embodiedness* (Heery & Bugental, 2005). From moment to moment, we experience the dualities of hunger and satiation, pleasure and pain, robustness and illness, high or low energy. Over time, our bodies grow, mature, and age, continually reminding us that life is change.

Some people spend much time caring for and enhancing their bodies. This can become an obsession; a desperate act to pretend there is physical permanence in the face of inexorable physical change. Psychological distress often arises when one denies or confronts the impermanence of the body. No one is immune to this.

2. Finitude

As each now-moment slips away into the next moment, we continually experience the given of *finitude*, the limitedness of life (Heery & Bugental, 2005). We face loss with situations beyond our control and with continual change. Yet we seek certainty in a variety of ways: by training to become a therapist, passing exams as a student, or buying fine furniture for our office. We try to avoid unwanted contingencies, but there are always circumstances beyond our control.

The one finitude that lurks beyond our control is our death. The awareness of death is the ultimate experience of finitude. We do not know when, where, or how we will die. We do know that we will die. Listening to concerns of death is a reminder of one's own death (Heery, 2001). The simultaneous certainty and uncertainty of death impacts us powerfully. Each of us is impacted differently in the way we live our lives. Some of us seek certainty by saving money, while others risk money by gambling or investing in the stock market.

We can view both the risk taking and security seeking as attempts to deal with the ultimate finitude of death. Everyone lives accompanied by the shadow of death, regardless of social status or culture.

3. Choicefulness

Life presents us with choices on every front, from what to eat for breakfast to what to do with the rest of our lives. This is the given of *choicefulness* (Heery & Bugental, 2005). It is paradoxically and inextricably interwoven with our experience of finitude: The choices available to us may not be endless; nonetheless, even declining to choose is making a choice.

Traveling to different countries and teaching psychotherapy is a choice. Picking up this book and reading this chapter is a choice. And to stop or continue reading this chapter is a choice. We have the capacity of choice no matter what we face; there is always a choice. Inherent in our choosing is our responsibility for acting or not acting. No matter where you live or under what circumstance you find yourself, no matter how limited the circumstance may be, there is always the element of choice. And the limited circumstances can leave limited choices but choice is still present.

4. Being a part of and apart from

Being *a part of* and *apart from* is another given of the human condition that existential-humanistic psychotherapy recognizes (Heery & Bugental, 2005). Just as life continually presents us with choices, so we continually face the experience of feeling *a part of* some situations and *apart from* others. This given involves a paradox: We can no more feel connected with everyone and everything around us than we can feel disconnected from them. We connect with humanity all the time, yet we are each uniquely apart from it at the same time.

Teaching in different countries can be enriched by being a part of different students' and therapists' journeys in learning. When I complete a training and wave good-bye to my colleagues at the airport, I turn to myself. I am surrounded by other travelers, but I sit alone. I look out the airplane window remembering all the shared moments of honesty, vulnerability, and courage. I may or may not ever see those individuals again. There is a sharp aloneness that I recognize. I, along with everyone else, ultimately arrive in this world alone and leave alone. Life is with others, yet each of us is ultimately alone. This paradox of being *a part of* and *apart from* follows each of us no matter where we live.

Authenticity Remembered

As I look over my shoulder at my international teaching experiences, I see faces, stories, tears, laughter, and so much more all weaving the givens of the human condition. I am humbled by the depth of each story, and by those who reached deep inside themselves in front of primarily strangers to make meaning of their lives.

I remember a tall well-dressed Russian woman. The suit she wore every day was the same and in perfect order. I noticed her physical appearance each day and wondered about her. I remember her certainty and her quiet manner. I trusted she would speak in time, which she did, and there was the surprise.

On the second day of the training, I began speaking to the given of finitude and how each of us carry the fact of our death. She raised her hand and said with certainty that she had cancer and might be dead in a few months. She continued to share that she was making the best of each moment, which included looking her best and being as honest as possible in all relationships. She actually felt grateful for her cancer because it added depth to her present appreciation of life.

I shared through my translator how deeply moved I was by her honesty and courage. Since I do not speak Russian, I relied on my intuitive sense to connect with her and the participants during this vulnerable moment. I was sensitive to the depth of her sharing, looking closely in her eyes and gently moving my eyes to each participant. The caring from participants was palpable. Some eyes were moistened and all were obviously moved. I invited the participants to share their feelings with her if they felt moved to do so. One person who knew the Russian woman spoke with great depth of appreciation. First, she thanked her for her honesty. Then, with great emotion, she shared how important she was to her in deciding to stop complaining about her life and, instead, live with appreciation. By watching her friend face her cancer with dignity, she had gained a new life. As others followed and movingly shared their feelings, the group drew closer together.

The experience of sharing a life-threatening illness with a group is powerful no matter what country or circumstance. In this teaching situation, the students immediately experienced the connection of sharing the possibility of an individual death. In teaching, there is "talk about" a subject and a "lived experience" of a teaching.

This experience took place many years ago and I do not know if this participant lived or died. I do know that her vulnerability brought the group into an immediate depth of authenticity that I had seen in many other groups in many other locations. The fact of her possible death and what she chose in facing her death was a huge piece of global authenticity. The possibility of her death brought us each into the reality of death. Even now eight years later, I can still see her in my mind and hold this experience close to my being. The courage to share her confrontation with her own death with mostly strangers has been engraved on my heart.

My memories of authenticity were captured in other surprises. Preparation for all my international teaching has been arranged primarily through e-mail. The fabric of trust and responsibility is woven through this electronic medium. On my first trip to Russia, I had not met some of my organizers so when I arrived in the airport and was greeted by no one, I realized I did not know what they looked like. They did know what I looked like from a video I sent but still there was no one there greeting me.

My fear began to rise as I looked through the sea of unknown faces. Then a striking blonde woman emerged from the crowd. She looked at me and said in clear English, "Seminar, seminar?"

"Oh yes, yes, seminar," I gleefully responded.

I restrained myself from embracing my apparent rescuer and we politely shook hands. In broken English, I was introduced to a gentleman whom I took to be the professor who had been e-mailing me.

We laughed about our e-mail. Then they asked where the other person was. I explained with the help of my fingers that there was only one, never two people. We proceeded to the sidewalk with my luggage. I was then informed that the seminar started that night. This was not what we had arranged, but I let this communication pass as the language barrier seemed insurmountable in my tired state. They said they would take me to my hotel. As the door to the car opened, I communicated as clearly as possible that in the last e-mail, we had confirmed my staying with the professor and his family. They assured me this was absolutely not true. I stepped back from the car. The woman then said in very clear English, "Football seminar!"

I responded, "Psychology seminar!"

They rushed back toward the terminal. I stood on the sidewalk with my luggage and looked at the distant terminal, with no clue about my next step. I could not help but laugh as I thought of missing my son's football game that day. And yes, if I had come for the football seminar, I might actually get some fame and money. My journey was definitely not one for the ego. At this point, I would need some heavy reliance on my soul.

It was certainly an existential moment. What were my choices? I decided to return to the terminal and wait by my arrival gate. As I pulled my bag, I looked into the terminal. For the first time, I had the very sharp awareness that the area I was walking into was filled primarily with men. There were very few women. The voice of fear came up. What am I doing here? Then a wave of courage and determination that I knew I could depend on overcame the fear. I had come to know this part of myself in many other circumstances in my life. I knew I would be fine. I could meet this situation with quiet resolution.

Within minutes after I got to the gate, another blonde woman arrived, and said to me, "Seminar?"

This time I responded, "Psychology seminar?"

She smiled and immediately hugged me. I felt a physical relief for both of us as we stood for a few seconds longer in our shared hug. In excellent English she said, "Myrtle, welcome to Russia. I am so sorry we are late. There was a terrible traffic problem."

The story of my arrival would be told and retold in Russia and America. It would be a central thread in my adventure. In so many ways, all of the human emotions that needed to come up for me did so during this airport experience. My fears, doubts, mistrusts, excitement, humor, and hopes were all present. My ability to make choices, to take responsibility, and to recognize the limits of my situation were all present. The knowns and unknowns were present. My capacity to transcend the boundaries of the present moment was supported by a deep reverence and trust for life. (Heery, 2001).

There were so many more experiences that brought surprise in connection with other human beings. I remember running with a Chinese student in Beijing to catch an underground train and her shouting, "Professor is late, please." And so many people moving aside to let me get in the train first so I could quickly get to the university. The respect for me as a professor still brings tears to my eyes as I recall this experience of global authenticity.

Global Authenticity in the Psychotherapy Room

I invite you now into the lives of two American psychotherapy clients. Their stories might surprise you. In fact, you may begin to see yourself through their stories no matter what country you are living in or in what language you are reading the story. You will begin to see the face of global authenticity, sometimes harsh and sometimes soft.

At 47, Ron entered therapy. His wife was exasperated at the renewed drain on the family income, which was comfortable but had never permitted the little extras she thought their ages and position should have warranted. Ron heard her out, promised to try to keep the cost of therapy down and maybe to earn a little extra to pay for it and then dismissed the matter. In therapy, Ron insisted he could afford no more than one visit a week and formed a strong bond with me, while still retaining a distance. We worked together well in some ways, but therapy with Ron was a frustrating experience for me. He was pleasant and appreciative; confirming what is known and avoiding the unknown. There were no surprises. This case was challenging. The questioning of what stops us and what moves us is part of our great quest for authenticity in living. This fact of living gets put to the fire in an authentic psychotherapeutic relationship.

At 45, Vicki entered therapy with me. Her husband had very little tolerance for her therapy, stressing that they could not afford to pay for it. Vicki heard him out and made a plan to pay for the therapy herself. In therapy, Vicki insisted that she could not afford more than one visit a week and the therapy began under these restricted conditions.

Vicki was eager to work, yet she stayed at a distance. At first this seemed to be due to the time restrictions on our sessions, but it turned out that the distance was the actual work: why was Vicki keeping distance from living her life fully? To bridge this distance, we worked in many ways to get through her resistance to deeper life-changing processes, but nothing seemed to help. Vicki was very compliant in many ways and her compliance frequently put her in a rather passive role during the therapy hour. This was a clear mirror of how she lived her life outside of therapy. I could describe how we attempted to work through her passivity, but that would not surprise you. Instead I would like to turn your attention to the larger story that helped her see deeper and differently.

Very similar to Ron, Vicki was a "good client," following what she thought to be the rules of therapy. Coming faithfully once a week, reporting her life story for that week, and paying for her therapy on time. Both clients filled their therapy rooms with boredom. I thought more than once of suggesting that Vicki stop coming — but I did *not*. This *not* with both clients is what I want to share with you

Ron and Vicki had some similarities in lifestyle. Both were married with children. Their lives were good by many standards: owning their own homes, successful jobs, and steady marriages accompanied by all the material things that are supposed to make people happy. However, both were unsatisfied and reported being at odds with their outer lives and wanted to change how they were living. Before entering therapy they had individually decided to break away from their ordinary lives and take a week's vacation alone. To break away from their respective lives even for a week — especially alone — was enormous but they each surmounted the hurdles to it.

Their individual experiences alone for a week opened their eyes to a world that they had previously known only as a fantasy, but now was a reality. Their perspective days began and ended as they chose, with no expectations, obligations, or responsibilities to or from others. Now Ron and Vicki did not know each other. There were similarities and differences with these two individuals that drew a deeper search. This deeper search brought them each into therapy. In my listening to their respective recounting of their one-week vacation, I consistently found a quality of timelessness that filled each of their days on this vacation, a quality which both reported had renewed and awakened them.

They each had experienced their lives from inside — not out, a primary step in the journey toward authenticity (Bugental, 1965). There is a story of Native Americans in Oklahoma who had lived in hovels for many years and then became suddenly very wealthy from oil rights. They hastened to buy radios, washing machines, and other gadgets of affluence with which they stocked their homes. But they had no electricity!

The deeper implication here is that the present global collection of material objects can only be created by and tolerated by people who are in large part dead to focusing on their inner potential. In that statement I include us all, certainly myself as much as anyone. We each intend to start living authentically one day, but when? There is an inner terror that is happening across the globe, the terror of not living our given life.

I have said that Ron and Vicki came to some awareness that they were dead, were non-being. The reasonable question is why don't they change? Since they know how dead they are as individuals and obviously want to be more alive, what stops them? What stops each of us?

No matter where you are physically living, there is a fear of authentic living in each one of us.

> For fear, real fear, such as shakes you to your foundation, such as you feel when you are brought face to face with your mortal end, nestles in your memory like a gangrene: it seeks to rot everything, even the words with which to speak of it. So you must fight hard to express it. You must fight hard to shine the light of words upon it. (Martel, 2001, pp. 160-161)

In Ron's and Vicki's search for an authentic life, they each found on their individual retreats a quality of timelessness that filled their days with a sense of renewed life. They both felt awakened. When they returned to their ordinary lives they felt stuck again and again. They were unable to take the risks in the everyday moments to be authentic. Their retreats had given each a glimpse of the possibility of authenticity, but how could they realize that authenticity in their daily lives of work and family? They were awakened to their human potential out of context, yet fell back asleep when they returned to their ordinary lives. Both individuals faced fear concerning the limitations of being human.

As I see it, Ron and Vicki both faced an existential crisis. Each given of the human condition was in operation: being finite, being able to choose and be responsible, and somehow being related to others even as they experienced the concurrent gulf of separateness that divided them from others. Each of these conditions gave rise to the fear and anxiety each experienced. To the extent that they meet this anxiety head-on and incorporate it with courage into their very being, to that extent Ron and Vicki may be said to be authentic.

"Vicki, how is it serving you right now, in this moment, to not look at other choices you have concerning your work?"

"Oh, I appreciate your thoughtfulness about possible other work for me, but gee, I think it might be best if I just settle back into my work and stop all this complaining."

"Vicki, that is your choice to settle back. The question remains how do the choices you are making serve you? It is your life we are speaking to in this moment."

This vignette shows us how Vicki's resistance moves her away from the deeper search for an authentic life. It shows how the therapist's job is to *hold to the possibility of the authentic* Vicki by questioning the moment, "How does your choice serve you in this moment?" Hopefully, Vicki will not stand apart from her life but rather experience *how* standing apart interferes with her living. It is her life. Her family relations, her work, her recreation — quite literally all that she does — are expressions of her search for or flight from authenticity. Every choice is present in the moment in psychotherapy and our job as psychotherapists is to mirror and question those choices in the moment, in the room. We are not asking about her work or about her family of origin. We are asking *how the choices she is making in this moment are serving her.* I take small steps with Vicki, noting the resistance patterns that interfere with the searching process in the here and now. In time, Vicki will come to experience the interference of limiting her choices here and now and begin to choose for herself a life in the actual moment (Bugental, 1999).

I experience being a part of Vicki's dilemma. I encounter Vicki. This does not mean a kind of exhibitionism or display of myself. It does mean a willingness to *be there* with her, to confront her directly as shown above, to take responsibility for my own thinking, judgments, feelings, and to be authentic in my own person with Vicki. My model of authenticity has a curative effect on Vicki. Our work is real. Vicki's ways of relating to herself and her world are continually challenged through our relationship until she begins to open to other possible choices in her daily life, not just on a week's vacation. Through *a challenging relationship of psychotherapy* Vicki begins her small steps toward an authenticity that are as real to me as it is to her.

We all know too well these choices of Ron and Vicki. It is not unusual for people with very busy lives to take a week's vacation on their own and to find when they return they are starved for more in the life they have chosen. These dilemmas are pervasive in all we say and do. We cannot stand apart from the issues of inauthentic being, for indeed our lives are caught up in just such matters. Ron, Vicki, and Myrtle have a common plight of authenticity. When I return from each international teaching, I face bringing my expanded awareness into my daily life. It is a challenge I face each time I teach internationally. Will I return and if I do, where will I be inside and outside?

This commonality is essential to the therapeutic alliance, where the therapist recognizes how he or she, too, struggles with similar issues. This recognition is often renewed in consultation with other therapists. During these consultations I openly discuss my deep concerns and uncertainties that continually renew my journey full of all its foibles. I must dare to walk my talk. The walk of authenticity is a courageous walk full of paradoxes. As I share these thoughts with you today, I hold the very real possibility that my life will end one day. And, my mentor, James F. T. Bugental, PhD, age 92, has just died. His death was not a surprise, yet I miss his physical presence. I celebrate his courageous, authentic life with each of you now as I share the awesome potential of living with the search for authenticity, both globally and individually.

In order for any individual to make this leap into authentic being, he or she must be willing to hold uncertainty. This is the paradox of authenticity — we want authenticity. We also want certainty. Embracing authenticity is a great act of faith, an act of embracing uncertainty. Just as we do not know when we will die, we hold the fact that one day we each will die.

> We are floating in a medium of vast extent, always drifting uncertainly, blown to and fro; whenever we think we have a fixed point to which we can cling and make fast, it shifts and leaves us behind; if we follow it, it eludes our grasp, slips away, and flees eternally before us. Nothing stands still for us. This is our natural state and yet the state most contrary to our inclinations. We burn

with desire to find a firm footing, an ultimate, lasting base on which to build a tower rising up to infinity, but our whole foundation cracks and the earth opens... (Pascal, 1662/1966, p. 63)

Everyone faces this authentic paradox every moment. We each live on a very thin thread. The conditions of being human are not unique to the client but rather are held as a mutual reality in the therapeutic alliance. The therapeutic relationship holds the power to heal the individual through this present tense authentic relationship. I recognize the finiteness of this relationship and paradoxically the continued healing of this relationship in other relationships beyond my knowing.

Holding the unknown is what we each face in becoming globally authentic. And the surprises emerge from the unknown and become known, part of the tapestry of our lives that are so interconnected.

Response and Responsibility

My international teaching and my therapy work with Ron and Vicki so clearly reminded me of and renewed my own search for authenticity. Vicki and Ron renewed their lives in their own unique ways, making creative decisions about their daily lives by learning to listen to their truth and follow their truth more and more. Understanding the imperfection of this listening is part of their individual authenticity.

One of the forms of genuine authenticity in the therapist is his or her acceptance of the fact that the therapist has but limited knowledge of the client. Since the therapist gets to know his or her clients so much more thoroughly than others, there is an illusion that the therapist knows the client fully. Therapists never know all about their clients, only some aspects. These may be terribly important aspects and certainly significant to know, but the full knowledge of the person is not known.

What we experience as an essential quality of authenticity is humility, of allowing ourselves to not know and be humbled by the not knowing for others and ourselves. Certainly this has been very true in my international teaching.

Along with the humility of uncertainty, there is the solidity of responsibility. We each have a life to live. To pick up our lives with full responsibility is an authentic life. I want to invite you to explore your responsibility as an authentic therapist.

What are the "rights, responsibilities and privileges" associated with being a psychotherapist? I believe that the rights and privileges of being a psychotherapist in private practice, research, or teaching bring a responsibility to make good use of the knowledge and skills we have each acquired. What does "good use" mean in today's world?

Our "good use" is joined by a long line of distinguished professors, researchers, and clinicians who have made excellent use of their knowledge and pursued their goals with passion for many decades. We are grateful for this foundation. Our profession of psychology is gifted with the extraordinary ability to understand human beings and to communicate that understanding to others. We often make judgments without the comfort of stable rules and categories, and navigate uncertainty without a map — and without guarantees. Yet, we proceed with our passion for our work, moving forward through the unknown to the known and back again.

If you are a traditional psychologist reading this chapter, I invite each of you to look closely at the choices available to you, to think outside of the box as you reflect on the "good use" of your knowledge of people and your knowledge of communication in today's world. I invite each of you to take off your glasses and see beyond the therapy room, the classroom, or your research. I encourage you to envision the intention of your work reaching out of the room of one-on-one psychotherapy or even from the classroom to the community in which you live and work, into the state in which you live, the nation you are citizen of, and the world in which we each live.

We each have a choice about how to respond to challenges. My invitation to you is the same I ask of my clients: look closely at how you usually hold and react to your world and embrace new ways of being over and over in each challenge you face. Each time a challenge comes, begin opening to the choices and their consequences. This process of facing challenges by holding choices mindful of the paradoxes of freedom and human limitation is the fundamental work of becoming authentic.

On an international, national, and local level we are now experiencing a major crisis in our response to terrorism and economic crisis. This present us-versus-them response of pointing at the bad guy works to continue war and catastrophe. The question is whether we can use this crisis to develop new choices that reflect wisdom, or whether our choices polarize the world. What does psychology have to offer in this continual crisis of who and what is the bad guy?

And what if we chose to not use the language of the good guy and bad guy? This is a question we often search deeply and naturally in our profession. If we as a profession are so adept at this searching process, how can this search inform our larger community? Is this a responsibility of our profession? If so, how can you participate? What I am proposing is *global authenticity* of the twenty-first century. Who we thought we were and who we can become as a profession is being challenged and require authentic responses.

I know many clinicians who have responded by picking up a mantle of responsibility reflecting their individual passions; working with hospice, proposing alternative global economic plans, addressing the aging crises, and more.

Clinicians are trained to listen to the good guy/bad guy conversation with their clients. My spouse, my ex-, my boss or my co-worker, my child or aging parent can easily fill an hour of being the bad guy. Listening to this story's endless variations with a trained ear, eye, and heart, you may interrupt at a moment that brings the client face to face with the ever-present option of authenticity. We invite an inner search, a deeper awareness of the story, going to the inner pain behind and underneath the concerns, giving rise to care, hope, and commitment for something more. We hold hope for change, with certainty that the individual can own the darkest part of his or her painful story and be transformed, to use that story as a creative resource for wholeness, not separation from self and others. This is the work of becoming authentic.

In exploring the self, we need to look at the client's relationship not only with the therapist but also the world in which the client lives. We must address integrating gains as a goal every bit as important as making gains. We need to be vigilant in communicating responsibly in the families and society in which the client lives. To be an authentic human means not only being attentive to the care of self, but also to the self in relation to the world in which the client lives, to embody concern about our world and caring toward others. Authenticity is not limited to the therapy hour or the classroom; it is a deeply human process of bringing forth all we are made of — inwardly and outwardly — into the world in which we live.

I have had the great honor of teaching many helping professionals, including psychologists, teachers, and hospice workers across this beautiful globe. Wherever I have traveled, I have always enjoyed a large piece of humble pie, eating it frequently as the unknown stands both quietly and loudly beside the known.

In each country I have taught, my heart has been deeply touched by stories filled with joys and sorrows. I am consistently moved by the sincerity of each person I have taught and how each person continually teaches me. We are searching together for all the possibilities of each moment. These authentic searchers represent an emerging global family which goes beyond race, nation, color, or gender, and unites us in our condition of being human. Out of all these searches, I have developed trainings for helping professionals with the signature name, *Unearthing the Moment*. This large family that continues to grow is a mirror of *global authenticity*.

Let us each find our common ground as helping professionals, as people serving each other for the full potential latent within ourselves. Let us celebrate this grand and glorious experiment of human potential with all of its paradoxes. To do so we must honor and fight vigilantly for the things that unite us rather than focus on what separates us.

Successful responsibility is the ability to respond to life within your own world. Becoming an authentic human being is the first step toward creating an authentic nation and world.

It is in this deep concern for living authentically which, as psychologists and psychotherapists, we have moved into the world with all that we have been trained. Forming the International Institute for Humanistic Studies resulted from our ability to respond, to be responsible, and to actualize our global authenticity in the world. I support people in expressing their uniqueness and help them to listen to themselves, others, and the world with hope, compassion, courage, resilience, and tolerance. This invitation to live global authenticity is not limited to psychotherapists and their clients, but to people in many professions: ministers, doctors, teachers, politicians, everyone who is seeking wholeness and peace.

I believe that changes in individuals lead to changes in small groups of people, which contribute to major shifts in a society. I trust psychotherapy to enhance individual changes and open people to the journey of authenticity. From this perspective of personal and social interconnectedness, therapy is not only a tool for psychological help and change, but is also instrumental in bringing about social transformations that enhance authentic cultures. I am aware of our professional potential as well as our responsibility to participate in promoting a society that embodies humanistic values.

I am inviting being *magnanimous*, to be open to the unknown, to share in the moment with all you have. We are each doing work that benefits the whole (Potter, 2004). The authenticity of psychology is to step outside the walls of academia and the consultation room, to put our knowledge and skills to good use in the marketplace by building bridges of communication among a large variety of professions. The invitation is open-ended—to advocate, question, listen, and inspire. This is the work of becoming authentic individuals, authentic cultures, and an authentic world.

References

Bugental, J. F. T. (1965). *The search for authenticity,* New York: Holt, Rinehart, and Winston.

Bugental, J. F. T. (1999). *Psychotherapy isn't what you think*. Phoenix, AZ: Zeig Tucker & Co.

Heery, M. (2001). Inside the soul of Russian and American psychotherapy trainings. *Journal of Humanistic Psychology, 42(2),* 89-101.

Heery, M. & Bugental, J. F. T. (1999). Unearthing the Moment. *Self and Society, 27(3),* 26-27.

Heery, M. & Bugental, J. F. T. (2005). Listening to the listener: An existential-humanistic approach to psychotherapy with psychotherapists. In J.D. Geller, J.C. Norcross, & D.E. Orlinsky (Eds.), *The psychotherapist's own psychotherapy* (pp. 282-296). New York: Oxford University Press.

Martel, Y. (2001). *Life of Pi*. Orlando, FL: Harvest..

Pascal, B. (1966). *Pensees* (A.J. Krailsheimer, Trans.). New York: Penguin Group. (Original work published in 1662)

Potter, R. N. (2004). *Authentic spirituality*. St. Paul, MN: Llewellyn Pub.

Yalom, I. (1980). *Existential psychotherapy*. New York: Basic Books

10

Zhaungzi's View of Freedom

Zhaohui Bao
Translated by Jennifer Tam

During the Warring Period, about the same time as Aristotle in the West, a philosopher in China (368–286 BC) named Zhaungzi proposed ways of attaining a sense of freedom during a period of time ravaged by war. In his writings, Zhaungzi did not use the word "freedom;" instead he used the word "wandering" to represent his idea of the basic existence of life. Statistically, the word wandering appeared more than 100 times in the book of *Zhaungzi* (Zhaungzi, 1994). He titled his first chapter "Carefree Wandering" to emphasize the concept of wandering. The concept was further developed twice more in this chapter. In fact, wandering was the main theme in six out of the seven chapters of the book. In the chapter titled "On the Equality of Things," Zhaungzi (1994) emphasized "wandering beyond the limits of this mundane world." The chapter "Essentials and Nurturing Life" described the state where there was "plenty of room for the blade to wander." In "The Human World," he promoted "simply riding along with things as you let your mind wander. Entrust yourself to inevitability thereby nourishing what is central." The chapter "Symbols of Integrity Fulfilled" emphasized "wandering among grace and harmony" and finally "The Great Ancestral Teacher" and "Responses for Emperors and Kings" described the possibility of someone achieving the state of "wandering between heaven and earth" and "wandering between existence and non-existence." Zhaungzi promoted the state of wandering as a way of life in the pursuit of freedom and peace of mind.

Zhaungzi's Reasons for Choosing Freedom

According to Zhaungzi, the reason why people failed to wander was because of too little room in their hearts (Zhaungzi, 1994). They did not achieve the state where their hearts had enough space for wandering— the reason being that their hearts were tied and bundled up, having submitted themselves to worldly perspectives and popular thinking. People became exhausted from chasing after worldly standards. They were not willing to allow their hearts to settle. Such worldly people chased after their own shadows for a living without the awareness that they were actually afraid of their own shadows. They became disgusted with their style of living and sought to escape their current uneasiness. They searched endlessly in the external world for a place to settle. They ran ahead fast, followed by their shadows, which they were unable to shed, so they ran even faster. In the end they would run out of breath and die. They were unable to see that happiness and freedom was in fact within oneself.

In his chapter "An Old Fisherman," Zhaungzi (1994) stated,

There was a man, who, afraid of his shadow and disliking his own footprints, tried in vain to run away from them. But the more he ran, the more footprints were created. And the faster he ran, the closer his shadows followed. He thought he was going too slow, so he kept running faster and faster without stopping, until dying of exhaustion. The man failed to realize that, by staying still, he could have expunged his footprints. Such was the extent of his foolishness.

People in the world chase after worldly things. We do not even know if these popular things fit us or not. We forget who we are and what we experience in the midst of following what is considered trendy. Zhaungzi offers the following parables. In his chapter "Autumn Floods," he stated,

Haven't you heard of the young lad from Shou ling who tried to learn to walk the way people do in Hantan? Yet, before he was able to acquire this new skill, he had forgotten how he used to walk. So all he could do was to crawl home on all fours. (Zhaungzi, 1994)

"Symbols of Integrity Fulfilled" (Zhaungzi, 1994) also recorded a man called Cheng Tse Tsan who went to learn the Tao from Hunbowuren so that he could increase his understanding of the essence of the mental/spiritual world. But Cheng chose to be influenced by popular thought. He was proud of his physical health and bragged about his status as a high government official. He despised his contemporary, Sin Tao Yia, who had no status and was physically disabled. Cheng admonished Sin for being rude to him because he did not pay his respects to Cheng. But Sin replied that Cheng should not to use physical appearance and status to measure Sin's worth. If Cheng had truly learned and embraced the way of the Tao, he would not be judging Sin's worth based upon physical appearances. Cheng felt ashamed after hearing this.

Those who follow worldly thoughts and ideas are like "someone who knows nothing about the cause of being" (Zhaungzi, 1994). They are lost in the "worldly standards of right and wrong and do good out of obligation" (Zhaungzi, 1994). They are living a life with no self-reflection. They have lost themselves to the material world and are not able to live a free and pleasant life.

People are slaves to their own desires. They are unsettled because they are trapped by their desires of their physical needs and lured by the desires of their eyes. This sense of being unsettled is triggered by worldly desires. According to Chi Wu Lun, a philosophical perspective titled "The Equality of Things,"

> Once people have received their complete physical form, they remain conscious of it while awaiting extinction. In their strife and friction with other things, they gallop forward in their course unable to stop. (as cited in Zhaungzi, 1994)

As a result, "their contacts turn into conflicts, each day involving them in mental strife." Zhaungzi deplores such a way of living. He asks, "Isn't this sad? We toil our entire lives without seeing any results. We deplete ourselves with wearisome labor not knowing to what it all adds up. Isn't this lamentable?" (Zhaungzi, 1994). In its place, Zhaungzi (1994) advocates in his chapter "The Great Ancestral Teacher," "I detach myself from my body and my desires, dim my intelligence, depart from my form, leave knowledge behind, to become identical with the Transformational Thoroughfare."

When people surrender themselves to the social standards and ideas of others., they lose their authenticity. In the story of "The death of Wonton," the emperor of the Southern Sea, Lickety, who represented social effectiveness and success in the world, joined with the emperor of the Northern Sea, Split, in mutual desire to reward the supreme emperor (Wonton) for his goodness. They decided to transform 'Wonton' according to popular opinions and social standards. They believed that human beings are unique because they have a total of seven orifices: ear, nose, mouth, etc. So they tried to dig openings one a day for a total of seven days.

Wonton died. In understanding this parable, the American scholar Girardot (1983) suggested:

> What is implied is that a civilized condition does not necessarily bring about the fulfillment of human nature. Indeed, from the Taoist point of view it amounts to the fall of man from the godlike condition of the paradise time. (p. 94)

The emptiness before civilization was similar to our time in heaven, symbolizing the authentic state of human existence. Humankind's false heroes, Lickety and Split, made the mistake of relying too much on the value of human civilization, which they relied upon to replace the most pure, spontaneous, inner values of humankind. This resulted in the loss of sacredness for humankind.

The worldly perspectives and popular ideas require us to be useful through contributing ourselves according to societal standards. These standards may result from fame, profit, money, power, status, nationality, or race. They turn us into slaves of others or society; slaves to schools of thoughts; slaves to pragmatism; slaves to enterprises or structures. Zhaungzi espoused that nothing was useful. He believed that existence in and of itself was sufficient; that the meaning of one's existence did not depend on one's usefulness to society. In his chapter "The Human World," through the stories of the "rubber tree and forgotten wood,' Zhaungzi (1994) revealed the secret of the useless rubber tree and it's meaningful existence. In the fourth story of this chapter there was a carpenter named Si. He was on his way to Nation Chi and passed by the trunk of a big tree. This tree was so big that it could offer shade to thousands of cattle. Si told his apprentice,

> ...this tree is not useful. If you use it to make it into a boat, the boat will sink. If you made it into a coffin, the coffin will wear out. If you made utensils out of it, the utensil will break. If you use it to make windows, the windows will shatter. If you use it as a pillar, the pillar will soon be consumed by termites.

Then one day the rubber tree explained the importance of its uselessness to Si in a dream. The carpenter at last sadly expressed that if he were to follow the rationale of the world in understanding the rubber tree to be useless, then they and his apprentice will be unlikely to find out the secret and value of this tree.

The next story is about a wise man called Nam Pau Tze. He traveled to the Shang qiu city in He nan Province (是南籍市). He understood the secret and value of the useless tree. At Shang qiu city, all the trees were very big; big enough to shelter thousands of horses. However, these trees could not be made into pillars or coffins, and their leaves had no taste or scent. But according to Nam Pau Tze, these qualities are what made the trees unique. He viewed human life the same way–of high value. If one does not surrender to the standards of the world--namely that one's worth is tied to one's usefulness to the world-- then like both of the trees mentioned above, one can avoid being taken away by the world. They grow in their own ways, not under the influence of any other. The other trees such as pear, orange, and pomelo tress rely on the standard of the world. They become useful when ripe. But then their branches got chopped off, their fruits are picked. Zhaungzi offered to people the choice of growth and freedom. He selected these trees as symbols to remind us of the way we should grow. He reminded us to stay away from being possessed or encumbered by worldly concepts and popular ideas. Zhaungzi exposed the usefulness of uselessness. Life itself and integrity is far more important than investing oneself to attain a particular goal or function.

Zhaungzi chose a life of freedom, but not life according to the required life style as defined by others. He made the important decision to withdraw from this noisy/busy world to follow his inner heart. Originally Zhaungzi had the opportunity to become useful in the eyes of others. During Zhuangzi's time, intellectuals were respected by the authorities. The Nation Chi had set up the Jixia Academic Center (稷下宮) to nurture the best talents of the nation. Many of the brightest minds were invited to the center to apply their talents in service to the nation. Freedom was in the air and intellectuals had their own liberty, such as Mencius and Chung Lin, who each had a similar personality as Zhaungzi. Both chose not to worship high officials on bended knees and worked at the academic center. Zhaungzi could have chosen the same path if he so desired. Similarly, a good friend of Zhaungzi named Wai Tsu worked at the royal house in the nation Leong. Zhaungzi had the same opportunity to work as a high commissioner for Nation Chu. But Zhaungzi believed in his chapter "Autumn Floods" that the commissioners in Nation Chu were like the dead tortoises from 3,000 years ago: "the king stores them (the tortoise bones) in his ancestral temple inside of a hamper wrapped with cloth…. Do you think these tortoises would rather be dead and have their bones preserved as objects of veneration?" (Zhaungzi, 1994). To the contrary, Zhaungzi desired freedom and a life filled with vitality. He chose be a living tortoise, "rolling around in the mud and muck" rather than receive the venerations accorded to tortoises that are long dead (Zhaungzi, 1994). So Zhaungzi withdrew from the noisy/busy world and chose a life of poverty without fame.[1] His lived in a poor house, married, and had a child. He made grass shoes for a living and humbled himself to borrow grain from the marquis, the overseer of a River, when he was hungry. Although he was occasionally rejected, overall he lived a pleasant life: he went fishing and had fun with fishes; he listened to the wind; he pursued a life without burden.

Zhaungzi gave us a model on how to actualize our human nature. We first need to learn how to retreat from this noisy/busy world and not be tied up in it. In order to cultivate that inner peace, it begins with finding external places of solitude. Only in such places of peace and quiet are we able to transform the external solitude into inner tranquility. In retreating from his noisy/busy world, Zhaungzi modeled for all of us how to experience quiet times in our own environment. We need to learn to do nothing, even if it causes us pain. Sometimes we need to just sit, allow ourselves become a slow person, and learn to let go of what we have; let go of things such as the present-day orientation toward success, hard work, and achievement. While under such contemporary influences, we cannot avoid our feelings of guilt and we are thus tied up by our work and fast paced life.

Retreating from the world will allow us to detach from its influences and swayed value systems. Furthermore, it will prevent us from imposing our views upon others. In this way, we not only set ourselves free, we are also able to set others free. Zhaungzi's books have a number philosophical parables to remind us that human beings have created numerous unanticipated consequences. Despite our best intentions, bad things still result. For example, in the parable of "The Marquis Birds" in the chapter "The Human World," Zhaungzi (1994) wrote of the Marquis of Lu who welcomed birds in his ancestral temple. He prepared a party with food, wine, and music to welcome the birds. However, the eyes of the birds were glazed over with sadness as they were unwilling to eat so much as a single sliver of fish, nor drink a single drop of wine. Three days later, all the birds died. The Marquis Lu made the mistake of nourishing the birds with his own nourishment. He did not nourish the birds as birds.

In the same book, Zhaungzi wrote a similar parable about a person who was extremely fond of horses, so much so that he bought an

---

[1] In Zhaungzi's time, especially compared to the pervasive influence of the Confucius and Mohist schools of thought, Zhaungzi was without fame and influence, he had only one student whose name was LinQie recorded in "Zhaungzi."

expensive container to collect the horse's wastes. Consequently, horseflies gathered and began to annoy and torment the horse. The owner then frightened the horse while slapping the flies away. Consequently, the frightened horse broke the expensive container and inadvertently treaded on the owner. Both the marquis and the horse lover were filled with good intentions, but painful unanticipated consequences resulted nevertheless.

Zhaungzi's extreme poverty and self-imposed limitations motivated him toward his pursuits. The Japanese scholar Fukunaga Mitsuji (1969) suggested,

> Zhaungzi was able to contemplate his freedom because of a history of living under such extreme poverty and facing the realities that come from such extreme limitation without freedom. Zhaungzi's situation differed from monks who lived in monasteries while mediating on freedom and ordinary people who lived in a stable society while contemplating their freedom. According to Friedrich Hegel, freedom was impossible while living under the ugly reality of ancient Chinese tyranny. Therefore, people struggled for freedom. This is what Zhaungzi referred to as the freedom within non-freedom and he viewed this as a vital character of freedom. (p. 5)

Fukunaga's views were only partially accurate in regards to Zhaungzi. He failed to account for Zhaungzi's will and choice. While it was true that Zhaungzi lived in a society without freedom, thus motivating him to reflect and write about freedom, Zhuangzi did not submit himself under the popular concepts of that worldly rule. He chose a life of poverty with freedom. He desired a life of freedom and therefore made his decision to retreat from the world. Zhaungzi's views toward freedom did not result from extreme poverty; instead, they resulted from his will to choose poverty and lead a simple life.

After Zhaungzi attained inner peace and freedom, he traveled the world with this peace of mind and sense of freedom. Regardless of where he went or what he did, he chose to co-exist with the noise and stress from the external world.

The Origin of Zhaungzi's Freedom and Problems

According to Zhaungzi (1994), human freedom originated with the genesis of the world: "Heaven and earth were born together with me and the myriad of things are one with me." When our hearts are joined with the world, we can find the way to the origin of all matters that then lead us back to dwell in the Tao. Within the Tao, matters exist in authenticity. In the chapter "On the Equality of Things," Zhaungzi (1994) emphasized the uniqueness of existence: "All things are possessed by that which we say is so; all things are possessed by that which we affirm. There is nothing that is not so; there is nothing that cannot be affirmed." All things exist with affirmation and admiration. Zhaungzi also emphasized that Tao is everywhere. Tao is among the low and the high with the same value and "is indifferent to baseness and honor...." (Zhaungzi, 1994). In other words, in Tao all things do not require an external factor to determine the value of self. The self is valuable because of its pure existence, like "the voice of the pipes of earth" and "the voice of the pipes of man" with their original pure form of existence. They reach "the voices of the pipes of heaven" (Zhaungzi, 1994).

The Tao is the way. It is a way to perceive things. Only those who perceive the Tao can let go of their stubborn attachments to material values. "Only the perceptive understand that all things join in unity. For this reason they do not use things for themselves but lodge in commonality" (Zhaungzi, 1994). Those who are able to perceive the Tao are willing to let go of their own perspectives and believe in observing things around them. The goal of their observation is to let things be as they are—like the beauty and strength of the osmanthus flower shining through between its bloom and wither. For those who are unable to perceive things, they are stuck because of their stubbornness regarding their perceptions. They are unwilling to let go, like the conflict between the Confucius and Mohist schools of thought during the period of war.[2]

In the chapter "On the Equality of Things," Zhaungzi (1994) revealed that things are integrated and share the same origin. Life and death is simply a transition from one stage to another, all belonging to one large cosmic world. "Life and death are predestined. Their constant alternation, like that of day and night, is determined by heaven" (Zhaungzi, 1994). To individuals, life and death are temporal, ordinary; just like the night, they comes and goes. Although human beings only live and die once, it does not

---

[2] The conflict between the Confucius and Mohist schools of thought revolves around status. Confucius advocated a form of filial piety and society love based on clearly defined status and hierarchy whereas Mohists advocated an egalitarian social structure within the family and society. Similarly, Confucius advocated for extravagant burial ceremonies where as Mohists preferred burial ceremonies that are characterized by practicality and simplicity.

impact humanity at large. Therefore, individual men and women are like travelers of the world, passengers in transition. When the time comes, individuals will return to the yellow earth. "That which we borrow to maintain our lives is merely dust. Life and death alternate like day and night" (Zhaungzi, 1994). "Ultimate Joy" recorded that when Zhaungzi lost his wife, not only he did not cry, he even "sang with the drum." He used the same principle of cosmic integration to respond to his wife's transition from life to death.

> I reflected on her beginning and realized that originally she was unborn. Not only was she unborn, originally she had no form. Not only did she have no form, originally she had no vital breath. Intermingling with nebulousness and blurriness, a transformation occurred and there was vital breath; the vital breath was transformed and there was form; the form was transformed and there was birth; now there has been another transformation and she is dead. This is like the progression of the four seasons–from spring to autumn, from winter to summer. (Zhaungzi, 1994)

Zhaungzi used the principle of cosmic oneness to give order to a confused and uncertain world. Human beings thus can let go of suffering and settle in this cosmic order.

However, Zhaungzi also knew that sometimes it can be difficult to give order to destiny, not even the Tao can do so. To him, people lived in mystery. This can be very difficult to understand. These mysteries and uncertainties are beyond human comprehension. Sometimes destiny is determined by the Tao. Zhaungzi understood that one can only learn to accept helplessness when confronted with higher guidance, particularly facing life and death. In "The Great Ancestral Teacher," Zhaungzi (1994) mentioned a man who was physically deformed because of disease. When this man confronted the meaninglessness of his unreasonable illness, he was only left with sarcasm as a form of acceptance.

Besides the mystery of Tao, which is beyond anyone's comprehension, the brutal political suppression and killing during the war period also enhanced the sense of uncertainty and powerlessness. Zhaungzi lived in a dark era. There were numerous wars among nations. Various emperors were fighting for their sovereignties. The emperor of Yee, Wei, and Chung all devalued the lives of the peasants. Even the contemporary of Zhaungzi, Mencius, in his book "Mencius" also commented and endorsed that "All the authorities was like to kill and

Peasants were the abused." He thought this was the worst period of time. Zhaungzi wrote a number of parables describing such kinds of brutal acts in this dark age.

When facing the gigantic wheel of destiny, Zhaungzi adopted the attitude of acceptance. He admitted that human beings were powerless and without control in the face of uncertainty and the higher power. He focused on the passive nature and dark side of the mystery of human destiny. It is regrettable that Zhaungzi did not discover the other side of human destiny. It is through disasters, suffering, and adversity that individuals are able to strengthen their beliefs and find unexpected courage. In fact, Zhaungzi himself modeled for us how to face one's own suffering and adversity with great faith and courage. He paid a handsome price while preserving his belief in living a life which valued freedom. The price paid was his perseverance in living a life that was not driven by the values of the world. He chose to retreat from the noisy/busy world and live a modest life. He could have gone further. The reason why he retreated from the world was because he wanted to preserve his own freedom as well as protect himself from being harmed by the world. Yet Zhuangzi's pessimism was also evidence of his lack of courage for he did not persist in maintaining his determination and courage in pursuit of freedom. In other words, he protected himself by giving in too easily to pessimism and failed to pay enough attention to the potential of human faith and courage. He overlooked the potential manifestations of faith and courage in human sufferings, adversity, and disasters. Because of his pessimism, Zhuangzi was unable to uphold his moral courage when confronted by his own destiny and social conscience. He was not as consistent as Confucius, who devoted himself to promoting moral conscience to various nations, even though he was unsure how to accomplish his task. This was what was missing with Zhaungzi--the same things that are missing within the Chinese culture at large.

In the end, through Zhaungzi, we are able to find out where to locate freedom–freedom comes from being aligned with the Tao. Through aligning with the Tao, Zhaungzi was able to find the ways of freedom as well as the meaning and value that are attached to it. But his view of freedom did not inspire the great faith or courage that can be gained through suffering. Because of his understanding of the order of Tao, Zhuangzi anticipated and accepted death as an attitude of living. Actually, this can diminish the wish for living as well as the value of living. Zhaungzi held a conscious and desperate attitude toward life. Zhaungzi never mentioned love or hope, both of which have tremendous power to activate faith and courage. In the end, Zhaungzi did not further reflect on how we can preserve freedom, relate to it, and apply it in society. Zhaungzi's sense of freedom remained individualistic because he failed to inspire society to a greater sense of collective freedom.

References

Mitsuji, F. (1969). *Chuang-tzu: Ancient Chinese existentialism* [福永光司《莊子古代中國存在主義》], Chen Guanxue [陳冠學譯], Taibei [台北: Sanmin Publishing House [三民局].

Girardot, N. J. (1983). *Myth and meaning in early Taoism*. Berkeley, CA & Los Angeles, CA: University of California Press.

Guo Qingfan 郭慶藩. (1961). *The complete works of Chuang Tzu* [《莊集》]. Wang Xiaoyu [王者, Beijing: Zhonghua Publishing House [點校原中華局].

Zhaungzi. (1994). *Wandering on the way: Early Taoist tales and parables of Chuang Tzu*. (V. H. Mair, Trans., from the original book Zhaungzi in Chinese.) Hawaii: University of Hawaii Press.

11

A Contemplative Approach to Existential Psychotherapy:
Mindfulness as Existential Praxis

Michael M. Dow

In recent years, psychotherapy approaches that incorporate or are inspired by the Buddhist practice of mindfulness (Germer, Siegel, & Fulton, 2005; Hayes, Follette, & Linehan, 2004) are proliferating rapidly. What is perhaps less appreciated is that mindfulness, properly understood, is at heart an existential practice, which is to say as much about death as it is about life, and less about "getting better" than it is about "living fully." Mindfulness confronts one experientially, as opposed to abstractly, with not only the alarming automaticity of one's habitual mental patterns, but the pain and ungraspability of the nature of existence itself, as revealed in each successive moment of awareness.

This paper argues that mindfulness and existential psychotherapy make for complementary if also contradictory partners. Mindfulness provides a praxis with which to experience one's existence with immediacy and without filters. Existential therapy provides an interpersonal context in which to understand experience. Both orient the individual toward a relationship to experience characterized by "being" as opposed to "having" (Batchelor, 1983). But there will always be a necessary tension between these two approaches drawn from East and West, between daring to articulate the self and letting go of the self altogether; between "just noticing" without interpreting, and consciously seeking reparative interpretive self-narratives. We might conceive of a mindfulness-oriented existential therapy that integrates both, which is oriented toward developing both existential meaning and experiential immediacy and helps patients to live with both awareness and authenticity.

Existential psychology, as defined by Yalom (1980), attempts to help patients confront the four ultimate concerns of life: death, freedom, existential isolation and meaninglessness. Although such a therapy sounds far from cheery, the idea here is that if existential concerns can be faced directly without suppressing them from awareness, untold reservoirs of energy will be released that allow one to live more freely and joyously. de Wit (2008) and others have argued that most of our suffering is neurotic, which is to say created unconsciously and defensively as an attempt to ward off the pain of existence. On top of the pain of existence we heap the suffering of resisting that pain: wishing, hoping, and otherwise pretending that life could be without limitation, pain, and disappointment. There are other possibilities, however. It is probably axiomatic that nothing inspires one to live life fully more than accepting the reality of death, which will come sooner than we think.

Buddhism, from which mindfulness is principally drawn, takes the analysis to another level. It is not so much that the self's vitality is hampered by suppressing awareness of death and associated existential angst, but the very notion of self, and especially the centrality of that notion to our awareness, is itself seen as symptomatic of a reflexive contraction away from reality. At every moment we are turning away from the "great, blooming, buzzing confusion" (James, 1890/1950, p. 488) and withdrawing into the artifice of "self." Mindfulness, and Buddhism in general, practiced with an existential frame of mind (Batchelor, 1983, 1998), provides a practice as opposed to an intellectual exercise for both clients and therapists to reverse that resistance and experience the reality of moment to moment awareness directly.

Mindfulness

Mindfulness is a translation of the Pali word, *sati,* which comes from the Sanskrit *smrti*, both of which originally meant something akin to "memory." The Buddhist use of the word came to mean something closer to the quality of mind that facilitates memory, both in terms of retaining new memories and recalling old ones (Sujato, 2005). A popular contemporary translation of mindfulness that reflects this original meaning of "memory," while also giving a flavor for the Buddhist usage, is Chogyam Trungpa's "recollecting the present" (Trungpa, 1995, p. 66). In traditional Buddhism, mindfulness is conceived as the ability to stay with the object of attention without, as usually happens, getting lost in self-referential associations and abstractions that miss the naked moment of perception (Wallace, 2006). It is both already there as part of the perceptual process and something that one must cultivate over time. In Buddhism, the cultivation of mindfulness is done in the context of a simultaneous cultivation of ethics and wisdom/compassion, known collectively as *The Three Trainings*, and in more detailed fashion as *The Noble Eightfold Path* (Rahula, 1974). It can be seen as a remedy for and a direct contrast to

Heidegger's (1998/1946, p. 250) "forgetfulness of being," in which we retreat from the authentic questioning of our existence into the ready made answers of various ideologies. Practiced with correct understanding, that is, without a desire for anything in particular to happen, mindfulness moves one in the direction of authentic being-alone and authentic being-with others (Batchelor, 1983). This authentic being stands in opposition to our more typical mode of "having," the consumer driven orientation of getting and spending which can never be fully satiated.

In the context of psychotherapy, clinicians applying mindfulness have emphasized the importance of a component of acceptance or nonjudgment (Germer, 2005; Kabat-Zinn, 2005), also termed *maitri* or compassion (Wegela, 1997). This emphasis has been important to counter the self-aggressive tendencies that "pure mindfulness" can at times elicit (Germer, 2005; Linehan, 1993). Germer (2005) helpfully defines so-called therapeutic mindfulness as consisting of three components: awareness, a present moment focus, and an attitude of acceptance.

Mindfulness, to simplify, gets us out of our heads and into our senses. But whereas mindfulness is a conscious de-coupling from the endless activity of storytelling of our minds, a therapy alive to existential concerns picks up those threads and from them helps clients weave and enact a subjective narrative of meaning. Both are important for a vibrant and vivid life: to disconnect from our default mode and rest in *self-as–context* (rather than *self-as-content*; Hayes, Strosahl, & Wilson, 1999), and to wrest a deeply felt intersubjective narrative that sustains and propels one further into the chaos of what comes next.

Dialectical Tension Between Mindfulness and Existential Therapy

These two modes of understanding the self are, unsurprisingly, at odds. But both modes, when held together, may provide a generative dialectical tension. Mindfulness arose, at least initially, within a collectivist worldview with little focus on a well-differentiated individual self; existentialism arose, at least initially, within an individualistic worldview with little focus on letting go of self-oriented awareness (see Hoffman, 2008, for more discussion of this issue). The whole point of mindfulness meditation is, in a sense, to drop the search for meaning, which, in itself, can be seen as a strategy to avoid suffering. The search for meaning is seen as part of the illusion of ego that creates a false separation between one's self and one's life:

Existential philosophers have largely missed this point. Their effort—to live authentically by finding individual meaning in a chaotic universe—presupposes that we are separate from the world we experience. To live authentically, we have to stop trying to avoid suffering and death by looking for meaning. We have to enter into the mystery of life itself. (McLeod, p. x, 2001)

And yet, patients come to therapy because they no longer know how to tell a story about their lives that works for them. Their narrative, their meaning-making machinery, has ceased to function smoothly, or perhaps never has functioned well at all. Patients come to talk and be heard, and through that process of talking and being heard learn new ways of doing both. Therapy, after all, is made of words. Although patients always both want and resist change, the change needed, one might say, is an orienting framework—call it a sense of meaning, positive introjects, secure attachment, a coherent self-narrative, schemas, etc.---that allows them to settle and feel more deeply into the intensity of their lives. The therapist helps to co-construct such a framework with the patient, again, by using words, at the right time, and infused with the right feelings. Paradoxically for the patient, this likely involves both tolerating a wider range of feelings without understanding them and putting that non-understanding into words.

As previously mentioned, it can be argued that there is a revolution going on in the behavioral sciences occasioned by mindfulness-based therapies and that, at heart, it is an existential one. A symptom reduction focus is fast losing its appeal as the limitations of such are being shown by empirical studies (Baer, 2003; Segal, Williams, & Teasdale, 2001). The focus in academic research psychology is shifting away from cognitive-mediated change and toward strategies that direct one to experience difficult thoughts and feelings with acceptance. Acceptance and Commitment therapy, for instance, a new mindfulness-based behavioral therapy with a growing evidence base, in consonance with existential approaches, is explicitly geared toward accepting rather than reducing anxiety (Hayes, Strosahl, & Wilson, 1999; Bunting & Hayes, 2007). Clients are encouraged to clarify and commit to their values and to move toward them regardless of anxiety. Dialectical Behavior Therapy (DBT; Linehan, 1993) and Mindfulness-Based Cognitive Therapy for Depression (MBCT; Segal, Williams, & Teasdale, 2003) are likewise, because of their mindfulness focus, more concerned with developing an openness to experience than with explicitly, or only, reducing symptoms.

Psychodynamic therapy informed by Buddhist meditation similarly tends to eschew interpretations in favor of both direct and indirect "emotional communication," and principally trains therapists to remain open to the range of feelings and associations "exchanged" in the therapeutic encounter with a client (Kaklauskas, Nimmanheminda, Hoffman, & Jack, 2008).

Parallels between Existential Philosophy and Traditional Buddhism

Though there are very important differences between traditional Buddhism and Western existential psychology (notably their understanding of the self, see also, Hoffman, 2008), there are some interesting parallels regarding the nature of existence being avoided. In traditional Theravadin Buddhism, the goal of developing mindfulness is to stabilize the mind so that one can then examine awareness with precision and develop insight or *prajna* into the nature of existence. Particularly the insight sought is regarding what are known as *the three marks of existence*: suffering (*dukkha*, Pali), impermanence (*anicca*, Pali), and no-self (*anatman*, Pali) (Rahula, 1974). A deep insight into the three marks leads to liberation from attachment or clinging to experience, otherwise known as enlightenment. Although these themes are generally not specifically emphasized in Buddhist-inspired psychotherapies (as of yet), there may be a parallel in this traditional Buddhist formulation with the four existential themes as outlined by Yalom (1980).

In Buddhism, the primary insight is into the non-existence of not only a separate permanent self (*anatman*), but the non-existence of any separate, permanent thing altogether. It is because of the lack of self or the lack of a separate essence inhering in any phenomena that the second mark of existence, impermanence (*anicca*), is true. Things arise and pass away in interdependence on one another, and do not stay because there is nothing to stay. It is even more complex than that, because no separate things are said to exist that arise or pass away in the first place. Suffering (*dukkha*), the third mark of existence, arises because we grasp onto phenomena that do not exist (in the way we think) due to our ignorance or rejection of these first two marks. Freedom or liberation comes from a deep non-conceptual realization of these three marks (Rahula, 1974).

In Yalom's summary of existential thought there are also three marks of existence: death or human limitation, existential isolation, and meaninglessness. We can similarly only move toward freedom by accepting the fundamental limitations of existence and abandoning our fantasies of perfect oneness, limitless achievement, painless existence, etc. (see Yalom, 2000). Only by accepting limitation and death can we reclaim passion for life. Only by acknowledging our existential isolation can we become truly intimate, and only by taking responsibility for authoring meaning that does not come pre-ordered can we move toward freedom.

Interestingly, there is a lot of overlap between the marks of existence as seen from East and West, with one notable exception. Although suffering and impermanence are not exact equivalents of death and isolation, one can easily imagine both Buddhist and existential thinkers agreeing on these. But whereas Buddhist thought has little to no emphasis on the need for the individual to craft meaning (deriving as it does from a collectivist culture), existential thought tends to miss the aspect of no-self (Batchelor, 1983). From a Buddhist perspective, existentialism might tend toward a nihilistic depression: suffering and impermanence are acknowledged by a very real and very separate self. From an existential perspective, Buddhism might tend toward passivity: one confronts death and isolation, but lacks the courage to boldly create (or discover) meaning from an inherently meaningless world. As Sartre (1957/1987) argues, "Man is nothing else but what he makes of himself. Such is the first principle of existentialism" (p. 15).

Buddhism and existential theory then suggest different, but perhaps complementary avenues for facing existential reality. Buddhism suggests the practice of mindfulness, which allows one to experience that we are more than just our thoughts, we are more than just our feelings, and we are more than just our sensations, or anything else that passes through our awareness, because, logically, if we are aware of something, than we cannot be that thing of which we are aware. Mindfulness gradually (and suddenly) allows us to see through the illusion of a self that is separate in any fundamental way from the world and thus to discover compassion and spontaneous non self-oriented action to help others.

Existential therapy suggests a different path toward facing existence. Existentialism encourages us to boldly craft meaning and direction from our lives, in spite of or even because of the uncertainty and ambiguity inherent in being alive. It is up to us to be who we are and to create tradition anew from an engagement with the concrete givens of experience. As James Joyce (1916/1993) wrote in true existentialist fashion, "Welcome, O life! I go to encounter for the millionth time the reality of experience and to forge in the smithy of my soul the uncreated conscience of my race" (p. 379).

Case Example[1]

At this point, it might be helpful to discuss a clinical example to see how these different but complementary approaches might be integrated. Mary was a talented writer and poet whose career had stalled due to years of struggling with alcohol addiction. When she presented for treatment she was newly sober, but struggling with powerful and shame-fueled urges to use, which often were accompanied by fragmented images of abuse she had suffered in childhood. We worked, initially, on using these urges as an opportunity to briefly practice mindfulness. Although she could only tolerate doing so for a few minutes at a time, she would practice shifting her focus away from the images to just noticing the sensations in her body without attaching a story line to them. In introducing this exercise, both during and between sessions, I also stressed the concept of being kind and gentle with herself (*maitri*). We devised mindlessness exercises to turn down the volume on her distress, such as gripping an ice cube, going for a walk, swinging her arms, watching television, etc. Knowing she would be able to effectively turn down the distress later, helped her to tolerate mindfully "leaning into" the difficult feelings associated with the memories/cravings.

During these mindfulness exercises, Mary learned to let go of the story line around the craving/traumatic memory and just to experience the craving as pure sensation. Her ability to shift into feeling her cravings rather than acting on them, was made possible, I think, only by the practice of *maitri*. Additionally, it was helpful that she knew that immediately after "mindfully feeling" the craving, she could do something distracting to effectively take her mind off of her distress. She had a number of distressing relapses, where she would "disappear" for months at a time, and return to treatment with intense crippling shame. Eventually, she became able to sustain a longer period of sobriety. She experienced that the more she practiced her mindfulness/mindlessness exercises, the more able she was to have her feelings and thoughts about using without feeling compelled to act on them.

Working with Mary, my countertransference was powerful. I found myself identifying with her quite a bit, having aspired to be a writer myself

---

[1] The following is a composite of different clients with identifying information changed to protect confidentiality.

in my early 20s. I found myself thinking at times that "we're just alike." Mary never objected to any intervention, and would sometimes go to great lengths to emphasize my rightness on some point. Any relapse she blamed wholly on herself. But while I found myself looking forward to our sessions, which were always intellectually and emotionally lively, this sense of "sameness" was also somehow frightening. I wondered if such fear was an *exchange*[2] with how Mary might be feeling. She seemed vigilant to erase any potential space of difference. Was she afraid of being separate from me, that she would be rejected or not tolerated if she expressed any aggressive or separateness energy? Somatically, I would tend to feel very relaxed and then quite suddenly my stomach would get tense as Mary shifted the topic suddenly from an area I hadn't suspected was sensitive.

Mary had another lengthy relapse, but this time continued to come in for sessions. As her situation worsened, I started to feel complicit. I had a strong sense of being violated myself during one session in which Mary gleefully recounted her drinking and driving. She agreed to enter a 30-day alcohol treatment center, but I realized that there were some difficult feelings of violation and aggression that needed to be dealt with in treatment.

When again Mary returned to outpatient treatment, she was better able to tolerate distress and craving through her continued engagement of mindfulness exercises. But whereas mindfulness had been helpful and key thus far, in many ways Mary's therapy was only beginning. When the struggle with alcohol slowly slipped into the background, although still a bright, attractive woman, she realized she was almost 40, without a family, friends, or career. Existential anxiety about death, isolation, and meaninglessness began to overwhelm her. Mindfulness had, in a sense, allowed her to stabilize enough so as to be able to confront these existential issues more directly.

In addition to talking about these concerns directly, sensing that my exchange of sameness was key, I began to use the relationship more. Inviting conflict and disagreement with me, interestingly, was not successful, indicating to me that she needed more time being somewhat fused or identified with me (see Spotnitz's [1979] "narcissistic defense"). Instead, I emphasized joining with her, and found small but subtle ways to suggest that differences between us were not necessary, unless she wanted them. At times I might ask her some form of, "What makes you

---

[2] *Exchange* refers in psychotherapy to "the direct experience of someone else" (Wegela, 1996, p. 127) unmediated by cognition that is made possible by the fact, according to Buddhism, that the self does not exist in a separate, solid permanent way.

think we need to be different?" I was attempting to support the resistance to separateness, so that when she felt ready to express difference, it would be her choice and not mine.

Interestingly, the less I resisted the feeling of sameness with Mary, the more she began to disagree with me in small ways. I made a point of being very encouraging and curious about these small disagreements, while also careful not to collapse the space of difference between us. In the process, she gradually became more open to addressing her sense of loss during the past 10 years and her fear of a future alone and without meaning. A sense of imminent death began to haunt her and she vacillated between feeling that it was too late to do anything with her life and taking small, tentative steps toward future possibilities. Rather than denying this sense of death, or encouraging her sense of imminence about it, we talked about what she would like to be able to look back on in her life when it was her time to die.

Although, at times, these fears were overwhelming for her, Mary slowly was able to define a life trajectory for herself. Appropriately, contrary to my desires for her, it had nothing to do with writing. As she came to terms with the depth of her suffering and loss during the past decade, she felt a yearning to help others and decided to pursue a career in nursing. Her involvement in Alcoholics Anonymous (AA) led her to re-consider her Christian faith, and she joined a local church while continuing to use her mindfulness exercises. Her use of mindfulness started to evolve away from a distress tolerance technique and more toward a sort of brief but restorative contemplative prayer. A few years into her sobriety, she was accepted into nursing school in another state and terminated treatment.

Discussion

There are a number of ways that mindfulness and an existential orientation might inform the course of a psychotherapeutic treatment. We might see mindfulness as serving either a stabilizing or alternatively a deepening adjunct to an existentially oriented psychotherapy. In Mary's case, mindfulness was essential at the outset as a technique to help her stabilize her mind and life enough before existential and relational issues could be addressed. In other cases, mindfulness, either taught to the client directly or used relationally (see Surrey, 2005), could come into play later in the treatment and function more as a deepening factor. Many patients have problems that are more due to repressed anxiety than a surfeit of it. Mindfulness can come into play in such cases as a way to contact the dimension of being more directly, and in the process to bring repressed existential anxiety to the surface.

In any case, mindfulness is best applied individually, depending on the presenting issues of the client. Often, mindfulness can be incorporated into treatment without using the word, but suggesting exercises that have some configuration of Germer's (2005) three components of noticing, present moment direct experience, and acceptance. Additionally, the most useful and immediate application of mindfulness to existential therapy is as a practice for the therapist. The ability of the therapist to be present with their experience in the therapy room without conceptual filter (greatly assisted by mindfulness practice) allows one to be open to the always present but fragile dimension of exchange, wherein therapist and patient experience is simultaneous and nonconceptual. Allowing and using these moments of exchange (which from a Buddhist perspective are often happening outside of awareness) can help patients to contact repressed or unacknowledged aspects of their existential experience.

Conclusion

Both mindfulness and existential therapy suggest that the domain of being is more fundamental and more inherently open and undefined than the realm of doing or having, with which we usually identify. Both suggest that we are more than what we think, and that this "more than" has little to do with thinking. But due to their different cultural backgrounds, mindfulness and existential therapy propose differing conceptions of the self. Mindfulness helps us to see through the fiction of the self; existential therapy challenges us to re-author that fiction ourselves.

How these two philosophies or theories or techniques might work together clinically is various and dependent on the needs of the presenting patient. The suggestion here is not prescriptive, but merely that a treatment that holds both perspectives in mind is most likely to benefit individuals, because it acknowledges and engages the full depth and breadth of human experience. Mindfulness and existential therapy in different ways help patients to accept the necessary realities of existence and to live fully in the midst of those realities.

References

Baer, R. (2003). Mindfulness training as a clinical intervention: A conceptual and empirical review. *Clinical Psychology: Science and Practice, 10*, 125-143.

Batchelor, S. (1983). *Alone with others: An existential approach to Buddhism*. New York: Grove Press.

Batchelor, S. (1998). *Buddhism without beliefs: A contemporary guide to awakening*. New York: Riverhead Books.

Bunting, K., & Hayes, S. C. (2007). Language and meaning: Acceptance and commitment therapy and the EI model. In K. Schneider (Ed.), *Existential-Integrative psychotherapy: Guideposts to the core of practice* (pp.217-234). New York: Routledge.

de Wit, H. F. (2008). Working with existential and neurotic suffering. In F. Kaklauskas, S. Nimmanheminda, L. Hoffman, & M. Jack (Eds.), *Brilliant sanity: Buddhism and psychotherapy* (pp. 3-17). Colorado Springs, CO: University of the Rockies Press.

Germer, C. K. (2005). Mindfulness: What is it? What does it matter? In C. K. Germer, R. D. Siegel, & P. R. Fulton (Eds.), *Mindfulness and psychotherapy* (pp. 3-27). New York: Guilford.

Hayes, S. C., Strosahl, K. D., & Wilson, K. G. (1999). *Acceptance and commitment therapy: An experiential approach to behavior change*. New York: Guilford.

Hayes, S. C., Follette, V. M., & Linehan, M. M. (2004). *Mindfulness and acceptance: Expanding the cognitive behavioral tradition*. New York: Guilford.

Heidegger, M. (1998). Letter on "Humanism." In W. McNeill (Ed. & Trans.), *Pathmarks* (pp. 239-277). Cambridge, UK: Cambridge University Press. (Original work published 1946)

Hoffman, L. (2008). An existential framework for Buddhism, world religions, and psychotherapy: Culture and diversity considerations. In F. Kaklauskas, S. Nimmanheminda, L. Hoffman, & M. Jack (Eds.), *Brilliant sanity: Buddhism and psychotherapy* (pp. 19-38). Colorado Springs, CO: University of the Rockies Press.

James, W. (1950). *The principles of psychology* (Vol. 1). New York: Dover. (Original work published 1890)

Joyce, J. (1993). *A portrait of the artist as a young man*. New York: Penguin. (Original work published 1916)

Kabat-Zinn, J. (2005). *Full catastrophe living: Using the wisdom of your body and mind to face stress, pain, and illness*. New York: Random House.

Kaklauskas, F., Nimmanheminda, S., Hoffman, L., & Jack, M. (Eds.). (2008). *Brilliant sanity: Buddhism and psychotherapy*. Colorado Springs, CO: University of the Rockies Press.

Linehan, M. (1993). *Cognitive-behavioral treatment of borderline personality disorder*. New York: Guilford.

McLeod, K. (2001). *Wake up to your life: Discovering the Buddhist path of attention.* New York: HarperCollins.

Rahula, W. (1974). *What the Buddha taught* (Rev. ed.). New York: Grove Press.

Sartre, J. (1987). *Existentialism and human emotions.* New York: Citadel Press. (Original work published 1957)

Segal, Z. V., Williams, J. M., & Teasdale, J. T. (2001). *Mindfulness-based cognitive therapy for depression: A new approach to preventing relapse.* New York: Guilford.

Spotnitz, H. (1979). Narcissistic countertransference.*Contemporary Psychoanalysis, 15,* 545-559.

Sujato, A. (2005). A history of mindfulness: How insight worsted tranquillity in the satipatthana sutta. Retrieved September 2, 2008 from http://www.dhammaweb.net/dhammabook/view.php?id=95

Surrey, J. (2005). Relational psychotherapy, relational mindfulness. In C. K. Germer, R. D. Siegel, & P. R. Fulton (Eds.), *Mindfulness and psychotherapy* (pp. 91-112). New York: Guilford.

Trungpa, C. (1995). *The path is the goal.* Boston: Shambhala.

Wallace, B. A. (2006). *The attention revolution: Unlocking the powers of the focused mind.* Boston: Wisdom Publications.

Wegela, K. (1996). *How to be a help instead of a nuisance: Practical approaches to giving support, service & encouragement to others.* Boston: Shambhala.

Yalom, I. D. (1980). *Existential psychotherapy.* New York: Basic Books.

Yalom, I. D. (2000). *Love's executioner: & other tales of psychotherapy.* New York: Harper.

12

In and Out of the Distress:
A Survival Philosophy of Shi Tie-Sheng

Wensheng Wang
Translated by: Joseph Siu

Shi Tie-Sheng (Shi) is regarded as an outstanding writer who is worthy to be studied by modern psychologists. The characters in his writings provide us with great insight into the psychology of human nature, both the benign and the pathological. At the same time, his literary writings contain a number of existential philosophical themes that deepen our understanding of the nature of meaning in existential psychotherapy.

Shi was physically disabled and remarked that he chose writing as his career because it "kept him from taking his own life" (Shi, 2001c, p. 19). Shi identified strongly with his characters who were often afflicted with physical disabilities such as cancer or blindness. In 1972, when he was 21 years old, Shi suffered from a tumor in his spinal cord that caused the lower half of his body to be paralyzed. Shi's paralysis caused him a great deal of distress and impelled him to question his existence. Suddenly confronted with his helplessness, he felt completely hopeless. He had to come to terms with the fact that he would never be able to stand up again. He had to give up the opportunity to receive a college education. He lived like in invalid without the ability to obtain a decent job in society. Sadly, though many applauded his perseverance none would offer their daughters in marriage. (Shi, 2001b, p. 152)

During his hospitalization, Shi shared his pain with and befriended a number of his fellow patients. There was a seven-year-old boy from a remote village who became paralyzed for life after falling out of a car while playing. The boy struggled mightily with accepting his painful reality. He was forever regretful. There was also a flourishing young man who had to give up a recent romantic relationship and his dream of studying abroad because of a medical mishap. These ordeals changed their lives forever. They reminded Shi of Heidegger's saying, "Man is abandoned onto the world," left to tremble at their encounters with an awesome transcend power.

Trembling best describes Shi's inner state when faced with this overwhelming force. It describes Shi's attitude as he begins his journey into his spirit/soul? Because of this attitude, Shi's soul searching is distinguished from others in that he seldom raised the questions, "Why Me? Why this suffering?" Instead of looking for reasons, Shi searched for the meaning of his suffering. Shi's reflections did not arise out of his Chinese tradition with words of wisdom such as, "Out of the depth of misfortune comes bliss" (否極泰來) or "Blessing is the flip side of misfortune." (禍兮福之所倚). Instead, Shi's comprehension derived from his understanding of the book of Job in the Bible. This is evident from the fact that several quotations from the Biblical character Job can be found in Shi's writings including, *A Patient's Notes*, (病隙碎笔) and his novel *My Ding Yi Journey* (我的丁一之旅).

The book of *Job* in the Bible provides a narration of the mystery of suffering. Suffering is a difficult theological topic. In reading the *Job*, Shi noticed two important themes that provided a mental map helping him cope with suffering. The first theme was the sovereignty of God. Shi's character Ding Yi ponders, "what or who is causing me to suffer for my sin? For what purpose?" Shi recaps the story from the Bible which "occurred long before Ding Yi's time wherein God asked Job 'Where were you when I created the Universe?'" (Shi , 2008). The second theme which helped Shi to cope with suffering was Job's faith.

> Job had a genuine faith towards God. Job's faith was not built on promises of blessings, instead it was tested with unceasing tribulations.... God's revelation of His almighty creation to Job allowed Job to gain perspective and submit to the mighty reality that suffering is an integral part of world and cannot be taken away. (Shi, 2002, p. 5)

Shi acknowledged with awe and respect that any causation of sufferings ought to be in the mystery of God. In addition, Shi also realized that Job's faith and his life were purified by his trials--the real meaning of suffering! This revelation subsequently led Shi to accept his persecutions as that from which he could discover the true meaning of his own suffering.

Original Sin, Predestination (原罪·宿命), one of Shi's novels, was initially regarded as a fatalistic analysis in suffering; however, its tenets are quite different from fatalism. The narrator began his tale from the end of the story to explain how his tragedy was predestined. He ruminates,

> Because I was late for that one second, or if only I could have waited one more second, or in other words, because I departed one second too soon or if only I could have departed even one second earlier, then I could have avoided a lifetime of being paralyzed. (Shi, 2001d, p. 158)

The ultimate meaning of the story boiled down to a puzzle within the author's mind "Why did the ordeal happen?" (Shi, 2001d, p. 163). "The past merely vanished into thin air (烟消雲散). And the cold, inhumane callous world turns its back on you, leaving you utterly alone" (Shi, 2001d, p. 161). It can also be seen that the life of the fine young man, who had accomplished so much in regards to his plans to study abroad, was turned upside down in the wink of an eye; from prosperity to adversity in a second! Whose fault is it? Blame it on the distraction of the loud and passive fart from the dog which provided the momentary distraction that caused the tragic and life-changing delay. It concerned none and was no one's fault. Such things happen sensibly. Nonetheless, tragedy occurs. Could it be true that their destiny was altered by the fart?! Who could control a fart of a dog? Fatalists would explain this in terms of predestination. They might view that man is merely a pawn in human destiny. One's significance has nothing to do with whatever occurs. To this, Shi sighs asking:

> Why? Why? Why? Why the fart?"
> Why ask why?
> God said, Let there be fart. There was fart. And God saw that it was good. That's the way things are. There were evenings and there were mornings. All this happened in the days following the seventh day of creation. (Shi, 2001d, p. 170)

Shi's insights regarding the meaning of suffering make him a writer distinct from the fatalists. In many of his writings, Shi makes sustaining arguments for the necessity of suffering. An individual's life is like a play on the stage, a spectacle unto the world. There are many roles to be acted out in the play. Without exception, both the fortunate and the unfortunate have their roles. Accordingly, Shi discovers the mission of his life. That is, to endeavor to fulfill his role and the suffering that has been commissioned by

God. This renders his life worthy and gives meaning to his existence. His commitment to his role not only enables him to flee from self blame, despair, and hopelessness, it also increases his self-esteem. As one of the many roles designated by Sovereignty, the disabled helps those who are normal, without physical handicap, to count their blessings. Thus, the disabled are accorded their full dignity and are deserving of respect by the world.

To those who ask, "Well, who is to suffer?" Shi would repeatedly refer to the fortuity regarding God's random arrangement. This has nothing to do with justice. In this regard, Shi's concept of suffering is seemingly more pessimistic than the Christian view of suffering. In the Gospel of John (9: 1-3) in the New Testament, Jesus' disciples asked him, "Rabbi, who sinned, this man or his parents, that he was born blind?" Jesus replied "Neither this man nor his parents sinned, but this happened so that the work of God might be displayed in his life." Beyond this biblical view in the Gospel of John is the core belief of the incarnation of Christ, who died on the cross for the sin of all people. The Divine Himself in Christianity had to carry his own cross and take up the bitterness and tribulation for all who suffered.

Even so, in regards to affliction, Shi did not clearly define the relationship between suffering and grace. He asked, "Where can we find salvation for all of our ill fates?" Shi sometimes expressed his pessimistic view regarding men:

> Men will perish, the earth will be destroyed, the universe is approaching a deathly silence. Then, what is the value and meaning of all our wisdom and wit, striving and toil, luck and success? Where are we going to and heading towards? What is our goal? Where is our joy and happiness? Where is the way of our redemption? Are we headed towards an impasse and finding nowhere to go? Truly, we are in a hopeless situation. (Shi, 2001c, p. 101)

Ignoring the relationship between grace and suffering, Shi emphasizes the need for individual works of self-transcendence and the importance of the "process" of overcoming one's own troubles. In the midst of suffering, the process becomes alive wherein individuals can surpass themselves, eventually attaining joy through suffering.

Popular belief states that a noble objective is a prerequisite for a meaningful life. However, Shi does not hold such an ontological perspective. To him, the existence of the world itself does not require an objective. The only significance of the end objective is to justify the ongoing process. In other words, the ends justify the means, or the end gives meaning to the means. The goal is in fact nonexistent. It is entirely presupposed to give meaning to the process. Regardless whether the goal was presupposed or the process created, both are in fact created by human beings. Hence, Shi placed his redemptive hope clearly onto individuals themselves instead of following the example of Job who looked upon God for hope.

In regards to the redemptive hope to be found within individuals, Shi emphasized the wisdom of survivorship. In his book *Ming Ruo Qin Xian* (命若琴弦) (Life resembling a zither-liked, plucked instrument), a prescription in the form of a blank piece of paper passed down through succeeding generations of the blind represented the wisdom of survivorship. It was a perfect goal prescribed for all those who desperately wanted to see. The goal of sight was prescribed in the rules, which stated that the cure for blindness to be found on that piece of paper can only be granted after a thousand of strings of the *qin* (琴) were broken through play. As a result, performing *qin* in public was no longer just a means to earn a living given that the act had been given a higher meaning. It became the motivation and full incentive for blind old men playing their *qin* during the next seventy years.

The story revealed that an old blind man had finally achieved the target in breaking a thousand strings of his *qin*. Wryly, he realized that what he really received was merely a blank paper which contained no words. Despite his despair at discovering that the piece of paper was actually blank signifying that in actuality there was no "cure" for blindness, nevertheless, the old blind man chose to follow the example of his old master and gave this same blank piece of paper to his young apprentice advising him just as his old master had prescribed. Fully cognizant of the ruse, the old blind man knew that the pull and hope of the distant promise of cure can become the driving force in the life of the young blind apprentice. The old blind man, after a lifetime of earning the prescription, chose to engage in the same duplicity in helping the apprentice to live his life. Rather than exposing the apprentice to the despair of reality, which in turn may lead to further desperation, the old man in turn allowed his young apprentice to live happily in hope.

Ming Ruo Qin Xian (命若琴弦) speaks of Shi's understanding of the existence of humankind, suggesting that the establishment of a life goal is an essential strategy for survival. Shi does not attempt to make sense of the life goal in terms of eternal meaning, nor does he presume that people are born to a purpose. Nonetheless, Shi does show empathy toward the concept of nihilism. In other words, Shi believes that "All goals are vanity. Life has only one reality. The meaning of this reality can only be found in achieving a higher level of awareness in regards to one's spirit and soul" (Shi, 2001c, p. 40). In his discussion of the goal of life, Shi's view is somehow contradictory. On one hand he emphasizes his belief that individuals can only be spurred through trials by holding firm to an objective; on the other hand, he alludes that the goal is more or less a vanity. How then can one determine if the empty goal is real or not? Shi offers an allegory.

> We woke up in our primitive dream and were faced with an unfathomable loneliness. However, life becomes colored and enlivened when we tell ourselves lively myths. These myths protect us from our primitive loneliness. In their pilgrimage, people galloped towards the charming myth which promised to bring them ultimate and genuine gaiety and felicity in life. (Shi, 2001c, p. 41)

Shi's objective in life can be found in this adorable tale. He holds that individuals have to discover their life's meaning in the walk and circumstances of their daily experiences, very much like the old blind man. Even though his life goal involved deception, the happiness experienced each time he broke the string was real. These hopeful and joyous experiences sustained him and gave his life meaning. However, the old blind man's dream was smashed when the secret was disclosed. In a moment, he lost the drive as well as the meaning to his life... until one day he discovered that his young apprentice needed his help and consequently, the blind man regained his meaning and purpose. He was once again able to stand on his own. Guiding his young apprentice out of distress became his sole mission. In this respect, we can understand the suffering of the blind apprentice as meaningful. It was the existential value of the young disciple.

Ming Ruo Qin Xian (命若琴弦) was Shi's search for a solution to humankind's distress. Regardless of whether the purpose originated with the self, or with others, individuals who can dedicate themselves to a mission will always find hope in the midst of hopelessness. It is in their love of offering meaning to others that allows people in distress to see their accountability and commitment. As Friedrich Nietzsche, the German existential philosopher said, "He who has a *why* to live for can bear almost any *how*" (as cited in Frankl, 1993, p. 59). This life philosophy fits well with Logotherapy, which was developed by the existential psychiatrist Viktor E. Frankl. In brief, "the utmost importance is not what we hope for in life but what life hopes for us" (Frankl, 1993, p. 59).

In Shi 's point of view,

> a person in despair has two options if he or she wants to escape the temptation of death. The first option is turn him or herself into an idiot. Or, the person can come to an understanding of how the process is always after the goal. (Shi, 2001b, p. 155)

Of course Shi recommends the latter approach.

> God arranges many hurdles and hardships in the process of life, so that human beings may experience joyfulness and pleasure…. If someone could not taste and experience such blessings and joy, life becomes a ridiculous, laborious assignment filled with bitterness. (Shi, 2001b, pp. 157-158)

This is Shi's existential philosophy. He believes that the existence of suffering and death is predestined. People do not have the liberty of fleeing from tribulations; however, they do have the freedom to choose how they will face their difficulties. This internal frame of mind so often determines the outcome of various situations.

Upon the discovery of his paralysis, Shi revealed his desire to end his life through suicide in his writing of the *Four Pieces of Dialogues* (對話四則). When asked why he did not commit the suicide, Shi replied with the words of Charlie Chaplin, "Why hurry? Sooner or later man will die." This excuse prevented Shi from killing himself and turned him into an outstanding writer. His novel *Poison* (毒藥) is a story about dying in order to live. The narrator in the story wanted to end his life and obtained two poison pills that can kill without pain. Paradoxically, the narrator did not die but continued living his life filled with blessings. This was because of the comfort provided by the two poison pills. Whenever the narrator encountered difficulties, he would take out the two poison pills for a glimpse. They reminded him that death is always waiting at his doorstep. Ironically, what was intended as an agent of death became a catalyst for life and inspired the narrator to do all that he can to live. Shi henceforth remarked that "though death is despairing, Chaplin's statement nonetheless transform it into hope" (Shi, 2001b, p. 155). With the existence of this hope, people are empowered to live on.

Shi interprets Chaplin's lines in the following ways:

> One begins first by assuming an attitude of acceptance for when you are near the end of your life, rest assured that death will naturally reach out to rescue you. Second, being fully aware of the certainty of death, why not give life your best try? You might even have some fun with it. Your life is already tough enough. As death is so reliable and certain for a dying man, what does one have to fear? What is there to lose? (Shi, 2001b, p. 155)

Ordinary people are used to the "reduction method" of viewing their lives. That is, they calculate what will be leftover after summing up their troubles. Particularly for those who are devastated, they will consider that there is too little of their lives left for them to count on. On the other hand, Shi shares Chaplin's wisdom, which encourages people to embrace the "adding-up" method for living. The baseline is that we are standing at the edge of death and indeed we are in possession of nothing. Having this perspective, we will learn to begin to add up all the possibilities in our lives. This summation of life not only sheds light on the hope for living, it also provides courage for people in despair.

Shi's philosophy of survivorship addresses the necessity for love. "The magnificent and unified cosmic message is fragmented and shaped into flesh which requires love to help complete and integrate our fragmentation" (Shi, 2001c, p. 261). Shi is also a man of affection, surrounded by people who love and care about him. Recalling the days of his hospitalization at the age of 21, Shi realized that "his friendships kept him alive" (Shi, 2001a, p. 39). In his book, *The Year When I Was 21* (我二十一歲那年), Shi recounted many of his lovely classmates and applauded the nurses and physicians who quietly offered him care and support during his recovery. Further evidence of Shi's affectionate nature can be found in *My Faraway Qing Ping Wan* (我遙遠的清平灣), which reflected Shi's rural sense of innocence and purity and *The Silk Tree* (合歡樹) and *I and the Earth Temple* (我與地), which portrayed Shi's affections toward his mother. Indeed the maternal love Shi received was a main reason for his survival.

Shi always felt grateful and lucky for having a satisfying, loving relationship. In his letter to a friend Li Jian Ming (李健鳴), Shi wrote about his own love story.

Somewhere in the past, Yi-Tong (一同) and I sat together alone in silent companionship, comforting each other, submitting to fate (聽天由命). This silent companionship allowed Shi to feel the breadth and width of love. Shi compared the gap between sex and love to the chasm between the finite and the infinite. This is why the experience of suffering is deeper and wider than the experience of attraction. Attraction cannot prove love whereas suffering can. (Shi, 2001c, 254-255)

According to Shi's life experience, disability and love are "the two fundamental sacred codes divinely inscribed into humanity" (Shi, 2002, p. 65). Shi likens the two codes to the concepts of original sin and redemption.

Love belongs to the spirit. She is a dream and hope for human perfection and fulfillment. It is boundless and it renders the possibility in the breakthrough of our limitations and constraints. It also compensates for man's imperfections and disability. (Shi, 2002, p. 65)

Hence, love has the power of redemption. No wonder Shi has expounded so much in his writings regarding the rights for the disabled to love. People have often been suspicious of the ability of the disabled to love. From this, Shi has been able to discern a deeper form of discrimination against the disabled. However, Shi's emphasis upon the alienable rights for the disabled to love comes not out of his own disability nor people's deep prejudices against the disabled. Instead, Shi's motivation for championing for the rights of the disabled arises out of a deeper metaphysical conviction regarding the humanity of the disabled. Shi is most concerned with the relationship between disability and love. He is not limiting himself to just physical disabilities but includes all those who are impaired and bound by external bondage and imperfections. People are isolated and desolated because of their limitations as well as their disabilities. And a loving relationship can be viewed as a call for reconciliation, wherein our other half is found to possess a similar soul yearning in loneliness. Shi thus professes that when it comes to loving relationships, people's hearts are in heaven even if their bodies are mired in the abyss. Shi realizes this to be the fulfillment of love in religion. The possibility and hope of human redemption is to be grounded on the possibility of the disabled to love.

In summary, the aforementioned acceptance of suffering, the analysis of meaning for individuals in despair, the prescribed goal of life, the life process creation, as well as the redemptive power of love, are all characterized in Shi 's philosophy of life. They also form a structure to his idea of survivorship. In reading and reflecting upon these ideas, we see Shi's wisdom and the effectiveness of his life meaning analysis for overcoming men's distress. The intellectual insights formulated in Shi's survivor philosophy incorporate values from both Western Christian culture and Chinese traditional philosophy. Although Shi rarely elicits the latter, from his emphasis on the survivor wisdom, his pursuit of happiness and his praise for the efforts for the individual, we understand that his propositions have their roots in the Chinese traditional culture. With these attributes in place, Shi's writings can be recognized as useful learning materials in the development of an indigenous Chinese psychotherapy.

References

Frankl, V. E. (1993). *Man's search for meaning*. Beijing: China Translation & Publishing Corporation.

Shi, T. (2001a). *Acacia*. Jinan: Shangdong Literature Publishing House.

Shi, T. (2001b). *Dialogue practice.* Changchun: Shidai Literature Publishing House.

Shi, T. (2001c). *Writing as destiny.* Jinan: Shangdong Literature Publishing House.

Shi, T. (2001d). *Zhong Sheng.* Taiyuan: Beiyue Literature Publishing House.

Shi, T. (2002). *A patient's notes*. Xian: Shan'xi Normal University Press.

Shi, T. (2008). *My Ding Yi journey*. Beijing: People's Literature Publishing House.

Part 3

Existential Perspectives on Eastern and Western Myths

13

Gordo's Ghost:
An Introduction to Existential Perspectives on Myth

Louis Hoffman

> There can be no stronger proof of the impoverishment of our contemporary culture than the popular--though profoundly mistaken--definition of myth as falsehood.
> ~ Rollo May, 1991, p. 2

> Our greatest challenge today... is to couple conviction with doubt. By conviction, I mean some pragmatically developed faith, trust, or centeredness; and by doubt I mean openness to the ongoing changeability, mystery, and fallibility of the conviction.
> ~ Kirk Schneider, 1999, p. 7

> What is the ideal for mental health, then? A lived, compelling illusion [or myth] that does not lie about life, death, and reality; one honest enough to follow its own commandments: I mean, not to kill, not to take the lives of others to justify itself.
> ~ Ernest Becker, 1973, p. 204

Myth is at the core of Rollo May's (1961, 1991, 1999a, 1999b) conception of meaning. Meaning, in return, is the central element in the existential perspective of mental health. This can be seen dating back to Nietzsche (1889/1999) as reflected in his famous statement, "If we possess a *why* of life we can put up with almost any *how*" (p. 33). This same sentiment is later reflected in Becker's (1973) statement, "Man cannot endure his own littleness unless he can translate its meaningfulness on the largest possible level" (p. 196).

Meaning provides a stabilizing and centering effect in a world that often is dizzying and disorienting. From an existential perspective, meaning is the ultimate "coping mechanism," but it is also so much more; meaning is a basic human need. Meaning, too, is a central motivating factor that stands behind many behaviors, both constructive and problematic. In one stance, meaning drives us to the most humanistic of ideals; it inspires us to seek great personal change, to serve the greater social good, and to have compassion for the less fortunate. Yet, in the lack of sustaining meaning, the inner experience of emptiness and meaninglessness can drive individuals to destructive pursuits of power, pleasure, and dangerous degrees distraction. As May (1991) states,

> I speak of the *Cry* for myths because I believe there is an urgency in the need for myth in our day. Many of the problems of our society, including cults and drug addiction, can be traced to the lack of myths which will give us as individuals the inner security we need in order to live adequately in our day. (p. 9)

The lack of myth reflects a lack of meaning. And a life without myth sets the foundation for many types of pathology, from the personal to the social.

This leads to the questions, "What, then, is a myth?" and "Why is it the ideal of meaning in existential thought?" A myth is a collection of related symbols that create a worldview or meaning system. It serves as a reference for the way we see the world and as an interpreter of our experiences in the world.

The confusion around myth as a meaning system is reflected in the quote by May at the opening of this chapter. Today, myth is often misunderstood as something that is false or deceptive. Instead, May (1991) illustrates that *myth* refers to a meaning system in which the content cannot be *proven* true. It is not that myths are false; rather they are a matter of faith or belief. But even the idea of faith, whether interpreted in a religious sense or not, has been distorted over time. Faith, which traditionally was understood as believing in something that cannot be proven, often is interpreted as factual knowledge today. Indeed, the idea of the "certainty of faith," which is a common today, is *contra*-faith!

Myth, however, is more powerful than knowledge or facts; it provides a deeper and more holistic sense of meaning and security (Hoffman & Fehl, 2008; Hoffman & McGuire, 2008). Knowledge is concrete; it involves one element of our being: cognitions. But faith is holistic; it is a matter of belief (cognitions) and emotion. Faith, as Tillich (1957) states, necessitates a degree of doubt. Doubt, in return, brings with it an element of anxiety. And as has been discussed earlier in the book, anxiety is not, of itself, pathological. Anxiety, as with doubt, becomes pathological when we resist or deny it. Anxiety, therefore, is a basic emotion that can either help us thrive or lead to our demise. When the reaction to anxiety is to rid oneself of it through convincing oneself of the certainty of what, in actuality, is not certain, then it becomes destructive. But anxiety can also bring vitality to our beliefs; it motives us to continue in our pursuit of meaning and/or spirituality.

As should now be evident, myth is a healthier meaning system than knowledge because it has a degree of openness, doubt, and humility. In other words, myth can hold together the paradox of conviction and mystery. It allows us to have passion without certainty, "truth" without oppression, and faith without arrogance. Schneider (2005) refers to this openness to mystery as "awe." Drawing on this language, the difference between the dry lifelessness of concrete facts is much less inspiring than the anxiety filled conceptions of mystery and awe.

Religion provides a good illustration of this application of myth. Applying May's (1991) conception to religion, it could be stated that all world religions are myths. This is not stating that religions are false, it is merely acknowledging that they cannot be proven true. Stated differently, *religion is a matter of faith, not knowledge.* Historically, this was not such a threat to religion as some may interpret it today. In the early premodern period, religion was a matter of faith; however, as premodernism progressed and then gradually was replaced by modernism, the idea of faith and belief was replaced with of the same content that is now understood as knowledge or facts (Hoffman & Kurzenberger, 2008). In other words, history turned mythos (i.e., myth) into logos (i.e., knowledge) and thereby changed the very nature of religion and faith.

Whether religious or not, it is difficult to deny the powerful, healing, and transforming qualities that religion and spirituality have in many people's lives. But we should not be naive about religion; it can serve destructive purposes as easily constructive ones. When religion has gone astray, it has been at the root of many harmful judgments such as hate crimes, and some wars. This use of religion has killed just as it has saved. Religion, when understood as a myth, is something that is powerfully constructive; however, when religion is turned into a rigid, definitive belief system it more often does harm than good.[1]

---

[1] This is the essence of the understanding of how "religion" and faith have changed and provides the foundation for the distinction between the religion and spirituality in our

In a sense, May's (1991) recapturing of this classical Greek understanding of myth is a call to return to faith, although not necessarily a religious faith. Similar critiques could also be made of science. Science, at one point, was understood as progressive and continually reformulating its ideas and hypotheses. There was no end to science because science was continually re-envisioning itself and reinterpreting the "facts" it discovered in the world. This is evident in the way Einstein spoke of science, which was to be awe-based, as opposed to the way science is often portrayed in very stale characterizations today.

Science, like religion, can be constructive or destructive. It is interesting that science is often used today to delimit and restrict the pursuit of knowledge. Rigid protocols, similar to religious laws, are applied to how knowledge should be pursued. The label of being "unscientific" is often intended as a very damning judgment. *Science, which Freud argued would replace religion, has too often instead become a religion!* We need to return to mythical understandings of both science and religion to save them from the destructive and constricting ends they often serve today.

Surprised by Myth: Why Stories Impact Us So

Many existentialists believe in the constructive power of the unconscious, or in the *wisdom of the unconscious*. Instead of something to be feared, we can learn to use the unconscious productively. This is particularly true in the realm of myth. For instance, myths can be useful in helping to understand why stories, movies, or other forms of art impact our lives.

Myths originate out of a need or a struggle by providing meaning, that is, a framework for understanding what the individual is experiencing. Often, these needs or struggles are connected to the existential givens (death/finitude, meaning, freedom/responsibility, relationship/isolation, and embodiment).[2] Indeed, sustaining myths are those that help bring meaning to the givens of existence. This, in part, explains why certain pieces of literature and art have sustaining meaning over time; they have provided meaning in the face of the existential givens. May (1991), in *The Cry for Myth*, provides examples of many myths of Western culture that have survived the test of time. The mythical nature some of these is evident, such as Dante's *Divine Comedy*, Goethe's *Faust*, and Fitzgerald's

---

contemporary usage of these terms. Historically, they were not separated. Over time, they were separated, in a sense, to *save religion through spirituality* (see Hoffman & Fehl, 2008).
[2] See chapter 1 for a more detailed discussion of the givens.

The Great Gatsby, all of which are great pieces of literature. Other myths are more allegorical and abstract, such as the myths of the frontier in United States history, the devil, and individualism. These stories and collective ideas reflect that they have been able to provide sustaining meaning for many individuals. Their ongoing popularity reflects that these have been effective meaning systems in the face of the starkness of the givens. For example, the myth of the devil has been a way of dealing with issues of freedom and responsibility around the issue evil; individualism has been a popular way of dealing with the reality of existential isolation; and Dante's *Divine Comedy* has touched on the value of painful or challenging aspects of self-awareness.

This aspect of myth elucidates why we often have powerful emotional reactions to art, literature, and movies without knowing the cause. On the unconscious level, we are recognizing the meaning level of the myth, particularly as it relates to the existential givens. For example, in Chapter 15, Calvert and colleagues discuss the movie *American Beauty*, which was very popular in the United States across several generations. Many individuals, however, would struggle to identify what made this such an engaging movie. Its popularity was not based on action, comedy, or high drama; instead, the draw of movie was more subtle: *American Beauty* illustrated themes that many Americans struggle with when facing the givens of existence. At the same time, it may not seem as relevant to those not familiar with American culture; it is a uniquely American response to the givens.

This power of myth can be particularly useful in therapy. In recent years, several books have been written on the use of cinema therapy, or integrating the use of movies in psychotherapy (Hesley & Hesley, 2001; Solomon, 1995; Wedding, Boyd, & Niemiec, 2005). Although the approach these books use is different from an existential approach to cinema therapy and other uses of movies in mental health, they represent the power and influence that this form of art possesses. From an existential approach, cinema therapy and other forms of art therapy are used to promote exploration, engagement, and encounter. For example, a therapist may encourage a client to identify art, literature, or aspects of a movie that have impacted him or her and use these points to explore the meaning it holds for the individual. The therapist could even be more specific by asking the client to identify art or movies that inexplicitly impacted him. Or, the therapist may "prescribe" a movie instructing the client to pay attention to what stirs his emotions. The therapist may also use movies, art, or literature to illustrate themes which emerge naturally in therapy. In essence, movies can be used to help the person explore and engage in various existential themes.

Universality and Particularity in Myths

A central tenet of this chapter, and the final section of this book, is that *myths represent the universality of the existential givens and the particularity of cultural responses to those givens*. This is principally true of the more sustaining myths. In the rest of this section, various myths are explored in the context of their meaning systems. For example, Cowan illustrates how several novels provided powerful therapeutic effect for him in his struggles with aloneness and existential isolation. As May indicated, often the most powerful and innovative work being done on understanding human nature comes from literature and art departments at universities, not the psychology departments (E. Mendelowitz, personal communication).[3] The novels Cowan discusses are direct in their engagement with the existential givens and were able to assist him in finding meaning in his experience. These novels, in particular, address a Western approach to dealing with the existential given of isolation.

In the East, many myths center on themes such as harmony, interconnectedness, and choices that value the collective. Westerners will notice that the answers to existential givens are quite different than those represented in Western myths. For example, the frontier myth of the United States represents a conquering and control of nature. In Eastern myths, similar to many Native American perspectives, the idea of harmony with nature is emphasized. Freedom and power often is used in the West to exert power over or mastery over others. Conversely, in the East, the motivation is to use one's freedom to choose to be part of the larger whole, or to be in harmony with nature and one's culture. In the East and West, these values can be seen in the different political structures, different family constellations, and different values regarding material possessions. Many Eastern perspectives emphasize choices that reflect the collective first and individual second, which is the opposite of what is seen in Western myths.

Cleare-Hoffman, in Chapter 20, uses the Bahamian myth of Junkanoo to illustrate a response to the existential given of freedom and responsibility in a way that is neither Eastern nor Western. Junkanoo originated as an expression and celebration of freedom during the

---

[3] Mendelowitz notes that this was a common theme when May spoke, but that he was less direct about it in his writing.

oppression of slavery. The Bahamians celebrated the little freedom they had, while Westerners too often take for granted or give up their abundance of freedoms. This illustrates the paradox that a genuine appreciation of freedom is often held more firmly when one's freedom is greatly restricted or taken away. This is very different than the Western ideas of freedom that often idealizes political freedom while neglecting and giving up personal freedoms at the same time.[4]

Although myths can be personal or collective, they always emerge from a particular culture and point in history. Myths that provide particularly poignant responses to the existential givens, such as those represented in the major world religions, have a greater ability to sustain over time. Myths may be adapted, as May (1991) illustrates in the various versions of *Faust*, or they may be reinterpreted, as we often see in the sacred scriptures of the world religions. However, myths must stay relevant to maintain their sustainability for individuals.

Some myths are able to transcend culture, at least to a degree, while others are very culturally limited. Hoffman, Stewart, Warren, and Meek (in press) address this in their discussion of "myths of self." They illustrate that the ideals of the self are drastically different in the East and the West. For example, Eastern cultures tend to value the collective over the individual. Some perspectives, such Buddhism, value the idea of "no self." In the West, the self is central to the Western psyche and often aggrandized. This has powerful implications for mental health.

Western psychology has been built upon the idea of the centrality of the self and self-esteem. This may not be appropriate or may require significant modification when working with people from the East who may perceive this as unhealthy attachment to the self or the individual. According to Hoffman et al. (in press), the implications is that what is psychologically healthy for people from Western cultures may not be psychologically healthy for people in Eastern cultures. A danger exists in exporting Western psychology with its implicit values without considering whether or not it is appropriate for the culture in which it is being exported. Similarly, it is dangerous for Eastern countries to import a Western psychology uncritically.[5] This danger exists with existential psychology, too. Hopefully, it is evident throughout this book that the

---

[4] I am not intending to devalue political freedom; however, I do intend to contrast it with personal freedom, which one has regardless of one's political condition.

[5] The same could be noted about importing Eastern ideas to the West; however, this has not happened to the same degree and, when it has occurred, it has not been in such a forced or uncritical manner.

approach of the editors and contributors is to be sensitive to this issue. Existential psychotherapy should not be practiced the same in the East as it is in the West. We hope that this book represents the beginning of the journey to make the appropriate adaptations for practicing existential therapy in the East. Additionally, we believe that scholars and practitioners in this book have addressed these issues in sufficient depth to begin Eastern applications of existential therapy. Yet, this still is the beginning and we implore the readers to continue the journey.

Learning to See Through Myths

Existential psychology, more than any other major theoretical approach to psychology with the possible exception of Jungian analysis, emphasizes the importance of engagement with philosophy, literature, and the arts as part of the training process and ongoing professional development of the therapist. This seems odd to many, but remains essential to the process of becoming an existential therapist. I would go as far as claiming that no existential psychotherapy training is complete without direct engagement with the arts.

This engagement is evident throughout the writing of Rollo May. In May's final book, *The Psychology of Existence* (1995) written with Kirk Schneider, the reader is introduced to the major philosophical and literary figures that have contributed to an existential understanding of the human condition. This remains an important introduction to the existential thinkers. Such themes are also seen in books such as Schneider's (1993), *Horror and the Holy: Wisdom Teachings of the Monster Tale*. But the question remains as to why philosophy, literature, and the arts are so important to existential psychology. The answer is twofold.

First, existential psychology is a holistic approach. One problem with Western psychology today is its myopic focus on understanding human beings as a distinct biological entity with firm boundaries between itself and the world. Also, drawing from its roots in the physiology of Wundt and the internalized personality theories of early psychoanalysts, contemporary psychology continues to both subtly and not so subtlety envision the individual as if in isolation. Western psychology could learn a great deal from the Eastern perspectives, as well as many other cultural views, that emphasize the interconnected aspects of being human. Although there are some signs that many in the West are beginning to consider these non-Western ideas, the entire basis of its psychological system has been built upon the foundation of Western thought. It may be that a dramatic re-envisioning of Western psychology is necessary to move away from these limitations.

When one knows only a single approach to the human condition, such as the biological, it deceptively appears very easy to understand the essence of the human condition. When one explores what it means to be human through multiple perspectives, it becomes evident that the ontological nature of being human is incredibly complex. This is radically evident in many approaches to "pop psychology" and even many scholarly approaches to psychology in which the individual has been deeply rooted in a singular subfield or specialty in psychology. Routinely, I find it much more difficult to learn from even the most brilliant of scholars if they are not rooted in the breadth of interdisciplinary study. Their assumptions are too narrow, too obvious, and too naïve. One should always be suspicious of anyone who thinks he or she has solved the human condition or can explain anything. And I would guess anyone who has made such claims has never read with any degree of seriousness or reflection the writings of Camus, Kafka, or Dostoevsky.[6]

This point is illustrated in a story told by Bohart (2008) in the Forward to Tom Greenings book, *Words Against the Void: Poems by an Existential Psychologist*. Bohart tells a story of sharing Greenings poems with a colleague who takes a rigid scientific approach to psychology. The colleague responds with mockery and questioning why a psychologist would waste his or her time with poetry when he or she could be engaging in the productive activity of research. In response, Bohart says, "For me, I would prefer a world where some insights are best conveyed through poetry, and where some experiences can only be captured in words and not numbers, although I am not opposed to numbers" (p. vi). This openness to learn from both numbers and art is a broader, more holistic way of learning. I have no doubt that someone who can learn from scientific research as well as various forms of art is much more prepared to sit across from the rich complexities and nuances of a human being with some understanding of what it means for that person to exist. Existence can never be reduced to numbers or biology without the loss of its soul,[7] the very essence of what makes one human.

---

[6] To give due credit, it should be noted the Freud (1928/1961) also gave consideration to the power of art and, in particular, referred to Dostoevsky as a literary figure particularly attuned to the human condition.

[7] "Soul" here is not used necessarily to metaphysical or non-material soul. This is one interpretation of the soul; however, today the soul is often understood as something that emerges from the material, but cannot be contained by the material. This compares to the

Second, philosophy, literature, and the arts help us to improve our *psychological vision*; they help us see the human within the human condition. As alluded to earlier, we see only those aspects of being human that we are prepared to see. In part, this is about our own emotional health; sometimes we do not see what we are not emotionally ready or able to see. However, we also cannot see those aspects of the human condition that are outside of our referential frame. For example, when working with students learning to identify the themes connected to the existential givens in therapy, they often struggle the most in identifying death issues. This, at times, is because of their countertransference about death issues. However, most of the time, this occurs because they have never learned to identify or see death issues. Although reading a book such as Becker's (1973) *The Denial of Death*, may help the student in identifying death issues, the more effective tool so often is the literary one. Reading Kafka's (1946/1999) *The Trial* or Camus's (1957/1988) *The Stranger* may be a more powerful tool in helping students to understand the human condition, including the death issues—both symbolic and literal.

For several years I have led a monthly existential reading group through the Depth Psychotherapy Institute. Initially we focused on reading the classics of existential psychology while mixing in a few books on existential philosophy. However, at one point we switched to rotating between a theory book, a novel, and a movie. It has been amazing how the depth of the dialogue has been enriched. I am certain that the participants, including myself, are gaining a much deeper appreciation for the human condition as we have broadened the scope of our exploration to include fiction and movies. Theory is brought alive through art and creativity.

I firmly believe that therapists can *see* their clients better when they are engaged in music, poetry, literature, and other forms of art. The training of an existential therapist is never complete, in my mind, until they have engaged in this aspect of their training; nothing can substitute for the arts. In the next section, I will attempt to illustrate this through the use of a classic folk song that deals rather directly with the idea of vision and the ability to see the other person beyond the surface levels.

Gordo's Ghost: Therapy and Vision

Gordon Lightfoot's (Gordo) song, "If I Could Read Your Mind" is a beautiful illustration of myth. Although the song is about a failed romantic

---

Gestalt idea that the whole is greater than the sum of the parts. In other words, if the soul is rooted, or even contained, in biology, it still cannot be reduced to being *just* biology.

relationship, in many ways the song parallels the story of psychotherapy. The song begins with the woeful strumming of the guitar, then Gordo's voice breaks in full of soft emotion and heartbreak. The song begins in a story of isolation. Although the couple is still together, Gordo is painfully alone and trapped. At the end of the first stanza, Gordo sings of a ghost chained up in a dungeon, setting the stage for the song's most powerful lyrics:

> You know that ghost is me
> And I will never be set free
> As long as I'm a ghost you can't see

These three lines speak powerfully to the existential condition of isolation, but also to psychotherapy.

A primary reason many clients enter psychotherapy is because they feel that no one sees them. Friends, family, and often even their therapists have been unable or unwilling to truly see them, to look beyond the mask. There is no greater loneliness than the one experienced in the presence of those who are supposed to love you the most. Yet, it seems this is one of the most common forms of loneliness.

It takes courage to allow oneself to be seen. Many clients choose to hide behind masks and heavy garments to protect themselves from being truly known. In therapy settings, I have often encountered clients who reported feeling vulnerable with the receipt of my gaze and they will often comment that they believe I can "see right through them." This is not uncommon for therapists. Clients often project special powers upon the therapists, believing that the therapist can see right through their defenses. Although many therapists are quite adept at picking up subtle cues and insights about the client, we hold no special powers and often are wrong in what we see. Clients can all too easily hide away if we are not able to provide a place where they can become comfortable in their vulnerability.

But it is not hiding that makes Gordo's ghost so elusive; it is the lack of vision by his partner. Just as much as it takes courage to allow oneself to be seen, it also takes courage to see. Too often we do not want to see what is there; we do not want to see the pain, the suffering, the scars. This is true even of therapists. So we hide it away. We tell the other, "Its okay," "It will pass with time," or "It's for the best." All these seemingly well intended statements give the message that it is not okay for the other to see us; we tell the ghost to continue to hide away. Or we may stick with detached cognitive analysis or dialogues rooted in our theories and psychobabble; anything to avoid engaging in the pain and suffering inherent in existence.

Gordo goes on to tell the next stage of the story that takes us back to an earlier time when he was idealized as the hero, just like in the "drugstore novel." But the hero does not save the day:

> When you reach the part where the heartaches come
> The hero would be me
> But heroes often fail

The drop in Gordo's voice when singing "heroes often fail" can be felt, as well as heard; it embodies the cliché of the heart dropping. In all relationships, for them to reach the point of genuineness, we must see beyond the idealized hero. In therapy, this is illustrated time and again. Many couples who enter therapy have reached the place where the heroic transferences begin to fade. As Robert Murney (personal communication) was fond of saying, "We all marry our idealized mate and then sometime after the ceremony we meet the one we married." This is a painful time for most couples and many do not survive. They may begin again searching for the hero that will never fail, but at some point they are forced to realize that what they need is not another hero; they need is a fellow sojourner just as imperfect as they are themselves.[8] We all fail; it is a part of the human condition. But only when we accept our partners as flawed beings can we experience a genuine relationship with them. There is no true intimacy when relating to the idealized other. Authentic intimacy occurs only with the human behind the mask and underneath the projections.

The same is often true in psychotherapy. Clients project many idealized images upon the therapist, such as super-human levels of intuition, knowledge, and advice. For some therapists, this may feel good. Many therapists spend their days hiding behind these idealized images, basking in the deception that our clients, who love and idealize us, are the ones who truly know and understand us. But this is not therapeutic for the client, and not healthy for us. For therapy to succeed, our clients need to

---

[8] It has often been stated that a therapist cannot take a client beyond where they have been themselves. I disagree. Although there are certain advantages to having already been down that road, in reality, each client will be further along in some aspects of the journey than the therapist. What is essential, in my view, is that the therapist, too, is on the journey. The adage I would suggest as a replacement is that *we cannot guide a client on a journey we are not willing to go on ourselves.*

be in therapy with a real person. It is our job to break through the idealizations and create a genuine relationship with the person who also happens to be our client. When this does not occur, the next lines Gordo's song become haunting:

> And you won't read that book again
> Because the endings just too hard to take

For individuals stuck in the cycle of idealizations and fallen heroes, they eventually back away from relationships with depth. They continue to interact with others, and may even be quite social and popular, but they no longer allow themselves to be vulnerable enough for true intimacy.

The paradoxical nature of relationships is such that the more deeply we love, the more deeply we can be hurt. Intimacy requires vulnerability, but so many choose to hide behind false intimacies in hope that they will never be deeply hurt. But this shallow existence has few rewards other than the surface smiles that hide the empty feelings behind them. They are alone behind the ever-present tragic smile.

In my own life, I can remember boldly thinking that I could endure any loss and suffer through it relatively unscathed. In part, this was due to having developed a rather existential approach to suffering early in life. When I experienced pain or loss, I boldly journeyed into it and found that the pain was never so bad when I faced it directly. But it was also due to routinely choosing "safe" relationships in which I was never asked to be vulnerable. In the later part of this phase of my life, I encountered two friends who invited me to be more present, and gently called out my hiding. This prepared me for my next lesson. It was later, after I married my wife, that I first became terrified of a loss. Although I had been bold in my vulnerabilities and brash in my love in prior relationships, it had never been to the same depths as with my wife. For the first time, I recognized that there was a potential for loss in my life of which the mere prospect was terrifying. The depth of her love and her courage to truly see me changed everything. Yet, at the same time, the beauty she has brought to my life would make every tear, no matter how unbearable, worth what I would have to face. Our relationship is far from perfect, but we have learned the sublime art of being broken together.

Not all relationships reach the depth of intimacy we have with our loved ones. Certainly, we do not love our therapy clients in the same way. But hopefully we love our clients enough to truly see them, and to offer them a genuine relationship with us where we are not hiding behind heroic projections. It should be clarified that the genuineness and breaking of idealization talked about here is not suggesting that we disclose our scars and wounds to our client; it is not about personal disclosure at all. Rather, it is about being vulnerable in the moment, about allowing ourselves to be fully present with our clients as fallible, imperfect human beings.

As Gordo's story progresses, the relationship becomes entangled in patterns that are not so easily broken. At different points he laments,

> I never thought I could act this way
> And I've got to say that I just don't get it

and

> I never thought I could feel this way
> And I've got to say that I just don't get it

The patterns have been set in the relationship and now they are difficult to break; they have become part of the couple's destiny. This pervasive pattern itself is a given; all relationships develop patterns that are hard to break, and they are more difficult to break when the patterns are not understood. Gordo recognizes the feelings and behaviors, but he does not understand them. These become additional chains on Gordo's ghost, keeping him bound in the dungeon, below the surface of conscious awareness.

As the song ends, there are no signs of hope. Gordo is alone and unseen; accompanied only by the experience of profound loneliness. There is a despondent feeling as if he knows the pattern is bound to reappear. But this, too, is life. For many, they begin to accept patterns as if that is all there is and they no longer seek new ways of being and understanding. It is not clear if Gordo's ghost even wants to leave the dungeon; maybe he is content with this pattern his life. Maybe the security of the cold, damp dungeon is easier than being exposed by the light.[9]

For a more hopeful ending, it is necessary to go beyond the story of Gordo's ghost. There is a degree to which we all are like Gordo's ghost; never fully seen by others no matter how vulnerable we are and how hard the other person tries to see us. But there is hope. As therapists our job is to *see* our clients, even at those times when we would rather look away. It

---

[9] It could be noted that the dungeon could also be interpreted as Gordo's unconscious. In this interpretation, Gordo is not able to see himself and is bound by his own lack of awareness.

is through our mutual fierce vision that clients discover choice and meaning.

From an existential perspective, therapy does not really begin at a deep level until we begin to see the client as they truly are. This is not to deny the inherent impossibility of ever completely seeing others, but rather focuses on the necessity of seeing for many types of healing to occur. As discussed earlier, it is often myths such as Gordo's ghost that help us develop our therapeutic vision that better enables us to see our clients.

Conclusion

Gordo's ghost is a story about the interface of existential isolation and interpersonal isolation, but it is also a story about existential or ontological vision. We can never be completely seen and we can never completely see another person. This, in part, is why existential isolation can never be fully overcome. But, we can be more seen and we can learn to see others more completely. As therapists, our therapeutic vision is essential not because it gives us any special knowledge or interpretive powers, but because it is necessary to encounter our clients on a deeper level and allow them to encounter themselves and their world more fully, honestly, and meaningfully.

References

Becker, E. (1973). *The denial of death*. New York: Free Press.

Bohart, A. (2008). Forward. In T. Greening (Author), *Words against the void: Poems by an existential psychologist* (pp. iii-vi). Colorado Springs, CO: University of the Rockies Press.

Camus, A. (1988). *The stranger*. New York: Random House. (Original work published in 1957)

Freud, S. (1961). Dostoevsky and parricide. In J. Stratchey (Ed. & Trans.), *The standard edition* (Vol. 21). New York: Norton. (Original work published in 1928)

Hesley, J. W. & Hesley, J. G. (2001). *Rent two films and let's talk in the morning: Using popular movies in psychotherapy* (2nd ed.). New York: Wiley.

Hoffman, L. & Fehl, S. (2008). *Spiritualizing the unknown*. In J. H. Ellens (Ed.), Miracles: God, science, and psychology in the paranormal (Vol. 3, pp. 194-209). Westport, CT: Praeger Books.

Hoffman, L. & Kurzenberger, M. (2008). The miraculous in mental illness. In J. H. Ellens (Ed.), *Miracles: God, science, and psychology in the paranormal* (Vol. 3, pp. 65-93). Westport, CT: Praeger Books.

Hoffman, L. & McGuire, K. (2008). Are miracles essential or peripheral to faith traditions? In J. H. Ellens (Ed.), *Miracles: God, science, and psychology in the paranormal* (Vol. 1, pp. 221-240). Westport, CT: Praeger Books.

Hoffman, L., Stewart, S., Warren, D., & Meek., L. (in press). Toward a sustainable myth of self: An existential response to the postmodern condition. *Journal of Humanistic Psychology.*

Kafka, F. (1999). *The trial.* New York: Schocken Books. (Original work published 1946)

May, R. (1961). The meaning of the Oedipus myth. *Review of Existential Psychology and Psychiatry, 1,* 44-52.

May, R. (1991). *The cry for myth.* New York: Delta.

May, R. (1999a). Oedipus and self-knowledge. *Review of Existential Psychology and Psychiatry, 24,* 10-16.

May, R. (1999b). The healing power of symbols and myths. *Review of Existential Psychology and Psychiatry, 24,* 17-24.

Mendelowitz, E. (2008). *Ethics and Lao Tzu: Intimations of character.* Colorado Springs, CO: University of the Rockies Press.

Nietzsche, F. (1990). Twilight of the idols. In R. J. Hollingdale (Ed. & Trans.), *Twilight of the idols and the anti-christ* (pp. 31-122). New York: Penguin Classics. (Original work published in 1889).

Schneider, K. J. (1993). *Horror and the holy: Wisdom teachings of the monster tale.* Peru, IL: Open Court.

Schneider, K. J. (1999). *The paradoxical self: Toward an understanding of our contradictory nature* (2nd ed.). Amherst, NY: Humanity Books.

Schneider, K. J. (2005) *Rediscovery of awe: Splendor, mystery and the fluid center of life.* St. Paul, MN: Paragon House.

Schneider, K. J. & May, R. (1995). *The psychology of existence: An integrative, clinical perspective.* New York: McGraw-Hill.

Solomon, G. (1995). *The motion picture prescription: Watch this movie and call me in the morning: 200 movies to help you heal life's problems.* Santa Rosa, CA: Aslan Publishing.

Tillich, P. (1957). *The dynamics of faith.* Harper & Row.

Wedding, D., Boyd, M. A., & Niemiec, R. M. (2005). *Movies and mental illness* (2nd ed.). Cambridge, MA: Hogrefe and Huber.

14

On Existential Aloneness: The Earthly Pilgrimage

Emory G. Cowan, Jr.

> Who indeed knows the secret of the earthly pilgrimage?
> Who knows for what we live, and struggle, and die? Who
> knows what keeps us living and struggling, while all things
> break about us? But this, the purpose of our lives, the end
> of our struggle, is beyond all human wisdom. Oh God, my
> God, do not Thou forsake me. (Paton, 1948, p. 94)

The Beginning of Memory

My earliest memories are of reading the daily comic .strips. I warmly reminiscence of moments with my family and of lying on the living room rug reading what we then called "the funny papers" in the daily newspaper. The comics not only provided me with reading skills, they provided motivation to learn and discover the world. Folded into those pages were humor, irony, mystery, intrigue, and adventure. As I read, I began to come to consciousness about the world. I was already playing with those concepts and constructs and perhaps understanding relationships with people better than I might otherwise have. I must confess that reading the comic pages is still part of my daily ritual and it is the first thing I look for in the newspaper.

That experience of learning to read was an integral part of the formation of my self. Reading became my escape into the world. As a lonely teenager on a farm, encyclopedias were my window to lied beyond the pastures. Tales of intrigue and adventure permitted an exploration of far away places and cultures that I could never imagine seeing or experiencing. My memory formation was more than real time life experiences; it was the sum of all experiences of thought, and the adventure and imagination that came from thought. No one else had the same thoughts or interpreted their experiences as I did mine. And, in a strange way, reading stimulated my thoughts and raised my consciousness to the fact that I was ultimately alone on my journey of life.

Understanding Ultimate Aloneness

I recently read a well written blog on *Existential Loneliness*, but from my perspective the author confused loneliness and aloneness as do so many writers. Loneliness is a transient condition in life marked by a longing to be connected with other humans. Yalom (1989) described it as, "The lonely *I* dissolving into the *we*." "It's the common denominator of every form of bliss – romantic, sexual, political, religious, mystical. Everyone wants and welcomes this blissful merger" (p. 43). All people experience loneliness from time to time, but it is not a constant state as is our ultimate aloneness.

If you want to understand your own experience of ultimate aloneness, you will be hard pressed to find a definition or an explanation of the experience. There is little in the literature that addresses the problem of existential aloneness. Moustakas's (1961) book *Loneliness* approached the issue by distinguishing between existential loneliness as being a part of human experience, and "...loneliness anxiety as self-alienation and self-rejection." Moustakas states loneliness anxiety is "...not loneliness at all, but a vague and disturbing anxiety." (p. 24). And he describes Existential Loneliness as:

> an intrinsic and organic reality of human life in which there is both pain and triumphant creation emerging out of long periods of desolation. In existential loneliness man is fully aware of himself as an isolated and solitary individual while in loneliness anxiety man is separated from himself as a feeling and knowing person. (Moustakas, 1961, p. 24)

Nevertheless, there seems to be a difference between what Moustakas (1961) was trying to explain and the problem of aloneness as a condition of being human. Moustakas makes an attempt to address aloneness by stating that "Every man is alone. Ultimately, each person exists in isolation. He faces himself in silence, wending his way in individual pathways, seeking companionship, reaching out to others" (p. 54). That being said, Moustakas resumes his exploration of loneliness without pursuing the real nature of aloneness.

For me, existential aloneness means that regardless of how close we become to another person, there is always a distance. We can touch, be close to, and soothe the wounds of loneliness, but there is always a barrier to that full connection with another person. Only in Roddenberry's (1966) science fiction fantasy world creation, *Star Trek*, does Commander

Spock have the ability to perform the Vulcan Mind Meld and be totally connected to the sum of the thoughts, feelings, rationalizations; the sum of the memory of another person. Even then, Roddenberry's Spock finds the experience of knowing the memory of another, with all its emotions, overwhelmingly painful and exhausting.

Frustrated in my attempt to find a clear understanding of the problem of existential aloneness, I turned to literature. Although I have read most of my life, I did not understand the hidden existential themes in the great works of literature until I reached my early-thirties. Bultmann, Barth, Buber, and Tillich were my guides in my first career as a pastor and chaplain. Freud, Jung, Rogers, Whitaker, May, Frankl, Yalom Bruner, Kozol and Conant, were my guides in my second and third careers as a psychotherapist and as an educator. Each contributed to my understanding and formation of my *self* and my awareness of my ultimate aloneness. Nevertheless, it was in the great works of fiction that I began to see stories similar to mine and understand more of my own journey of ultimate aloneness.

Three Works of Fiction

In my early 30s, I took an informal course that explored the themes of some great pieces of fictional literature. Among them, three stand out because of the existential themes intrinsic to the life journey of the protagonists. These three works have informed me more about my life, and my ultimate journey of aloneness, than anything else. They have helped me make meaning from the fragments and pieces of my memory.

The first was Eric Maria Remarque's *All Quiet on the Western Front* (1929), which I believe is the definitive expression of human experience in combat. It is Remarque's own memory of the horrors of World War I (As a soldier in the German Army he was wounded five times) as told through the experience of his character Paul Baümer. At the urging of his schoolmaster, Baümer, only 18 years of age, enlisted in the German Army along with six of his schoolmates. He and his comrades had dreams of glory and aspirations of serving the Fatherland. Yet at 20, the promises of glory, heroism, and pride had faded. Baümer loses all of his friends, his youth, his innocence, his hopes and ambition, and finds himself in despair, alone and facing his own death. In the midst of the terror of memory that he is living through, Baümer reflects on his aloneness.

> My strength is exhausted as always after an attack, and it is so hard for me to be alone with my thoughts. They are not properly my

thoughts; they are memories which in my weakness haunt me and strangely move me. (Remarque, 1929, p.119)

Reading the story evoked terror laden combat memories of my own. Once again I tasted the stench of death; experienced feelings of fear, hopelessness, and despair. Like Baümer, my memories include the closeness of friends, acts of unbelievable courage, times of joy, and moments of horror. There are also the smells of blood and feces, cries of pain, and the sounds of gunfire and explosions. But unlike Remarque's Baümer, my memories have to do with jungles, rice paddies, thatched hut villages, alluvial plains, and rubber tree plantations. There are noises, sights, and smells that can trigger for me what I call a Past-Now-Time experience. Although these are 38-year old memories, they are closer in time for me than the events of last week. I have never liked the term "flashback" because it implies going back to something and remembering the time as a vivid experience. A Past-Now-Time experience is memory coming into the now in such a powerful presence that it is being lived again, and not relived as some would surmise.

When I returned from Vietnam in 1971, my second tour in Southeast Asia, I did not realize how profoundly depressed, hopeless, guilty, joyless, and weighted with ontological anxiety I was. For years, I struggled to outrun depression. Surprisingly, it was not through therapy but in reading Remarque's work that I discovered the meaning of my depression; my fear of living. It was in the futility of Baümer's dreams that I came to accept my experience of ultimate aloneness.

> I am very quiet. Let the months and years come, they can take nothing from me, they can take nothing more. I am so alone, and so without hope that I can confront them without fear. The life that has borne me through these years is still in my hands and my eyes. Whether I have subdued it, I know not. But so long as it is there it will seek its own way out, heedless of the will that is within me. (Remarque, 1929, p. 295)

The second important discovery for me was Albert Camus' *The Fall* (1956). Camus provided another insight into my journey of aloneness. His protagonist, Jean-Baptiste Clamence, once a successful Parisian attorney, now holds court as a judge-penitent in the Mexico City Bar in the red light district of Amsterdam. Through Camus we hear one side of Clamence's dialogue with a stranger as he confesses and justifies his narcissism and life of debauchery. As an allegory of the Biblical story of the fall from grace in the Garden of Eden, Clamence attributes his professional demise to his failure to try to rescue a woman whom he believed had committed suicide by jumping into the river Seine. Her cries torture him. He hears voices laughing at him and is confronted with his own hypocrisy. The tyranny of his memory haunts him, propels him to reject his successful life, leave his friends, and flee Paris. He becomes a prisoner of the Germans in North Africa where his fellow prisoners elect him as a pope. In this role he decides who among them gets the scarce water and food; who shall live and who shall die.

Although a person who prefers the heights of ships decks and mountain peaks, Clamence ends up in Amsterdam, a city below sea level that consists of concentric canals reminiscent of Dante's view of Hell. There, as the judge-penitent, he confronts strangers with their hypocrisy. There he laments:

> Then please tell me what happened to you one night on the quays of the Seine and how you managed never to risk your life. You yourself utter the words that for years have never ceased echoing through my nights and that I shall at last say through your mouth: 'O young woman, throw yourself into the water once again so that I may a second time have the chance of saving both of us!' (p. 147)

People of conscience, no matter how fragile the artifact is, question their lives, their motives, and their perception of themselves. They delve into their memory to explore and explain their behavior, their courage or lack thereof, their inactivity, and their relationships. The echoes in my own mind of regretful things said, or not said; things done, or not done, are very few, but they are significant to me. Therefore, while they can gnaw at my conscience, no one else could ever possibly understand them. The actions of a person's past are evidence of ultimate aloneness for they are, despite explication, explanation and justification, known only to the one with the memory of them. They are etched in the individual's memory and no other person has full access to what is in memory.

It is the third work, however, that speaks most profoundly to me and my journey in life. In 1948, Alan Paton published what would become a classic of 20th century literature; *Cry, the Beloved Country.* Set in his homeland of South Africa, the story centers around the life of a Black (Zulu) Anglican pastor, Stephen Kumalo, a deeply pious servant of his congregation, whose beloved son Absalom has left his homeland to journey to the great bustling city of Johannesburg. Notified by a fellow priest that his youngest sister, Gertrude, is ill, Father Kumalo takes what meager savings he and his wife have accumulated and makes the long journey by train to find his sister and her child. His trip, however, becomes an opportunity to connect with his brother, John, and search for his son, Absalom. Nevertheless, the journey comes to a heart wrenching culmination when he discovers that Absalom has been accused of murdering a prominent White man. Kumalo watches helplessly as Absalom is tried, convicted, and sentenced to death.

In addition, with all that has happened to him, Kumalo experiences a great betrayal by his own brother, John, a successful labor leader. John saves his own son from murder charges, but lets his nephew, Absalom, carry the guilty verdict alone.

Paton also tells the story of James Jarvis, the White land owner whose only son was murdered by Absalom. After his son's death, Jarvis comes to understand his own son's progressive position toward relations with the native population, his son's views on the origins of crime, and the extensive impact of the destruction of tribal and family life. Jarvis and Kumalo touch each other because of their mutual loss. Filled with hurt and pain, they are ultimately kind, helpful, and respectful of one another. But each of them is still alone with the loss of his son. Each still lives with the memory of his little boy. For example, in the home of his murdered adult son, Jarvis walks down the stairway.

> He took off his hat and looked down at the dark stain on the floor. Unasked, unwanted, the picture of the small boy came into his mind, the small boy at High Place, the small boy with the wooden guns. Unseeing, he walked long the passage and out of the door through which death had come so suddenly. (Paton, 1948, p. 180)

Kumalo, facing the hanging of his son for that same murder, climbs to a mountain top near his home the night before the hanging is to take place in the far off city of Pretoria. The mountain top is a place to which Kumalo has gone to on several occasions to pray: the first time when Absalom was a small boy close to death, and once when tempted to commit adultery.

> It was an angle in the rock, sheltered from the winds, with a place for a man to sit on, his legs at ease over the edge. The first of these occasions he remembered clearly, perhaps because it was the first, perhaps because he had come to pray for the child that no prayer

could save anymore. The child could not write then, but here were three letters from him now, and in all of them he said, If I could come back to Ndottsheni [his village] I should not leave it any more. And in a day or two he would receive the last letter he would ever write. His heart went out in a great compassion for the boy that must die. (Paton, 1948, p.308)

Sitting alone Kumalo prepares for the sunrise. But he does more than grieve his loss of his son. He confesses his own sin, an act of recalling memory, and then he gives thanks for the many people who have loved him, provided for him, welcomed him, and supported him in his travail. He remembers his journey.

Paton's work was at once a cry against the (late 1940's) emerging injustice in the call for Apartheid in his country, and his hope that the returning World War II veterans would have none of it. It was written out of his deep sense of the struggle that was changing tribal life, families, and the church for both Blacks and Whites. His love for the people and the land, and his hope for South Africa are clearly evident in this work. Nonetheless, amid the backdrop of the growing call of Whites for Apartheid, the story's existential theme of aloneness is amplified to an almost painful crescendo.

This story touched me because I grew up in the Southern United States in the era of racial segregation when the prevailing view was that White people were superior to Black people and that separation of the races was the rule. I remember very clearly, even the date of December 13, 1948, coming to consciousness about the issue of segregation in the South. I knew something was wrong with this way of thinking and living. That night, while Christmas shopping with my family in Atlanta's Sears Roebuck department store; a White male sales clerk grabbed me by the scruff of the neck as I started to get a drink from the water cooler. "What's the matter with you boy? Can't you read that sign? That there is a colored drinking fountain." At almost eight years old, I had the awareness that I was alone in my feelings; I became acutely aware of the great injustice to Black people

I went to college and seminary during the 1950's and 1960's, but I never heard of Apartheid, *Cry the Beloved Country,* or the history of the Union of South Africa for that matter. Nevertheless, like Kumalo, I did know what it was like to be ultimately alone. First as an associate pastor and later as the pastor of an inner city Atlanta church during the Civil Rights struggle of the mid-1960's, I was ridiculed in the press, and scorned by some parishioners when I tried to establish a dialogue between the races in our religious community. Although Apartheid in South Africa and Racial Segregation in the U.S. had different antecedents and roots, the effect was the same. They both divided communities, destroyed families and lives, and fostered hatred and mistrust.

It Is Aloneness Not Loneliness

Like the protagonists of these stories, I have experienced times of hurt, despair and isolation. There are times when I too feared that God had indeed forsaken me. In addition, like the protagonists, I have also experienced the great pain of betrayal by close friends and loved ones. May I say that it is my belief that a person can only be betrayed by a close trusted friend or loved one. Betrayal is a violation of the profound trust we place in one so close that we think we know that person intimately. That is why it hurts so much when it happens. However, when a person known to you to have a characterlogical problem wrongs you, that is not betrayal, it is only behavior that you should have expected.

Nevertheless, it should be clear that in this essay I am not talking about personal experiences of loneliness. Although I have experienced periods of profound loneliness in my life, as I believe all people have, for the most part I am seldom lonely. My life has been filled with joy by the love of a wonderful, selfless, caring woman; my wife of 24 years. I have been renewed by the innocent laughter and goodness of my grandchildren and their parents. I have been strengthened by wonderful, close, supportive friends whose love has empowered and lifted me in times when I could have easily given way to despair. Indeed, like Kumalo, Baümer, and even Clamence, I am surrounded by good loving and faithful people. And like Father Kumalo, I give thanks for them.

Memory Creates Our Aloneness

For 46 years as a pastor, soldier, psychotherapist, and educator I have learned from the stories of people that we are each ultimately alone in our life's journey. I have also discovered in these and other works of fiction that my journey, indeed your journey, is unique. Like a fingerprint, a retinal scan, or the unique growth of dendrites from new learning, no one else will ever have your memory or be able to replicate it. Yet, we are all desperate to know and be known by another. Therefore, like small lifeboats on the turbulent ocean, we may touch for a time, but ultimately our journey is one of aloneness.

In reflecting on the journey of existential aloneness, I have concluded the red thread woven in each of the stories previously cited, and indeed in each of our stories, is that of the uniqueness of our individual memory. Baümer, Clamence, and Kumalo, like you and I, have unique memories. It is the simple, unique, infallible memory of the events of their individual journeys, and ours, which produce existential aloneness. Because my memory is unique to my interpretation of my experience, and because it is infallible, that is it is not subject to review and alignment with the reality of others, I am ultimately alone with it. No one else has had my journey or your journey of experience. Others may have shared the same touch points of experience, as Baümer's friends did with him in the trenches, as Clamence's fellow prisoners did with him in the concentration camp, or Kumalo's fellow priests did in Johannesburg rectory. But they could not ascribe the same meaning that Baümer, Clamence, or Kumalo did to the same experience.

For example, Clamence, in his reverie, laments that he did not act to prevent a suicide. In this lament he not only ascribes meaning to the woman's behavior (as a suicide), he places a moral judgment on his own behavior, and both occur as a result of his memory of the event. He feels guilt for failing to act, for being afraid, for being hesitant. Kumalo's and Jarvis' reverie for the youth and innocence of their sons; Baümer's memory is of the closeness he felt toward his dead friend when they stole a goose and spent the night cooking and then eating it. Each character ascribes meaning to the sights, the sounds, and the total experience recorded in their individual memory. Thus memory, although a distorted recording of reality, is infused with phenomenological experiences of sights, sounds, smells, touch and tastes. In addition, memory is interpreted by our intrinsic value judgments: It was good, it was bad, I am good, I am bad.

Memory is the Key

I wish Descartes had said, I *remember,* therefore I am. Perhaps that is what he meant to say. Nevertheless, it is our memory, and of course, our thoughts about that memory, that signifies our existence. Although memory can be corrupted by a cardiovascular accident, the deterioration of our aging process, or even by interference from outside sources as was discovered in the "brain washing" experiments during the Korean War, or more recently in the false-memory conundrum of the 1990's, it is still the memory and not necessarily the reality of the individual experience that is important.

Therefore, to make a quantum leap, it seems to me that it is not the fear of death per se, or the fleeting thought that at some point we will not *be* that evokes ontological anxiety. On the contrary, it is the fear of not being able to remember beyond life that does so. We fear the loss of the one faculty that makes us an *I am*. The existential question that seems to be the central struggle of all great religions of the world is, Do I remember me beyond death? Will I continue to be an *I am*? Or will I cease to be an *I am* and be absorbed or adsorbed into nothingness. Most religious traditions and rituals in general are centered on remembering. We celebrate by remembering our ancestors, the acts of our deities, the promises that beyond death we will not just be remembered, we will indeed have memory.

Yet, as humans, we also struggle with the tyranny of memory, the terror of memory, and the hurt of memory as it affects our lives. All three are reasons we go to therapy or do therapy with others. We seek to calm the tyranny, make the terror less disruptive, and heal the hurts of memory. In a way, we make new memories from the dreams and reflections about our memory, and we call that making meaning from our experiences. For me, memory is the only truly individual activity that we possess, and understood in this way, I am not averse to calling a suicide the murder of memory.

Over the past 40 years, cognitive psychology and neuropsychology have contributed to our growing, but as of yet incomplete, understanding of what memory actually is. In my neuropsychology courses I learned that memory, simply put, is our ability to store and recall sequences of experience as they are fixed chemically to neuronal communication, first in the frontal lobes, and then in the other lobes where sensory information, visual, auditory, gustatory, smell, and tactile experiences, and the accompanying emotions of the event, fear, hurt, frustration, joy are also affixed. Finally, as an intrinsic part of the memory, we include an overlay of our value judgments about the event and our behavior. What is then essentially brief or short-term memory, depending on its importance to us, can move to long-term storage. Other physical structures of the brain such as the amygdala and hippocampus assists the process of moving memory from short-term to long-term storage by changing neural connections, creating new pathways, and spreading memory throughout the brain. I leave all of that to my more scientifically minded colleagues, who are exploring this three pound universe called the human brain, and the ethereal mind that is the keeper of the memory.

Summary

Existential aloneness is a constant of human existence. It is not dependent on loneliness or the lack thereof, our proximity to a loved one, or even to those who might betray or revile us. It is simply our human condition, spawned and maintained by our memory, which is the only legacy of our life's journey. What I have proposed in this essay is that the factor that makes us uniquely human is our ability to reflect on our journey and realize that we are ultimately alone. It is memory that is the vehicle by which we do this reflection. Alas, ultimate aloneness is our existential condition. Because of the uniqueness of our memory, of our journey, no one else can ever fully know us, which leaves us ultimately alone. To be sure others, including therapists, can categorize, diagnose, and reduce us to interpretation, but they can only know what we reveal to them from our memory. Even then they cannot possibly understand our individual experience in full. Perhaps that frustration is what leads many therapists to simply employ their tool bag techniques to change behaviors in people rather than journey with them in the effort to make meaning from the experience of memory.

Nevertheless, the most important factor in this essay may be my conclusion that anxiety about physical death is not the ultimate anxiety we as humans experience. In our existential condition of ultimate aloneness, it is our fear about loss of memory, of ceasing to be an *I am* that is the basis of real ontological anxiety.

References

Camus, A. (1956). *The fall.* (J. O'Brien, Trans.). New York: Vantage Books.

Moustakas, C. (1961). *Loneliness.* New York: Prentice-Hall.

Paton, A. (1948). *Cry, the beloved country.* New York: Scribner.

Remarque, E. (1929), *All quiet on the Western front* (A. W. Wheen, Trans.). New York: Ballantine.

Roddenberry, G. (Producer). (1966). Star Trek [Television series]. Los Angeles: NBC.

Yalom, I. (1989). *Loves executioner: And other tales of psychotherapy,* New York: Perennial.

15

The Myth of Obedience:
An Existential Analysis of *American Beauty*

Cathy Calvert
Kate Calhoon
Steve Fehl
Christin Gregory

A recent search on Amazon.com (2008) identified close to 162,000 titles dealing with the concept of obedience. In this first decade of the 21st century, the nature and meaning of obedience has become a hotly debated issue in Western society whether it is politics, spirituality, family relations, or cultural diversity. In this chapter, obedience will be discussed in light of Rollo May's concepts of freedom and responsibility utilizing images and characters from the 1999 Academy Award winning film, *American Beauty*.

Myth

In his 1991 book *The Cry for Myth*, Rollo May explored the power and evolution of myth in human existence, in particular as it relates to American culture. Contrary to today's common use of the term "myth" as a falsehood or popular fictitious belief, May described myths as important shared stories of a society and a way of making sense of our lives. May believed that myths give individuals a template for building their own values. In addition, myths provide relief from anxiety and guilt by helping the individual explain the how and why of what he or she thinks and does. Myths can be empowering, as well as limiting, depending on how they are used by individuals and the culture at large. For May, how an individual understands the concept of freedom and responsibility determines the way in which obedience is exercised and demonstrated. Because the terms freedom, responsibility, and obedience are used in such a variety of ways in current Western society, we will be using these three terms in the following manner.

Freedom

Freedom, at its core, is the capacity to accept, bear, and live with anxiety. This freedom is anchored in the centered self that consciously chooses to be responsible for the interactions one has with the culture or society. Freedom and responsibility always imply each other and are inseparable. Freedom is experienced in choosing to accept our limitations and the choices we have made in the past, engaging in critical thought, and allowing ourselves the space to feel all that life has to offer; pain and joy, sorrow and ecstasy, as well as engaging in the possibilities of the unknown that lay before us (May, 1979).

Responsibility

To be responsible is to take ownership for one's own choices and their consequences, including the person an individual chooses to become. In addition, to be responsible is to consciously engage the world, of which one is a part; as well as to look past one's immediate needs, wants, or desires and, instead, think in long-term consequences. This conscious engagement accepts that there are limits to how one interacts with the culture or society (May, 1979).

Obedience

Obedience, for our purposes, is understood as the active participation and/or conscious choices one makes with his or her thoughts, words, and actions in relationship to an individual's culture or society. In order for obedience to be exercised willfully and meaningfully, the person must have the choice concerning whether he or she comply. When an individual is free, he or she is able to reflect on the system of beliefs before him or her, weigh out the options, as well as the possible consequences. Once the person has gone through this process, he or she can take action based on his or her own personal beliefs and values. Making such a conscious choice, knowing the possible outcomes of the choice, is exercising obedience with freedom and responsibility.

Obedience and Western Culture

Existential ideals about obedience as an experience of choice and empowerment are often lost in the more common usage of the term "obedience" to denote submission or compliance to the commands or standards of another entity, individual, or authority. Furthermore, Western culture sends confusing, even conflicting, messages about the value and benefits of obedience. On one hand, the culture celebrates "fierce individualism" (May, 1991, p. 109) with its inevitable side effects of narcissism, isolation, and an insatiable quest for success. At the same time, however, Western measures of success are remarkably universal and narrow in scope — money, titles, SAT scores, etc. In the end, hordes of "rugged individuals" find themselves racing like lemmings off the cliff of uniformity.

In Western culture, how one speaks, works, plays, eats, presents oneself, and engages the world can be judged against a sometimes rigid set of acceptable standards. "Don't be rude." "Don't rock the boat." "Don't overdo it." "Don't question authority." "Go with the flow." "Do the right thing." "Be all you can be." "Never let them see you sweat." Our culture applauds the obedient child, the tireless worker, and the toned musculature and discipline of athletes. The rugged individual is affectionately embraced only when he or she does not challenge the majority too much or create discomfort with dramatic new ways of being. To understand obedience in Western society, it is important to look at the societal expectations, or dogmas, that are constricting and ultimately killing the spirit of freedom and responsibility for individuals.

American Beauty and the Myth of Obedience

The film *American Beauty* chronicles one year in the life of an upper middle class suburban family, their neighbors, and a few adolescent friends. The storyline centers on Lester and Carolyn Burnham, who find themselves 20 years into a marriage that has lost its vitality as they have lost their own sense of freedom, choice, and self. In different ways, the film's characters demonstrate blind obedience, disconnection, awakening, and a struggle with the dawning awareness of individual freedom and its inevitable joys and pitfalls.

Each of the film's characters has something important to contribute to our understanding of the myth of obedience. The main character, Lester Burnham, refers to himself as a loser; he describes his life as "closely resembling Hell," with a loveless marriage to a woman he views as a "bloodless, money grubbing, freak," a daughter from whom he is completely disconnected, and a job he views as meaningless and insignificant. Lester appears bitter and resentful about the state of his life, a feeling which up until relatively recently he has repressed. He "bought into" the American Dream which stated that if one follows the norms for Western society, happiness is the end result. Lester is not happy. As Lester is on the verge of losing his meaningless job, his bitterness and resentment turn to anger, and his perception of himself begins to change.

In the meantime, the mother character in *American Beauty*, Carolyn, holds her choices of obedience in high regard and wishes to be recognized in society for her success as the "perfect" wife, mother, and businessperson. However, Carolyn, like many others who choose this path of acceptance, is willing to be obedient, believing that her approach will provide the desired freedom. What is demonstrated throughout the movie is Carolyn's struggle to accept and live with the anxiety, which comes from not being true to oneself. While she engages in the world, she is not willing or able to show her vulnerability to create meaningful relationships.

The Burnham's' new neighbors consist of a rigid ex-military father, a sedated and dissociated mother, and their pot-smoking, free thinking, loner son Ricky. The Western concept of obedience is evidenced in a scene from the film with the Colonel and his son:

COLONEL: You can't just go around doing whatever you feel like, you can't--there are rules in life... You need structure, you need discipline.

RICKY: Discipline. Yes, sir, thank you for trying to teach me. Don't give up on me, Dad.

The Colonel speaks for much of Western society today. For many, obedience means following a dogma, a set of rules and regulations established by an external authority. If one disagrees, or worse yet, disobeys these rules he or she is branded as defiant, rebellious, unpatriotic, or other negative conclusions. When individuals act disobediently, there frequently is swift judgment exercised, whether by a court of law or a group of vigilantes taking discipline into their own hands.

Just prior to this dialogue in the film, the Colonel has burst into Ricky's room and punched his son in the face. What had Ricky done to deserve such strong discipline? Ricky had gone into a curio cabinet holding items the Colonel had collected during his military service to retrieve a piece of china from the third Reich that Ricky wanted to show his girlfriend. In this father-son relationship, obedience is strictly understood as an unquestioned allegiance to specific rules and beliefs the father has established. Ricky demonstrates his understanding of the Colonel's dogma by the way he responds to the Colonel. Ricky has learned there is no sense in trying to argue the point or even defend his perspective; rather Ricky simply capitulates to his father's outburst in order to protect his physical well-being.

However, obedience in its truest form is rooted in an individual's freedom to choose and then taking responsibility for the choice he or she makes. Only when an individual has the option to follow or not follow a set of guidelines or regulations is obedience truly and meaningfully exercised. When a person is coerced either by authority or by peer pressure to obey, obedience is reduced to acting out of fear and self-preservation. As is demonstrated in an encounter between the Colonel and Ricky later in the film, it is not until Ricky is willing to take responsibility for his choices that he is able to confront the Colonel and his disdain for the Colonel's values and beliefs.

While on the surface this Western perception of obedience appears to provide a sense of well-being and stability, a release from anxiety – it is strictly superficial with shallow roots. Ultimately, when an individual encounters the struggles and paradoxes of life, this superficial sense of security gives way and robs the individual of both well-being and stability. When the person adopts a dogmatic understanding of obedience, he or she creates a set of barriers that close off the ability to identify options and explore possibilities. All maneuverability is lost and the individual becomes a prisoner in a prison cell he or she has created. The basis of this closed perspective of obedience is fear, a fear of losing connection with an *ultimate truth*. In order to maintain this connection the individual believes he or she must establish and adhere to a set of hard and fast beliefs.

Isolation

Obedience may offer the promise of acceptance and "fitting in" with prevailing standards and expectations. However, ironically, obedience can result in disconnection with self and others if an individual prioritizes doing the "right" thing over doing the thing that is most meaningful and true to oneself. Early in the movie, Lester's robotic existence leaves him disconnected from everyone. Carolyn's social nature is a thin disguise for the isolation she experiences in her tireless pursuit of projecting an image of success at all times. She confuses her success with joy. She cannot experience an authentic moment or connection because she is distracted by her own persona and its maintenance.

Carolyn Burnham's fear of being perceived as anything less than perfect in the eyes of societal standards has created a lack of trust of others and she believes she must rely on herself to make a place in this world. She allows no one to truly help her and she is afraid of others' needs. She tells her daughter in one scene that, "You can not count on anyone except yourself" and those words describe Carolyn's perception of the world and how to survive. While she is actively pursuing this societal obedience, she is unable to engage in meaningful relationships. This inability creates mistrust and reinforces, for Carolyn, the concept that she must do it on her own, which then becomes a vicious cycle.

It initially appears that Carolyn's obedience provides comfort and stability for her, but her obedience has no depth. Without the depth of true freedom and responsibility, she cannot reach deep enough within herself to allow others to be a part of her life. The barriers created by Carolyn's desire to be a part of society, through the choices made with her responsibility, freedom, and obedience has led this character to her ultimate fear - loneliness.

While an individual may assume if he or she follows societal expectations and dogma he or she will gain relationships and be a part of the group, the reality is that following the societal rules creates little space for the development of significant relationships. Conformity strips a person of his or her unique self, as well as the uniqueness of the person to whom he or she is trying to attach.

The hope for many in Western society, who follow rules or beliefs dictated by society, is that their efforts will provide success and acceptance into a group. The desire to not be isolated and alone can be a tremendous impetus to keep one following the rules. This doctrine suggests that successful living will lie within the rules and expectations of society and not within the ideals of each person's conscience. Carolyn lived and breathed this belief; she actively participated in Western society's worldview. Her expectation, which is similar for many, is to follow the rules of an upper middle class working mother in order to create the perfect home, family, career, success, beauty, and confidence. Without those perfections, she is nothing, and if she is nothing then she will not belong and will be alone.

Sedation

The isolation one experiences in the quest for obedience is both a cause and byproduct of a loss of self and feeling of sedation. The person who practices blind obedience sleeps through significant decisions about life. Sedation may be relaxing in terms of avoiding the anxiety of choice and responsibility; however, this sedation of self robs the individual of the energy, awe, and emotions of life. Many characters in the film *American Beauty* are sedated into a lifestyle that lacks feeling or self-expression.

Returning to the character of Lester Burnham, we find this middle-aged, married father realizing his efforts to obey his wife, boss, and society's demands of his upper middle class existence have transformed into a slow death over the last 20 years of his life. His choice of blind obedience leaves him feeling dead inside until he finally awakens to true choice, responsibility, and the opportunity that awaits him every moment of the day. Lester speaks to this phenomenon as demonstrated in the following quotes from different moments in the movie,

LESTER: It's the weirdest thing. I feel like I've been in a coma for about 20 years and I'm just now waking up.

LESTER: I've lost something. I'm not exactly sure what it is, but I know I didn't always feel this… sedated. But you know what; it's never too late to get it back.

LESTER: It's a great thing when you realize you still have the ability to surprise yourself. It makes you wonder what else you can do that you forgot about.

Lester is not the only character in *American Beauty* who struggles with obedience to the point of sedation. Although his wife, Carolyn, in all of her perky phoniness appears quite different from Lester's dead eyes and monotone voice, she, too, is a prisoner of conformity. Perfect clothing, flawless gardens, and an image of success do little to assuage her anxiety and leave her struggling to maintain a rigid and unreal facade that alienates her from her husband, daughter, and herself. Carolyn relinquishes the power of choice in favor of the power of perfection and conformity. Her intense and ever-busy disposition may seem anything but sedate; however, she chooses to indulge in diminutive original thought, emotion, or action. Instead, Carolyn allows the autopilot of obedience to dictate everything from her choice of relationships to her color coordinated garden clogs. Like Lester, Carolyn rediscovers the world of choice through a forbidden sexual opportunity, but lacks Lester's carefree attitude toward its consequences.

Letting Go of Society's Myth of Obedience

Lester recognizes he has been lulled into submission by consumerism; acquiring things had replaced meaningful interaction with himself as well as others. At one point in the film, Lester is trying to connect with his wife in a deeper way than she is use to when his wife shuts him down because he is about to spill beer on the sofa. Lester tells his wife "this is just stuff; it's not your life." The more Lester abandons his fear of losing (things, societal standing, image, etc.) the freer he is to accept responsibility for what he has created for himself and to make changes that reflect his deepest desires. Lester was willing to follow his desires into the unknown. Often, the individual can only know what his or her true desires are if he or she allows him or herself to experience them, or at least acknowledge that he or she has these desires. For example, Lester honestly believes that he wants to be sexually intimate with his daughter's adolescent friend. However, as he allows himself to walk down this road, he discovers that sexual intimacy with an adolescent is not at all what he truly desires.

Only when Lester seizes his freedom of choice and rejects blind obedience does he finally begin to connect in an authentic way with others and himself. His dramatic transformation is not welcomed by his wife or daughter, but he seeks comrades in unlikely new places like the fast food drive through manager and the teenage drug dealer next door. These new acquaintances do not hold Lester to any traditional standard. In some ways, he becomes obedient only to his "id" after 20 years of service to his superego.

Lester's awakening is triggered by his lustful fixation with his daughter Jane's adolescent schoolmate, Angela. This catalyst itself flies in the face of obedience to politically correct values about lust and underage girls, and yet it taps a more primal, even mythological, male attraction to youth and beauty. A near complete rejection of his obedient past and a newfound embrace of choice and its consequences follow Lester's awakening. Lester quits his job, confronts his wife, buys his dream car, smokes pot, and works out in order to "look good naked" for his fantasy dream girl. Lester decides that the myth of obedience is a raw deal and not one he chooses to make a part of the next chapter of his life.

As Lester "snaps" in his bosses office, he appears to be experiencing a healthy anger that Rollo May (1981) refers to as "an anger that pulls the diverse parts of the self tighter, that integrates the self, keeps the whole self alive and present, energizes us, sharpens our vision, and stimulates us to think more clearly" (p. 42). Even though Lester expresses himself in ways that might be viewed as unhealthy by mainstream Western society (blackmailing his employer, smoking marijuana, and lusting after his daughter's adolescent friend), he begins to accept responsibility for himself and the decisions he has made in his life. He then commences to live as a free man. As he lets go of the expectations society has placed on him (conforming to a narrow role as an upper middle class, Caucasian, married, middle-aged male), he immediately experiences an increase in his self worth. Lester views himself as no more or no less than anyone else. He states that he is "just an ordinary man with nothing to lose." Here he rejects the Western myth that implies the individual must compare who he or she is and what he or she does with everyone else in society, to see how he or she measures up.

Lester is awakening to the fact that he is okay just because of who he is not because of his accomplishments; he is realizing that self worth has very little to do with one's success. He illustrates this by leaving his well paying job to work at a fast food restaurant, signifying that he is aware of exactly where he is in life and has rejected the myth of entitlement that states one must have something which is *better*. He has actively chosen to engage with his internal self, and has accepted a job with the least responsibility required in order to devote his time to what is meaningful to him. This shift from focusing on the outward self to the inward self is quite significant. Lester starts to be fully present in what he is doing.

The film leads us to believe that Lester Burnham would not have traded his new freedom to engage with himself for anything; even death. Lester Burnham found what he was looking for: acceptance and engagement with himself.

However, as May (1991) suggests, the demise of myth can be disorienting and devastating when it leaves society without reference, values, structure, and responsibility. Lester seeks freedom without limits and pays the ultimate price. At the movie's end, a misunderstanding leads to Lester's murder, suggesting that reckless abandonment of obedience confuses others and can be downright dangerous. Nonetheless, for the year preceding his death, Lester had finally exercised his choice and freedom and showed a newfound or rediscovered range of experience, including joy, rage, lust, disappointment, wonder, and power. It may be no wonder that Lester dies smiling. In death, Lester appears content.

The individual's willingness to live out what is meaningful to him or her takes a great deal of courage, and is in direct opposition to blind obedience where one lives for an illusion of something someone else states as the norm. So here again we, as human beings and individuals, need to allow ourselves the experience, not just limit ourselves to what others dictate we should or should not do.

Gratitude

The film, *American Beauty*, informs and illuminates the almost lost myth (in the positive sense) that brings knowledge of the importance of things that are not seen. This film asks the question, "Will we let go of things and the American Dream (a negative myth in this culture) to embrace those things that cannot be named?"

In the end, all eight main characters (Lester, Carolyn, Jane, Angela, Ricky, Ricky's father and mother, and Buddy) are impacted, in varying degrees, by the awakening that occurs in Lester's life. One can only speculate about what influence Lester's awakening and then sudden death will have on Carolyn. Within the context of the developing relationship with Ricky, Jane, Lester's daughter, begins to embrace her authentic self in ways that free her from the Western myth of beauty. She begins to accept her perceived flaws and admits to herself, Ricky, and Angela, that she would rather be a freak than to continue to try to fit into Angela's external and shallow world of normal. Ricky is very familiar with pain and suffering, and seems to have embraced pain in a way that allows him to open to that which is beautiful, but unseen. Meaning is created in Jane and Ricky's relationship as Ricky truly "sees" Jane and the pain she is in. He is then able to appreciate that quality in her as something which adds, not subtracts, from who she is. Ricky finds her quite beautiful. It is as if pain is a gift that refines and informs one about the hidden beauty within the individual; it sharpens one's awareness of him or herself and allows him or her to see beauty in the mundane. Perhaps, as a human being, one does not have the ability to truly see beauty without embracing suffering and pain.

Lester Burnham's life illustrates a significant shift in consciousness; where once there was only fear that left him completely constricted, he moved into the realm of expanse. Expanse allowed him to become open to the authentic. As Lester is no longer resisting, and moves into expansiveness, he now walks in the consciousness of the absolute. In the end, Lester Burnham saw the beauty in all -- not by adhering to a narrow and rigid predetermined script of what is beautiful, but as it is; no more, no less. He was thankful for all aspects of his life. At the end of the movie Lester appreciates the stars at Boy Scout camp, the yellow leaves of a maple tree, his grandmother's hands, the first time he saw his cousin

Tony's brand new Firebird, as well as his daughter Jane and his wife Carolyn.

In death, Lester states that it is "hard to stay mad when there is so much beauty in the world," and that sometimes he feels like he is seeing it all at once, and his heart fills up like a balloon about to burst, then he remembers to relax and stops trying to hold on to it; then it flows through him like rain. He recognizes the life behind things, just as Ricky did. Lester concludes by saying he, "can't feel anything but gratitude for every little moment of my stupid little life." Lester Burnham is the real American Beauty.

Conclusion

As with many individuals, there are events that change everything and what one believes to be the path of obedience can be shaken. The myth of obedience lies in its promise that doing the "right thing" will give us comfort and confidence, maintain order, reduce anxiety, and garner admiration. It may deliver on some of these outcomes, but it is not guaranteed and not without costs. Furthermore, obedience comes in many shades of gray, not simply black and white. Nevertheless, black and white hold the allure and illusion of certainty, as well as the avoidance of anxiety of the unknown and choice. Therefore, we seek the comfort of the myth of obedience and all of its gifts until we are shaken into the awareness that sometimes the costs are too high, we have gone too far, or we are just plain missing a fuller life of unknown beauty and experience. Such is the case in *American Beauty*.

References

Amazon.com. Retrieved August 12, 2008 from http://www.amazon.com/s/ ref=nb_ss_b?url=search-alias%3Dstripbooks&fieldkeywords= Obedience

Cohen, B. & Jinks, D. (Producers), & Mendes, S. (Director). (1999). *American Beauty*. DreamWorks.

May, R. (1981). *Freedom and destiny.* New York: Norton & Company.

May, R. (1979). *Psychology and the human dilemma*. New York: Norton & Company.

May, R. (1991). *The cry for myth*. New York: Norton & Company.

16

Brokeback Mountain:
A Gay and Universal Love Story[1]

Ilene Serlin

A young, gay client left my office, and I reflected on her urgent questions. She was intent on explaining to me the difference between enjoying being submissive in sex and enjoying the dominance or cruelty of her partner. One of her main issues, she said, is that she cannot have an orgasm or feel passion with this partner, who is stable and loves her greatly, but only with someone who is emotionally cruel or unavailable. My client was turning 30 years old and wanted to settle down. She had been with the same partner for three years and was desperate at her inability to feel passion. Although I appreciate the importance of these subtle distinctions of sexual identity, equality, and love, I am also aware of the many gaps in my own understanding and of the stereotypes that I, as a heterosexual psychotherapist, hold.

Looking at *Brokeback Mountain* as a lesson in sexual identity and relationship issues is only one of the ways it would be useful for psychologists to discuss this film with clients and one another. We should be as informed as possible about the nuances of all kinds of love and be aware of our own biases and perspectives. But are the concerns in this film only about gay love? I believe that the issues raised by this film are compelling and universal themes of passion, authenticity, loneliness, and partnership. These are the very human questions that show up in all great dramas: Can any romantic love that is fueled by challenges, secrecy, and idyllic settings live in the real world? Does domestic routine always kill passion? Is romantic love inevitably tragic?

Setting

Brokeback Mountain is an exquisite story about two cowboys who fall in love. It is based on a short story written by Wyoming resident E. Annie Proulx, who won the Pulitzer prize for *The Shipping News*. First published in *The New Yorker* in 1997, it also appeared in the book *Close Range: Wyoming Stories*. The screenplay was adapted by Larry McMurtry and Diana Ossana, and the film was brilliantly directed by Ang Lee, director of *Crouching Tiger, Hidden Dragon* and *Sense and Sensibility*. The score was created by Gustavo Santaolla (*Motorcycle Diaries*) and contains excerpts from Merle Haggard, Willie Nelson, and Rufus Wainwright. Poetic visual images of the Western landscape iconography were created by Rodrigo Prieto. The film was produced by James Shamus, is rated R, and runs for 134 min.

The story is about two young men in 1963 who are hired to work for a rancher in Signal, Wyoming. The inarticulate and solitary Ennis Del Mar, played by Heath Ledger, and Jack Twist (Jake Gyllenhaal) both come from families of emotional cruelty, and one stormy night they find refuge in their tent and each others' arms. Although Ennis immediately says, "You know I ain't queer," and Jack says, "Me neither," their passion continues to smolder. After the summer, Ennis returns home to marry his childhood sweetheart (Michelle Williams, Ledger's real-life partner), and Jack goes to Texas and marries a rich boss's daughter (Anne Hathaway). Over the next 20 years, they continue to meet periodically for "fishing trips" on their idyllic *mountain*, while their respective marriages deteriorate. Scenes of silent male camaraderie taking place in wide open spaces are juxtaposed against images of the banality of domestic family life.

Brokeback Mountain: Why Is It Relevant?

I went to see the film on the evening after I met with my client, and the 10:00 p.m. showing was sold out in San Francisco. Although *Brokeback Mountain* has sold out houses in liberal New York and Los Angeles, it is not just a gay or liberal film. It won seven Golden Globe nominations and was screened at the Venice International Film Festival, and more advance tickets for *Brokeback Mountain* were sold in a metroplex in Plano, Texas, than for the blockbuster film King Kong. Other movies with gay characters this year, such as *Capote and Rent,* had urban or campy settings, but Brokeback Mountain takes place in America's heartland. It is impossible to dismiss the film as a plot designed by latte-sipping liberals or Chelsea faux cowboys. Set in the same year as Martin Luther King, Jr.'s march on Washington and the publication of Betty Friedan's book *The Feminine Mystique*, the film shows the heartening progress we have made on civil rights since 1963. Even though the film was released around the time that the president "cynically flogged a legally superfluous (and unpassable) constitutional amendment banning same-sex marriage for the sole purpose of whipping up the basest hostilities of his electoral base" (Rich, 2005, p. 13), polls are nevertheless showing that a large majority of Americans support equal rights for gay couples if the relationship is not called marriage.

Brokeback Mountain: Psychological Issues

The film's postmodern layering of perspectives and issues about identity, alienation, and the need for connection (Gergen, 1991) is revealed by a look at the fascinating array of review titles. Some examples include "Masculinity and Its Discontents in Marlboro County" (Dargis, 2005), "Two Gay Cowboys Hit a Home Run" (Rich, 2005), "Cowboys, Just Like in the Movies" (Trebay, 2005), and "Love Story with One Difference" (2005). Robert Roten (2005), from the *Laramie Movie Scope*, called it a "modern story about 'star-crossed lovers,'" a modern "Romeo and Jack." Rob Nelson called it "Midnight Cowboys, Lonesome Doves," and Roger Ebert said it was "as observant as work by Bergman" (*Brokeback Mountain*, n.d.).

Reviewers and writers have quite different ideas about what the film is about. Proulx, the author of the short story on which the film is based, has said that it is "about two confused young men 'beguiled by the cowboy myth'" (Dargis, 2005, p. 13). The irony is that the protagonists are not actually cowboys but technically shepherds. Dargis noted that *Brokeback Mountain* is a film about identity ("On Brokeback, the two men are neither straight nor gay, much less queer; they are lovers, which probably accounts for the category confusion that has greeted the film"; p. 13), and Rich (2005) made the same point tongue in cheek, calling it "a heavily promoted American movie depicting two men having sex" (p. 13). Epidemiologists attempting to categorize sexually transmitted diseases have the same problem with mixed identities, having no categories for men who have sex with other men but do not identify as gay. Being gay in American poses special questions and challenges about identity formation (Cass, 1979; Coleman, 1982; Isay, 1996).

Brokeback Mountain is also a film about the challenging societal factors that impinge on gay relationships. The film has been called a "landmark in the troubled history of America's relationship to homosexuality" (Rich, 2005, p. 13); Proulx's story "*Brokeback Mountain*" was written six years before Stonewall became a new frontier for gay rights, and gay student Matthew Shepard was murdered near Laramie, Wyoming, on October 6, 1998, the year after the story was published. Shepherd was pistol whipped by two men he met at a bar, tied to a split rail fence with his own shoelaces, and left to die in the cold. Consensual sex between two men was still a crime in some American states until 2002, when the Supreme Court reversed the sodomy laws; therefore, critic Trebay (2005) called the film a documentary that shows the violence so often part of gay men's experience. Other reviewers have pointed out that the problem in the film is not caused by the wife and family of the men but by their bullying bosses and shaming fathers-the patriarchy itself.

Noteworthy for clinicians are also the terrible alienation, depression, and loneliness that come with being gay in America (Herek, 1989). The name of one of the two protagonists, Ennis, brilliantly played by Ledger, means *island*, and we see him as unable to fully connect with either Jack, his wife, or his children. Jack, the other protagonist, played seductively by Gyllenhaal, is also lonely in his cold family, his wealthy and insensitive wife and in-laws. Both men live a secretive double life, and neither is able to commit authentically to either life. One rancher from Wyoming who was interviewed in a review (Trebay, 2005, p. 1) spoke of his great loneliness and said that he had considered suicide.

Another theme of *Brokeback Mountain* is purely a visual element-the power of nonverbal communication. From the grunting and wrestling between the two men and their use of silence, pauses, and body language, we feel their bond (Birdwhistell, 1970). They use understatement to make their points, as when Jack summarizes the whole story of the relationship as, "That ol' Brokeback got us good." The camera work echoes the poetic use of imagery, lingering on distant mountaintops and clear streams. The imagery even gets campy, as when the smoldering looks and shots of men's butts in tight jeans have the audience snickering. In psychotherapy, the nonverbal level is often minimized by our verbal, goal-directed, male therapeutic model. Because nonverbal and visual imagery are so directly connected to dreams and the unconscious, it would be helpful for therapists to be aware of this aspect of the therapeutic process.

Another layer of the film is archetypal. The image of the Western frontier is mythic in the American imagination, and the film shows the power of the imagination over reality. For example, the era of the cowboy actually existed for a relatively short time in American history-from the end of the large-scale cattle drives after the Civil War to the advent of the use of rail to move cattle. By the time movies were created, this era was over. The myth of wide open spaces lives on in the collective unconscious and symbolizes freedom to be oneself, away from the stifling conformity of domesticity and technology. Part of this myth shows the conflict between nature and culture in the human psyche. Other Western films that show this conflict and also have sexual overtones include John Wayne and Monty Cliff in *Red River*, Gary Cooper and Lloyd Bridges in *High Noon*, and Rock Hudson and James Dean in *Giant*. Outsiders have always been drawn to this freedom, as shown in the John Wayne genre. Even artists who perpetuated the myth, such as Aaron Copland, who wrote *Billy the Kid* and *Rodeo*, were outsiders; Copland was a Jewish boy from Brooklyn who was a Communist sympathizer and more comfortable in Paris than the West (J. Weisgall, personal communication, December 26, 2005). Agnes de Mille, the choreographer of *Oklahoma*, was the ugly duckling and outsider of the famous Hollywood de Mille family, and Oklahoma was one of the first American musicals that captured the hearts and minds of the American public. In the political arena, Ronald Reagan and Arnold Schwartzenegger (Serlin, 2003) posed before pictures of Teddy Roosevelt, evoking the myth of the rugged individualistic cowboy. However, the myth of freedom is an ideal and not real; for example, cowboy Rock Hudson spent his life living in the closet. The myth of the wild West shows the tension between the real and the ideal.

As Carl Jung (1958), Rollo May (1975, 1991), and others have shown, the influence of mythic images is as significant as the reality of human thoughts, feelings, and behavior. Mythic images can be used in psychotherapy as a template to see one's own personal mythology (Feinstein & Krippner, 1988) and also images of male partnership (Beebe, 1993). In the case of my psychotherapy client, for example, her mythology was partly about her need for freedom, commitment and flight, and doomed love. Myths capture the paradoxical complexity of human nature, whereas much modern psychology emphasizes a one-dimensional approach to diagnosis or treatment. For example, the trend toward manualized methods that help clients replace negative thoughts with positive ones, or those that emphasize happiness while leaving out tragedy, miss the drama of human life. Instead of fixing symptoms, a mythic approach to psychology aims to help people deal with the real complexity between individuation and adjustment to reality, freedom and fate, and multiple selves and identities. From a mythic perspective, as

Shakespeare wrote in *As You Like It*, "all the world's a stage," and we play many roles.

Finally, a mythic perspective allows us to see that, like great art, life comes in genres. Is *Brokeback Mountain* a tragedy? Both heroes leave the community and go off to the island or paradise to find themselves a theme often found in Shakespeare. Yet can they individuate, or are societal factors such as homophobia and intolerance too strong? Greek tragedies portray the tension between freedom and fate. Is *Brokeback Mountain* in the genre of forbidden love?

Because everything else in the cowboys' life changed, but their love lasted all their life, I see this film as showing the enduring power of love. The director set out to sympathetically portray the challenges of two men in love and the human need to live an authentic life. To this end, he succeeds magnificently. The acting by Ledger may win him an Academy Award nomination, and the score and cinematography support the action seamlessly. In short, *Brokeback Mountain* introduces many complex psychological issues that would be valuable for psychologists to see and understand.

References

Beebe, J. (1993). Towards an image of male partnership. In R. Hopcke (Ed.), *Same-sex love and the path to wholeness.* Boston: Shambhala.

Birdwhistell, R. (1970). *Kinesis and context: Essays in body motion communication.* Philadelphia: University of Pennsylvania Press.

Brokeback mountain (2005). (n.d.). Retrieved January 30, 2005, from http://www.rottentomatoes.com/m/brokeback_mountain/?beg=75&int=28&page=4

Cass, V. C. (1979). Homosexual identity formation: A theoretical model. *Journal of Homosexuality, 4(3),* 219-235.

Coleman, E. (1982). Developmental stages of the coming out process. *Journal of Homosexuality, 7(2),* 31?43.

Costigan, M. (Producer) & Lee, A. (Director). (2005). *Brokeback mountain* [Motion picture]. United States: Universal Studios.

Dargis, M. (2005, December 18). Masculinity and its discontents in Marlboro country. *New York Times,* p. 13.

Feinstein, D., & Krippner, S. (1988). *Personal mythology.* Los Angeles: Tarcher.

Gergen, K. (1991). *The saturated self.* New York: Basic Books.

Herek, G. M. (1989). Hate crimes against lesbians and gay men: Issues for research and policy. *American Psychologist, 44,* 948-955.

Isay, R. (1996). *Becoming gay: A journey to self-acceptance.* New York: Pantheon Books.

Jung, C. G. (1958). *Psyche and symbol* (V. de Laszlo, Ed.). New York: Doubleday.

"*Love Story with one difference.*" (2005, December 23). Palm Beach Post.

May, R. (1975). *The courage to create.* New York: Bantam Books.

May, R. (1991). *The cry for myth.* New York: Norton.

Rich, F. (2005, December 18). Two gay cowboys hit a home run. *New York Times,* p. 13.

Roten, R. (2005, October 9). *Brokeback Mountain*: A song of doomed love for cowboys. *Laramie Movie Scope.*

Serlin, I. (2003, October 10). Image vs. reality: Daddy will take care of you. *San Francisco Chronicle.*

Trebay, G. (2005, December 18). Cowboys, just like in the movies. *New York Times*, Section 9, pp. 1, 6.

17

In Harmony with the Sky, (天, Tian, Universe): Implications for Existential Psychology

Albert Chan

Although the word psychology had not been introduced in Asia until more recently, I have always thought that Chinese psychology has developed over the thousands of years of Chinese culture. It integrates science and the laws of nature, agriculture and industry, philosophy and poetry, history, and politics. This psychology favors the collective and social aspects of humans, their relationship with each other, and their harmony with the ever present symbolic and mythic principles of sky nature (天, Tian, universe)(He 2007; Wang, 2008). In Chinese psychology, personal phenomenological and ontological experiences of the individual have been neglected and/or compromised.

In this respect it is very different from many modern Western clinical theories that are based in a scientific mythology based in the separateness and discreteness of each individual. Since Descartes famous statement of "I think therefore I am," Western psychology has been focusing on individual consciousness and individualistic expressions of emotion, thoughts, and behaviors. These experiences are reduced, defined, measured, and analyzed, but rarely realigned with the whole person or the larger society context. This minimized psychology has helped to capture the label of a scientific discipline, but shuns addressing the larger questions of existence and how one lives a meaningful life.

On the other hand, Chinese psychology has more directly sought a more holistic, experiential, and embodied understanding the psyche (Bond, 1986; 1993; Wang 2008). However, this approach to existence has been deeply, and to a large degree subconsciously, subjected to the ideas of Confucianism, and more specifically Confucianism's view of collectivism. In this chapter I am going to analyze the Chinese ideas and myths of the importance of humans being in harmony with the sky nature (天 Tian, universe), and its implications on existential perspective of psychology. I believe that this foundational idea of finding harmony within the sky nature, has influenced the Chinese development of their collective psychosocial and political psyche, and in turn has an immense impact on Chinese cultural context, individuals' social relationships, and individuals' relationship with themselves. Collective and social harmony surely develops under such context, but at the cost to the personal individuation of each member of society.

Returning Home

I was born in Hong Kong, but spent most of my adult life in the Western communities of England, the United States, and Canada. Two years ago I returned to Hong Kong. On the surface, my return was for new opportunities to teach and lecture, but in my heart I have discovered hidden meanings. Living in Hong Kong makes me feel like I am already home, but sometimes I feel like I need to return to Canada where I found my individual 'self.' Perhaps, in the depth of my Chinese psyche I am yearning to be completed with a collective order, a collective sense of psyche that Jung (1965) emphasized, but my individual self keeps questioning the validity of my yearning.

Recently I have been supervising a group of students in Shenzhen. We meet in a hotel named *Harmony*. The Chinese name is "Tien, Die, Yen" hotel, whose direct translation is "Heaven, Earth, and Man." When I travel in China and I have seen similar names in different provinces and cities throughout the country. It makes me wonder if we, as Chinese, are yearning to be at peace with the universe, or in a more holistic sense are we reminding ourselves that we are part of the universe? My curiosity sets me venturing into the Chinese mythology.

Sky

Sky (天 Tian, universe) bears the synonym of nature (He, 2007; Wang, 2008). It is the dominant force regulating the cosmic order. Besides being the home of the god and goddesses, Sky encapsulates moral commands, from on high one might say. The ancient agricultural Chinese culture developed and co-existed with the sky. The importance of coexisting with and being in harmony with the sky nature, the sky cosmic orders, and the sky moral commands is embedded in the Chinese collective culture. Sky nature has been ingrained in each Chinese life for thousands of years. I believe this sky nature belief system provides insight into the Chinese personality, and is vital to understand and consider when working with Chinese clients in psychotherapy.

In Sichuan

After the earthquake in Sichuan, on May 12, 2008, I went up to Chendu, where the disaster response center was located. Many Tibetans, one of the minority people of China, live in Sichuan. In my travel there, I had the fortune of having a dinner with a Tibetan family. The family organized a traditional BBQ lamb dinner for travelers, and over the generous and delicious meal I was told about the "Sky Burial."

My hosts explained to me that Tibetans live at very high altitude; the average elevation is 4,900 meters (16,000 ft). It is the highest region on Earth and is commonly referred to as the "Roof of the World." Tibetans rely on herding sheep and cows on the plateau grasslands. They believe their lives are dictated by nature, the mountains, the sky, and the rivers. Tibetans believe that humans have two lives; a physical life and a spiritual life. The spiritual life is everlasting and death is the beginning passage. When someone is dying the passage from the physical life to the spiritual life breaks open. A close family member or a friend will gently talk to the dying person that his or her physical life is coming to the end. The dying person will be reminded to let go of the earthy physical body and enter to the spiritual world, to mingle with the sky and the true nature of all existence.

A sky burial scaffold is built halfway up the mountain away from chilly winds, and from there the spirit will ascend to heaven to join the gods and goddesses. The burial ritual is performed by a Tibetan Buddhist priest in three stages. First, the corpse with a cloth covering the head is put on the scaffold naked and facing downward toward the earth. Then smoke is raised to attract eagles to snatch the outer flesh. After this initial clearing of the flesh, the priest then uses a surgical knife to separate all the bones, organs, and tendons to allow the eagles to full access to the body. Finally the priest removes the cloth covering the face and head. It is believed that the faster the physical body is decimated, the sooner the spiritual body will start the homeward journey to heaven.

Sky Burial sounds both mysterious and horrific. I was told about this ritual just after dusk and I felt the spirit world that they were explaining all around me. Tibetans believe humans are created by the nature of all things and that our spirits return back to this nature. Death and the decomposition of the body allow us to achieve harmony with nature, the natural order of things. The inevitable cycle of life and death provides the ground for deep meaning in our limited time in human form (Ga, Cai, & Ge, 2000). Although this is a Buddhist ritual, it echoes the Taoist understanding of our search to be united with sky, heaven, nature (He 2007; Ho, 1995; Wang, 2008).

This cross cultural and cross religious Chinese belief of being reunited with nature has developed from the Chinese philosophy (He 2007; Ho, 1995; Wang, 2008). It is believed that humans, as finite beings, need to rely on the unlimited sky to be complete and to become in harmony with the nature. These ideas are found in all the major religions of China: Confucianism, Taoism, and Buddhism. Although there are differences between each understanding, I want to draw focus to the similarities.

These ideas could be simply explained in that sky nature dictates the fate of humans and at the same time grants blessings on us. We are dependent upon and part of the sky nature. A human life is finite, but the sky is infinite. These concepts emerged during the period when China was primarily an agricultural society. Nature provided the resources for survival, while at the same time nature constricted the communities with impervious destructive forces such as drought, fire, and disease. Sichuan had just experienced recent economic growth that was lost in the aftermath of the deadly earthquake.

Infinite sky nature sets boundaries on humans, but we are not helpless. Humans have an endless reservoir of spirit that allow us to adapt and adjusts to changes and to coexist within these contradicting tensions. The sky nature does not necessary stand in opposition to the human existence, but co-exists with us. The sky nature is the passage between the infinite and the finite (He, 2007; Ho, 1995; Wang, 2008).

In Harmony with Sky

The concept of humans seeking to be in harmony with the sky nature has existed since ancient China. We have had to find a way to exist despite, and in co-existence with, the contradicting tensions between the infinite sky nature and human limitedness. The Chinese farmer has always given blessing to this the infinite sky nature as it provides all the necessary resources for life: soil, rain, crops, and livestock. Simultaneously, the farmer is also at the mercy of the unpredictable and unwelcome aspects of sky nature: drought, sickness, earthquakes, and death.

While I was traveling from Hong Kong to Macau to teach at Macau Inter-University Institute, I met a coarse looking man with tattoos on both of his arms. I had been talking with my dean about a student and had not realized that he had been listening to our conversation. He came up to us and asked my profession. I told him I was a lecturer at a university and family therapist, and he took this as an opportunity to educate me about sky nature. He was like a modern sage that I met not on the ancient Silk Road, but on a state of the art hovercraft. He explained he retired as a fisherman nine years ago because the sea gave less fish than ever before. He said he was not so brash and foolish as to compete with the sky nature.

He described his experience of fishing. He would go to sea with his crew for a week at a time. He would travel into the ocean, where there was only the sea and sky as far as he could see in all directions. He awoke each day at dawn, and worked until dusk when he would be rocked to sleep by great waves. He said that although he made a living, he understood that he risked his life each trip. He felt tremendous humility in the power and vastness of the sea, but his greatest respect went to the sky. He said no human could complete with the nature. Many of his friends had lost their life to the sea as sky nature did not give mercy to them. He believed that his life and his livelihood depended on the blessing and mercy of the sky. He praised the sea goddess for her generosity, but feared the sky immensely.

He explained that each time at sea he would struggle and maneuver with and within sky nature to maximize his catch. He made clear that I understood that he was not only talking personally, but mythically. "This is not only the fate of the fisherman, but this is all of life." The immense contradicting tensions were shown in the lines of fear and gratitude in his face. On each journey he was hopeful and hopeless, assertive and subservient. I finally understood what the spiritual traditions of China had been trying to teach me: One must find a union with oneself and sky nature. This is the essence of harmony.

Chinese culture and collectivism has been built upon this foundation. Perhaps only through the notions of harmony and being in collective can humans survive. Striving for this harmony is a pragmatic journey, as it supports the individual but also the timeless Chinese collectivist values and institutions of family structure, social order, and survival. This shaped our shared and complicity agreed upon ethics and morality.

Grand Dad Sky

The following sky myth illustrates how earnestly the Chinese desire harmony. The story was told to me by a student I supervised. In his village, they have an annual festival for the *Grand Dad Sky*. It is the most important festival of his village; all households have to participate. All have to contribute food that gets redistributed after the celebration. The priest leads the worship and has the obligation to be fair in the redistribution of food, as *Grand Dad Sky* is fair. During the ceremony, the priest invites the gods and goddesses from heaven to give blessings to the village.

The annual festival recognizes the infinite of the sky nature. A myth that humanizes the gods and goddesses accompanies the celebration. The community is destined receive both blessings and curses from the gods and goddesses. Therefore, by offering food, the community tries to bribe them to provide only blessing. The resolution comes as they meet in the middle. If the community agrees to be submissive to their orders and be harmonized with the sky nature, the gods and goddesses will be less wrathful.

Chinese Collective Foundation

I believe that the phenomena I have described form a significant part of the foundation for the prevailing cultural collectivism, belief systems, and myths of contemporary Chinese civilization (Wang, 2008). The co-existing tensions and blessings between human beings and the sky nature (天, Tian, universe) are endless. To be in harmony with nature without disturbing the blessings and good faith from the sky (天, Tian, universe) nature is the destiny of human beings. This belief is core in Confucianism and Taoism: the union of humanity and the sky (天, Tian, universe) nature is the essence of harmony. These concepts continue to influence Chinese civilization and culture. Therefore, Chinese existence is based on harmony with the collective context and in relating to nature. The Chinese psychological sense of collective security has been developing on the platform of harmony within collectivism (Gou, 2008; He 2007; Wang, 2008). Chinese security has emphasized its collective roots and skirted the Western individualism that has been exported globally by way of global mercantile structures and mass media. We recognize, however, that many Western ideas have already permeated the social organization of the East and that there will be a continued mutual interpenetration of ideas resulting from our increasing contact through commerce, tourism, and the media.

The Self and the Collective

In my heart and through my contemplations, I believe individualism is a given. But in the Chinese cultural collective, context and individualist concepts have to be endorsed and legitimized by the rulers of the social order and in turn legitimized by the sky (天, Tian, universe) nature. This legitimizing of hierarchy is analogous to that achieved by ancient Chinese emperors. The worship of the sky (天, Tian, universe) in China was started with the Emperor of Huang, (Huang Di) (He 2007; Wang, 2008; Ho, 1995). He built the worship altar not only to use it for worshiping the sky (天, Tian, universe), but also to ask heaven to legitimize his ruling legacy. Confucius stated that worshiping heaven signified emperors receiving the blessing and heavenly orders to rule their kingdom. This ritual signified the emperors of ancient China gaining the passage to rule. Those who received the blessings would rule, and those who lost the blessings would lose their kingdom in chaos and die. Chinese culture thus embraced harmony, which enabled everyone to live cooperatively.

Ancient Chinese history records that emperors sent their daughters to marry the neighboring princes in order to establish a harmonized relationship between territories. If this harmony was not established, Chinese rulers were obligated to prevent chaos by any means at their disposal. The 1989 Tiananmen Square incident provides a recent and well documented example of the dynamic. The Tiananmen Square incident represented the moral voice of the people, including the students, intellects, workers, and even some of the government officials looking for more social, economical, and democratic political changes in face of corruptions. Unfortunately, the ruling party leaders ultimately saw this as a potential for chaos which threatened the harmony of the society and led them to their choice to call the military.

The Great Wall was built under the command of many Chinese rulers between the 600 BC and the 16th century. The goal was to protect the northern borders of the Chinese Empire and to ensure harmony. We could say that these emperors merely did not want to be attacked, but psychologically, it bears the symbolic meaning of guarding the harmony. I believe that Chinese emperors feared the disharmony, chaos, and consequences of war.

Confucianism: Preservation of Order and Harmony

Chinese psychologically fear chaos and conflicts. They endorse a collective psyche and consequently a strict social order rooted back to the rise of Confucianism. At that ancient chaotic time, centuries before the birth of Christ, order set the boundaries that preserved individuals and the collective. Confucius wanted to have a social order in which everyone was in harmony. Fear is evident throughout history in seeking peace and harmony. The values of Confucianism, like the Great Wall, have preserved Chinese social, political, and family structures over millennia. Confucius constructed five relationships to which he wanted the Chinese to strictly adhere. These are relationships between: ruler and subject, father and son, husband and wife, elder brother and younger brother, and friend and friend (Bond & Hwang, 1986). With strict obedience to these five social orders, the harmony of the collective society will be preserved.

Filial piety, the father-son relationship, is considered the most important among the five Confucian relationships. Historically, a central Chinese value is the strict family structure that requires devotion and obligations of children to their parents. It is parallel to the strict devotion and loyalty to the emperor from officials (Bond, 1986; Bond & Hwang, 1986; Gou, 2008). Confucian filial piety provides an example of culturally defined intergenerational relationships with absolute obedience. Although some of its component ideas (obedience, for example) are shared by other cultures, filial piety surpasses all other ethical prescriptions in its historical continuity, the proportion of humanity under its governance, and the encompassing and imperative nature of its precepts. The attributes of intergenerational relationships governed by filial piety are structural, enduring, and invariable across situations within Chinese culture. They may be generalized to apply to authority relationships beyond the family and they are thus potent determinants of not only intergenerational, but also superior-subordinate interactions.

I remember when I was a child; my father was, in a typical way, the outsider to the family. He worked and we had a very distant relationship that appeared harmonious but had unseen tensions. He wrote on a board in our home that "when a family is harmonious everything is perfect and when a family is problematic there will be unceasing conflicts." In my father's eyes, "harmony" among family members was not just a central guiding principle, it was the essence of his existence. His beliefs were deeply reinforced in the collective perspective that the security of the collective is rooted in harmony within the family. At this stage of my life, having been a father myself, I understand and am deeply moved by this paternal essence. At the same time I am conflicted by the attitudes I absorbed in my journey of adulthood in individualist communities of the West. Sometimes I am puzzled by several notions: Do we become secure by first being self-differentiated and later are enabled to be united and connected with others in a more intimate union? Or do we find our integrity by playing the strict, assigned role and through acceptance of it come to appreciate the collective security of being? Or can both collective and individualistic natures of human being co-exist, in a paradox of human nature, and thus be cherished by human existence? When these two "natures" are in conflict, it seems that the contraction within self could broaden to conflicts in other intimate relationships and may eventually result in conflicts between groups and even nations. Nonetheless, in a family systems perspective, emotional conflicts and projections within the cross generational and nuclear Chinese family will generate the sense of a deep need for harmony and a fear of chaos and conflicts (Bowen, 1994). Hence, I believe my father desired harmony and feared conflicts.

During my studies in the West, I came to adopt Bowen's ideas of self differentiation; that the individual self is both intrapsychic and interpersonal, that is both individualistic and collective. It is the ability to reflect on an individual's wish and feeling but not respond automatically to emotion. Perhaps the debate of individualistic and collective culture is only a rhetoric expression; the consciousness of a human self embraces both individual and collective meanings. Leading existential psychologists, Ed Menedelowitz (2008) and Kirk Schneider (2008) ground the examination of the nature of self in ideas similar to Martin Buber and contemporary Buber scholar Maurice Friedman (1999), who have an implicit recognition of these dual aspects of human nature. For a mature individual, one needs the blessing found in the paradox of individual independence and collective interdependence.

Emotion in a Chinese Mind

For the Chinese people, showing emotions is risky business. Emotions are dangerous because they demonstrate individual desire and chaos; both of which are threats to relational and collective harmony. Consequently, emotions need to be suppressed, denied, ignored, and jettisoned from the self experience. From a tradition Chinese medicine perspective, emotions are evidence of internal imbalance. Therefore, emotions are signs of illness (Bond, 1993; Kleinman, 1986). Strong feelings are dangerous because they may be contagious.

When compared to the West, emotions are less valued and relevant in the Asian psyche (Potter, 1988). The expression of emotions has no social value, nor do they move the individual or the collective toward any possible constructive outcome. For example, unlike Westerners who engage with the emotional expressions of others, the Chinese believe that the open expression of feelings should be met with only indifference. My early training in emotional constriction served me poorly when I moved to the West, but the openness I worked hard to attain has often been met with concern and confusion when I returned to Asia. When I urge students to embody and passionately engage with the psychological concepts they are learning, they look at me as if I am speaking a foreign language and not our native Cantonese.

In the West, I learned to communicate in a more transparent, assertive, and candid manner. It was not an easy task. It was filled with false starts, awkward moments, and profound self doubt and conflict. Not only did I have to fight against my internalized cultural bias, but I believe my temperament has always been introverted and shy. However, I learned that only through sharing my opinions that my knowledge and wisdom was expanded and enriched. Only by sharing myself did I move toward the true intimacy I longed for. When I returned to Hong Kong with my new skills, I experienced a cultural shock. Chinese colleagues and students desired hierarchy and harmony within the education context, not the interactive and fiery discourse I learned to admire in my Western education.

At first I could not understand why students remained silent when I asked for their opinions and experiences, but after one class a brave and insightful student shyly approached me. She said that although the students appreciated my invitations they dare not disturbed the classroom by interrupting the teacher to ask a question. They had never experienced a pedagogy in which their opinions were valued. This experience helped to reacquainted me with the power of filial piety and its psychological consequences. Within a collective learning context, a student never draws attention away from the teacher's expertise. Students may have questions, doubts, and even feelings, but these must remain secret as individual learning is subordinate to the social order. In Chinese culture, feedback and complaints must only be given by those higher in the collective social order. Therefore, despite my repeated invitations, I rarely receive the honest feedback from students that would improve my teaching. It is a closed system that does not engage in process and consequently limits progress.

Professors are seen as the knowledge and wisdom experts, therefore acceptance and patience without contesting is the most respectful and harmonious attitude. It nullifies the possibility that the harmony within the learning environment will ever be disturbed. This sheds new insight into my understanding of the Chinese personality. The Chinese character reveres harmony and subverts itself to the societal and cosmic hierarchy. The Chinese have blindly accepted an oversimplified understanding of the Taoist beliefs that to be harmonized with the natural order is the supreme way of being.

Avoidance of Conflicts

According to Tao, to avoid unnecessary controversy and to be in harmony with one's world is the goal of life (Gou, 2008; Ho, 1995). It is also a pragmatic way of life. The Tao is quintessentially Chinese allowing its adherents to attain harmony with the universe, the social orders, and with nature. If we seek harmony, we can alleviate and avoid suffering. A negative definition is adopted because, as in physical illness versus health, people more readily agree on what psychological suffering is than they do on happiness. Moreover, just as physical well-being is achieved in medicine through the prevention and cure of illnesses, so we shall attempt to achieve psychological well-being by the avoidance and alleviation of suffering. One is not just a metaphor of the other. From an evolutionary point of view, physical and psychological well-being go hand-in-hand. What is good for the body usually makes us feel good emotionally, and vice versa. The so-called pragmatic philosophies of Taoism and Buddhism as understood in China reinforce this belief.

All these stories reflect deeply the ancient Chinese belief that an individual becomes mature as his or her life harmonizes with heaven. These same ideas continue to be elaborated by modern Chinese philosophies (Gou, 2008; He 2007; Wang, 2008; Ho, 1995). When people become mature, their minds will have integrated with the cosmic orders. Once they achieve this maturity, they breathe with the cosmic rhythms. I have found that my context has profoundly influenced my beliefs; as I settle more into my new life in China I discover a deeper appreciation of these beliefs.

Existential Givens in Chinese Psychology of Harmony

Recently, a couple sought my services to assist with their eldest son. He had not eaten for five days and had not spoken to them for over a month. I will call this family the Voiceless Family. There are four members in the family: the father is Chinese, the mother is Filipino, their eldest son (the identified patient), G, is 32 years old, and his brother is two years younger. The parents met in Canada and have been married for more than 33 years. Mr. and Mrs. Voiceless worried that their son's condition has worsened over time. In Hong Kong, where they now live, crisis workers are not readily available. Since I had worked as a crisis therapist at a hospital in Toronto for several years, they were able to locate me in Hong Kong.

G studied in primary and secondary schools in Hong Kong. He then went abroad to attend college before returning home. After school, G had worked as a computer technician until he was laid off in 2007. Since then G had stayed at home with his parents. It was apparent that his mental health was declining. Mr. Voiceless, afraid that his sons would lose their facility with the Chinese language and forget their cultural roots wanted them to return to Hong Kong.

G first returned from Canada when he was 3 years old. Both Mr. and Mrs. Voiceless went to work and put him and his brother under the care of his grandmother and aunts. Such familial support is common in China and indeed is virtually mandatory. The extended family was initially disturbed that G did not have the mastery of Cantonese that was typical of other three year olds in their community. He was told that he was dumb because his language skills did not meet the family's expectations. Moreover, he looked different since his mother was Filipino. As G matured he became markedly quiet and reserved. In his adolescence, he would later try to defend the insults cast upon him by stating that he was introverted and shy like his father. Throughout his development, G rarely raised his voice to assert his ideas and tried to avoid of conflicts with his family and peers. Apparently, Mr. Voiceless was the biggest avoider.

My initial phone conversation was with G and his mother. G said that he did not really know his father. Mrs. Voiceless quickly discounted G's experience and stated that their boys love both their parents. G quickly asserted back that he did not know what love his mother was talking about. The mother then attacked her son again by retelling an earlier consultation with psychiatrist in which G was labeled as capable of rationality, but incapable of having feelings. I did not engage in the dynamics over the phone and just arranged a time for me to visit family in their home.

As I traveled to meet the family I was not sure what to expect. I had the recollection of being struck by a paranoid youth twenty-five years earlier when I had just began my career. As I entered the home, Mr. and Mrs. Voiceless looked worried and pointed me to G's room. When I entered the small room, G was sitting on the floor. He did not rise to greet me nor did he look at me. He was quite slim and a sad and suspicious face stared out at the wall below his greasy hair. My instincts told me to sit on the floor near the door and not force communication. In our silence, we heard voices of the family talking about him.

After a few minutes I introduced myself and explained that I was invited by his parents to assist him and his family. He now had the choice to either engage with me or to ask me to leave. His first statement was, "Nobody listens; I have nothing to say." While I felt like perhaps I should get up and leave, I continued to sit with him silently. He soon began to talk directly and deeply with me. He stated that he was physically abused by his grandmother and aunts, and that he was teased and bullied by schoolmates because he looked different. He said that the best way for him to keep peace was to be silent. He only liked to go out late at night when there was no one on the street. He put his head down which seemed to symbolize that he was finished talking with me for now.

I returned to the living room and was met by Mr. Voiceless who quickly told me that G, like himself, does not like conflicts, keeping the peace in vital to his family's survival. Mr. Voiceless went on to explain that his brothers and sisters have land in the New Territory that is very valuable and that it is essential that his wife and sons do not create trouble in his extended family. Mr. Voiceless explained that his brothers and sisters can be abusive and make his family the objects of their jokes. Mr. Voiceless tried to minimize contact with his extend family, but G protested that he did not want to see any these relatives, not even once a year on the Chinese New Year. Mr. Voiceless admitted that there is conflict among his siblings about the land, but he accepted the way his family was. He denied that he was afraid of asserting his opinions with his family, but stated that he chooses to make peace and avoid conflict. He accepted the collective family decisions even though he is not convinced that they are fair. He asked me if I understood that the collective co-existence prevails over any *individual*'s desire. I asked whether he had internal conflicts between his own needs and his family's collective decisions. He then put a smile on his face that did not mask his underlying bitterness.

Mrs. Voiceless came and joined us. She stated that her husband never talks to her about his family, the land, or the conflicts that trouble his own family. She quickly became emotional. She said that she loves her husband and sons and feels that she did the best she could as a wife and mother, but now feels that her job is done as her sons are adults. She desires to move forward into the next stage of her life with or without her family, although she worries that if she left her sons would not be able to withstand the collective emotional ridicule from her husband's family. She has grown resentful of her husband's silence. In consequence, she also learned to be voiceless and therefore her sons are the same. Now each of her sons has turned into a "hiding youth," a new contemporary term to describe youth with emotional problems whose refuge is their room where they spend their days playing computer games.

According to Mrs. Voiceless, her husband has been living a life without direction or meaning. He refuses to change or grow. She gave the example that he will order dim sum every time the family goes out for lunch because that is the family tradition, even though neither he nor his family actually enjoys this traditional meal. He lives and breathes, but has not done anything since he returned to Hong Kong. He just eats, sleeps, and gambles to pass time. She claims to be the one tackling life pressures and conflicts. Unfortunately, he quietly demands that his wife and sons live as he has lived. If they do not comply, he verbally attacks them, accusing them of being angry people and then withdrawals again.

In discussing the harmony with the sky (天, Tian, universe), I wonder how much China's way of collectivism stifles individuals' authentic self as proposed by existential psychotherapy. In my sessions with the Voiceless family, we explored these themes. I have asked them if love could only be expressed through obedience; if life could be harmonious when life is only half lived, fulfilling prescribed roles; if harmony can only be achieved by sacrificing one's self and one's family?

Rollo May (1981), regarded freedom as "man's capacity to take a hand in his own development. It is our capacity to mold ourselves" (p.7). In Mr. Voiceless's situation, he blindly followed his destiny without question and without allowing himself or his sons to grow. Tragedy happened not only to him but to his next generation.

Any values that a person develops will be based upon his or her experience of autonomy and the sense of personal power and possibilities. G was not able to express himself. His voice and experience were not being heard and consequently he chose to shut down. I suspect that freedom is enhanced when one's expression is recognized regardless whether it is accepted or rejected.

G's first statement to me was, "Nobody listens I have nothing to say." May (1981) suggested that freedom is life's creative goal and coercive destiny is the opposite because it "leads to decay" (p. 19). Therefore, freedom gives meaning to destiny. As there is no freedom or meanings in G's life, he chose to avoid life, to become a breathing corpse.

In terms of love, G has not felt loved. According to Eric Fromm's (1956/2000) *Art of Loving*, G has not felt the experience of an exchange of respect or the cherishing of self and other's ideas, desires, thoughts, life-goals, and performance. I asked Mr. Voiceless if he ever wanted his father to tell him about his internal emotional life. Mr. Voiceless quietly admitted his wishes. I simply asked Mr. Voiceless if he could do this for his sons. Over time, Mr. Voiceless and G began to speak more honestly and openly with each other. Although Mr. Voiceless did not change his stance of trying to maintain peace and harmony with his extended family, he was able to let the rest of his family make their own choices of not visiting with this side of the family.

Mr. Voiceless also began to identify and question the conflicting family roles he adheres to. Does he want to be the well behaved younger brother of his family or would he prefer to be his sons' father. Does he want to lose his wife because she does not comply to the ideas of obedience that are not part of her culture, or is he willing to feel the anxiety of doing something new, uncharted, alive, and even passionate. Mrs. Voiceless also found more of her voice. She clearly stated that she is no longer participating in a life of obedience and silence, and that she would like him to join her in the time they have left. While his father struggled with changing the strict societal roles, G surprising bloomed. The idea of creating his own destiny was not dissimilar to his journey in the computer games he used to use for escape, but G wanted to try this in his own life. He left the family home, returned to work in software engineering, and when I last meet with him he was embracing the Filipino and Western elements of his heritage. He also found some balance with his Chinese roots that had held him and his family as prisoners.

Chinese Psychological Freedom

I have encountered many clients that have difficulties making decisions due to limited resources and difficult social situations. They usually feel trapped and believe that they do not have free will to choose their destination in life. On the other hand, some clients with more impulsive or narcissistic qualities may abuse their free will and end up in overwhelming destitution. I suppose the virtue of freedom depends on how much we can handle; a little child does not have the maturity of judgment to handle momentous issues, and a non-benevolent dictator will abuse freedom. We see this not only in individuals, but also in a collective form. Various empires in history have abused freedom, imposing their will on other countries, which resulted in devastating consequences for all involved.

I appreciate the mistrust between East and West that has developed in the past few centuries. The transparency, openness, and idealism (at least in principle if not always in practice) of individualistic societies purport to equip the democratic social and political system with the means to promote equality for all. In an individualistic society, communities need to have idealistic forces to make individuals accountable to one another. However, in major portions of the Chinese population, it is the strict social orders, roles, and implicit moral codes that militate against malfeasance and disturbing collective harmony. The concept of individual growth is foreign to these populations. The self-actualization and growth of individuals are based on the well being of the community rather than on the transcendence of the individual.

In China, the minority of people who promote creativity, freedom, and individualism do not find acceptance. In some cases, they are exiled to prisons or other countries. The lives and work of two of China's greatest poets Li Bai (李, *the god dismissed from heaven*) and Du Fu (楠, *the poet of history*) provide poignant examples. However, when we primarily seek universal harmony and obedience, we compromise the necessities of individual differences, personal freedom, and creativity. Thus, traditional Chinese arts are sometimes regarded as only crafts. Although beautiful in their classic style and technical mastery, they lack the creativity and originality that has become increasing important among present-day Chinese artists. Contemporary film maker, Ang Lee (李), however, is an excellent example of how many of China's current cultural visionaries integrate traditional and modern sensibilities, individualism and collectivism, Eastern and Western influences in their art.

Chinese individualized transcendence is a union with the sky (天, Tian, universe) nature as a collective union. This notion, deep rooted in the Chinese collective psyche, has inhibited the Chinese people from speaking up boldly and being assertive. This generated internal tensions between wanting a collective harmony and pursuing one's personal wishes. However, even today many Chinese prefer the collective ideal and grow indifferent within themselves and with the larger society. This internal chaos and disharmony within the self can often leak out onto the collective society that they are trying to protect.

May (1981) similarly challenged the one dimensional aspect of traditional American psychology that had been deeply rooted for decades in biological, experimental, and behavioral theories used in academia and research institutes. To some degree, psychology at its best will always challenge the cultural norms, even if in other places being a prime example of them. May's notion of freedom and destiny not only wakes up the soul of human existence in psychological terms, but also includes the moral and philosophical, and spiritual quest that exists in current psychology.

I was recently supervising a team of young social workers in Shenzhen. Social work is a new profession endorsed by the central government in Beijing and Shenzhen is a testing region for this profession. I appreciate that the government wishes to bring in this new discipline for the harmony and well being of the community. I have found that many young social workers are disappointed with the limited vision of their emerging role in China. Like many Western social workers and therapists, they complain that most of their time and energy gets used up in primarily administrative tasks rather in the engagement with individuals, families, and communities. What has complicated this matter is that these young social workers are suspiciously received by the existing government services. Under my encouragement, they have become more courageous in asking for appropriate social work assignments. To my surprise, the reviews have been very positive across individual, family, community, and governmental rating questionnaires. These young visionaries and hard working social workers are forging important new ground in China. They have found the balance of helping individuals and the collective in a harmonious manner. They are viewed as both culturally cooperative and agents of change and growth.

Conclusion

I have discussed the strengths and limitations of collective harmony in China. The strict moral and social codes of Confucianism need to be examined in light of our modern era. I believe the cross cultural dialogue between East and West has had a positive effect in both societies. This interchange has helped to highlight the timeless wisdom in the various views of both traditions, while also exposing the myopic vision inherent in each of them. From my experience of *being in* and *in between* both cultures and traditions, I believe that individualism and collectivism are continuous variables. No person or community can be characterized as being entirely one or the other. At its best, the collective society allows families and communities to share life experiences, care, love, cooperation, responsibility, and meaning closely with one another. At its worst, collectivism can suffocate creativity, freedom, individual and collective growth. The sense of harmony needs to be achieved not only through strict social codes, but also through the processes of interpersonal engagement, discussions, mutuality, intellectual and emotional fearlessness, and appreciation and acceptance of our individual differences.

As for the individualistic perspective, I believe life starts with the blessings of collective unions, deep attachments, social supports, mentoring, and love. A self differentiated person needs to connect not only to his or her personal wilderness, but also to the larger collective. Freedom, courage, commitment, humanity, compassion, integrity, and love are all necessary for the general well-being of oneself and one's community. As Alfred Adler (1929/1969) taught, interest and involvement in the full life of one's community is characteristic of the healthy person. A good life is predicated on this spiritual-psychological dimension. We need to embrace and seek to understand the individual and collective tensions within ourselves, within our cultures, and within our global community. If we are accountable to ourselves and others, this is the good life; individuated and connected.

References

Adler, A. (1969). *The science of living.* New York: Anchor Books. (Originally published in 1929).

Bond, M.H. (Ed.). (1986). *The psychology of Chinese people.* Hong Kong: Oxford University Press.

Bond, M.H. (1993). Emotions and their expression in Chinese Culture. *Journal of Nonverbal Behavior, 17* (4), 245-62.

Bowen, M. (1994). *Family therapy in clinical practice.* Lanham, MD: Jacob Aronson

Freidman, M. (1999). *The affirming flame: A poetics of meaning.* Amherst, New York: Prometheus.

Fromm, E. (2000). *The art of loving.* New York: Harper Perennial. (Original work published 1956)

Ga, Z. Cai. D., & Ge, S. B, (2000). *Sky burial, Tibetan funeral culture.* LanZhou: Ga Su Cultural Press.

Gou, S. (2008). *The way of heaven and holy word, A comparative studies between Zhuang Zi and Bible.* Beijing, China: Religious and Culture Press.

He, X. L. (2007). *Nature worship in China.* Nan Jing, China: Jiang Su People Press.

Ho, D.Y.F. (1995). Selfhood and identity in Confucianism, Taoism, Buddhism, and Hinduism: Contrast with the West. *Journal for the Theory of Social Behaviour, 25, 115-138.*

Jung, C. G. (1965). *Memories, dreams, reflections.* New York: Vintage Books.

Kleinman, A. (1980). *Patients and healers in the context of culture.* Berkeley: University of California Press.

Potter, S.H. (1988). The cultural construction of emotion in rural Chinese social life. *Ethos, 16,* 181-208.

May, R. (1981). *Freedom and destiny.* New York: Norton.

Mendelowitz, E. (2008). *Ethics and Lao Tzu: Intimations of character.* Colorado Springs, CO: University of the Rockies Press.

Schneider, K. J. (2008). From segregation to integration. In K. J. Schneider (Ed.), *Existential-integrative psychotherapy: Guideposts to the core of practice* (pp. 15-22). New York: Routledge.

Wang, S. N. (2008). *Confucius: On being human.* Beijing, China: Chiang On Press.

Wang, L. L. (1999). *Interpersonal harmony and conflict in Chinese culture.* Taipei: Guerin Guan.

18

Building the Great Wall of China
Postmodern Reverie and the Breakdown of Meanings[1]

Ed Mendelowitz

I

In the midst of his short story "Building the Great Wall of China," Franz Kafka (1971) relates the following parable:

> The Emperor, so it runs, has sent a message to you, the humble subject, the insignificant shadow cowering in the remotest distance before the imperial sun; the Emperor from his death bed has sent a message to you alone. He has commanded the messenger to kneel down by the bed, and has whispered the message to him; so much store did he lay on it that he ordered the messenger to whisper it back into his ear again. Then by a nod of the head he has confirmed that it is right. Yes, before the assembled spectators of his death—all the obstructing walls have been broken down, and on the spacious and loftily mounting open staircases stand in a ring the great princes of the Empire—before all these he has delivered his message. The messenger immediately sets out on his journey; a powerful, an indefatigable man; now pushing with his right arm, now with his left, he cleaves a way for himself through the throng; if he encounters

---

[1] This essay has been "built" out of fragments, much like Kafka's Great Wall of China itself.

resistance he points to his breast, where the symbol of the sun glitters; the way is made easier for him than it would be for any other man. But the multitudes are so vast; their numbers have no end. If he could reach the open fields how fast he would fly, and soon doubtless you would hear the welcome hammering of his fists on your door. But instead how vainly does he wear out his strength; still he is only making his way through the chambers of the innermost palace; never will he get to the end of them; and if he succeeded in that nothing would be gained; he must next fight his way down the stair; and if he succeeded in that nothing would be gained; the courts would still have to be crossed; and after the courts the second outer palace; and once more stairs and courts; and once more another palace; and so on for thousands of years; and if at last he should burst through the outermost gate—but never, never can that happen—the imperial capital would lie before him, the center of the world, crammed to bursting with its own sediment. Nobody could fight his way through here even with a message from a dead man. But you sit at your window when evening falls and dream it to yourself. (p. 244)

This parable, sometimes found standing on its own as "An Imperial Message," is a fragment that reflects perfectly the essence of the larger piece in which it is set. It is a quintessentially Kafkan meditation, its modernist message, paradoxically, the loss of revelation in a world cut off from sustaining meanings and forms. Kafka has been called, in this regard, "the exemplary modernist" (Alter, 1991, p. vii), a "post-traditional Jew" (Alter, 1991, p. viii)—a scribe who waits interminably for a message from on high while knowing full well that it will never arrive. "We are," as I have myself written in *Ethics and Lao-Tzu* (2008, p. xiii), "survivors in an endlessly expanding universe of ever-diminishing returns." Messages of definitiveness are now, irretrievably both behind and beyond us. How on earth is the bereft human specimen going to make it from here?

Ejected from Eden or, in Chinese terms, a Golden Age of harmony, peace and prosperity, nothing proceeds as it should. Like the actual Great Wall of China (whose construction began in the 6th century BCE), Kafka's Wall is built with the goal of fortification in mind, protection against fearsome "peoples of the north" (Kafka, 2007, p. 113). Is this not what is always at stake: our frantic quest for safekeeping during the course of our fitful earthly sojourn, shelter from the omnipresent metaphorical storm, our insatiable desire to have precisely what we cannot? In Kafka's telling of the tale, the grand design begins resolutely enough, the northernmost point of the Wall being joined at its apex with sections from the southeast and the southwest. From this starting point, however, the building of the Great Wall proceeds, not systematically, but rather according to a system of "partial construction," gangs of twenty workers apiece sent off into the vast expanse of China to erect random five hundred yard sections while an adjoining gang then constructs a section of equal length to meet it. In this manner, original order is compromised and finally lost:

> But then, after the juncture was accomplished, the construction was not continued at the end of these thousand yards, as you might expect; instead, the groups of workers were sent into quite different regions to continue work on the Wall. In this way, of course, numerous large gaps came about, and these were only gradually and slowly filled in, many only after the Wall had already been announced as completed. Indeed, it is said that there are gaps that have not been filled in at all; according to some people these are much larger than the completed sections, although this assertion may be only one of the many legends that have grown up around the Wall and which, given the length of the Wall, is not something one person can verify, at least

with his own eyes and by his own
standards. (Kafka, 2007, p. 113)

Grandiose schemes devolving into intractable confusion. The unreliability of stories and words. More gaps (or is it only another legend?) than wall. Do these images not evocatively depict an essential aspect of the state of things as we know it? Certainly, muses the Chinese narrator of our tale, it would have been more advantageous to "build continuously" or, at least, "continuously within the two main sections" rather than this strange method of "partial construction" (Kafka, 2007, p. 113). Such piecemeal proceedings can never afford adequate protection from enemies without and the gathering storm. And, yet, return to a "fixed place" (May, 1991, p. 53) of substance is a thing fanatically sought even as chances for attainment become increasingly remote. "I have been forty years wandering from Canaan," Kafka (1949/1988, p. 213) opines in his diary. This is our acutely modernist/postmodernist predicament. It is also what makes Kafka indispensable and palpably present.

Exile and the impossibility of return. The breakdown of meanings and forms. Our disconnection from Original Sources, the succor of traditional wisdom assumedly afforded in more coherent times. With Kafka, we are a long, long way from the world of the master builders with their blueprints and graphs, their raceways to expedient arrival, their voluble pronouncements seeming almost to command adjustment if not utter happiness in the midst of retreating voices and signs from beyond. "It is indeed a kind of Wandering in the Wilderness in reverse," muses Kafka, (1949/1988, p 213), of our post-paradisiacal, post-Canaan/canonical world. Those looming capitalizations ("Wandering" and "Wilderness"), a kind of gnostic shorthand disclosing an urgency concerning what is at stake. "Not "castration," suggests Rollo May (1991, p. 81), "but *ostracism*." Enter a brave new world from which God has departed, leaving in her or his absence manifold truncations in which nothing completely adds up. Kafka, explorer of a vast new space of a world on the lam and the mortified mind, sheds light on dark truths that science itself does not adequately broach. Unlike the academics, Kafka is reverential, even penitent—like some latter-day and literary Darwin—before the gravity of his ordeal. While realizing that the past may never have been exactly what we remember, Kafka nonetheless embraces this desolate landscape with a countenance of awe and dread. "Kafka," sighs the Italian critic Pietro Citati (1991, p. 171), "the man who has taught us to coexist with the death of the gods."

II

Scarcely known in his own time, Kafka's name has (like the legends of China) spread far and wide, his star rising posthumously to astronomical heights even as Freud's has notably declined. Kafka seems to me to be the truer conquistador of modern-day consciousness, whereas Freud and his disciples—their sizable accomplishments notwithstanding—find touchstones significantly in shibboleths of the past. (*"This is how eager we are,"* reflects the narrator of our tale, *"to wipe out the present."*) In his survey of a world in which scripture is lost and meaning no longer coheres, Kafka lays bare our own lives in much the same way, as Auden keenly observed, that Dante and Shakespeare had those of their own epochs and place. With Kafka, we gaze dumbfounded at a world from which God has departed, "the single divine Truth decomposed into myriad relative truths parceled out by men" (Kundera, 1986, p. 6). What we are left with, to quote a prescient William James (1961, p. 335), is a "string of facts," "provisional and revisable things."

The French literary critics Deleuze and Guattari (1986, p. 41) are wrong to project into Kafka an embrace of "socialism" or "anarchism" to be found in their own theoretical writing and minds. Still, they are right when they note that Kafka "laughs with a profound joy." "I can also laugh," Kafka (Wagner, 2007, p. 303) once wrote to his fiancée Felice; "have no doubt about this." Walter Benjamin (Alter, 1991, p. 21), too, posits, counter-intuitively, that the key to Kafka's work may reside in deciphering *"the comic aspects of Jewish theology."* "And from one end to the other," Deleuze and Guattari (1986) note, Kafka is "a political author, prophet of the future world" (p. 41). A political author, yes, in his unflinching gaze into the manifold conundrums of authority and meaning, spirit and self on a planet without compass that has seen better days. By no means, however, a proponent of newly minted systems to replace the "various, perhaps contradictory, statements" concerning "the obscurity of ancient times" (Kafka, 1954/1999, p. 9). We have only to think of this 21st century that has so fitfully commenced and our own tenuous ties to worlds inside and without when considering our narrator's reflections on Chinese emperors real and imagined and the lingering desire of the lowly individual to commune with what is deemed high:

> Just so, as hopelessly and hopefully, our
> people view the emperor. They do not
> know which emperor is reigning, and there

> is even doubt about the name of the
> dynasty . . . In our villages, long-dead
> emperors are set up on thrones, and one
> who lives on only in song has recently
> issued a decree that the priest reads aloud
> in front of the alter. Battles from our most
> ancient history are just now being fought,
> and with glowing cheeks your neighbor
> bursts into your house with the news.
> (Kafka, 2007, pp. 120-121)

With Kafka, we approach the numinous "limits of understanding" (Benjamin, 1968, p. 124). Even matters of leadership (where thoughts of current emperors merge beguilingly with memories of the dead ones) and transmission of knowledge, pressing as they are in an age of radical complexity, may be simultaneously matters of levity and even awe— touchstones not only for vagary but, ultimately, for reverie as well.

Intimations of the spiritual are in Kafka everywhere implied yet remarkable for their insubstantiality and lack of fulfillment.

> In the leadership office—where it was
> located and who occupied it, no one I have
> ever asked knows or knew—in this office
> there surely revolved all human thoughts
> and desires and, in countercircles, all
> human goals and fulfillments; but through
> the window the reflection of divine worlds
> fell on the hands of the leaders as they
> drew their plans. (Kafka, 2007, pp. 116-
> 117)

Founding fathers, mothers, and architects, their plans gently illumined by the gods. "Camouflaged within the social order," observes Roberto Calasso (2005, p. 23), "the cosmic order continues to exist and operate. After all, it has dealt not only with stars and spheres but also with powers and archons." It is precisely the manner in which divinity is intimated (merging seamlessly, albeit inconclusively, with authority) yet never disclosed that holds us eerily spellbound, as though we were witnessing in Kafka a mythology perfectly reflective of our own frenetic experience and nebulous time. "Anyone intent on concluding . . . that we have no emperor at all," our narrator (Kafka, 2007, p. 122) coyly informs us, "would not be far from the truth." The mysteries of Time, the mysteries of Space, the mysteries of God and Authority as hearsay replaces scripture and human beings now pose as gods.

III

And, so, connections are lost not only temporally but, also, hierarchically with incorporeal leaders replacing deities of old. Kafka's world is typified throughout by the loss of what the German sociologist Arnold Gehlen (in Wagner, 2007, p. 308) has called a "grand key attitude." As such it constitutes a hallmark expression of the "general uncertainty" (Kafka, 2007, p. 120) of our own experience and time:

> And while it is mainly the fault of the regime, which in the most ancient empire on earth has always been unable, perhaps through neglect of this concern in favor of other matters, to develop the institution of empire with such clarity that it would exercise its influence immediately and incessantly as far as the realm's most distant frontiers. On the other hand, this attitude also exhibits a weakness of imagination or conviction among the people, who are unable to embrace the empire obediently, in all its liveliness and presence, raising it from its submersion in Peking, and yet the subjects wish nothing more than just for once to feel this connection and drown in it. (p. 123)

No direction home commingling with a subjectively experienced imperative of right of return. A "hierarchically structured purposelessness" (Bauer, 1999, ¶ 6) and, consequently, the "search for a fixed spot in an otherwise chaotic" (May, 1991, p. 53) world. Yet, also, this notion that the problem may reside, ultimately, in our own "weakness of imagination." It is a point to which we will return in due time.

IV

The German-Jewish literary critic Walter Benjamin (1969), contemplating a painting he had purchased by the Swiss modern artist Paul Klee entitled *Angelus Novus,* once wrote down these words:

> A Klee painting named "Angelus Novus" shows an angel looking as though he is about to move away from something he is fixedly contemplating. His eyes are staring, his mouth is open, his wings are spread. This is how one pictures the angel of history. His face is turned toward the past. Where we perceive a chain of events, he sees one single catastrophe which keeps piling wreckage upon wreckage and hurls it in front of his feet. The angel would like to stay, awaken the dead, and make whole what has been smashed. But a storm is blowing from Paradise; it has got caught in his wings with such violence that the angel can no longer close them. This storm irresistibly propels him into the future to which his back is turned, while the pile of debris before him grows skyward. This storm is what we call progress. (pp. 257-258)

Throughout his abbreviated life, Benjamin carried on a passionate epistolary dialogue with Gershom Scholem, scholar of Jewish mysticism, centering (it should hardly surprise us!) often on Kafka. His insights into the modernist seer and postmodern psyche remain astonishingly brilliant to this day. Both men shared an evolving perception of Kafka as the artist who had, above all others, "mapped out the spiritual territory of the modern condition" (Alter, 1991, p. 14). Benjamin sensed in Klee's painting the essence of what the Jewish genius had spent his life pondering: the longing for paradise/revelation/Canaan and the gathering storm we mistake for progress. Benjamin used the painting as a mandala of sorts, an object for focus and reverie. After his suicide (when attempting to flee the Nazi occupation of France—the sinister face of totalitarianism and the obliging bureaucratic/clerical mind is everywhere lurking in Kafka—he was turned back at the Spanish border), the painting joined his friend Scholem in Jerusalem where it remained until Scholem's own death many years later. Robert Alter (1991) beautifully tells the whole story in a slim and relevant book entitled *Necessary Angels: Tradition and Modernity in Kafka, Benjamin, and Scholem.*

Diaspora, a dispersion into Wilderness or Desert; the spiritually/metaphorically wandering Jew. "Losing one place without gaining another," reflects Zadie Smith (2008, p. 17) in her recent essay on Kafka. In Kafka's story, too, as in the Tower of Babel, there is a vision of harmony never finally attained: "unity! unity! breast on breast, a round dance of the people, blood no longer confined in the meager circulatory system of the body but rolling on sweetly and yet returning to its source through the infinity of China" (Kafka, 2007, p. 115). Indeed, among the many legends that sprout up around the Great Wall is one that claims that it is itself to become the foundation for a new Tower of Babel. Once again, the hubris of mortals who, in their irrepressible childishness, haven't yet realized their bankruptcy and the impossibility of agendas. "Human nature, giddy at heart, a thing of flying dust, cannot endure being fettered; if it fetters itself, it will soon go mad, begin to rattle its chains, and tear to pieces wall, chain, and itself, scattering them to the winds" (Kafka, 2007, p. 116). And, so, the desire not only for unthinking loyalty to the Emperor but also, by extension, the Universal Project, even though collective life remains unredeemed. "Not system," cautions Scholem (in Alter, 1991, p. 86), "but *commentary.*" It is an essentially Hebraic (and also modernist) point of view.

V

Now, surely, there must be some kind of message here for modern-day China as well. The rest of the world stands rapt before the burgeoning nation reborn now with newfound resources and intoxicating powers, its teeming populace and its great expanse. As I write these words, the sprawling city of Beijing, the rest of the planet in its thrall, prepares for its forthcoming Olympics. On the cover of this morning's Sunday edition of the New York Times, I peruse, coincidentally, another meditation upon Chinese architecture and design. In "The Changing Face of Beijing, A Look at the New China," Nicolai Ouroussoff (2008) writes with awe and irony about arrival at what is now the largest airport on earth:

> If Westerners feel dazed and confused upon exiting the plane at the new international airport terminal here, it's understandable. It's not just the grandeur of the space. It's the inescapable feeling that you're passing through a portal to another world, one whose fierce embrace of change has left Western nations in the dust. (p. 1)

Dazed and confused. It is, of course, the contemporary state explored unflaggingly by Kafka. And with Kafka, too, one feels oneself passing, inexorably, through a portal to another world.

Reflecting China's "embrace of the modernist creed," Ouroussoff (2008) notes, also, the majestic new airport's "real precedent" in Albert Speer's (Hitler's chief architect) Tempelhof Airport in Berlin, a monument conceived by the Third Reich as the "gateway to a new Europe." "Both," writes Ouroussoff, "are part of a vision of a mobile society, one that extends back through Grand Central Terminal to the great train halls of Paris" (p. 1). With this harking back to traditions both grand and disarming, we are, here, in today's American newspaper, very close to the spirit of Kafka:

> Guided by twinkling lights embedded in the terminal's ceiling, arriving visitors glide up ramped floors and across broad pedestrian bridges before spilling out onto the elevated concourse. From there they can disperse along a fluid network of roads, trains, subways, canals and parks whose tentacles extend out through the region. (Ouroussoff, 2008, p. 1)

In Kafka's fiction, such movement is relentless, even ominous, yet devoid of ultimate destination or import. (*"There is a destination but no way there,"* Kafka once wrote in his diary; *"what we refer to as way is hesitation."*) For Ouroussoff (2008), too, China's velocity and scope is breathtaking but disconcerting, its future forebodingly uncertain: "Everything is possible here from utopian triumphs of the imagination to soul-sapping expressions of a disregard for individual lives" (p. 14). China, the "great laboratory for architectural ideas," holds within it intimations of "a vast propaganda machine" (Ourossoff, 2008) just as well. Even in the glittering metropolis there are tenements and gaps.

VI

Writing in his diary under an autobiographical group of entries called "He," Kafka (1971, p. ix) contemplates his destiny and craft:

> All that he does seems to him, it is true, extraordinarily new, but also, because of the incredible spate of new things, extraordinarily amateurish, indeed scarcely tolerable, incapable of becoming history, breaking short the chain of the generations, cutting off for the first time at its most profound source the music of the world, which before him could at least be divined. Sometimes in his arrogance he has more anxiety for the world than for himself.

In the modernist/postmodernist world, as R.D. Laing (1962) had informed us, even dissociation becomes part and parcel of normative experience. Looking at himself as if he were another, Kafka dwells here with fear and trembling on his fateful vocation and prophetic role.

In the *Fourth Blue Octavo Notebook*, the seer of Prague (Kafka, 1954/1999) further elaborates his calling and path: "I have not been guided into life by the hand of Christianity, admittedly now slack and failing, as Kierkegaard was, and have not caught the hem of the Jewish prayer shawl, now flying away from us as the Zionists have. I am an end or a beginning" (p. 51). Calasso (2005) elaborates on the universal implications in Kafka, man and woman's tenuous place in the modern-become-postmodernist world—a sphere in which, between private and collective realms, no reliable demarcation any longer inheres:

> With Kafka a phenomenon burst onto the scene; the *commixture.* There is no sordid corner than can't be treated as a vast abstraction, and no vast abstraction than

> can't be treated as a sordid corner. This
> phenomenon isn't a reflection of the
> writer's personal inclinations. It's a matter
> of fact. (p. 22)

This *commixture* of elements is precisely what typifies modernist/postmodernist existence and consciousness—what James, always ahead of his time, had called the "blooming buzzing confusion." "Experience is vague," observes Gavin (1992, p. 29), "in the sense of being richer than any formula." This may be good or bad depending on capacity and moment, but privacy and Cartesian clarity are now things of the past.

VII

In 1922, suffering with tuberculosis and immersed in the writing of his final novel in the Bohemian town of Zurau, Kafka notes in his diary having suffered a nervous breakdown only one week before (Greenberg, 1965). As he ponders his plight, his thoughts turn on two possibilities. First, he imagines, and genuinely fears, that his fanatical inner/modernist "chase" may end in utter isolation or madness. If he is able, however, to "hold up even the littlest bit," letting himself be "borne along by the pursuit," there exists the possibility of a sort of triumphal "assault against the last earthly frontier," a journey through the vagaries of the modern world and jumbled mind to a forbidding yet new horizon:

> All this writing is an assault upon the
> frontiers, and if Zionism hadn't intervened
> might easily have developed into a new
> secret doctrine, a Kabbalah. There are
> beginnings in that direction. Of course, it
> needs an almost inconceivable genius that
> would be able to strike root again in the
> old centuries, or would create the old
> centuries anew without using itself up in
> doing so, but would only then begin to
> flower forth. (Greenberg, 1965, p. 216)

Here we are again. The quest for a new mythology that does not lose itself in political movement ("if Zionism hadn't intervened") on the one hand nor end in dissolution ("without using itself up") or madness on the other. Awe before mysteries both cosmic and terrestrial, the "reinstatement of the vague" (James, 1950, p. 254).

In a world without revelation, redemption may be gleaned through reverie and the alternating receptive/creative spirit. Although modest in decorum almost to a fault, Kafka realized the enormity of what had been lost and the consequent gravity of his task. "Art like prayer," he once told his youthful friend and admirer Gustav Janouch, "is a hand stretched out in the dark seeking to catch something from grace in order to transform itself into a giving hand" (as cited in Bauer, 1999, ¶ 4). The ascendancy of imagination, however fleeting, and the act of a genuinely personal expression (thereby rekindling the possibility of encounter) counterposes even the darkest truths. Dark truths have, in turn, their ennobling aspects simply by virtue of being disclosed: there is truth after all. A *"sense of being,"* teaches May (1983, p. 15), "the ontological sense."

Kafka did consciously seek to write a kind of "new mysticism, a Kabbalah" for a world shorn of moorings and in alarming disarray, doggedly exposing the extreme states of anxiety and confusion, the augmented self-consciousness ("a sensitivity," John Updike notes, "beyond usefulness") that typifies the collective modernist/postmodernist psyche. Janouch (1971/1985) once suggested to him that his oeuvre constituted, perhaps, "a mirror of tomorrow" (p. 150). Upon hearing these words, Kafka covered his ears with both hands, exclaiming, "Please, don't go on." He then continued himself: "You are certainly right. Probably that's why I can't finish anything. I am afraid of the truth . . . One must be silent, if one can't give any help. No one, through his own lack of hope, should make the condition of the patient worse" (p. 150). Max Brod, Kafka's friend and confidante, thankfully disregarded Kafka's deathbed instructions that his unpublished manuscripts be burned after he had passed away. It was a happy instance of disobedience, noted the Argentinean master Jorge Luis Borges, thereby preserving "the most singular works of our century."

VIII

It has been said that in Kafka we witness the seamless merging of reality and dream. The oneiric state is itself a merging of realty with the unencumbered mind. One day, my patient Kristina, a multiple personality, sets down the following dream about alternate/parallel worlds and selves, dissolution of self/world and engulfment by larger bodies and forces— intimations of forthcoming intrapsychic/cataclysmic events, dissociation/escape and resultant macroscopic/global perspectives. Note here, as in Kafka, the Chinese connection and, also, the vagaries of a world in peril without sure beacons to guide our way:

I was living way out in the Far East, in China on an island. I was surrounded by all these people who didn't speak the same language as I did except for one person who acted as my translator and guide. I didn't go anywhere without him because I'd get lost or wouldn't be able to communicate with the people around me. I lived in a house with him and a woman who couldn't speak our language either. She was always sitting on a couch in front of a large picture window watching American television, even though she couldn't understand what was being said. I could never figure out why she liked watching it so much. She was older than the man; her hair was already turning grey.

The house that we lived in was small, and it seemed like we lived at the end of a jetty. Three sides of the house looked out upon the ocean. The side of the house with the picture window looked west, so we always saw the sun setting against the horizon. There was another window that was fairly large, looking out onto the sea.

One day I was sitting with the old woman and the man came in and sat down. He told me that the island was slowly sinking into the ocean and that each day the water came closer and closer to the house. He told me that soon the water would overtake us and the house would be lost to the sea. Eventually the whole island would be buried under the sea. Of course, I was saddened to hear it. It was a beautiful place to live, and I couldn't imagine how we could leave it and travel to another island to live. Days went by and, sure enough, whenever I went to the water's edge, it was closer and closer to my home. If I looked to the west, I could see the horizon, and to the right were enormous cliffs. Maybe we could move there and then we would be safe. The man told me that even these places would eventually be swallowed up. He said we would move to America. I asked him why we had to move so far, and he told me the whole continent would be buried, not just our island.

One day the water reached our steps. It rose and kept on rising. We took everything we had and we moved. We flew to America where we soon settled on the East Coast. We moved into a house right along the water, just as we had in China. Again we lived on a jetty, the water surrounding us on three sides, with one large window looking to the west and the setting sun. I asked the man, still my only companion (for even in America they spoke a language I did not understand), what would happen when the continent drowned. He told me that he did not know, that we would have to wait until it happened to find out. The woman still lived with us, and she still watched television, only now she watched Chinese television! One day the man finally told me that the time had come when the whole continent would be swallowed up. I asked him again what would happen. Surely there would be a massive tidal wave. Would it come all the way to America? Would it swallow us up? Who would survive such a wave? Questions all to which he shrugged his shoulders. We would wait to see.

Then I flew out of my body. At first I hovered over the house and the ocean, and then I hovered over America and then over the whole world. I could see China and

> Europe and Australia and Africa sinking. It happened slowly at first. Then, as the time grew longer and longer, it happened faster and faster. I knew that when everything had disappeared under the waves, the suction of the sinking would cause a disturbance in the sea. Still I was unsure of exactly what it would do. So I just hovered in outer space looking at the world. Then it began. The whole globe started to wobble and ripple and fall in upon itself. I watched horrified above the earth, waiting to see what would happen next. It seemed as if the whole earth would collapse upon itself. I was terrified because I knew it meant I would be dead.

Kristina's dream projects upon a planetary canvas an intrapsychic architecture founded on two interior (*altered*) "worlds" or "houses." Red and blue, blood and tears, action and reaction: an inner sanctuary of makeshift form and "sanity" in the face of overarching chaos from without. As psychotherapy progresses, there is a shift from presenting alters of Kristina's "blue world" of presentation to an earlier "red world" of original pain. Our work together (for, surely, I am the accompanist and guide who has, nonetheless, scant awareness of what exactly happens next) changes qualitatively as primal trauma is encountered face to face. In Kristina's dream, this shift in alters is mirrored in the relocation from China to the States. Insofar, however, as the precariousness of the outer world continues unabated, the dreamer finally leaves her body outright as she hovers now precariously high above the globe. Dissociation, mastered in early childhood, remains the only means of escape. Yet once the body is abandoned absolutely (just as the nations of the world now abandon Mother Earth), there is no place left to go. All that remains is an apocalyptic flood.

IX

Louis Sass (1992), in his erudite book *Madness and Modernism*, explores the manner in which modern forms of insanity appear to be epiphenomena (a sensitivity beyond usefulness) of the manifold complexities associated with modern-day existence itself. Mostly, it would seem, there is a retreat from a world of exponentially increasing cacophonies and crosscurrents into a solace afforded by the hypertrophied head. In the *Third Blue Octavo Notebook,* Kafka (1991) writes:

> In one and the same human being there are cognitions that, however utterly dissimilar they are, yet have one and the same object, so that one can only conclude that there are different subjects in one and the same human being. (p. 34)

And concerning, specifically, the theological connection, Kafka (in Smith, 2008) observes:

> With their posterior legs they were still glued to their father's Jewishness, and with their waving anterior legs they found no new ground. (p. 17)

Here again, the loss of tradition and, as in our dream, the impossibility of effectively moving on. Kabbalah, it is interesting to note, means, literally, "oral received tradition." And, so, the complexities not only of the ambiguous postmodernist world but also of the polymorphous postmodernist self.

X

Yet if revelation is no longer within reach, what then remains? During those contemplative days at Zurau, Kafka (2006) reflects on the possibilities inherent in Exile:

> The Expulsion from Paradise is eternal in its principal aspect; this makes it irrevocable, and our living in the world inevitable, but the eternal nature of the process has the effect that not only could we remain forever in Paradise, but that we are currently there, whether we know it or not. (p. 65)

We are reminded here of Dostoyevsky's observation that we are all happy if we but knew it. Perhaps a Golden Age of perfection is unnecessary. Perhaps it is possible to momentarily rise above what cannot in any case be repaired, finding nobility of spirit, even fleeting triumph, in presence and awareness. Kafka (1954/1999), indeed, seems quite intoxicated with this idea:

> Beyond a certain point there is no return. This point has to be reached.
> The decisive moment in human evolution is perpetual. That is why the revolutionary spiritual movements that declare all former things worthless are in the right, for nothing has yet happened. (p. 16)

And once again:

> There are two cardinal human vices, from which all the others derive their being: impatience and carelessness. Impatience got people evicted from Paradise; carelessness kept them from making their way back there. Or perhaps there is only one cardinal vice: impatience: Impatience got people evicted, and impatience kept them from making their way back. (Kafka, 2006, p. 15)

Even "psychology," suggests Kafka (1954/1999) provocatively, "is hesitation" (p. 15). Perhaps, in other words, we have already what we need.

XI

One day Janouch brought Kafka a German translation of the *Tao te Ching* popular among mystically inclined westerners at the time. Kafka, familiar with Lao-Tzu's little wisdom book, and contemplating the epigrams within its pages, cautioned the youth still in search of methodology:

'They spell out—as you can see here—transcriptions of reality from translations of ancient Chinese instead of quietly reading the original text of their own lives and responsibilities. To them the day before yesterday seems more accessible than today. But reality is never and nowhere more accessible than in the immediate moment of one's own life . . . All it guarantees us is what is superficial, the façade . . . [O]ne must break through this. Then everything becomes clear.'

'But how does one do that? How does one proceed? Is there some sure guide?'

'No, there is none,' said Kafka, shaking his head. 'There is no route map on the way to truth. The only thing that counts is to make the venture of total dedication. A prescription would already imply a withdrawal, mistrust, and therewith the beginning of a false path. One must accept everything patiently and fearlessly. Man is condemned to life, not death.' (Janouch, 1985, p. 156)

The immediacy, again, of experience in lieu of traditional comforts afforded once in another time. Kafka's sensibility is, in fact, exceedingly close here to the essence of Taoism, with which he acknowledged being involved "quite deeply and for a long time" (Bauer, 1999, ¶ 5). So much so that the Bulgarian-Jewish novelist Elias Canetti (1974) once cited Kafka as "the only writer of the Western world who is essentially Chinese" (as cited in Bauer, 1999, ¶ 5). "Knowledge we *have*," muses Kafka (1954/1999) in the *Third Octavo Notebook;* "Anyone who strives for it with particular intensity is suspect of striving against it" (p. 39). Experience no longer mediated by arbiters of the past but written, as we read in Jeremiah (17:1), "upon the tables of [one's] heart." "*New* . . . insights and possibilities," states May, (1991. p. 86); the ineffable and numinous NOW.

In the *Fourth Octavo Notebook,* Kafka (1954/1999) returns again to the place of reverie in a world of exile:

> Contemplation and activity have their apparent truth; but only the activity radiated by contemplation, or rather, that which returns to it again, is truth. (p. 49)

> There is no need for you to leave the house. Stay at your table and listen. Don't even listen, just wait. Don't even wait, be completely quiet and alone. The world will offer itself to you to be unmasked; it can't do otherwise; in raptures it will writhe before you. (p. 54)

The consolations and, yes, even possibilities, of a world without revelation or gods. "Vagueness," elaborates Gavin (1992) in his excellent book on James, "is not, ontologically speaking, a fall from grace" (p. 179). The secret lies in *attentiveness*, "the natural prayer of the soul" (Benjamin, 1965, p. 134).

And, so, the Great Wall of China will never be complete, just as the Law will never be fully rendered and the Castle walls never breached. Still, there is something holy in it all for the attentive spirit and inspired mind. A secret doctrine, a Kabbalah. Modernist/postmodernist epiphany in a world without final directives and forms. There is great joy at last in Kafka. The exquisite ecstasy of writing, a concomitant tribulation notwithstanding, is always in evidence just beneath the surface. This new kind of writing with its message of opacity could never have taken root in more coherent times. Kafka's graceful "posture of doubt," reflects Irving Howe (in Kafka, 1930/1992), amid "the vast indifference of the cosmos" (p. xviii). "A word, a glance, a sign of trust," (p. 262) says an official named Burgel in Kafka's final novel. Mysterious yet moving, even hallowed, words.

XII

It is a unique admixture of horror, grace and courage that allows Kafka to gaze unblinkingly into the Void while succumbing to neither System Replacement nor Nothingness. We find no comforting philosophy in Kafka. What we find, paradoxically, is something both more and less: awareness and the inspired act of creation out of notable decay. Kafka in "his twenty-first-century aspect," states Smith (2008, p. 17), becomes an "existential prophet" for each one of us, as sinking into the warm bed of the past becomes a quaint yet no longer realistic thought. "These days," Smith (2008) notes, "we all find our anterior legs flailing before us." Kafka's message, though never wholly spelled out (it becomes, paradoxically, more difficult to fathom as it is expressed with increasing precision) and (like the myriad villagers of China) interpreted differently by each one who comes to him, seems all the more profound all the same. Wagner (2007) has, perhaps, stated it as well as anyone:

> And the outcome? Instead of directing his readers to this or that country on the ideological map . . , Kafka offers them another attitude toward the complexity of modern knowledge, a new economy of knowing, based on a way of reading his stories: like the Chinese architect, readers are invited to travel through them, across new provinces of knowledge, feeling the risk of the journey and noting the importance of small differences and, occasionally, of laughter, against the backdrop of an age of violent uniformity. (pp. 320-321)

"Only by abandoning all pretended 'groundings,'" Bauer (1999) adds, "can one attain the freedom out of which authentic existence gives itself a finite meaning" (¶ 8). Reverie in place of revelation. "The world will not yield to lucidity," observes Howe in his fine essay on Kafka, yet we may find there a kind of metaphysical sublimity nonetheless. "The poignancy of the transient" (in May, 1991, p. 294); a sense of being, the ontological sense.

And only now can we more nearly grasp the observant, indeed worshipful, manner in which Kafka (1949/1988) approached his sacred craft:

> The strange, mysterious, perhaps dangerous, perhaps saving comfort that there is in writing: it is a leap out of murderers' row; it is a seeing of what is really taking place. This occurs by a higher type of observation, a higher, not a keener

> type, and the higher it is and the less within reach of the "row," the more independent it becomes, the more obedient to its own law of motion, the more incalculable, the more joyful, the more ascendant in its course. (p. 423)

The modernist scribe, was, after all, setting down a new mysticism, a Kabbalah, as recompense for a liturgy lost and had, as a consequence, a message at once hallowed and, in a sense, strangely simple to convey.

The Great Wall of China. A new age of radical ambiguity, manifold gaps, and the gathering storm. This storm is what we call progress.

References

Alter, R. (1991). *Necessary angels: Tradition and modernity in Kafka, Benjamin, and Scholem.* Cambridge, MA: Harvard University Press.

Bauer, J. E. (1999). *Franz Kafka: Power, religious minorities and the inception of existence.* Paper presented at the CESNUR International Conference, Bryn Athyn College, Bryn Athyn, PA.

Benjamin, W. (1969). *Illuminations: Essays and reflections* (H. Arendt, Ed.; H. Zohn, Trans.). New York: Schocken Books.

Calasso, R. (2005). *K* (G. Brock, Trans.). New York: Alfred A. Knopf.

Canetti, E. (1974) *Kafka's other trial: The letters to Felice* (C. Middleton, Trans.) New York: Schocken Books.

Citati, P. (1990). *Kafka* (R. Rosenthal, Trans.). New York: Alfred A. Knopf.

Deleuze, G. & Guattari, F. (1986). *Kafka: Toward a minor literature* (D. Polan, Trans.). Minneapolis: University of Minnesota Press.

Janouch, G. (1985). *Conversations with Kafka* (G. Rees, Trans.) London: Quartet Books.

Gavin, W. J. (1992). *William James and the reinstatement of the vague.* Philadelphia: Temple University Press.

Greenberg, M. (1965). *Kafka: The terror of art.* New York: Horizon Press.

James, W. (1950). *The principles of psychology* (Vol. 1). New York: Dover Publications.

James, W. (1961). *Psychology: The briefer course* (G. Allport, Ed.). New York: Harper Torchbooks.

Kafka, F. (1992). *The castle* ((W. Muir & E. Muir, Trans.). New York: Everyman's Library. (Original work published in 1930)

Kafka, F. (1988). *The diaries of Franz Kafka.* New York: Schoken Books. (Original work published in 1949)

Kafka, F. (1999). *The blue octavo notebooks* (E. Kaiser and E. Wilkins, trans.). Cambridge, UK: Exact Change. (Original work published in 1954)

Kafka, F. (1971). *The complete stories* (N. Glatzer, Trans.). New York: Schocken Books.

Kafka, F. (2006). *The Zurau aphorisms* (M. Hoffman, Trans). New York: Schocken Books.

Kafka, F. (2007). "Building the great wall of china." In *Kafka's selected stories*. (S. Corngold, Ed. & Trans.;   pp. 113-124). New York: W. W. Norton & Company.

Kundera, M. (1986). *The art of the novel* (L. Asher, Trans.). New York: Harper & Row.

Laing, R.D. (1962). *The divided self.* New York: Pantheon Books.

May, R. (1983). *The discovery of being.* New York: Norton and Company.

May, R. (1992). *The cry for myth* New York: Norton and Company.

Mendelowitz, E. (2008). *Ethics and Lao-tzu: Intimations of character.* Colorado Springs, CO: University of the Rockies Press.

Ouroussoff, N. (2008). The Changing Face of Beijing, A Look at the New China. In *The New York Times,* 7/13/08.

Sass, L. (1992). *Madness and modernism.* Cambridge, MA: Harvard University Press.

Smith, Z. (2008). "F. Kafka, everyman." In *New York Review of Books,* LV:12, 14-17.

Wagner, B. (2007). No one indicates the direction: The question of leadership in Kafka's later stories. In *Kafka's selected stories* (S. Corngold, Ed. & Trans.; pp. 302-321). New York: Norton & Company.

19

Kisagotami, Buddha, and Mustard Seeds:
An Existential Psychological Perspective

Francis J. Kaklauskas
Elizabeth A. Olson

Dew world
It is a dew world
It is what it is
~ Issa Kobayashi [1]

As interest in Eastern thought continues to increase in Western societies, psychologists and psychology students in India, China, Japan, and other Asian countries are rigorously studying the history and methods of the Western tradition as the use of psychotherapeutic interventions is rapidly expanding there. This cross cultural dialogue is becoming more frequent and lively as clinicians and researchers travel more regularly between cultures. Curiosity and dynamism continue to hold off the dogmatism that can be present in both traditions, and due to their open-mindedness, Western existential psychology and Eastern Buddhism seem to be at the forefront of this exchange.

In fact, many of the fundamental questions and conclusions of existentialism and Buddhism are analogous. While both traditions value rigorous scientific and philosophical examination, both also use the creative arts and narratives to go beyond reductionist paradigms and engage multiple ways of knowing. This chapter recalls some common stories about Siddhartha Gautama, the Buddha, to highlight these similarities and to consider their implications for the practice of psychology and psychotherapy. While some fundamentalist Buddhist scholars

---

[1] This was written after the death of his two year old daughter. The dew reflects the water covering the grass and vegetation in the morning, the sadness in his heart, and the inevitability and acceptance of death and suffering, all interconnecting in one personal phenomenological moment. Translated by Francis Kaklauskas, 1988.

prescribe to singular interpretations, or even a literal understanding of these stories, the vast majority of teachers and scholars encourage students to contemplate their meaning not only intellectually, but personally. In fact, the historical information about the actual life of the Buddha, similar to that regarding the life of Christ, was not codified until after his death. The earliest biographies of the Buddha were written more than five hundred years after his death and most stories have multiple versions, each of which has been influenced by the culture, historical background, and the interests of the writer.

One of the best examples is the multiple versions of a story of Kisagotami. Depending upon the source, Kisagotami can be described as tall, thin, restrained, and unattractive (Hecker, 1982), or pretty, well-spoken, and a cousin of the Buddha (Tisdale, 2006). While these details may carry important information for cultural studies scholars, from a general existential perspective, and particularly for the purpose of this chapter, they are tertiary, as the poignancy of the story transcends these demographic variables. The following summary is drawn from multiple sources in order to capture the essence of the existential messages of the story with particular emphasis placed on the translations from the earliest Pali version (Bhushan, 2008; Gyasto, 1992; Hecker, 1982; Lillie, 1881; Murcott, 2006; Nikaya, 1930; Therigatha, 1883; Tisdale, 2006; Udana, 1948; Weeraperuma, 2006).

Kisagotami

Kisagotami was from a poor family and, given the culture of ancient India, she was expected to marry and to have children. After several false starts, and despite her lessening hopes, she eventually married a man from a wealthier class. When she had difficulty bearing a child, her in-laws began planning for their son to find a new bride. Unexpectedly, Kisagotami became pregnant and had a son. She loved her son very much and her wealthy husband and in-laws became supportive. She was relieved, knowing she had secured a financially sound future for both her son and herself.

When her son died unexpectedly in his sleep, Kisagotami was inconsolable. She carried his corpse from home to home asking for a medicine to revive her son. She was eventually directed to the Buddha. By the time she met the Buddha in the forest, she was exhausted, dirty, and becoming physically ill herself. Her son's body was decaying badly with maggots running across his flesh. When she approached the Buddha, she told him that she had heard that he was a very special healer and would he cure her son.

Observing the situation, the Buddha told her to put her son down and he would watch after him. He then instructed her to collect just a small amount of mustard seed from the homes in her village that had not had a death. Kisagotami set off to her village. She thought that because mustard seed is such a common spice that the task of collecting a few seeds would not be difficult.

When she came to the first house, she asked if she could have a few mustard seeds and she was quickly given a few seeds. Then Kisagotami asked whether anyone had died in their home? She was told that the family's father had died in the home just four months ago. Leaving the seeds behind, Kisagotami rushed off to the next home.

In home after home she was told of the parents, the sons and daughters, and the friends who had died in each home. Some had died by falling from a tree or a roof, some from animal attacks or other wounds, others from malnutrition, one from suicide, and still others for reasons no one could name. Everywhere she went she discovered the experience of death. Not only the death of the elderly, but the loss of adults in their prime, children, infants, mothers, fathers, daughters, and sons. Everywhere she went she heard stories of death and grief.

Even before she had finished visiting every home in her village, she returned to the Buddha. She reported that she had been selfish in her grief, that the living are few and the dead many. She brought her dead son to the carnal ground, buried him, and said good-bye. She stood above his grave and said the universal law for all things is impermanence. Change. She then returned to the Buddha and renounced her former life with her husband and in-laws.

Her grief further lifted when she heard the Buddha say that the person who lives one hundred years and does not understand the realities of human existence would be better to have lived just one day and beheld the truths. Kisagotami lived the remainder of her long life as a renowned, compassionate nun.

Existential and Buddhist Themes

The story of Kisagotami is, in many ways, a perfect existential myth. The story is simple, yet leads one to consider many of life's most difficult challenges. The story also outlines many of the existential givens as understood from the Buddhist perspective. Although this story is set over

2,500 years ago and comes from Pali texts of the first century, Kisogotmi's grief, insight, and journey are universal.

Suffering

Buddha's first teaching was on suffering, pain, or *duhkha* (sanskrit). This is the first noble truth: Pain is the unavoidable companion of existence. Not only is suffering reliable, but it comes in an unlimited variety of flavors. Kisogotami experienced many types of suffering. Prior to marrying, she experienced anxiety about her future, class discrimination, and cultural expectations dictated by her gender. During her marriage, she experienced the pain of being negatively judged by her in-laws and the despair of possibly being infertile. As a mother, she experienced perhaps the greatest suffering one can know, the death of a child, and the resultant despair, confusion, grief, and existential angst.

In many Buddhist traditions, this existential suffering, or all pervading pain of separation, loneliness, and dissatisfaction, is stressed (Trungpa, 1976). On a cognitive level, one is inevitably uncomfortable with the understanding that life can be difficult, complex, unpredictable, and finite. On a physiological, emotional, and spiritual level, existence can feel similar to anxiety; the bubbles of disappointment inevitably rising up to the surface. From both existential and Buddhist psychological perspectives, this experience of dukkha is the uncomfortable foundation of human experience that we defend against and push away. As a consequence of this experience, we can negatively judge both ourselves and our environments as the cause of our suffering, as opposed to directly accepting the inevitability of this experience.

Impermanence

The story of Kisagotami is filled with change. She experiences the great joy of motherhood and the deep despair of grief. But even the depth of her grief is not permanent. Her understanding, acceptance, and adaptation to the realties of life are, moreover, also not permanent. She lived, and like everyone else, she died. Her life, her form, arose and dissipated, leaving only this brief story for the living to consider. Furthermore, for the Buddhist, like the existentialist, the knowledge of the shortness of our lives and the knowledge that our death will come unexpectedly lead to questions concerning life's meaning and our free will (Gyatso, 1984). Kisagotmi chooses a life of spiritual engagement rather than returning to a life designed to meet the expectations of her culture.

In the Buddhist traditions, the truth of impermanence directly flows into the idea of egolessness or no self. On a relative level, this concept is easy to digest. Even if we have the same job, home, and community, each day we are, in at least some minor way, different than the day before.

On an absolute level, the self is only an inaccurate construction of reality. In fact, all people and things are dependent upon a limitless network of factors. We only exist because our parents existed, because we have air and food, and because we have an earth to live on. The progressive meditation on this topic asks one to contemplate if any part of us represents a continuous enduring self. If we lose a limb or our sight, if we lose our memory or our minds, are we still the same? If we lose our skin, which creates the visual illusion of separateness, are we still a discrete self? If we get an artificial heart, does our essence of selfhood continue? From the Buddhist view, since no singular part cannot be removed, the self has no essence. From the existential psychology perspective the questions of the self have no dogmatic answer and should be examined not only from a theoretical perspective, but also on a personal level. Everyone should consider one's existence, who they are, and what they believe to be real as part of the journey towards understanding and freedom (May, 1966).

Phenomenological Consideration

Phenomenology comes from the Greek word meaning "that which appears" (Smith, 2007). In the West, questions about the nature of existence, what is real, and the interplay of the mind and the world are generally the pursuit of academic philosophers, neurologists, and physicists. In Buddhism, however, the examination of such questions is encouraged for everyone. Through meditative practices, philosophical discourses, and myths and stories, one thoroughly absorbs the complexity of these perhaps unknowable questions, and becomes comfortable living in a world that is beyond our understanding

If, as Heidegger (1927) asserts, methodology creates phenomenology, in the West the majority of phenomenological explorations are focused on a kind of rationalism. Although Buddhism has a rationalistic and reductionist tradition that at least equals that of Western philosophy (e.g. Nagarjuna, Yogacara), this element has been balanced by the various meditation and yoga practices. The Western dilemmas of subject/object and existential/theoretical have been the common focus of meditative contemplation for thousands of years. The limitation of rationalism and the wisdom of experience were originally addressed and abandoned by Western scholars. William Wundt and his students tried to journal the experience of consciousness and address the emerging subject-object dyad, but it was felt, given the limits of methodology and scientific instrumentation, that this pursuit was best suited for later psychologists (Hunt, 1994).

Phenomenological philosopher Edward Husserl imagined a philosophy not estranged from everyday life and one that incorporates the existential experience of each person (Rollinger, 2008). He sought to understand consciousness not through theoretical reduction, but rather through suspension of judgments. His pursuit of this state of existential consciousness beyond one's thinking was mocked by his contemporaries, including his student Heidegger. Husserl's pursuit has similarities to the Buddhist view and the meditation experience. But without the support of his culture and an experienced guide, he abandoned this pursuit, but retained the experience of consciousness as a core part of the self.

From the existential and Buddhist philosophical perspectives, a quality of skepticism is essential. In fact, much of psychotherapeutic theory embraces a stance of skepticism for both the clients and the clinicians. Whether one seeks to reveal the unconscious motivation of psychodynamic insight or to correct distorted cognitions, acknowledging that one not may be accurately understanding oneself and the world is a prerequisite for change and growth.

While the Buddhist traditions, particularly Zen, offer stories of immediate enlightenment, such epiphanies may be more the result of an accumulation of experience than an immediate transformation. As seen with Kisagotami, the need to experience grief is necessary to understand and to have compassion for others.

Ambiguity

From a Judeo-Christian point of view, Kisagotami and her son's souls would be everlasting, and depending upon the interpretation of different sects, they may be in hell, purgatory, or heaven. The Buddha, after trying the various Vedic experiential practices and logical arguments of his culture and time, felt that such metaphysical questions could not be answered with certitude. Life must be lived with this ambiguity and tension. The Buddha, however, prompted his followers to consider such questions for themselves and to believe nothing that does not seem to be in accord with common sense and experience. Given such freedom, various Buddhist sects have promoted different tenants. Many Tibetan Buddhists believe in reincarnation, while other Buddhist schools renounce such ideas as unknowable or unimportant (de Bary, 1972). This Buddhist ideal of independent thought has also allowed some of the Judeo-Christian faithful and even atheists to incorporate Buddhist principles that match their own experiences. In both Buddhism and existential thought, dogmatism is scorned in favor of individual exploration and experience.

Aloneness

From a phenomenological perspective, one's experience of one's life is unique, subjective, and beyond communication. Aloneness is not being without others, but the realization that although we can communicate well, have similar experiences, and have feelings of intimacy and closeness, the phenomenological experience of separateness endures. While Hinduism, Sufism, and even Buddhism promise glimpses of holism in which we transcend the subjective self, the fundamental and relative psychological aloneness returns. To deny this experience is to deny the reality of our lives, and this is as ridiculous as denying our deaths.

While Kisogotami undoubtedly received solace from sharing her grief with others, her grief remained her grief. Not even the experience of her husband or that of other mothers who had lost children can be the same. In the retelling of her story, one can see the struggle against this experience of aloneness. The methods of escape for her are no different than the methods used today. Marriage, children, community, and spiritual exploration can help us feel less lonely, but none can change the fact of our fundamental aloneness.

In both approaches, the path leads to a realization and acceptance of this human predicament. Like all existential and Buddhist givens, only through acknowledgment is there a hope for increased freedom. We are no longer stuck endlessly pursuing escapes from the prison of aloneness, but connect to the world and others more authentically from this experience. Krishnamurti lived a life that seemed to embody this view. While his ideas are similar to those found in both Buddhism and existentialism, he felt that his ideas, that each of our ideas, transcend the reductionism of labels and are, therefore, solely personal (Krishnamurti, 2004). He states,

> on the journey of life and death, you must walk alone; on this journey there can be no taking of comfort in knowledge, in experience, in memories. The mind must be purged of all the things it has gathered in its urge to be secure... There must be complete, uncontaminated aloneness. (p. 95)

Compassion

As Kisagotami's story unfolds, her compassion for others increases. While much of Buddhism strives to be non-metaphysical, the concept of compassion is an exception. Buddha, and most contemporary forms of Buddhism, understands compassion as the base of human experience. One does not develop compassion, but rather one works through obstacles to compassion. Kisagotimi comes to realize that her focus on her own grief limited her openness to the suffering of others. From both Buddhist and Western psychological perspectives, compassion can be seen as a measure of psychological maturity (Gilighan 1982; Kolhberg, 1981), and also a core human competency (Frankl, 1969; May, 1995).

Nietzsche, upon witnessing a horse being beaten by its master, realized the supreme harshness of the world and was inspired to search for an ethics and ontology that might account for this cruelty (Pearson, 1997). His interpretation, later found in the drive theory of Freud (1923), is that aggression is close to the human soul. Klein (1975) moved this aggression into a frustrated relational drive, while other theorists have abandoned this idea in favor of the ideas of self actualization (Adler, 1929), meaning (Frankl, 1969), or integration (Schneider, 2007) that might also make sense of our experiences. Regardless of how one understands human biological instincts, it is easy to see the external manifestation of multiple beliefs. These theories can be extremely helpful in psychotherapy and in the creation of personal meaning, if tempered. However, the leap from behavior to the latent construct of a specific drive remains filled with holes and cannot be at this time proven.

The concepts of compassion and altruism have gained some support. Both animal and human studies have or demonstrated altruistic and caring behavior (Baron & Burn, 2008). The experience of trauma stirs the heart to help others who are suffering (Batson, 1997), much like Kisogotami was moved to help others after her trauma and hearing of the traumas of others. The scientific case, however, for either aggression empathy/compassion as the core human instinct appears weak. One's personal experience, however, appears to be strongly linked with both the increase of aggressive behavior (Zimbardo, 2007) and compassionate behavior (Schore, 2003). While the Buddhists argue that through meditation and contemplation one comes to understand the encompassing power of compassion, it remains impossible to determine if this understanding is the consequence of uncovering a foundational universal principle or the result of having practiced a specific course of behavior. As

Heidegger (1927) concluded, "phenomenology is primarily a certain conception of method" (p. 27). If one practices meditations on compassion one is apt to feel more compassionate, if one is surrounded by propaganda and authoritarian rule, one can without difficulty become a murderer (Zimbardo, 2007).

Journey

The Zen teacher Shunyra Suzuki (1973) stressed that while philosophical understanding is good, experience is more important. While philosophical discourse sets forth logical arguments, the personal is often discounted. The personal and the theoretical, and the subject and object examination, can never be fully discrete and never fully explanatory without the other. Buddhist and existential writers have attempted to combine these dualities. The narrative and phenomenological journey is valued and given importance as an essential way of knowing. The core teachings of both traditions repeatedly use myth to help guide the reader or listener to a personal experience of a philosophical message.

The Buddha went through a series of life events that formed the basis of his philosophy. As a young son of a wealthy and over protected father, he was shielded against the painful reality of existence. He eventually snuck away from the grounds of his father's estate. On this journey he encountered individuals that were old, sick, dying, and dead. These experiences became the root of his teaching of suffering. The Buddha then encountered a yogi who was seeking to understand and transcend the suffering in the world. This became Buddha's path as this experience instilled both hope and a life mission in the young Buddha. He left his father's estate and sought the instructions of yogis, philosophers, and spiritual teachers. After years of rigorous training, he became learned and skilled at a variety of spiritual systems and practices, but remained insatiate. He set forth to discover his own path and truths.

Many of the great works of existentialism employ a similar narrative teaching methodology. Nietzsche's (1909/2005) Zarathustra, Camus' (1942/1989) stranger, Satre's (1947/1992) Mathieu, and a multitude of Kafka characters go through a series of events that inform their philosophies and behavior. This view of the journey is particularly important to the practice of psychotherapy. As the client and clinician review a client's experiences, new meanings and new ways of being emerge. The goal of existential and Buddhist influenced psychotherapy does not have predetermined destination. While valuing symptom reduction, both clinician and client must go beyond in search of meaning and purposeful action.

Prajna

In Buddhism, Prajna is the blending of compassion and skillful means. While stories of circuitous teaching methods that shock students into enlightenment abound in the Chinese, Tibetan, and Japanese traditions, the Buddha himself is generally understood to have been more direct and less dramatic. In fact, his choice to have Kisogotami search for mustard seeds is not typical of most of his instructions. However, as the story unfolds, this request was perhaps the wisest method. If Buddha had attempted to rationally explain the truths of existence as he understood them to her in her fragile state, the philosophical explanations would have been of little help. Through her search, she learned of the losses of others, released some of the pain of her own loss, and over time made meaning of her son's death.

This journey can be seen as having implications for the practice of therapy. In the legends of the Buddha, we encounter a master who offers various responses depending upon the individual and the circumstances. His approach to personal interactions is not unlike the use of ideographic case conceptualization and treatment planning. In the story of Kisogotami, she embarks on a journey that is filled with empirically supported therapeutic process factors. She catharts about her loss, connects with others, engages in exercise, has a definite goal and course of action, has insight, and uses language and cognition to integrate her experience into new learning.

Dynamism, Not Dogmatism

The fundamental questions asked by both Buddhism and existentialism are the timeless ones. What is reality? Who am I? What does it mean to exist? How should I act? While some traditions prescribe a codified belief system to address these questions which may reduce one's anxiety, the nobler goal is to practice living with these questions. When asked what Buddhism should do if science showed that some aspect of Buddhism was inaccurate, the Dalai Lama responded that if that were the case, Buddhism would have to change (Gyatso, 2005). The Dalai Lama continues to provide an excellent example of a multi-methodological approach towards finding truth. His explorations of Western philosophy, physics, neuroscience, and art suggest a desire to understand reality from multiple diverse cultures and systems.

The same is true for psychological science. The incorporation of multiple data streams allows for the most accurate understanding. Quantitative outcome research should be respected and employed, but balanced against the importance of qualitative depth, an increased focus on process and ideographic research, findings in other fields, personal and mythic narratives, and an openness to new ideas. Through integration, interrogation of previously held beliefs, and new discoveries, psychology moves closer to understanding the complexity of the world and the human psyche. The destination will continue to move and may never be reached, but day trips and bush-whacking should show us new ground and methods from which to redraw our maps.

Conclusions

Buddhism and existential psychology are truly compatible. The goals of understanding the world, acting in a meaningful manner, and reducing human and nonhuman suffering are ethical pursuits for this new millennium (Gyatso, 1999). Despite the variables of time and culture, the methodological approaches and resultant findings are shockingly similar and scientifically comforting. While an argument could be made that Buddha was an existentialist, he also could be seen as a scientist of the mind, a spiritual seeker, and by most accounts a hesitant teacher. The hope in this chapter is that through the stories and comparisons, the reader will become inspired to pursue their own journeys towards understanding and to seriously consider the ideas emerging from this and other cross cultural dialogues.

References

Adler, A. (1929). *The practice and theory of individual psychology.* New York: Harcourt, Brace & World.

Bhushan, N. (2008). Toward an Anatomy of Mourning: Discipline, devotion and liberation in a Freudian-Buddhist framework. *Sophia 47*(1), 7-69.

Camus, A. (1989). *The stranger.* (M. Ward, Trans.) New York: Vintage. (Original work published in 1942)

de Bary, W. T. (1972). *The Buddhist tradition in India, China, and Japan.* New York: Vintage.

Frankl, V. (1969). *The will to meaning.* Cleveland: World.

Freud, S. (1923). *Introductory lectures on psycho-analysis.* (J. Riviera, Trans.) London: Allen & Unwin.

Gilligan C. (1982). *In a different voice: Psychological theory and women's development*. Cambridge MA: Harvard University.

Gyatso, T. (1992). Introduction to Buddhism: An explanation of the Buddhist way of life. London: Tharpa Publications.

Gyatso, T. (1999). *Ethics for a new millennium*. New York: Riverhead.

Gyatso, T. (2005). *The universe in a single atom*. New York: Morgan Road.

Hecker, H. (1982). *Buddhist Women at the Time of the Buddha*. (S. Khema, Trans.) Buddhist Publication Society: Sri Lanka.

Heidegger, M. (1927). *Being and time*. (J. Stambaugh, Trans.) New York: SUNY.

Hunt, M. (1994). *The story of psychology*. Landover Hills, MD: Anchor.

Kafka, F. (1971). *The Complete Stories*. (ed. N. Glatzer) New York: Schocken Books.

Klein, M. (1975). *The writings of Melanie Klein*. London: Hogarth.

Kohlberg, L. (1981). *The philosophy of moral development*. New York: Harper & Row.

Krishnamurti, J. (2004) *On living and dying*. Sandpoint, ID: Morning Light.

Lillie, A. (1881) *Buddha and early Buddhism*. London: Trubner.

May, R. (1995). *The discovery of being*. Bel Air, CA: Peter Smith.

Murcott, S. (2006). *First Buddhist Women: Poems and Stories of Awakening*. Berkeley; Parallax Press.

Nietzsche, F. (2005). *Thus spoke Zarathustra*. (G. Parkes, Trans.) Oxford: Oxford Press. (Original work published in 1909)

Samyutta Nikaya. (1930). Translated by A. F. Rhys Davids & F. L. Woodward. London: Pali Text Society.

Pearson, A. (1997). *Viroid life: Perspectives on Nietzsche and the transhuman condition*. New York: Routledge.

Rollinger, R. D. (2008). *Austrian Phenomenology: Brentano, Husserl, Meinong, and Others on Mind and Language*. Frankfurt am Main: Ontos-Verlag.

Sartre. J. (1992). *The revival*. (E. Sutton, Trans.). New York: Vintage. (Original work published 1947)

Schneider, K. J. (Ed.). (2007). *Existential-integrative psychotherapy: Guideposts to the core of practice*. New York: Routledge.

Smith, D. W. (2007). *Husserl*. London: Routledge.

Suzuki, S. (1973). *Zen mind, beginner's mind*. Boston: Weatherhill.

Therigatha. (1883). Edited by H. Oidenberg and R. Pischer. London: Pali Text Society.

Tisdale, S. (2006). *Women of the way: Discovering 2,500 years of Buddhist wisdom*. New York: Harper Collins.

Trungpa, C. (1976). *The myth of freedom*. Boston: Shambhala.

Udana. (1948). (Edited by P. Steithal). London: Pali Text Society.

Weeraperuma, S. (2006). *The first and best Buddhist teachings: Sutta Nipata selections and inspired writings*. New Delhi: New Age.

Zimbardo, P.G. (2007). *The Lucifer effect: Understanding how good people turn evil*. New York: Random House.

Junkanoo: A Bahamian Cultural Myth

Heatherlyn Cleare-Hoffman

> History and culture are inseparable twins. The former conveys to a people a sense of where they have been, and the latter conveys a sense of where they are. If this concept is accepted, it can also be said that the history and culture of any people are essential to their holistic development.
>
> ~ McCartney, 2004, pp. 1-2

After months of preparation, the day before Junkanoo, Christmas Day, arrives in the Bahamas. The Junkanoo groups have been preparing since the day after the last Junkanoo drum sounded from the previous year's celebration. Families across the Bahamas celebrate Christmas in its usual fashion: church, gifts, food, and time with family. In the early evening, they take naps in preparation for the evening excitement. As it turns from Christmas night to Boxing Day, people begin to venture downtown for the festival.

At 2:00 AM, the first sounds emerge from the darkness. Hearts beat faster in rhythm with the drums. Anticipation builds as the sounds of the horns and cowbells soon follow. As the energy nears its height, bodies move to the rhythms and the dazzling colors start to peer through the night. A banner introduces the first Junkanoo group. With sight of the group's leader, the crowds come alive with cheers that fill the islands. The bright, vibrant cardboard costumes adorned with glitter, bright beads, and feathers fill the night with color.

Each of the four main groups – Roots, the Valley Boys, the Saxons, and the Music Makers – have more than 100 members and their own chant. As these groups near, their fans sound off their chant: Roots! Roots! The Valley! The Valley! Saxons! The chants dance through the night air with the music, coming together as one. The competition between groups is fierce, and tensions run high as dawn settles in. Later into the morning, the winners are announced to the frustration and celebration of the crowd. For winning groups, they now have a day to revel in their victory before putting on the final touches for the New Year's Day celebration.

Bahamian Culture

Long before Columbus arrived in the Bahamas, native tribes, such as the Lucayan Indians, thrived in the Bahamas. Although the Lucayans had a rich culture and societal structure, they were not technologically advanced. Various hardships that came with the Europeans caused the indigenous tribes in the Bahamas to become virtually extinct.

The islands were eventually settled by the British who imported many African slaves. Slavery continued in the Bahamas until 1838, when the slaves were finally set free. The Bahamas, however, remained a British colony. On July 10, 1973, the Bahamas gained its independence from Great Britain and became a culture predominantly of African decent. Despite the predominantly African heritage, the British influence remained strong, particularly in regards to religion. Today, the Bahamas is largely a Christian nation.

Although Bahamians of African decent share the history of being brought to the West Indies through the slave trade, there is a significant difference between Bahamian culture and African American culture. While African Americans have been a minority in the United States, those of African decent have been the culture of majority in the Bahamas, and have not been subjected to the same extensive history of oppression that African Americans have had to endure.

Bahamian culture is rich in tradition, which is a mixture of African and British influence combined with new Bahamian traditions (McCarthy, 2004). Religion has also been a central influence in the development of Bahamian culture. Early on, the British Anglican influence was the most dominant religious influence; however, this has diversified mostly through the introduction of other forms of Christianity.

The African influence is seen largely in the music and dance of the Bahamas. Junkanoo is just one example of this influence. Traditional African medicine, which includes many bush medicines, herbs, and teas, also continues to be popular in the Bahamas today (McCarthy, 2004).

The most familiar stereotype of the Bahamas, as well as much of the Caribbean, is that Bahamians are very laid back and, potentially, lazy. This is an unfortunate misperception. Although Bahamians have a more laid back approach to time (i.e., not as structured on time), they are a culture that works hard and tries improve their collective lot in life. Education is prized in the Bahamas, and many Bahamians attend colleges in Europe, Canada, or the United States.

Upon returning from college or graduate education, many Bahamians find employment in the two primary industries of their country: banking and tourism. Both of these industries cause the Bahamas to be highly dependent upon other countries. In banking, the private bank accounts draw many international customers. In tourism, the beautiful beaches and ocean are the primary draw. However, in the 1920s, the Bahamas Development Board sought to convert Junkanoo into a tourism attraction, which served to help convert the customs into the more elaborate and commercialized form today. Although Junkanoo remains primarily an attraction to the people of the Bahamas, there are many tourists who travel to the islands for the event.

The History of Junkanoo

There are many versions of the story of how Junkanoo came into existence, but most begin during the time of the slave trade. Junkanoo is thought to stand for "John Canoe," who is believed to be a successful African merchant in the early 1700s (Thompson, 2006). There are a number of resemblances between aspects of Junkanoo and the Masquerades that were part of West African culture. The link between African celebrations and Junkanoo is evident; however, it has also taken on some variations in form and meaning.

The Junkanoo celebration is also celebrated in other places, such as Jamaica, but the largest and earliest celebrations have been in the Bahamas, where the practice can be seen dating back to the 1600s (Thompson, 2006). Also, there are variations in spelling and culturally derived meaning between the different practices.

Early on, Junkanoo was something that was tolerated, but not embraced, by the authorities (Thompson, 2006). During these times, it was described as dangerous and was not respected by many. This led to the suspension of Junkanoo for several years by the authorities beginning in 1942. Six years later, in 1948, under pressure from individuals in tourism, Junkanoo returned to the famous Bay Street in Nassau. Since this time, its reputation has changed, and the event has grown in size, length, and reputation. Junkanoo has also become an intense mixture of competition and celebration.

Junkanoo and the Existential Givens

Junkanoo represents the height of Bahamian culture. Beginning with its African origins, Junkanoo has been intimately connected with issues of freedom, survival, and oppression on an individual and cultural level. In this section, I will talk about the way Junkanoo has helped Bahamians face three of the existential givens: freedom, isolation/relationship, and emotions/embodiment.

First, it is important to discuss the place of Bahamian culture in the context of a book dialoguing between the East and the West. Although located in the West and heavily influenced by British culture, *Bahamian culture rightly falls between the East and the West.* This is evident in a number of ways, but most noticeable is the individualism-collectivism dimension: It is more collectivist than the United States and most Western cultures, but more individualist than China and most Eastern cultures.

Within the Western cultures, Bahamian culture is more similar to the southern European cultures in the expression of emotion. Similar to African American and Latino culture in the United States, Bahamians are much more expressive of their emotions and more open to conflict than most Western subcultures, particularly those originating from northern Europe.

Last, Bahamian culture is located in a paradoxical position in regard to privilege. It is often referred to as a "third world country," but some Bahamians, including myself, take offense to this classification. We are not as developed in regards to technology and higher education, but have had these commodities readily available through Great Britain, Canada, other Caribbean countries, and the United States. In another form of privilege, Black people have been the culture of majority in the Bahamas, as mentioned earlier; however, as demonstrated in the world's response to Rwanda, the Sudan, Haiti, and other African tragedies, the world seems to be less interested in the rights of Black people around the world. For Bahamians, this has been a collective experience as well as an individual experience. Bahamians have survived as a mixture of privilege and oppression, freedom and subjugation. We have had our culture pride challenged through a history of slavery, but we remain a proud, celebratory people.

Freedom

Junkanoo, in the beginning of its history, represents a celebration of freedom while still under the tyranny of slavery. As Frankl (1984) stated in *Man's Search for Meaning*, at the very least, each individual retains the freedom to choose the attitude through which he or she will face his or her oppression. In the midst of the horrors of slavery, torture, and oppression, the African slaves celebrated.

It has not been a common narrative for people of European decent to be enslaved because of their group identity. Individuals were enslaved, not groups. For example, some White people *individually* bound themselves as slaves, or indentured servants, to get to the Americas; however, this was their individual decision and they were able to earn their freedom through years of service. For the African slaves brought to the Americas and West Indies, slavery was a cultural condition. Political freedom and rights were stripped away as were the clothes that left them bare and exposed to harsh leather of the whips that tried to break them of their personal freedom.

With Junkanoo, the Bahamians demonstrated the difference between this political freedom and the more intimate personal and collective freedom to which they firmly held. This stands in stark contrast to the condition of many around the world today who fight hard to maintain and expand their political freedoms all the while remaining unaware of their many levels of personal freedom (see chapter 1). It seems evident that for many born of privilege, they cannot truly understand and embrace their personal freedom until their political freedom has been taken away. Freedom, to them, has more of a symbolic nature than an embodied one.

When one comes from a history of slavery, freedom takes on a new meaning. The Bahamian slaves spent 362 days a year working, bound to the will of their oppressor. Three days a year, December 25, December 26, and January 1, they were allowed to rest or celebrate. It is quite amazing that these Bahamians chose to celebrate two of their three days of rest a year. After enduring so much externally imposed constriction, they spent two days embracing their expansive nature (see Schneider, 2008).

Isolation/Relationship

Junkanoo has become a solid, unifying part of Bahamian culture. It is a celebration that at once unifies, but often separates, too. The islands as a whole come together to celebrate, yet fierce competition remains between the groups, especially the four main groups previously mentioned.

James F. T. Bugental (1987) discussed the paradox of simultaneously being drawn toward being *a part of* and being *a part from* as part of the existential condition. In other words, our human nature places us in the paradox of continually trying to connect to others or a cultural group, while at the same time wanting to remain distinct or separate. Hoffman, Stewart, Warren, and Meek (in press) discuss this as being a basic difference between individualist and collectivist cultures. Although both have to wrestle with this paradox, individualist cultures place more emphasis on the being a part from while collectivist cultures emphasize being a part of more.

Junkanoo, with its mixture of celebration and competition, emphasizes both aspects of this existential given at once. From an existential perspective, the goal is not to solve the paradox, but to accept it and integrate both aspects. O'Donohue (1998), in his book *Anam Cara*, which means "soul friend' in Gaelic, emphasizes that being a part from is an aspect of being a part of. Stated differently, solitude is an essential part of intimacy, and separateness is necessary before coming together.

The a part of is more central in Junkanoo's function. The individual feels part of the Bahamian culture and part of the group that they are supporting, People unite around shared symbols, which generally represent something that they have in common: a location, a value system, or aesthetic preferences. In Junkanoo, there are various levels of symbolism. Within the group, their colors, costumes, and songs unite them. They have different roles, from dancers to those playing the drums and cowbells, but they have a shared purpose and they move in rhythm to one another.

Junkanoo groups also spend time together throughout the year building relationships around their shared goal. Family and friends, too, become involved by supporting the group in various ways from making costumes to providing food and encouragement. Then, during Junkanoo, they join in the chants with the group so that throughout the route, the fans in the crowd become part of the group.

Even the separateness of a part from serves a purpose of uniting, becoming a part of. In sports all around the world competition serves to pull together one team against another. The divisive part of competition can be harmful, however, if the opponent is demonized. This can be witnessed in many types of separateness seen all over the world including racism, gang violence, and even in the behavior of parents who become obsessed with their children's athletic teams. In Junkanoo, the overriding celebration is one focused more on a national uniting, therefore limiting, but not eliminating, the divisive potential.

Emotions/Embodiment

Individuals of African decent have been integrated into many cultures around the world. One consistent feature in these African threads throughout the world, particularly in the Caribbean and Americas, is that of embodiment. They tend to embrace emotion and to embody it. The colors, sounds, and sights of Junkanoo are but a more pronounced expression of what is present on a daily basis.

Bahamians are often viewed as a gregarious and vibrant culture; we are full of life and energy. This is very different than the British, American, and Canadian cultures with which we interact regularly. In Schneider's (2008) terminology, Bahamian culture tends to be much more expansive than these other cultures.

The expansiveness of Bahamian culture, which is something shared with African American culture, can create discomfort for those more accustomed to restricted emotion. I write this during the historic 2008 elections, which brings forth a prominent example. Michelle Obama, wife of presidential candidate Barak Obama, is a fairly self-possessed woman, especially for her culture. However, she has been labeled by some as an "angry black woman." Although the motivations for this may be political, it brings to light an important issue.

Bahamians and African Americans tend to be comfortable with stronger expressions of emotion when compared with most other cultures. This includes being more comfortable with higher levels of conflict and anger. Although this is a matter of culture more relevant to preference than ethics, there are some benefits and liabilities that come with it. This, in itself, is an important point. Although it is often viewed as politically correct to view cultural variations as value neutral, all cultures have their strengths and liabilities from psychological and other perspectives.

Existentially, it is important to integrate one's expansive and constrictive tendencies, finding a place for both of them. The liability in Bahamian culture is to ignore the constrictive tendencies, or to be too expansive. However, in many cultures, the opposite, being too constrictive, is the liability. Additionally, and more to the point with the example, individuals more comfortable with the expansiveness often create discomfort in individuals with a preference for a more constricted existence. It is easy to make value judgments about these different preferences that are often culturally influenced.

Junkanoo provides an important, healthy expression for the expansiveness tendencies in the culture. It also provides a particularly important illustration in that it connects the expansiveness to meaning. When a culture has been subjected to hyperconstriction, such as has occurred through years of slavery, the need for a healthy expression of the expansive tendencies is needed. As discussed in a previous section, Bahamian slaves chose to celebrate on two of the three days off of work they had each year. Junkanoo, in its early practice, was a healthy response to the constricted condition of slavery. Today, although the externally imposed constriction has been removed, Junkanoo continues to serve as a healthy expression of the expansive and celebratory tendencies.

A Bahamian in the West: My Story

I have lived in the United States for many years now; first as a student, now as a professional as well as being a wife and mother to Americans. Often I have been asked why I have not yet become a citizen. Although still considering the possibility of becoming a United States citizen, this is not an easy decision. Many from the United States are surprised to hear of my hesitancy.

It is often heard in the United States that it is "the greatest country in the world." In my experience, the United States has much to offer and I am thankful for the opportunities I have been given here. There are opportunities for me and for my sons that would not be available in the Bahamas. However, at the same time, I am often resistant to the idea of the United States being the greatest country in the world. After all, the Bahamas, with its rich culture, beautiful beaches, and tropical climate, is not such a bad place to live.

Remaining a Bahamian, and not a United States citizen, has a lot to do with the cultural myths. I am proud to be a Bahamian; proud of our legacy and proud of our country. It is important to me that my husband and children, who have been brought up in the United States, know my culture. As part of this, I want them to experience Junkanoo and understand its significance in my culture.

In the United States, I am often referred to as an African American and I generally correct this. I am not an African American and I could never fully understand what this label means. I have not been through their hardships, their struggles, and their oppressions. I have not been part of their victories in the civil rights movements and increased opportunities.

But neither am I African; I have never been to Africa and do not know their struggles or their realities. I refer to myself as being Black and I do feel a connection with Black people around the world. When watching the aftermath of Hurricane Katrina, it pained me to see that most of these ignored people were Black. When watching the movie *Hotel Rwanda*, I grieved at how easy it was for the world to ignore genocide when it involved Black people, knowing full well that the world has generally intervened much quicker when the skin tone of the people suffering is lighter. Today I wonder why it is so easy for many around the world to ignore the atrocities occurring in places in Africa, such as Darfur and Zimbabwe.

As a Black person, I know what it is like to not be seen when people are looking directly at me; I also know what it is like to be seen too much. In the Bahamas I was blessed with the luxury of being a person of majority. I was sheltered from many painful lessons that I cannot, and should not, protect my sons from; they must learn what it means to be African American even though neither their father nor I fall under this label.

Even if I become a United States citizen, I will always remain a Bahamian. The Bahamian myths, such as Junkanoo, are meaningful to me. I am not sure as of yet whether I can buy into the American myths. The American dream, for all its beauty, has not been my dream. It represents prosperity, but my life has been more about survival and I am content with that.

Conclusion

Junkanoo is the most central of all Bahamians myths. It connects us to our African heritage; tells the story of celebrating our freedom even when we were bound to slavery, and unites us as a people. Junkanoo is not just a celebration or parade. It is part of our way of life. It is the expression of who we are and what we value.

The greatest threat to Junkanoo is that it could become just another celebration. The commercialization may be great for tourism and our economy, but if that replaces the deeper meaning that Junkanoo has served in our culture it would be tragedy. We must retain its mythical nature, its meaning. If we do so, Junkanoo will continue to unite and inspire Bahamians for many years to come.

References

Bugental, J. F. T. (1987). *The art of the psychotherapist*. New York: Norton.

Frankl, V. E. (1984). *Man's search for meaning*. New York: Simon & Schuster.

Hoffman, L., Stewart, S., Warren, D., & Meek, L. (in press). Toward a sustainable myth of self: An existential response to the postmodern condition. *Journal of Humanistic Psychology*.

McCartney, D. M. (2004). *Bahamian culture and factors which impact upon it: A compilation of two essays*. Pittsburg, PA: Dorrance Publishing.

O'Donohue, J. (1998). *Anam cara. A Celtic book of wisdom*. New York: Harper Collins.

Schneider, K. J. (2008). Theory of the existential-integrative (EI) approach. In K. J. Schneider (Ed.), *Existential-integrative psychotherapy: Guideposts to the core of practice* (pp. 35-48). New York: Routledge.

Thompson, K. (2006). Junkanoo rush. *Caribbean Beat, 82*. Retrieved from http://www.meppublishers.com/online/caribbean-beat/archive/index.php?pid=6001&id=cb82-1-48.

Annotated Bibliography of Works
Related to Existential Psychotherapy

Christopher S. M. Grimes
Erica Palmer
Matthew Thelen
Michael Moats
J. M. Chavis
Ellen Marsalis

This selected annotated bibliography of works related to existential psychotherapy contains entries of scholarly books, journal articles, and popular novels which are relevant to existential psychotherapy.

Scholarly Books

Becker, E. (1973). *The denial of death.* New York: Free Press.
Becker provides a re-interpretation of ideas from Freud, Rank, Kierkegaard, and others into an original theory which states that culture and religion are elaborate philosophical systems designed to conceal the overwhelming reality that every individual will die. Humans, according to Becker, are dually comprised of a physical self limited by biological determinism and a symbolic self that seeks to either create or endorse symbols that represent immortality in order to prevent an eventual nullification of one's presence on earth. The goal of the symbolic self is to transcend death through some form of heroism, quest for immortality, or *causa sui* project; all of which can assume an infinite number of forms including the symbolic structures that support modern civilization. Becker explains how religion, sexuality, science, and psychology all attempt to suppress one's anxiety towards death albeit each system is never entirely successful in doing so. Becker hopes that increased awareness on how anxiety towards death is imbedded in all motivations will result in a more effective approach to improving the human condition. This is one of the most frequently referred to philosophical works in contemporary existential writing.

Bugental, J. F. T. (1987). *The art of the psychotherapist.* New York: Norton.
Bugental outlines his approach to *life-changing psychotherapy* asserting this approach gives primary attention to the subjective experience of the client. He does not dismiss the usefulness of objective approaches to psychotherapy and clearly states they are necessary and have significant value. However, he argues

that objective approaches to therapy are not sufficient to produce major life-changes. Life-changing psychotherapy does not refer to a theoretical orientation, but rather refers to a way of going about the work of depth-oriented therapy. Bugental provides a technical discussion of levels of communication and demonstrates with case examples how the therapist can guide the therapy conversation toward the subjective. He also provides insightful and practical advice on how to work with a client's resistances.

Bugental, J. F. T. (1999). *Psychotherapy isn't what you think: Bringing the psychotherapeutic engagement into the living moment*. Phoenix, AZ: Zeig, Tucker & Theisen.

This volume serves as a companion to Bugental's earlier book *The Art of the Psychotherapist*. Bugental stresses the importance of understanding the client's immediate subjective experience elucidating the therapeutic opportunities of working in the "living moment." He proposes to help therapists move away from an historical, information focused approach to therapy where change occurs as the therapist interprets current behaviors based on past experiences. He encourages therapists to build skills of attunement to the here-and-now experience of the client illustrating how this attunement benefits the therapeutic encounter. Bugental highlights his ideas with segments of client–therapist interaction which provide clear examples of the use of the here-and-now in the context of therapy. The technical examples are less cumbersome than those in *The Art of the Psychotherapist* providing a more user-friendly introduction to Bugental.

Cain, D. J. & Seeman, J. (Eds.). (2002). *Humanistic psychotherapies: Handbook of research and practice*. Washington, DC: American Psychological Association.

This groundbreaking compilation of research in the field of humanistic psychotherapy represents work done by current leading experts in this area of research and practice. In an attempt to expand and increase awareness of the humanistic approach to therapy, this volume has been created for use primarily in an academic setting. The editors of the work believe this is where change must begin in training humanistic therapists and increasing the presence of humanistic psychology as a more accepted approach to therapy. After laying the foundational background of humanistic psychotherapy, various authors address topics such as empirical research, specific therapeutic approaches and treatment modalities, and specialized applications within the humanistic framework.

Diamond, S. A. (1996). *Anger, Madness, and the Daimonic: The Psychological Genesis of Violence, Evil, and Creativity*. New York: State University of New York Press.

Diamond provides a powerful resource for students and professionals seeking a better understanding of the nature of rage and anger, particularly as it is related to the daimonic. America's plague of violence has left questions regarding how it is possible that society has spiraled so far out of control and who is responsible. Diamond writes of the often detrimental practices of psychology focused on eliminating the discomfort, minimizing the distressing responsibility for one's actions, or over-pathologizing the presence of anger and rage. He illuminates the overlooked constructive opportunities of anger and rage, and how productively channeling these passions have resulted in creative treasures, as well as personal growth. True to existential and other depth psychologies, Diamond's development of the daimonic and an existential perspective on anger and rage parallel's May's work to redeem the concept of anxiety.

Frankl, V. E. (1988). *The will to meaning*. New York: Meridian.
Frankl, a neurologist and psychiatrist contemporary of Sigmund Freud and Alfred Adler, developed Logotherapy as a result of working with fellow Jewish prisoners during World War II at Auschwitz and Dachau. Written following a series of lectures in 1966, Frankl defines in *The Will to Meaning* the existential foundations and applications of Logotherapy. The foundations include the freedom of will, the will to meaning, and meaning of life. These foundations may be applied in mental health treatment for noogenic neurosis, psychogenic neurosis, and somatogenic neurosis.

Frankl, V. E. (1984). *Man's search for meaning*. New York: Simon & Schuster.
This volume begins with Frankl's autobiographical reflection upon his experience in the Nazi's concentration camps during World War II. Frankl begins with obvious, yet profound, observations: Some prisoners maintained hope, others did not; some prisoners endured the camps while maintaining sanity, others did not. From his experiences and observations, Frankl determines there is much truth in Neitzsche's famous quote: "He who has a *why* to live for can deal with almost any *how*." Frankl concludes that those individuals who maintained a reason for surviving managed better emotionally than did those who despaired in meaninglessness and hopelessness. From these observations, Frankl outlines his theory of Logotherapy. Logotherapy focuses on the meaning of human existence and the individual's search for this meaning. Frankl's theory is based on the assumption that the individual's will to meaning is the primary motivation for his or her life, and frustration of the will to meaning can result in neurosis. This is one of the most famous existential books ever written.

Frankl, V. E. (2000). *Man's search for ultimate meaning*. Cambridge, MA: Perseus.
The 2000 edition of Frankl's *Man's Search for Ultimate Meaning* is a republication of the text which first appeared in English in 1975. The text presents Frankl's thoughts on Existential psychotherapy, and adds to his previous works: *The Will to Meaning* and *Man's Search for Meaning*. He discusses the limitation of a

mechanistic view of the human being, and argues for the field of psychotherapy to supplement its traditional emphasis on depth-psychology, as characterized in the psychoanalytic perspective, with a *height-psychology* that recognizes the higher aspirations of the human psyche including the human's search for ultimate meaning. For Frankl, the search for ultimate meaning is spiritual and he presents a model for understanding humans as principally spiritual beings with a psychophysical overlay. This book provides the most complete introduction to Frankl's existential psychology.

Heidegger, M. (1996). *Being and Time*. (J. Stanbaugh, Trans.). Albany, NY:
    State University of New York Press.
The thesis of Heidegger's book *Being and Time* can be summarized in his words, "Philosophy is universal phenomenological ontology, beginning with a hermeneutic of Da-sein which, as an analytic of *existence*, has made fast the guideline for all philosophical questioning at the point where it *arises* and to which it *returns*". The demanding focus required to abstract concepts from Heidegger's intricate text will likely exclude casual readers, but the essential questions and conclusions contained within his chapters will reward readers who have a persistent curiosity in defining the most primitive foundation of being human. The meaning of being, according to Heidegger, is to care for the future possibility of being, thus implicating the importance of time in the ontic foundation of being. Heidegger, a structural philosopher, investigates the primordial sequence of being through the ontological, phenomenological, and existential intellectual systems. Despite the many profound and sometimes controversial insights contained within, the only absolute truth of all may be that the questions posed are equally as insightful as the answers that may be.

Kierkegaard, S. (1981). *The concept of anxiety* (R. Thomte & A. B. Anderson,
    Trans.). Princeton, NJ: Princeton University Press. (Original work
    published in 1844)
Known as the "father of existentialism," Kierkegaard has written many volumes of philosophical thought uniquely integrated with psychology and Christian theology. In this text, he looks at anxiety from the perspective of its relationship with freedom and original sin. His assertion that anxiety was a forerunner to Adam's fall and is human beings' natural response to his expanse of freedom is followed by a discussion of anxiety as a consequence of sinfulness. The book concludes with the suggestion that this anxiety born of sin can be an individual's salvation and lead the sinner back to God. This circular interconnectedness is a central theme of this writing and speaks of the power of freedom as well as the value of anxiety. A precursor to Rollo May's writings on anxiety and freedom, it could be deduced that Kierkegaard's position regarding these phenomena may have laid the foundation for the subsequent existential writings of May.

Kierkegaard, S. (1985). *Fear and trembling* (A. Hannay, Trans.). New York:
    Penguin. (Original work published in 1843)
This volume is Kierkegaard's retelling of the biblical story of God's commandment
to Abraham to kill his only child Isaac. During Abraham's journey to Mount Mariah,
where he is to sacrifice his son, Kierkegaard explores the moral conflicts that
Abraham faces. Commonly the story of Abraham is held as an example of
unquestioning faith in God's will. Kierkegaard, however, points out that Abraham's
apparently adherent faith in God is actually mixed with fear and trembling towards
God. Yet, the magnitude of Abraham's faith in God is increased because he
continues to believe despite doubting the intentions of God. In contrast to the
existential presupposition that the individual is at the center of his or her own
existence, Kierkegaard asserts that God is at the center of human existence.
Although Kierkegaard did not intend for the role of God to be interpreted
symbolically, non-Christian readers can benefit from his assertion that beneath the
self-fulfilling desires of individuals is an eternal consciousness or moral code that
functions as a safe-guard from the collapse of civilization.

May, R. (1970). *The meaning of anxiety*. New York: Norton & Company.
    (Original work published in 1950)
May takes the issue of anxiety examining it from multiple viewpoints in this
volume. He compiles various theories from the great philosophers to the
psychological and sociological schools of thought prior to synthesizing his own
theory. May's recognition of the prevalence and significance of anxiety despite the
lack of attention toward understanding anxiety's purpose led to his assertion that
anxiety is not only brought to our awareness for the purpose of elimination, but is
acknowledged as a necessary and meaningful aspect of human existence. Case
studies illuminate the application of his integrated theories on anxiety and
poignantly display the importance of his endeavor. May aptly postulates that if
anxiety were to be treated as a simple, one-dimensional symptom to be readily
alleviated through a few psychotherapeutic techniques, client and therapist alike
would miss out on a profound experience central to being human.

May, R. (1969). *Love and will*. New York: Delta.
This volume addresses of the topics of love and eros emerging into awareness
during the 1960s and 1970s in Western culture as a more acceptable topic of
conversation. By this time, May had become a leading name in psychology,
particularly as a pioneer in existential theory, and this book became a bestseller
among professionals as well as the general public. He explores the possibility that
to love another within the context of our freedom of choice may be an illusion we
create for ourselves in an attempt to alleviate the pressing anxieties of the modern
world, becoming a source of problems rather than the solution. Within this text,
May introduces his innovative concept of the daimonic, which has since stimulated
much discussion and controversy, but ultimately has come to define May's

perceptions of human nature and to steer the course of existential psychotherapy. May also develops his conception of intentionality in this volume.

May, R. (1975). *The courage to create*. New York: Norton & Company.
May, in this volume, introduces creativity as a fluid process of life. The very production of this book was a source of existential angst which furthered the understanding that overcoming psychological inertia allows one to thrive in life's abundant opportunities to create. May challenges the cornerstone beliefs of logic, as a linear process controlled by form, in which he discusses the converse realization that creativity is the basis and catalyst of logical expansion. Whether discussing simple life decisions or Nobel Prize-winning advancements, it is the power of asking *what if* that creates the opportunity for growth, as well as the opportunity for vulnerability. May's inspiration to face one's fears of imperfection, incompletion, and potential displays the power that embracing and encountering latent, ego-bruising discomfort can have toward one's growth.

May, R. (1981). *Freedom and destiny*. New York: Norton & Company.
This volume shares the paradoxical nature of freedom and the importance of accepting one's destiny, or the influences upon humans that cannot be controlled. Through the multi-levels of influence that help to shape one's destiny come the opportunity for existential angst to occur. Only when one accepts his or her destiny can he or she begin to find freedom. The West has demonstrated a tendency for attempting to embrace freedom through beliefs that it is found through self-indulgence instead of understanding that destiny is interweaved with transcendence of self. Using a case study, Rollo May shares his insights into facing the struggle of attempting to find freedom through living one's destiny and finding comfort in the pause between stimulus and response. It is the emptiness of the pause, as May reflects on Lao Tzu's writings, which give value to the observed form. This volume addresses common misunderstandings existential views on freedom, particularly through dismissing the idea of absolute freedom.

May, R. (1985). *My quest for beauty*. Dallas, TX: Saybrook.
In a somewhat divergent turn from his previous works, May writes of his experiences while teaching in Greece for a three-year period after graduation from Oberlin College. During this time, he became aware of the physical beauty around him and subsequently interested in how an attunement with beauty and art could enhance mental health. Hearkening back to themes in *The Courage to Create*, May asserts that psychological well-being depends on the ability to create beauty in our lives. The creation of order from chaos, May contends, is the very essence of beauty. In a very personal way, he relates how his own discovery of art and beauty led him to improved mental health and to the conclusion that recognition of our individual creative beauty is imperative to our social existence. In this way, art is reflective of a culture's design and future direction. Whether with paint, music, language or in our life's work, art is an expression of beauty that is dependent

upon the freedom that May has previously defined for us as one of our ultimate human strivings.

May, R. (1988). *Paulus: Tillich as spiritual teacher* (Rev. ed.). Dallas, TX: Saybrook.

In this short book, May honors his teacher and mentor, Paul Tillich. May presents the story of Tillich's life including his professorship at Union Theological Seminary in philosophy and theology. In addition to presenting the biographical information, May also discusses Tillich's person and presence, his way of being, and his manner of impacting others. Tillich significantly influenced his fellow existential adherents, as well. May discusses how Tillich promoted the benefits of doubt and discussed how he sometimes felt it was his mission to bring to "bring faith to the faithless and doubt to the faithful." *Paulus: Tillich as Spiritual Teacher* won the American Psychological Foundation Gold Metal Award in 1987.

May, R. (1989). *The art of counseling* (Rev. ed.). Lake Worth, FL: Gardner Press.

The original edition of this text was published in 1939, and according to May's preface, was the first book on counseling produced in the United States. It provides a concise overview of May's humanistic-existential theory of counseling. *The Art of Counseling* could be classified as a handbook of basic counseling theory. It may be especially helpful for those who find themselves in a position of having to often provide a form of counseling without having the benefit of significant training in the field. Ministers, teachers, physicians, and attorneys, for example, could benefit from adding this text to their reference shelf. May begins with a summation of the underlying principles of counseling and then discusses the practical steps of the counseling process. His definition of empathy and his discussion on the importance of empathy as a key component of the counseling relationship is especially instructive. Of particular interest to clergy is May's discussion of the neurotic tendencies in religion, which he includes in the final section of this book.

May, R. (1991). *The cry for myth.* New York: Delta.

May defines myth as "a way of making sense in a senseless world." He promoted and encouraged dialogue among all peoples and emphasized the importance of seeking to give meaning to our lives. The purpose of myths, according to May, is to provide a sense of identity, to promote a sense of community, to undergird moral values, and to explore the mystery of creation. The first section of the book addresses myth's contribution to the exploration and potential answers to personal crises, the search for our roots, and mystery. Sections two and three review some American and Western myths, the voids they fill, and the explanations they offer to Western society. This book also provided the basis for section 3 of *Existential Psychology East-West*.

May, R., Angel, E., & Ellenberger, H. F. (Eds.). (1958). *Existence*. Northvale,
    NJ: Jason Aronson, Inc.
May, Angel, and Ellenberger are commonly credited as the first persons to introduce existential psychology to United States psychologists with this volume. In *Existence*, essays written by Ludwig Binswanger, Eugene Minkowski, Roland Kuhn, Erwin Straus, Werner Mendel, and Joseph Lyons are translated into English. Through his own contributions to the book, May asserts his mastery of existential theory and provides an alternative paradigm to the positivistic dominance in Western science and United States psychology. May's idea that even the most empirically based sciences are rested upon philosophical presuppositions regarding the meaning of being human served as inspiration to the first generation of United States existential psychologists.

Mendelowitz, E. (2008). *Ethics and Lao-Tzu: Intimations of character.*
    Colorado Springs, CO: University of the Rockies Press.
This volume is a colorful creation filled with poetic verse, client-originated artistry, and powerful quotes from brilliant minds. Mendelowitz shares his journey with his client, Kristina, as they travel together down a path of acceptance, understanding, and growth. The vulnerability and empathetic frustration Mendelowitz displays in his search for comprehension illuminates the process of existential therapy. The pages are filled with travels through poetry, art, and silence. His ability to collaboratively work with the presenting personalities of Kristina, who suffers from Dissociative Identity Disorder, demonstrates his passion for the person. Mendelowitz boldly challenges traditional approaches to therapy and the "experts" who were unsuccessful in connecting with Kristina. The style and process of this book not only demonstrate existential therapy at its best, but also why Schneider refers to Mendelowitz as the "poet laureate of existential psychology."

Moustakas, C. (1994). *Existential psychotherapy and the interpretation of*
    dreams. Northvale, NJ: Jason Aronson.
A leading figure in humanistic psychology, Moustakas is one of the first to conceptualize dream work from an existential perspective. Moustakas attempts to explain the significance of dreams within the context of meaning, existence, anxiety, and guilt, and other existential concepts. He examines how all of these are manifest in dreams and how this can be analyzed and processed in therapy. Moustakas begins by establishing a framework for existential psychotherapy, then proceeds to develop a foundation for analysis of dream meaning that incorporates established methods of dream interpretations by Freud and Jung. Although taking a substantial portion of the book to set up this foundational material, his conclusions regarding the implementation of existential theory in dream interpretation are innovative. The case examples are highly illuminative in demonstrating the process of existential dream interpretation.

Nietzsche, F. (1954). *Thus spoke Zarathustra: A book for none and all* (W. Kaufmann, Trans.). New York: Penguin. (Original work published 1892)

This volume is a loosely constructed novel that explores several themes through the eyes of the fictitious Zarathustra. These themes include: (1) the overman, a character who has become all-powerful and is nearly omnipresent through self-awareness; (2) the eternal recurrence, the concept that all events have happened and will happen again, repeatedly; (3) the will to power, the essential drive of human nature; (4) the descent and demise of Western religion, including the concepts of good and evil and the "lie" of the afterlife; (5) the dangers of conformity. This is often conceived as Nietzsche's most important book and one of the best overviews of the central themes of his thought. Many also consider this a great literary work demonstrating both Nietzsche's comprehension of the major religious and philosophical works of his time and his ability to blend fiction and philosophy (non-fiction) in a literary style that later existentialists attempt to replicate.

Nietzsche, F. (1966). *Beyond good and evil: Prelude to a philosophy of future* (W. Kaufmann, Trans.). New York: Vintage Books: (Original work published 1886).

In this sequel to *Thus Spoke Zarathustra*, Nietzsche criticizes various schools of philosophy, both old and new. He finds fault with stoics and scholars, with scientific anti-realism and contemporary religion. Nietzsche explores the concept that religion often is a dangerous and cruel form of control over the masses. Regarding European cultures, Nietzsche honors the Jews and renounces Arian anti-Semitism. He considers France to be culturally spiritual and refined and finds particular fault with the English especially the philosophers Bacon, Hobbes, Hume, and Locke. This provides a basis for an existential perspective on ethics, which goes beyond the morals codes often relied upon in Western culture.

Sartre, J. P. (1956). *Being and nothingness* (H. E. Barnes, Trans.) New York: Washington Square Press. (Original work published in 1943)

Many identify *Being and Nothingness* as the definitive text on existential thought. Although an important contribution, the elevation of this text as the definitive text on existential thought has created a great deal of confusion about the primary tenets of existentialism. It is more helpful to understand this as one important and influential approach to existential thought. According to Sartre, being must be understood in the context of nothingness, an idea that serves as the basis of the title. Sartre goes on to discuss his notion of "bad faith," which essentially delineates his thoughts on self-deception, a tendency most individuals are drawn toward. Next, Sartre develops many of his ideas on relationships, which demonstrate that Sartre's individualism is not as unbalanced as often portrayed by many who inaccurately portray existential thought. In the end, Sartre advocates for an extreme approach to self-honesty and overcoming self-deception that many think is too extreme. Sartre's approach shows less tolerance of the need for some defenses against the horrors of human condition. Many other existentialists, such as Becker and Nietzsche, provide a more sympathetic understanding of the need of some self-deception while also pursuing greater honesty about the human condition.

Schneider, K. J. *The paradoxical self: Toward an understanding of our contradictory nature.* Amherst, New York: Humanity Books.

Schneider introduces Kierkegaard's concepts of *infinitize* (expansiveness) and *finitize* (constriction), applying them to psychology, including concept of spectrums or continuums regarding mental illness and overall human behaviors. Schneider purports that existential-phenomenological theory and practice assumes a mind/body gestalt. Schneider continues referencing multiple scholars' writings that endorse the concept that human beings shift between the two poles: expansiveness and constriction. He summarizes the existential agreement that everyone has an individual center or centric (Schneider), also referred to as ego (Freud), centering (Lifton), presence (Bugental) or intentionality (May), depending upon the label provided by the given scholar. Finally, Schneider addresses optimal potentialities: personal, societal, organizational, health-centered, individual developmental, and worship.

Schneider, K. J. (2004). *Rediscovery of awe: Splendor, mystery and the fluid center of life.* St. Paul, MN: Paragon House.

The major threat to humanity, suggests Schneider, is intolerance of paradox. A mass movement towards extreme ideologies in religion, politics, and economics has left many people searching for meaning and happiness in life without success. According to Schneider, the path out of polarized institutions begins with a fluid centered approach to living which is characterized by searching for the mystery, reverie, and splendor in everyday living. The concept of living with a fluid center is based on the impression that the world appears to be an overwhelming and hostile environment, yet by embracing the paradox one is able to transform anxiety into excitement, grief into veneration, despair into hope, etc. Schneider points out social institutions such as government, schools, and business influence the ethical standards for individuals and recommends that a fluid centered approach be integrated into decision making processes in social, vocational, and educational settings. The fluid filled center is a contentious decision to expand and contract the reciprocity of influence between the environment and oneself for the purpose of enabling intellectual growth and emotional protection. This serves as the most important contemporary application of existential psychology to social issues, including education and ethics.

Schneider, K. J. (Ed.) (2008). *Existential-integrative psychotherapy: Guideposts to the core of practice.* New York: Routeledge.
This is an essential resource for students and practitioners of virtually any orientation. Schneider has created an important body of information that includes a blend of diversity, student viewpoints, and multiple case illustrations. Schneider has continued the legacy of existential collaboration in his attempt to advance the integration of existentialism with other orientations and diverse clientele by giving life to this book. The uniqueness of his work is that he demonstrates a value for various practices, but not without the ever-important significance of the therapeutic relationship and presence. Undoubtedly, this is a very important contemporary text in existential psychology, especially given its emphasis on the innovative and integrative potential of this approach.

Schneider, K. J., Bugental, J. F. T., & Pierson, J. F. (Eds.). (2001). *The handbook of humanistic psychology: Leading edges in theory, research, and practice.* Thousand Oaks, CA: Sage.
Some of the greatest contributors to humanistic and existential psychology contributed to this volume that begins with historical background and establishing basic theory, then leads the reader through methodological themes and applications to the practice of humanistic psychology. In an attempt to ground humanistic thought in today's society of practicalities and empirical research, the authors explore the possibilities of blending humanistic practice with emerging trends in neuropsychology, positive psychology, and postmodernism. Also included is an intriguing section of humanistic applications to settings outside of therapy, such as in education, the mind/body connection, and romantic relationships. This text is a revival of humanistic thought, which some believe is fading from contemporary practice, revealing its richness and value in a world where humanity is often overlooked. In closing, the editors reflect on the present place and future of humanistic psychology, effectively demonstrating its usefulness in professional practice by illuminating its place in our lives as essential to our very existence.

Schneider, K. J. & May, R. (1995). *The psychology of existence: An integrative, clinical perspective.* New York: McGraw-Hill.
This volume is a concise, yet comprehensive overview of the existential role in today's psychology movement. The text includes overview of existential contributions in literature, philosophy, and psychology. The theoretical and case illustrations provide the foundation of Schneider's more recent book, *Existential Integrative Psychotherapy: Guideposts to the Core of Practice.* However, the overview of literary and philosophical contributions maintains the important place of this volume.

Spinelli, E. (2004). *The mirror and the hammer.* Thousand Oaks, CA: Sage.
Spinelli challenged the very core of commonly accepted psychotherapeutic tenets and techniques from an existential perspective. The intriguing title is meant to

convey an image of holding up a mirror to the profession thereby gaining insights into its present state and taking up a hammer to shatter previously held perceptions to make way for the creation of something new. Spinelli proceeds to discuss the ways that contemporary psychotherapy has reduced the therapy experience in episodes of short-term problem solving when many problems that individuals face today are not easily solvable and at times are irreparable. He proposes that therapists engage with clients in their journey and help them to explore the possibilities and choices available, given that life is unavoidably uncertain at times. Through this framework, Spinelli challenges such icons of therapy as therapist disclosure, the self, the unconscious, the role of childhood experience, sexuality, and the problem of evil. Rather than taking in a skill set to "cure" the client, Spinelli urges that the therapist's role become one who engages in a mutual human experience with another individual, recognizing shared limitations and uncertainty on life's journey.

Tillich, P. (1952). *The courage to be.* New Haven: Yale University Press.
Tillich approaches existentialism from a theological perspective and provides valuable insight regarding the interconnectedness of the spirit and mind. In *The Courage to Be,* Tillich addresses the existential dread which all humans encounter and the courage necessary to carry on in the face of dread. Tillich identifies this dread as stemming from awareness of individual guilt, meaninglessness, and the threat of non-being. The courage to overcome this dread, or the courage to despair, requires faith in the Ground of Being which allows for self-acceptance and self-affirmation in the face of dread. This faith produces courage and allows the person to transcend fear and carry out his or her existence. Of Tillich's many contributions, this book has been the most influential with regard to existential psychology.

Tournier, P. (1957). *The meaning of persons.* New York: Harper & Row.
A medical doctor and general practitioner in Geneva, Switzerland, Tournier was unique in that he recognized the need of some patients for deeper and more personal interventions than those typically offered by the medical establishment. He was a self-proclaimed practitioner of the "medicine of the person," and combined his knowledge of the physical with his that of the psychological and spiritual nature of persons. In this text, he addresses basic existential questions of identity and being, one's place in the world, and in relationship with others. Distinguishing the person from our personages, Tournier examines the masks that we wear in everyday life and how difficult it often can be to identify the real person within. He goes on to explore the ways individuals attempt to interact with the world around them, particularly interpersonal relationships. He also gives examples of how an individual's physical being affects his or her psyche and spirit. Although Tournier speaks from a perspective of Biblical authority, he effectively melds this foundational belief system with scientific evidence and psychological constructs, while not neglecting the importance of spiritual concerns.

Van Deurzen, E. (1997). *Paradox and passion in psychotherapy: An
        existential approach to therapy and counseling.* New York: Wiley &
        Sons.
Van Deurzen, the leading figure in existential psychology in Great Britain, covers a
wide range of psychotherapeutic topics and situations in an existential framework.
Throughout the book, she challenges therapists to move closer to embracing
insecurity as opposed to falling into the trap of false confidence in systematic
methods. She reminds us that excessive grasping for control is not life enhancing
but dulling and deadening, and provides vignettes to illustrate this concept.

Yalom, I. D. (1980). *Existential psychotherapy.* New York: Basic Books.
Existential Psychotherapy has become a standard text for introducing students and
therapists to existential psychology. Yalom is clear that the existential orientation
is not right for every therapist and will not work for every client. However, for
those inclined toward an existential therapeutic orientation, this text is a
necessary read because of how Yalom thoughtfully and thoroughly summarizes
the existential point of view as it relates to psychotherapy. Yalom begins by
outlining the distinction between an existential orientation to therapy and the
classical Freudian drive model before focusing on an in-depth exploration of the
four ultimate concerns which contribute to existential anxiety in the individual:
death, freedom, isolation, and meaninglessness. In his discussion of these ultimate
concerns, Yalom lays out a comprehensive theory of existential psychodynamics
including a discussion of commonly used defense mechanisms, examples of
psychopathology arising from failure to deal with these concerns, and frequent
references supporting research and case examples.

Journal Articles

This section is very selective in identifying important articles on existential
psychology that introduce authors not identified in the scholarly books section,
important articles distinguishing existential psychology from other approaches,
and essential dialogues in the scholarly literature involving existential psychology.

Mahrer, A. R. (1989). The case for fundamentally different existential-
        humanistic psychologies. *Journal of Humanistic Psychology, 29,*
        249-262.
Mahrer outlines his case for a fundamentally different theory of existential-
humanistic psychology. His assertion is based in postmodern thought with respect
to previously held definitions of the term "humanistic," and whether those
concepts and constructs typically assigned to humanistic thought are provable
truths or if they can be reconstructed based on theories of relativism. Based on
this premise, Mahrer provides a foundation on which to build a new definition of

humanistic that can exist only if different answers are provided to the fundamental theoretical questions and only if different results or payoffs are offered. In making his case, Mahrer addresses the problem of our tendencies to accept a theory based on preconceived ideas without challenging the boundaries and limitations that may accompany those ideas. He opens up a new door through which existential-humanistic thinkers and practitioners can view their clients and the world.

May, R. (1961). The meaning of the Oedipus myth. *Review of Existential Psychology and Psychiatry, 1,* 44-52.

The Oedipus myth is intrinsically connected to the history of psychology. Freud used this to elucidate his theory of sexuality. The psychological literature is replete with reinterpretations of this myth. May provides a reinterpretation of the Oedipal myth that serves as a primary distinction between the psychodynamic and existential perspectives on the core conflict in human nature. For May, the Oedipal conflict illustrates the child's movement toward individuating from the parents and seeking a form of personal freedom. This article initiates May's thoughts on freedom and destiny, which also serve as an important distinguishing factor between existential psychology and the various deterministic schools of psychological thought.

Rollo May and Carl Rogers on the Problem of Evil

May, R. (1982). The problem of evil: An open letter to Carl Rogers. *Journal of Humanistic Psychology, 22,* 10-21.

Rogers, C. (1982). Notes on Rollo May. *Journal of Humanistic Psychology, 22,* 8-9.

May's article on the problems of evil is in response to a letter published in 1981 by Carl Rogers in a special issue of *Perspectives,* an excerpt of which was published in the Journal of Humanistic Psychology in 1982 along with May's response. May took issue with some of the statements and misinterpretations made by Rogers regarding the problem of evil. May takes this opportunity to clarify several issues such as his use of the term "daimonic," the necessity of those daimonic urges to be integrated into the whole person to counter potentially destructive forces, and the origin of evil. The primary issue of contention between May and Rogers is on the nature of being human as intrinsically good or if evil. While Rogers identifies evil originating in culture and social influences, May contends that there is an inherent potential for evil in all people. This contention sets the stage for an essential debate between existential and humanistic schools of thought and identifies the psychology of evil as an essential difference between humanistic and existential psychology. May ends the article making a plea for a more realistic view of evil, particularly by those of the humanistic movement, who in May's opinion often avoid the confrontation of the reality of evil.

Schneider, J. J. (1999). The revival of the romantic means a revival of
psychology. *Journal of Humanistic Psychology, 39,* 13-29.
Schneider elaborates the separation of existential psychology from its romantic roots; traces the progress and process of the theoretical separation from humanities and the arts: the losses resulting from abandoning literary investigation of human psychology; and discusses postmodern psychology as illuminated by romanticism.

Tillich, P. (1961). Existentialism and psychotherapy. *Review of Existential Psychology and Psychiatry, 1,* 8-16.
Tillich points out that a valid theory of being human is a necessary prerequisite for a valid theory of psychotherapy. One problem with constructing a theory of being human is that it is difficult to separate the difficulties that arise from individuals essential nature from those arising from his existential predicament. This philosophical problem is explored in-depth and with keen clarity, illuminating important questions and the existential foundation for understanding being.

Ken Wilber and Kirk Schneider on the Transpersonal Movement
Schneider, K. J. (1987). The deified self: A "centaur" response to Wilber and the transpersonal movement. *Journal of Humanistic Psychology, 27,* 196-216.
Schneider, K. J. (1989). Infallibility is so damn appealing: A reply to Ken Wilber. *Journal of Humanistic Psychology, 29,* 470-481.
Wilber, K. (1989). God is so damn boring: A response to Kirk Schneider. *Journal of Humanistic Psychology, 29,* 457-469.
Wilber, K. (1989). Reply to Schneider. *Journal of Humanistic Psychology, 29,* 493-500.
This dialogue serves as an essential guide to distinguishing between existential and transpersonal psychology, both of which are considered important branches of humanistic or phenomenological psychology. In particular, Schneider and Wilber debate the existential and transpersonal perspectives of *ultimate consciousness:* consummate human awareness that transcends time and space to complete awareness of the universe. While Wilber argues for the possibility of attaining ultimate consciousness, Schneider emphasizes mystery and human limitation in knowing. Schneider's contributions also serve to elucidate existential perspectives on topics relevant to religion and spirituality.

Novels

This section, too, is very select identifying the novels and works of fiction most commonly referred to in existential psychology and other works which have influenced existential psychology.

Camus, A. (1989). *The stranger* (M. Ward, Trans.). New York: Vintage.
(Originally published in 1942)

Camus' stranger is an anomic man named Meursault who struggles to feel any emotion while attending his mother's funeral and then many other aspects of his life experiences. Instead, his attention is focused on the perceptual sensations that surround him, such as the stifling temperature and his own physical discomfort. Similarly, he functions in his occupation, friendships, and romantic relationship with the same emotional detachment that alienates him from his own experiences. For Meursault, life is an incongruous collection of events that lack both logic and meaning. His perspective does not change until going through the process of being convicted of murder and sentenced to death. For the first time, he is forced to reflect on his responsibility for his actions and his own impending death. In the end, Meursault denies repentance for his crime and embraces his departure from the world that appears indifferent to human suffering. This illustrates existential concepts of responsibility and the necessity of engaging in self reflections in order to be responsible.

Camus, A. (1991). *The plague* (S. Gilbert, Trans.). New York: Vintage.
(Originally published in 1947)

This novel is about an Algerian town quarantined due to a plague outbreak. Camus explores the unique paths taken by different townspeople in response to the threat of death and suffering. The extremity of the situation brings the human existential predicament to the forefront in attempts to engage the reader in their own reflections on the existential condition.

Camus, A. (1991). *The fall* (J. O'Brien, Trans.). New York: Vintage. (Original work published in 1956)

The Fall is the story of Clamence telling his life story. At one time, Clamence was a person appearing beyond reproach, living a life that seemed to represent impeccable character. However, when he did not act to save a woman who died, he began to reflect upon his life and motivations for his many good acts. As he tells the story, he demonstrates that he is, and always has been, guilty. His motivations were always flawed and self-serving when engaging in his many good acts. The reader seems to be invited, too, to examine his or her own motivation for behaviors. As most of Camus's novels, *The Fall* illustrates that to be human is to be guilty; no one is perfect and no one is pure in their motivations. Moreover, through honest self-reflection, the individual is bound to recognize their guilt. This is an important work in understanding ethics from an existential viewpoint.

Dostoesky, F. (1866/1981). *Crime and punishment*. (C. Garnett, Trans.) New York: Bantam Books.

Crime and Punishment is a fictional story depicting the multiple causes of murder and the many possible forms of punishment that ensue. Following the murder of two women by a despondent student and the subsequent persecution of an innocent man, the reader is challenged to define the thin lines between perpetrator and victim, guilt and innocence, and lastly between judgment and justice. Through the use of multiple perspectives, Dostoesky meticulously records the self-destruction of a guilty conscious ending in a provoking conclusion regarding the salient consequences of moral guilt and the fallibility of social justice. It seems that any crime will always have two victims, the one who is violated and the one who's conscious is violated. Sadly, after it is too late, Dostoesky's characters realize that fear of the unknown does not exclusively assume tragedy, but that uncertainty for the future contains an equal potentiality for reverence.

Dostoyevsky, F. (1881/2003). *The brothers Karamazov.* New York: Penguin
       Classics
Dostoevsky's last novel, generally considered his masterpiece, follows the tale of four brothers who are each complicit to varying degrees in the murder of their father, a scoundrel. Throughout the novel, questions of God and faith are wrestled with through the narratives of the brothers, who each represent a particular aspect of humankind: flesh, intellect, spirit, and baseness.

Kafka F. (1992). *The trial* (W. Muir & E. Muir, Trans.) New York: Schocken
       Books. (Original work published in 1925)
A judicial trial is a powerful metaphor for the daily moral judgments that one must decide in order to live an authentic and meaningful life. This is the premise for Kafka, who overloads his morally weak protagonist, K., with the crushing weight of social judgment and drives him towards his own fatal conclusion that he is, in fact, guilty. The lesson learned is that if an individual forgoes the responsibility to make independent moral decisions, then liberty, freedom, and life will be likewise forfeited resulting in a symbolic if not literal death. The relinquishing of responsibilities for a self-determined life, Kafka warns, is a slow and subtle process that can deceive the innocent into believing in their own guilt. The simple plot line of *The Trial* becomes more complex should the reader attempt to name the range of responsibilities that an individual should assume in relation to the degrees of freedom that one can deservingly claim. Moreover, who, among all, should be appointed to judge another; and what, if any, responsibility does one individual have to another?

Kafka, F. (1926/1998) *The castle.* New York: Schocken. (Original work
       published in 1926)
The type of mindless, convoluted, and ineffective bureaucratic government depicted in Kafka's novel is increasingly easier to imagine. The premise of the story is that K., a land surveyor, is mistakenly called into service by the Castle government but lacking authorization to work. K. voluntarily pauses his life-goals waiting for permission to proceed, which will never come. For the rest of his life,

K., attempts to gain access to the Castle in order to receive his orders, but he is continuously refuted by the villagers who assure him that the Castle is a flawless government that cannot correct a mistake that it did not make. For many, the Castle is a metaphor for humankind's quest for salvation. Unfortunately, the novel was never finished by Kafka and many possible interpretations abound.

Sartre, J. P. (1947). *No Exit and three other plays: Dirty hands, The flies, The respectful prostitute.* New York: Vintage Books.

"No Exit" is a one act play in which three characters, a man and two women, find themselves in trapped in hell. They discover that they each need and utilize the other two in order to continue and realize the inevitable consequences of their pre-death immoral and self-serving behaviors. This illustrates existential themes of freedom and responsibility, along with the potential for change and facing suffering. "No Exit" is the most famous of the short plays in this section; however, the other three plays also illustrate many important existential themes, particularly of responsibility, morality, and ethics from an existential perspective.

Goethe, J. W. (1993). *The sorrows of young Werther.* (E. Mayer & W. H. Auden, Trans.). New York: Modern Library. (Original work published in 1774)

In 1774, Johann Wolfgang Von Goethe published his masterpiece novel titled, *The Sorrows of Young Werther* which is widely regarded by literary historians as the first psychological novel. The story is about two young lovers who attempted to bridge the cultural divide between upper and lower class membership in 18th century Europe. The novel inspired a cult following among young European youth who identified with the countercultural message that economic class divisions are unjust and that every individual should be granted basic civil liberties such as the right to marriage. Werther, the lower class protagonist in the story, committed suicide after he is denied marriage to his upper class lover Lotte. As a result, some followers of the novel committed suicide in allegiance to the principals that Werther appeared to represent: through death all humans become equal. Today, the Werther Effect refers to the apparent social contagion of suicides following the suicide of famous individual or when suicide is portrayed as an iconic gesture in any fictional plot. Existentially, Goethe raises the question whether or not suicide is the ultimate expression of freedom or the absolute loss of meaning in life.

Contributor Biographies

Zhaohui Bao, PhD, having obtained his degrees in Zhejian Normal University, Beijing Normal University, and Nanjing University, is currently teaching at Chinese Department of Nanjing University as an associate professor. His major area of research is Chinese Classical Aesthetics, especially Chuang-Tzu studies. In recent years, Dr. Bao shows special academic concern about disciplines relevant to human experience and spirituality, such as, literature, psychology, and theology. Dr. Bao has published over 30 articles and two books, *A Study of Chuang-tzu's Existential Aesthetics*. (Nanjing: Nanjing University Press, 2004) and *A Study of Popular Music*. (Kunming: Yunnan People Press, 2004). He also has two books on his publication plan: *The Spiritual Realm of Chuang-Tzu* and *Viewing Taoist Spirituality through Christian Perspective*.

Kate Calhoon, PsyD, is a psychological resident at the Center for Growth in Colorado Springs, Colorado. She provides individual, couples, and group therapy in Colorado Springs and Denver. Her doctorate and masters degrees in clinical psychology are from the Colorado School of Professional Psychology. For over 10 years, Dr. Calhoon served as an executive for The Change Companies, a national consulting and publishing company assisting individuals in making positive lifestyle changes. She authored many curricula publications for The Change Companies in the areas of substance abuse education and adolescent risk prevention. In addition, she was a contributing writer for "Voices: A program of self-discovery and empowerment" for adolescent girls authored by Dr. Stephanie Covington. Her undergraduate degree is in film from Northwestern University.

Cathy Calvert, PsyD, is a psychological resident at the Center for Growth in Colorado Springs, Colorado. She provides individual, couples, and family therapy in Colorado Springs with a concentration in working with Postpartum Depression. Dr. Calvert received her Masters degree in Psychology from the Colorado School of Professional Psychology and her doctorate in Clinical Psychology is from the University of the Rockies. Her bachelor's degree is from the University of Nebraska at Omaha in the field of Exercise Physiology. Cathy has co-authored a book review titled "Evolutionary and Neurocognitive Approaches to Aesthetics, Creativity, and the Arts in the book Evolutionary and Neuropsychological Perspectives on Art as Purposeful." Her research experience includes collaborating in a project examining the interplay of religious, spiritual, and psychological health in lesbian, gay, bisexual, and transgender (LGBT) individuals, which was presented as a poster session during the 115th Annual Convention of the American Psychological Association Annual Convention.

Albert Chan, MEd, is a marriage and family therapist. He lived and worked in Toronto, Canada for over 25 years. His master degree is in Counseling Psychology from McGill University. He is a clinical member and an approved supervisor of America Association for Marriage and Family Therapy. Currently, he is completing his doctorate degree in clinical psychology and a master degree in theology. Mr. Chan's clinical work has embraced client-centered humanistic approaches, systemic structural and strategic approaches, and emotional focused and constructive models. He is a past board member of Ontario Association for Marriage and Family Therapy, the past clinical director of Living Water Counseling Services, a Chinese counseling center in Toronto, and clinical manager at family services at York Region Family Services. He was also on the teaching faculty at Humber and Seneca College in Toronto. He relocated to Hong Kong in 2006, and he has been providing individual, marriage, and family therapy, giving consultation and trainings to non-governmental organizations and corporations, as well as teaching at University of Hong Kong, Baptist University, IIUM, Macau Inter University, and Olivet Nazarene University (Hong Kong Campus).

John Chavis, BA, is a student in the Clinical Psychology Masters Degree program at the University of Colorado at Colorado Springs. His interests include Jungian analysis, emotion-focused therapy, affective neuro-science, and the psychology of religion.

Heatherlyn Cleare-Hoffman, PsyD, is an adjunct faculty member of the University of the Rockies and the Director of Clinical Training at the Center for Growth in Colorado Springs. A native of the Bahamas, Dr. Cleare-Hoffman professional interests include diversity issues and international perspectives on psychology. She currently maintains a private practice, and her specialties include couples therapy, existential-humanistic psychotherapy, prepartum and postpartum depression, and providing clinical supervision.

Emory G. Cowan, Jr., PhD, is the founding President/CEO of the Colorado School of Professional Psychology (now the University of the Rockies), and served in that position for ten years. He holds an MDiv in Theology and Pastoral Care from Emory University, an EdM in Education from Boston University, and an MS in Education (Guidance and Counseling) from Long Island University. His PhD in Psychology is from Saybrook Graduate School in San Francisco. Academically, Dr. Cowan has served as a professor in several institutions of higher learning. His teaching interests are Marriage and Family Therapy, Qualitative Research, Personality Theory, and Professional Ethics. He is a Member of the American Psychological Association (APA), a Clinical Member of the American Association for Marriage and Family Therapy (AAMFT), and a Member of the American Counseling Association (ACA). Dr. Cowan is a retired U.S. Army Chaplain (Lieutenant Colonel) and a Vietnam combat veteran, and he was awarded two Bronze Star Medals and an Air Medal. He is also a Past President of The Psychological Society of the Pikes Peak Region of Colorado and he is the 2004 recipient of that society's Cornelia Sabine Award for outstanding contribution to the psychological community of the region.

Erik Craig, EdD, is a licensed psychologist with an independent practice in Santa Fe, New Mexico. Having mentored for several years each with Clark Moustakas, Paul Stern, Charles MacArthur, and Medard Boss, he has been teaching and practicing humanistic and existential psychotherapy for over 40 years, holding full time positions at Assumption College, University of New Mexico, and Pacifica Graduate Institute. More recently he has been studying Eastern approaches to psychotherapy, especially Tao Psychotherapy with its founder Rhee Dongschick in Seoul, South Korea. His primary interest is in developing phenomenological hermeneutic grounds for understanding critical issues in psychological theory, research, and practice with the hope of achieving a comprehensive, existential approach to depth psychology. In 1988 he edited a special issue of *The Humanistic Psychologist* entitled, "Psychotherapy for Freedom: The Daseinsanalytic Way in Psychology and Psychoanalysis," the culmination of his four years of study with Medard Boss and other daseinsanalytic colleagues in Zurich, Switzerland. Erik is currently the Secretary for the New Mexico Psychoanalytic Society and a past president of the Societey for Humanistic Psychology of the American Psychological Association as well as of the International Association for the Study of Dreams. You may contact the author at 113 Camino Escondido, #3, Santa Гe, NM 87501 or at DrErikCraig@aol.com.

Michael M. Dow, MA is a psychotherapist in Boulder, Colorado. Consonant with his strong interest in the interpersonal and community aspects of psychological health, he is currently involved in helping to establish a primary care program fully integrated with behavioral health at Clinica Campesina, a network of bi-lingual community health centers. He is a member of the National Health Service Corps (NHSC), the American Group Psychotherapy Association (AGPA), and the Colorado Group Psychotherapy Society (CoGPS). He is a doctoral candidate in clinical psychology at the University of the Rockies, completing his dissertation which is entitled, "What is Mindfulness? A Qualitative Study of Psychotherapists Integrating Mindfulness into Psychotherapy." He has recently presented in New York, Hong Kong, and Beijing on the intersection of mindfulness and Buddhism with contemporary psychotherapy. His publications included, "Buddhism, Psychology and Neuroscience: Towards a Neurobiologically-informed Contemplative Psychotherapy" in *Brilliant Sanity: Buddhist Approaches to Psychotherapy*, published in 2008 by the University of the Rockies.

Jennifer Christy Dyer, LCSW, PsyD, is a graduate of the University of the Rockies doctoral program in clinical psychology. She also holds a Masters of Social Work (MSW) from the University of Pennsylvania and a Bachelors of Arts (BA) in Chinese History from the University of California at Santa Cruz. Dr. Dyer regularly presents on a variety of topics related to psychology and psychotherapy In March 2008, she spoke on existential-humanistic psychology in Hong Kong and Beijing with a group of other graduate students and professors from the University of the Rockies. Most recently, she was a presenter at the 2008 Colorado Behavioral Health Annual Training Conference, where she conducted a workshop for mental health providers on geriatric depression. Dr. Dyer previous clinical experiences include working with adolescent, adult, and geriatric clients. She is currently in private practice specializing in existential-humanistic psychotherapy, bereavement counseling, and neuropsychological assessment. She also leads women's retreats for personal growth and renewal.

Steve Fehl, MA, is completing his doctorate in Clinical Psychology at the University of the Rockies and is currently finishing his psychology internship at the Center for Growth. Steve served Lutheran parishes in Texas, Michigan, California, Minnesota, and Colorado before beginning his doctoral work. He has a Masters in Psychology and has done additional graduate work at San Francisco Theological Seminary in San Anselmo, CA.

Nathaniel Granger, Jr., MA, received a Bachelor Degree in Psychology from the University of Colorado where in became a lifetime member of Psi Chi (The National Honor Society in Psychology), and later earned a Master's Degree in Counseling and Human Services. He has presented at the Humanistic Psychotherapies Conference and is interested in the areas of existentialism, diversity, men's issues, and forensic/criminal psychology. Nathaniel is an adjunct psychology instructor at Pikes Peak Community College and was recently awarded the J. Frank Rice, Ph.D. Memorial Scholarship for demonstrating academic excellence and dedication to the field as a person of color. Additionally, he was recently elected Vice President of the Student Government Association at University of the Rockies.

Christin Gregory, MA, is a psychological intern at the Center for Growth in Colorado Springs, Colorado. She provides individual, couples, and family therapy as well as group therapy services. Her areas of interest include depth psychotherapy, existential and humanistic therapies, LGBT issues, women's issues, and EMDR. She has a Bachelors of Science degree in applied psychology from Regis University and a Masters of Arts degree in clinical psychology from the University of the Rockies, where she is currently working on her doctorate degree in clinical psychology.

Christopher S. M. Grimes, PsyD, is the Clinical Director of the Psychology and Religion Program at Saint Louis Behavioral Medicine Institute. He specializes in working with individuals who wish to integrate their faith and spirituality into the therapy process, and maintains research and writing interests in the area of psychology and religion and existential psychology. Dr. Grimes is a graduate of the Forest Institute of Professional Psychology.

Myrtle Heery, PhD, is an Associate Professor of Psychology, Sonoma State University, Rohnert Park, CA., and Associate Core Faculty, Institute of Transpersonal Psychology, Palo Alto, CA. In addition, she is the director of the International Institute of Humanistic Studies (www.human-studies.com). For the institute she provides two year Unearthing the Moment trainings nationally and internationally leading to certification of in-depth communication in both individual and group settings. She has regularly provided psychology trainings internationally. She is in private practice in Petaluma, CA, leading consultation groups for therapists and seeing individuals and couples. She is a bereavement volunteer for Hospice of Petaluma for 19 years. She has published papers and chapters in psychology journals and textbooks on bereavement, existential-humanistic, and transpersonal psychotherapy and psychology. In addition, she was a contributing editor for the Yoga Journal. She studied and taught with James F. T. Bugental, PhD for over two decades.

Louis Hoffman, PhD, is a core faculty member at the University of the Rockies and adjunct faculty member of the School of Psychology at Fuller Theology Seminary in Pasadena, California. An avid writer, Dr. Hoffman is an editor and contributor to *Spirituality and Psychological Health, The God Image Handbook for Spiritual Counseling and Psychotherapy,* and *Brilliant Sanity: Buddhist Approaches to Psychotherapy.* In addition to serving on the editorial boards of the *Journal of Humanistic Psychology* and *PsycCRITIQUES: APA Review of Books*, he has written numerous book chapters and journal articles as well as regularly presenting conference papers in the United States, China, and Canada. Recently, Dr. Hoffman has begun collaborating to establish training opportunities in existential psychology in China that focus on integrating indigenous approaches to psychology in China with existential psychology. His professional interests include existential and other depth psychotherapies, spiritual and religious issues in psychotherapy, theoretical and philosophical issues in psychology, and diversity issues. Dr. Hoffman lives with his wife, two children, and two dogs in Colorado Springs.

Francis Kaklauskas PsyD, has presented at numerous national and international conferences including the American Psychological Association and the American Group Psychotherapy Association on topics including Buddhist psychology, group psychotherapy theory and research, comparative psychoanalytic theory, existential psychology, and human sexuality. Dr. Kaklauskas publications include being the primary psychological consultant and on screen presenter for the widely used three part video series, *Hooked: The Addiction Trap* (United Learning, 1999), co-authoring the Group Psychotherapy chapter in doctorate text book *The Handbook of Clinical Psychology* (Wiley, 2006), and serving as the lead editor of the book, *Brilliant Sanity: Buddhist Approaches to Psychotherapy* (University of the Rockies Press, 2008). He created the *Group Process Inventory*, a psychometric instrument that measures a broad range of group events that link process and outcome research variables. Dr. Kaklauskas currently teaches in the graduate schools of psychology at Naropa University and has a private practice in Boulder, Colorado, specializing in group treatment, depth psychotherapy, and clinical supervision and consultation.

Ellen Marsalis, MA, is a psychotherapist in Colorado Springs, Colorado. She specializes in individual therapy with people who have experienced trauma, especially childhood sexual and other abuses. Ellen's Master's degree in Psychology is from the Colorado School of Professional Psychology, University of the Rockies. Her bachelor's degree is from the Colorado State University at Pueblo in the field of General Physiology. Her research has included the propensity for people to lie to government officials and in abused women's perceptions of their personal strengths.

Ed Mendelowitz's, PhD, work resides on the gnostic frontiers of psychology in its eloquent blending of art, literature, music, cinema, religion, philosophy, and riveting clinical narrative with the more recognizable fare of theory and scholarship. His recently published *Ethics and Lao-Tzu* has been called "an "extraordinary moral narrative"" by Robert Coles and "a "remarkable book, a compendium of wisdom from an astonishing variety of sources"" by the late psychoanalyst Allen Wheelis; Louis Hoffman heralds it as "a monumental contribution to psychological literature" and Dr. Mendelowitz as, possibly, "the best contemporary writer in the field of psychology." Dr. Mendelowitz completed his doctoral studies at the California School of Professional Psychology where he worked closely with Rollo May. He is on the board of editors for the *Journal of Humanistic Psychology* and has been a contributor to the major compendiums of existential/humanistic/depth psychotherapy. He has presented numerous papers on psychology, psychotherapy and their respective relationships to the humanities in both the United States and Europe. Dr. Mendelowitz is Distinguished Visiting Professor at the University of the Rockies. He lives and works in Boston. Website: www.edmendelowitz.com.

Michael Moats, MA, has a Masters Degree and is currently pursuing a PsyD in clinical psychology from the University of the Rockies. He has presented at the 2nd Annual Conference for the Society of Humanistic Psychology and he is preparing to be involved in existential trainings for mental health professionals in China in the Spring of 2009. Michael's academic interests include how culture influences the definition of self.

Elizabeth A. Olson, LCSW, PsyD, received a master of social work degree from the University of Washington at Seattle and completed a Post Master's Internship in Clinical Social Work from the University of California at Berkeley. She completed her doctoral degree in clinical psychology at the Colorado School of Professional Psychology, a college of the University of the Rockies specializing in child and family assessment and treatment. She directs the group training program at the University of Colorado at Boulder's Psychological and Psychiatric Services and is adjunct faculty in the Naropa University's Contemplative Psychotherapy program teaching graduate Human Development and Family Systems courses. She has presented professionally at a varied conferences, including the American Group Psychotherapy Conference, on topics related to child and adolescent development, parenting, and group treatment. Her previous publications include book chapters on the integration of psychodynamic and mindfulness approaches to mothering and large group process. She has a private practice in Boulder, Colorado specializing in depth and psychodynamic psychotherapy, the treatment of women's developmental issues, eating disorders, self harm behaviors, and family and group therapy.

Erica Palmer, MA, research and professional interests include existential approaches to psychotherapy, spirituality, postpartum depression and women's wellness issues. She resides in Colorado Springs with her husband and four daughters. She is completing her doctorate in clincial psychology at the University of the Rockies and is an officer of the Graduate Student Association and serves as a facilitator of training classes for new practicum students.

Elizabeth Saxon, MBA, is. a former investment banker in New York City, and she received her MBA from the University of Southern California. She currently is comleting her doctorate in clinical psychology at the University of the Rockies in Colorado Springs, Colorado In March 2008, she traveled to China with Dr. Louis Hoffman and other graduate students from the University of the Rockies and spoke on existential-humanistic psychology in Hong Kong and Beijing. Most recently, she was a co-presenter at the 2008 APA Humanistic Conference in Boston on *New Directions for Mindfulness-Based Therapies: A Buddhist Critique*. Recently she co-authored a book review titled *Paradoxes of Time in Existential Therapy: Can a Time-Limited*

Existential Approach Work? published in APA PsycCRITIQUES . Her research interests include neuropsychology, trauma, mindfulness, and existential psychology.

Kirk J. Schneider, PhD, is a leading spokesperson for contemporary humanistic psychology. He is current editor of the Journal of Humanistic Psychology, vice-president of the Existential-Humanistic Institute (EHI), and adjunct faculty at Saybrook Graduate School and the California Institute of Integral Studies. He is also a Fellow of the American Psychological Association. Dr. Schneider has published over 100 articles and chapters and has authored or edited seven books (one more is in preparation), *The Paradoxical Self: Toward an Understanding of Our Contradictory Nature* (translated into Portuguese and Slovakian), *Horror and the Holy: Wisdom-teachings of the Monster Tale*, *The Psychology of Existence: An Integrative, Clinical Perspective* (with Rollo May; currently being translated into Chinese), *The Handbook of Humanistic Psychology: Leading Edges in Theory, Research and Practice* (with J. Bugental and F. Pierson), *Rediscovery of Awe: Splendor, Mystery, and the Fluid Center of Life*, *Existential-Integrative Psychotherapy: Guideposts to the Core of Practice* (currently being partly translated into Russian) and *Existential-Humanistic Therapy* coauthored with Orah Krug (in press for the APA, accompanied by a DVD demo). The book in preparation is *Awakening to Awe: A New Outlook on Health, Healing, and Spirituality*.

Ilene A. Serlin, PhD, is a licensed psychologist and registered dance/movement therapist who began her interest in existential/humanistic psychology studying and teaching with Dr. Laura Perls at the New York Gestalt Institute. She is Past-President and a Fellow of the Division of Humanistic Psychology of APA, and is currently President-Elect of the San Francisco Psychological Association. Dr. Serlin's publications include: "A Humanistic Approach to the Psychology of Trauma in *Living with Terror, Working with Trauma: A Clinician's Handbook;* "Humanistic psychology and women: A critical-historical perspective" in *Handbook of Humanistic Psychology: Leading Edges of Theory, Research, and Practice* (K. Schneider, J, Bugental, & J. Pierson, Eds.), "History of Division 32" in *History of Divisions* (Ed. D. Dewsbury, published by the American Psychological Association), and *Whole Person Healthcare* (3 volumes) (2007). She maintains a private practice in San Francisco and Marin County, and her website is ileneserlin.com.

Heyong Shen, PhD, is a Jungian Analyst (IAAP) and Sandplay Therapist (ISST/STA), Professor of Analytical Psychology at Fudan University, China and South China Normal University. He is the president of the Chinese Association for Analytical Psychology, speaker of Eranos (1997, 2007), main organizer of the International Conference of Analytical Psychology and Chinese Culture (1998, 2002, 2006, 2009). Heyong Shen has published several books in Chinese, including: *Sandplay Therapy, Theory and Practice; Jungian Analysis; Psychoanalysis and Analytical Psychology*; and *Psychology of the Heart*. A leading Jungian scholar, Dr. Shen has also helped translate writings of Rollo May and poetry of Tom Greening into Mandarin. He can be contacted at shenheyong@fundan.edu.cn.

Matt Thelen, MA, earned his BA in psychology from Augustana College. In 2007, he earned my MA in clinical psychology from the Colorado School of Professional Psychology. The title of his doctorate dissertation is *The good death: A cross-cultural comparison of expectations towards death.* His professional interests include community responses to individuals with mental disorders, suicide prevention, existential psychology, and psychological strategies for environmental sustainability.

Benjamin R. Tong, PhD, is Professor in the Clinical Psychology PsyD Program at the California Institute of Integral Studies, San Francisco. An emeritus faculty member of the Asian American Studies Department at San Francisco State University, he is executive director of the Institute for Cross-Cultural Research, a nonprofit organization for the advancement of indigenous mind/body health and healing practices. In the past twenty-five years, he has produced a host of symposium presentations, published papers, book chapters and critical reviews in such subject areas as race relations, cross-cultural psychology, and Taoist/Buddhist thought and disciplines. His current book in preparation include a volume on *Taoist Approaches to Psychotherapy*. Dr. Tong is Director and Head Instructor of the School of Taoist Internal Arts (San Francisco) which offers a program of Taoist studies, Tai Chi Chuan and Chi Gung, mind-body health, and personal consultation. He also maintains a private practice in existential psychoanalytic psychotherapy. Among other professional pursuits, Dr. Tong, along with Dr. Satsuski Ina, PhD, has been conducting group therapy/healing retreats for adult survivors of clergy sexual abuse. Website: http://drbenjaminrtong.com.

Wensheng Wang, PhD, is an associate professor of Chinese Literature at College of Liberal Arts, Nanjing Normal University. Her fields of research have been "the phenomenon of Chinese Literature during 1949-1966" and "comparative study of contemporary Chinese literature and Christianity," with articles and books published in the two fields. Her recent interest has begun to extend to existential psychology as an academic lens to view contemporary Chinese writers.

Xuefu Wang, PhD, having obtained his degrees in the fields of theology, literature, psychology and pastoral counseling, is the founder as well as the director of Zhi Mian Institute for Psychotherapy, Nanjing, China. At present, Dr. Wang is a visiting scholar at Fuller Graduate School of Psychology. His past experience has been teaching at universities, seminaries, and psychological institutions. Dr. Wang is an active promoter as well as a pioneering practitioner of professional counseling and pastoral counseling in China. He is also involved in international institutions as visiting clinical professor of Korea Professional Psychotherapy Institute, adjunct faculty of TCA College of Singapore, and editorial board member of *Pastoral Psychology*, USA. Dr. Wang has published numerous articles and two books, *A Fog-Shrouded Oasis – On Modern Chinese Literature and its Christian Culture Influence,* (Singapore: Big Idea Publishing House, 1996) and *Fallen Flowers—A Reflection of Life Experience and Spirituality,* (Haerbin: Heilongjian People Publishing House, 2008). His recent book, *Turning from Escape to Zhi Mian* (to be published), demonstrates indigenous Chinese experience of counseling and psychotherapy. Recently he is preparing a book, *The Zhi Mian Thinking of Lu Xun*, which draws referential view from existential psychology.

Mark Yang, PhD, is a licensed clinical psychologist from the United States. Currently, he is serving as the Director of Clinical Training for the Hong Kong Campus of Alliant University (formerly California School of Professional Psychology). The core of Dr. Yang's clinical experience has been working in University Counseling Centers where he conducted short-term individual and group psychotherapy for students and consulted with faculty regarding mental health issues. In addition, Dr. Yang has been involved in the training and supervision of psychology students. Dr. Yang's professional interests include: individual and group psychotherapy, grief and bereavement, existential psychotherapy, cross-cultural and organizational psychology. In regards to Cross-cultural and Organizational psychology, Dr. Yang is an entrepreneur who started his own business that has him working and living in Hong Kong and Dongguan, China for the past seven years. Dr. Yang earned his Doctorate of Psychology (Clinical Psychology) in 1994 from Fuller Theological Seminary's, Graduate School of Psychology. He earned his Bachelor of Arts in psychology from the University of California in Santa Cruz. Dr. Yang was born in Taiwan and immigrated with his family to the United States when he was nine years old. Dr. Yang embraces the fact that he is a dog lover and laments the fact that he is unable to properly raise a dog here in Asia. A broad range of interests keep Dr. Yang occupied during his free time – prime among them are tennis and ballroom dancing.

Index

Lightning Source UK Ltd.
Milton Keynes UK
UKOW06f1823190914

238900UK00004B/55/P